Rethinking Asian Tourism

Rethinking Asian Tourism: Culture, Encounters and Local Response

Edited by

Ploysri Porananond and Victor T. King

CAMBRIDGE SCHOLARS PUBLISHING

Rethinking Asian Tourism: Culture, Encounters and Local Response,
Edited by Ploysri Porananond and Victor T. King

This book first published 2014

Cambridge Scholars Publishing

12 Back Chapman Street, Newcastle upon Tyne, NE6 2XX, UK

British Library Cataloguing in Publication Data
A catalogue record for this book is available from the British Library

ISBN (10): 1-4438-6458-7, ISBN (13): 978-1-4438-6458-9

Table of Contents

INTRODUCTION: RETHINKING ASIAN TOURISM

VICTOR T. KING AND PLOYSRI PORANANOND

In recent years and for obvious reasons, given the rapid expansion in tourism outside Western Europe and the Americas, there has been an increasing number of contributions to the study and understanding of the characteristics, development and transformation of tourism in Asia and sub-regions within Asia, particularly Southeast Asia and the western Pacific Rim. Since the appearance of the co-edited book *Tourism in South-East Asia* (Hitchcock, King and Parnwell, 1993), now two decades ago, the study of Asian tourism has come of age. Victor King and his co-editors have developed this work further, and particularly in the field of heritage, with *Tourism and Heritage in South-East Asia* (Hitchcock and King, 2003, a special issue of *Indonesia and the Malay World*), *Tourism in Southeast Asia: Challenges and New Directions* (Hitchcock, King and Parnwell, 2009) and *Heritage Tourism in Southeast Asia* (Hitchcock, King and Parnwell, 2010). This current volume from Victor King and Ploysri Porananond is the latest development of on-going research on tourism in Southeast Asia and the wider Asia (in geographical terms there are chapters on Thailand, Vietnam, Indonesia, the Philippines, Malaysia, Hong Kong, Japan, Korea, but there are also chapters which examine cross-national encounters in Asia, including those between Japan and Thailand).

Moreover, during the past two decades several volumes on tourism in Asia, Southeast Asia, the Pacific and China have appeared which have focused on particular issues such as ethnicity and the state, cross-national interconnections, policy and management issues, heritage and cultural development, and domestic or local tourism within Asia; and there are those which constitute general multidisciplinary collections or surveys of the scope and scale of tourism, as well as issues, problems, prospects and policies related to tourism development.

An early contribution to the political dimension of Asian-wide tourism was Linda Richter's *The Politics of Tourism in Asia* (1989), an issue which has become particularly important in an Asian context with the invariable intervention of national governments in the development of tourism and in determining the ways in which tourism is used for purposes of national identity formation, national status and projection and for legitimising political regimes.

There was then a noticeable increase in scholarly interest in Asian tourism development from the late 1990s into the early 2000s. Some of the publications made important theoretical and empirical contributions; others were in the form of surveys, compilations and teaching texts, but were nevertheless worthwhile additions to the literature. Among others there were: Shinji Yamashita, Kadir H. Din and J.S. Eades, *Tourism and Cultural Development in Asia and Oceania* (1997); Michel Picard and Robert E. Wood, *Tourism, Ethnicity and the State in Asian and Pacific Societies* (1997); C. Michael Hall, *Tourism in the Pacific Rim: Developments, Impacts and Markets* (1997); C. Michael Hall and Stephen Page, *Tourism in the Pacific: Issues and Cases* (1997); F.M. Go and C. L. Jenkins, *Tourism and Economic Development in Asia and Australasia* (1997); Michael J. Hatton, *Community-based Tourism in the Asia-Pacific* (1999); C. Michael Hall and Stephen Page, *Tourism in South and Southeast Asia: Issues and Cases* (2000); K[aye] S. Chon, *Tourism in Southeast Asia: A New Direction* (2000); Peggy Teo, T.C. Chang and K.C. Ho, *Interconnected Worlds: Tourism in Southeast Asia* (2001); Jean Michaud and Michel Picard, *Tourisme et Sociétés Locales en Asie Orientale* (2001, a special issue of *Anthropologie et Sociétés*); Tan Chee-Beng, Sidney C. H. Cheung and Yang Hui, *Tourism, Anthropology and China*. (2001); and Alan L. Lew, Lawrence Yu, John Ap and Zhang Guangrui, *Tourism in China* (2003).

Of the most recent contributions there has been a clear shift to the concern with Asian travel, leisure and tourism within Asia itself, which raises all kinds of new and emerging issues in the field of tourism studies, as well as strong evidence of a continuing interest in such matters as cultural and heritage tourism. Among important recent volumes there are Tim Winter, Peggy Teo and T.C. Chang, *Asia on Tour: Exploring the Rise of Asian Tourism* (2007); Bruce Prideaux, Dallen J. Timothy and K[aye] S. Chon, *Cultural and Heritage Tourism in Asia and the Pacific* (2008); Janet Cochrane, *Asian Tourism: Growth and Change* (2008); and Shalini Singh, *Domestic Tourism in Asia: Diversity and Divergence* (2009/2011). There is also the recent *Routledge Handbook of Heritage in Asia* edited by

Patrick Daly and Tim Winter, and their introductory overview (Winter and Daly, 2012), which covers issues of tourism and heritage as well as intra-Asian tourism (2012); the volume also contains the important chapter by William Logan (2012).

Our present volume addresses some of the emerging as well as established themes and issues in Asian tourism, building on this substantial literature, with a particular focus on culture and heritage. It also pursues and provides case study material on a range of conceptual and empirical matters which have been raised in eloquent and searching terms by Tim Winter in his paper 'Rethinking Tourism in Asia' in *Annals of Tourism Research* when he says 'Despite the recent surge in the number of tourists originating from countries across Asia, the literature on tourism on the region, published in English, remains dominated by encounters between Westerners and their Asian hosts. As yet, little attention has been given to either the motivations and values of tourists from Asia, or the broader social, cultural, and political implications arising from this fast-growing industry' (2006: 27). The issues he raises were then further elaborated in his co-edited book *Asia on Tour* and particularly his concluding chapter entitled 'Recasting Tourism Theory towards an Asian Future' (2007: 315-325). In a subsequent article he urges a rethinking of the theoretical and analytical apparatus of tourism studies in that 'the ongoing rise of Asian tourism' has rendered this field of research 'institutionally and intellectually ill equipped to understand and interpret the new era we are now entering'. One solution, he suggests, is 'the cultivation of critical scholarship within the region itself [which] will not only help overcome the field's Anglo-Western centrism but also help us better comprehend the profound societal changes now occurring through Asian mobility'(Winter, 2009: 21). In a further contribution to these debates and reflections, King has also addressed the emerging agenda for future research in his review article 'Tourism in Asia: a Review of the Achievements and Challenges' in the journal *Sojourn* (2008: 104-136), which was a review article which addressed Janet Cochrane's 2008 book, followed by his reviews of Winter et al (2010) and Shalini Singh (2012).

Our current edited volume *Rethinking Asian Tourism* picks up on some of Winter's observations and those of other researchers who have focused on Asian tourists in Asia (see Cochrane, 2008; Shalini Singh, 2009/2011; and also Daly and Winter, 2012) concerning the need to address and develop our conceptual understanding of the character, experiences, encounters, perceptions and motivations of local, national and intra-regional tourism rather than to continue to base our concepts, perspectives, emphases and analyses on Western-Asian interactions and on transformations in the West (and see Lew, Hall and Williams, 2014). An important corollary of this shift in emphasis is to encourage the development of Asian scholarship on Asian tourism, which should not confine itself primarily to matters of policy, marketing, management, organisation and training in the tourism and hospitality industry (which is exemplified especially well in K.S. Chon's book, 2000) but should embrace multi- and interdisciplinary approaches and perspectives on critical issues to do with power and marginality, representation and imaging, and local community involvement. However, we are conscious of the problematical distinction which is still made between domestic and international tourism (or Asian and non-Asian) when the patterns of mobility, residence and work are increasingly shifting and unstable and the frequency and ease of movement have increased dramatically in the fast-moving post-modern world. Indeed, the categorisation of tourists into domestic (or local) and international (or foreign), though we use it as a short-hand in this volume, throws up a number of problems in a globalising, inter-connected world.

Not only is a clear-cut distinction difficult to make in that the categorical boundaries between domestic and international tourists are fuzzy and overlap, but the two categories themselves need to be unpacked and differentiated into a range of more subtly and finely tuned sub-categories. For example, there is now a rapidly expanding group of foreign, retired senior citizens who have settled in such countries as Malaysia and Thailand, and who come from other parts of Asia, from Australia and the West; with the considerable leisure time that they have at their disposal, they also undertake activities and pursuits which are tourist-like. There are in addition foreign sojourners who continue to reside in their home country but who will spend extended periods in another country; often they will have their own accommodation there (a holiday home, an apartment, or regular lodgings). On the other hand there are citizens of a particular country who now live and work abroad and return periodically to see family and friends, or they are part of Southeast Asian diasporas in Western Europe, North America, Australia and New Zealand, as well as increasingly in other parts of the world who return home for extended breaks from time to time. They may or may not retain citizenship in their country of origin. There are also now large numbers, and increasing numbers of expatriate workers in Southeast Asia, again residing there for extended periods of time, and who, during their leisure time, often do what tourists do.

Much has also been written about the different categories of international tourists: short-stay, long-stay, package (high-end) tourists, budget travellers, back-packers and independents, informed heritage and eco-tourists, relatively uninformed pleasure-seekers (the sun, sea, sand, shopping [and sometimes sex] syndrome), pilgrims, businesspeople with leisure time, those in search of themselves and hoping to find some meaning in their lives in cross-cultural encounters, those who remain untroubled about authenticity and meaning and are in search of new experiences and usually just plain fun, and then there are the further complications concerning those tourists who are from different ethnic, national, and social class backgrounds, of different gender and so on. Wikipedia now presents us with 83 different categories of types of tourism (http://*en.wikipedia.org/wiki/Category:Types_of_tourism*), and the number of publications devoted exclusively or in part to the classification of tourists and tourism, and of course the range of tourist experiences is truly substantial (see, for example, Cohen, 1972, 1979a, 1979b, 1984; Ning Wang, 1999, 2000).Von Egmond has revealed just how complex the category of 'Western tourists' is, let along tourists from other parts of the world (2007). And then take any category of tourist and tourism – cultural tourists, for example – and complexity abounds (McKercher, 2002). This complexity is intimately interconnected with the expansion and differentiation of the experience and contexts of personal mobility; many more of us are now on the move so that tourism becomes part of wider social, cultural, economic and political processes of movement and should increasingly be thought about within the sociological and geographical study of mobility. A significant voice in this field of research has been John Urry who has more recently moved on from his seminal concerns with the 'tourist gaze' (2000, 2007), and, in association with Kevin Hannam and Mimi Sheller, has been concerned to develop our understanding of what he refers to as the 'sociology of mobilities' (and see Hannam, Sheller and Urry, 2006; and Hannam, 2014). Erik Cohen and Scott Cohen have recently begun to build on Urry's work in the field of 'mobilities' to attempt a 'paradigm shift' in tourism studies (see, for example, 2012a).

The need to identify, name, delimit, and categorise particular phenomena is part-and-parcel of the sustained attempts not merely to handle complexity, but it is also part of the package of crucial analytical devices in much of tourism studies to objectify tourism 'as a thing, a product, a behavior….[and] in particular an economic thing' (Franklin and Crang, 2001:6). One major result of this tendency has been the impulse to classify types of tourist and to formulate different categories and sub-categories of tourism. As Franklin and Crang argue persuasively in explaining how research in tourism has attempted to address a rapidly expanding field of studies, we have witnessed the construction of 'ever finer subdivisions and more elaborate typologies as though these might eventually form a classificatory grid in which tourism could be defined and regulated' (ibid). Of course, as they (and we) recognise typologies do play a role in this research; they also tend to appear during the early stages of the development of a field of studies in order to arrange findings and data into some sort of graspable and comprehensible form. But in citing Löfgren (1999: 267), Franklin and Crang remark that 'the obsession with taxonomies and "craze for classification" seems often to produce lists that "represent a tradition of flatfooted sociology and psychology" which is often driven by "an unhappy marriage between marketing research and positivist ambitions of scientific labelling"' (ibid). Perhaps this observation is a little harsh, and one wonders about the relation which is posited between marketing research and positivist ambitions, nonetheless, Franklin's and Crang's criticism of the classifying impulse is well taken.

We have decided in this volume not to contribute to this substantial literature on classification and the devising of templates, categories and lists, but instead and quite simply to draw attention to the diversity of tourism types and experiences and of the motivations, characteristics and behaviour of tourists of all kinds. This exercise also involves us in taking more serious account of the work of Asian researchers on Asian tourism and to consider some of the ways in which this shift in interest and perspective can contribute to embellishing and embroidering the trajectories, changing characteristics and understandings of the cultural context of tourism experiences, encounters and local responses.

In pursuing the project to help 'Asianise' the field of Asian tourism studies most of the chapters in our volume give expression to Asian scholarship; 16 of the 17 chapters are written or part-written by Asian scholars working in Asia, and 15 of the 18 contributors are from the region. Several of the chapters also address the importance of understanding touristic encounters between Asians. One of the purposes of the international conference from which these papers emerged on 'Tourism and Culture in Asia', at Chiang Mai University, Thailand, 17-18 November, 2013, was also to establish a network of programmes, departments, and institutions involved in tourism studies and training across Asia to underpin the future development of cross-national collaboration in multidisciplinary research.

A focus on 'Asians on tour' also interrelates with certain issues which have been raised by recent theoretical developments in tourism studies. A paper by Erik Cohen and Scott A. Cohen in the journal *Annals of Tourism Research* (2012a: 2177-2202) entitled 'Current Sociological Theories and Issues in Tourism' captures much of what has been going on in the recent re-thinking of concepts, approaches, themes and issues in research on tourism (in Asia and beyond). The article addresses a very wide range of literature indeed, but what it draws attention to in particular is the movement away from earlier discourses and concepts to do with 'authenticity' (Cohen, 2007) and 'the tourist gaze' (MacCannell, 2001; Perkins, 2001; Sherlock, 2001; Urry, 1990 [2002]; Urry and Larsen, 2012) as well as with the too simple classification between 'hosts' and guests' (Smith, 1979 [1989]) towards what Erik and Scott Cohen refer to as 'three novel theoretical approaches' which are interrelated and which can be deployed analytically in tandem, viz. (1) the mobilities paradigm; (2) the performativity approach; and (3) actor-network theory (ANT) (2012a: 2180-2189).

What this paradigm shift throws into question is the problematical nature of 'tourism' as a defined and delimited field of studies, and the realisation that there is now a range of phenomena and activities which are included (or becoming increasingly so) within the category 'tourism', but which previously were considered within other forms of scholarly enquiry, or at least have been seen as partaking of or implicated in other areas of social, cultural, economic and political life. In this regard they are often referred to as 'new' or 'emergent' tourisms. As Franklin and Crang propose 'tourism is now such a significant dimension to global social life that it can no longer be conceived of as merely what happens at self-styled tourist sites and encounters involving tourists away from home' (2001: 7).

We have already referred to the turn in sociology and in the multidisciplinary study of tourism to 'mobilities' in the work of John Urry, and his collaboration with Mimi Sheller (and see, Sheller and Urry, 2004, 2006; and Sheller, 2011) and Kevin Hannam (Hannam, Sheller and Urry, 2006; and see Hannam and Knox, 2010). As Sheller indicates in a recent paper, citing Urry, the concept of 'mobilities', which, in our view, does not comprise a coherent theoretical model, but rather captures the coming together of disparate fields of study, 'encompasses not only corporeal travel of people and the physical movement of objects, but also imaginative travel, virtual travel and communicative travel' (2011: 3; and see Urry, 2007). Over a decade ago at the launch of the journal *Tourist Studies* Franklin and Chang had already presented a strong case for the location or relocation of the study of tourism within a broader conceptual and theoretical field because even then they perceived tourism as 'no longer a specialist consumer product or mode of consumption', as no longer an event, process or phenomenon of minor or marginally eccentric importance in post-modern life but as 'a significant modality' which was contributing to the organisation and transformation of people's everyday lives (2001: 6-7). In other words 'The majority of people are now part of the market aimed initially at visiting outsiders', indeed 'more or less *everyone* now lives in a world rendered or reconfigured as interesting, entertaining and attractive – for tourists' (ibid: 9). In this observation they refer to 'transnational' lives, but of course in the way in which tourism and leisure activities have been increasingly inserted into 'the everyday' these touristic experiences are enacted within as well as across national boundaries.

In turn they refer back to the important work of Chris Rojek (1995; Rojek and Urry, 1997) and Fred Inglis (2000) which had already argued that tourism could no longer be seen as a separable, discrete, exotic, extraordinary part of post-modern life, but as a set of activities, experiences, behaviours and processes which was intimately intertwined with other dimensions of people's everyday lives, and indeed their increasingly globalised lives. Franklin and Crang refer specifically in this context to the need to investigate 'the wider ramifications of tourism mobilities and sensibilities' (2001: 6), and, in capturing the importance of the characters and consequences of movements, to address such issues as 'migration', 'nomadism', 'travellings', 'homelessness', 'flight', 'circulation' and the 'flows' of goods, information, culture and people (ibid: 6-10). Indeed, they suggest tourism studies might seek relations with 'other mobilities such as commuting, mobile labour markets, migration and Diasporas' (ibid: 11). More than this '[t]he excitement of mobilities in these highly mobile times, structured by the language and practice of tourism, is that they generate new social relations, new ways of living, new ties to space, new places, new forms of consumption and leisure and new aesthetic sensibilities' (ibid: 12).

The 'performativity' approach is perhaps not as 'novel' as the Cohens want to suggest (2012a), and it seems to us to be a somewhat loose and slippery umbrella concept: it embraces a range of expressions and actions which include well established and familiar sociological concepts (behaviour and meaningful bodily movement, identity, symbolic and self-representation and -expression, staging, imaging). But importantly what this approach draws attention to are the ways in which performance is connected to the creation of places and identities (both for those living and working in the location and those who are visiting) and to the structuring and changing of relationships and meanings through an increasingly 'reflexive awareness' in tourist sites (Edensor, 2001, 2007; Franklin and Crang, 2001: 10). In other words, 'performativity' does not refer solely to the staging of tourist-related events, but to tourist or visitor behaviour and reflections as well (see, for example, Bruner, 2005). It also comprises the translation of symbolic categories and representations into concrete, observable acts which often form part of a repetitive cultural repertoire presented to and in interaction with tourists (who themselves perform), but which can also be subject to modification and change depending on consumer and market demands and on the reflections and perceptions of those involved in the staging of their cultures in tourist contexts. These concerns with 'performativity' can however be profitably brought into relationship with earlier concerns in tourism studies, exemplified in the stimulating work of Tom Selwyn on symbolism, images, myths, representations and semiotics (1996).

Similarly with regard to the Cohens' notion of actor-network-theory (2012a) we do not detect anything here that is especially original, although we accept that any analysis of tourist experiences will of necessity have to engage in the examination of relations between people/actors/translators and between people and things/objects ('thing-ness' and the role of objects are becoming increasingly important in tourism studies [Franklin and Crang, 2001: 15]); in this regard networks are usefully seen as project-specific, fluid, in flux, hybrid, and heterogeneous (and see van der Duim, 2007).

Our present 'rethinking' volume attempts to capture some of these concerns, particularly in relation to the theme of Asians on tour. There is first and foremost the issue of cultural expressions, performance and behaviour which are primarily designed to meet political, social, religious, and everyday economic objectives for a primarily local or national audience but which are also deployed in the interest of tourism development (as in the chapters by Ploysri Porananond and Mae Claire Jabines). Ploysri Porananond examines the context of the invention and political agendas in the Dum Hua procession in the Songkran Festival in Chiang Mai; this is an event which demonstrates the multi-vocal character of tourism and the ways in which public events are used politically. Originally it was a Northern Thai Lanna practice to pay respect to the elders. Subsequently it was introduced into the Songkran in 1964 and it became a political tool for the benefit of the city governor, who was appointed from Bangkok. Additionally, it has been deployed as a strategy by the provincial officers as representatives of the central government in Bangkok to reduce the power of the traditional ruler of Chiang Mai. The high ranking officials at the provincial and district level who also participate in the Dum Hua procession use it to express their authority. Several ethnic groups in northern Thailand have also seized this processional opportunity to temporarily displace their marginality and invisibility and demonstrate their cultural heritage and ethnic identity.

Mae Claire Jabines examines the socio-cultural and spiritual expressions and images of honouring saints in the Philippine province of Bohol through the institution of the fiesta and its contribution to the development of local tourism. The province of Bohol is widely known for its fiesta celebrations in much of the month of May. People come home for the fiesta, bringing along their friends and family, an occasion which also serves to promote the local tourism industry. There is a substantial increase in the arrivals of local tourists and other visitors at ports and terminals as the fiesta season starts.

Fiestas are common to predominantly Catholic countries, and the Philippines, as a former colony of Spain, celebrates these based upon the ecclesiastical calendar of the feast days of saints. However, this practice is not solely Spanish in origin because prior to their arrival, the Filipinos practised similar celebrations during the harvest season, when festivities were held to pay tribute and give their appreciation to the gods and ancestral spirits (*anitos*). They sacrificed chickens, pigs, or water buffalo (*carabao*) as a sign of gratitude for a successful harvest from the previous season. Importantly and intriguingly in an environment of globalising tourism, a cultural event of local significance becomes increasingly a tourism event of national and international interest.

In connection with the two studies above which address events of procession and celebration the study of Asian tourism in Asia also throws up issues to do with family-based travel where leisure time and the participation in religious events are experienced with family and friends rather than it being a purely touristic experience. Several chapters provide illustrations of these new and emerging activities in what are still usually conceptualised and analysed within the field of tourism studies rather than as being thought about in a more general field of 'mobilities' (see, for example, Hannam, 2014; Urry, 2007). One such chapter is that by Janianton Damanik which focuses on suburban family tourists from Yogyakarta. Increasing numbers of Indonesian people are becoming involved in tourism and leisure activities. In a national survey in 2007-2008 it was found that 52 per cent of Indonesians travelled away from their home and this number has since increased considerably. The survey, however, only presents a general overview of individual tourist activities. As studies of family tourism are few and far between, it is difficult to formulate the map of tourism needs for this sector and, following on from this, the policies for its promotion despite its phenomenal development in Indonesia. The tourism activities of individuals and families are also very different, and Damanik's chapter discusses the meanings of tourism for families and how these meanings are realised in destination choice and tourist activities, which include visiting natural landscapes and engaging in ecotourism as a break away from the densely populated urban areas of Java. The suburbs of Yogyakarta comprise residents with different economic, social and cultural backgrounds and most middle class families there visit other destinations in Java. Family tourism has three dimensions: enhancing the emotional ties and integration of family and relatives effectively; generating pleasure and entertainment, and giving gratitude to God.

There are other chapters which illustrate the diversification of phenomena which can legitimately fall within the field of tourism studies, but also lend strong support to the view that what has been commonly referred to as touristic activity is being increasingly incorporated into other fields of study (retirees and long stays in Chiang Mai, gastronomy in George Town, Penang, homestays in Java, popular culture in South Korea, and rural tourism and local branding of products in rural Japan). Furthermore, these diverse tourisms are primarily located within an intra-Asian arena of encounter and interaction. They are demonstrated very persuasively in Miwa Shibuya's study of 'long-stay tourism' or the International Retirement Migration of Japanese senior citizens. In her chapter she explores the migration experiences of Japanese retired people to Chiang Mai in northern Thailand. The retirees come from different socio-economic groups and they experience asymmetric relations and ruptures which arise from the demands of cross-cultural encounters. Consequently, the economically less-fortunate Japanese are prone to being rendered more marginalised in transnational contexts. Nevertheless, in exploring a more discretionary life overseas, many of them go through a process of self-emancipation and a reshaping of self-identity in their extended touristic encounter with Thailand.

Suet Leng Khoo provides us with an excursion into 'gastronomy' in Penang as a potential cultural strategy in tourism promotion.The chapter draws attention to the 'UNESCO Creative Cities' flagship comprising cities around the world which are formulating strategies to become creative cities in order to regenerate their urban spaces. Under this flagship, cities are branded accordingly based on their niche economic activities and the attractions that best promote and present their city to the globalised world. As a result, innovative and creative place-branding labels have emerged such as City of Fashion, City of Literature, City of Design and even an accolade bestowed on the gastronomic function of a city, thus, City of Gastronomy. Khoo argues that George Town's unique gastronomic prowess provides a strategy which can contribute towards the authenticity of the place, enhance tourism sustainability as well as strengthen the local economy. Yet this raises the question of what a World Heritage Site should embody and express, and should a UNESCO site be promoted in this way?

In relation to homestays in the community of Banjarnegara, located on the Dieng Plateau near Wonosobo in Central Java, Destha Titi Raharjana proposes that there are economic benefits for local people in developing homestay opportunities which host local as well as international visitors. Of course, homestays generate income for the local economy; they provide an environment within which there are positive interactions between hosts and guests; homestays also encourage the development of expertise and skills (including acquisition of other languages), as well as a mindset which is much more open to the reception and hosting of visitors. If their organisation and promotion depend on external agencies then they do not deliver the level of benefit for local people; ideally the services should be organised by the local community.

Continuing the theme of the Asianisation of Asian tourism Eoin Joseph Trolan examines the internationalisation of popular culture in the Republic of Korea which has served to make it a vibrant tourist destination for both regional and international tourists. He argues that Korean success in developing its tourism market has been based primarily on the concept of the 'Korean wave or *hallyu*'. The promotion of Korean drama, pop-stars and athletes has implanted the idea of Korea as a vibrant and significant tourist destination. The global infusion of K-drama, K-pop, and Korean sport (K-culture) has led to an increased desire to travel to Korea, and the increased attention to Korean culture and *hallyu* has led to the Korean government's encouragement of it in its tourism promotion strategies (Han and Lee, 2008). Trolan demonstrates that the impact of K-culture has changed the image of Korea. Whether it is in Vietnam, Thailand, Japan, or Singapore, K-culture stars are in high demand and as such the Korean government through its Ministry of Tourism and Culture has attempted to promote the stars' image as a positive element of Korean culture. This can be seen from the popularity of such performers as Girl's Generation, Super Junior, Beast, Big Bang, Rain, 2N1, and Psy. The image of these performers has changed the social and cultural image of Korea – it is now viewed as a place of wealth and opportunity and as such, a place where many want to visit to experience the concept of *hallyu*.

Finally in our excursion into new tourisms Yasuo Ohe has examined the complementary relationships among the direct economic effects of local branded farm products in agricultural cooperatives in Japan on income, employment and the social effects on the local community, as well as the development of tourism. A major finding is that local branding is a significant element in the diversification of farm and rural economies, and it provides opportunities for tourism.

These case-studies demonstrate above all that 'tourism' is an open-ended, shifting, fluid and complex category of phenomena just as is 'culture' and the related concept of 'heritage'. We suggest that these three crucial concepts need to be deconstructed and reviewed critically. So let us now move on to the problematical matter of the relationships between 'culture' and 'tourism' which includes the politics of identity construction and transformation, modes of cultural and ethnic representation, the role of the state and its policies in relation to cultural and ethnic processes, and the responses of local communities to tourism and national level policies and practices. There is also the need to return to the long-running issues of authenticity and what has been referred to more recently and more satisfactorily as the process of 'authentication' in relation to heritage (Cohen and Cohen, 2012b). Thi Hong Hai Nguyen and Catherine Cheung investigate tourists' perceptions of and the factors influencing perceived authenticity within the context of heritage tourism in Hong Kong. The question of authenticity in Hong Kong heritage tourism has particular moment because of the rapid transformation of this cosmopolitan city. This study discovered that about half of the respondents claimed not to have authentic heritage experiences. Nonetheless, authenticity is not always a major concern, but rather the study finds that aesthetics, novelty and relaxation play an important role for some tourists. This is a finding which is supported in many other studies of authenticity and the motivations of tourists.

A further chapter also addresses the issue of heritage and authenticity. King and Hitchcock focus on the region's 36 UNESCO World Heritage

Sites (WHS) and argue that they make a significant contribution to national identity, prestige and tourism development. Yet we do not know much about them in comparative terms. Once UNESCO has inscribed a site then it becomes 'a validation of quality' and confirms its 'authenticity'; these attributes provide significant attractions for the international tourism market, and governments use them for political and economic purposes. Moreover, they are both globally important but also local spaces for cultural encounters, social and political conflicts, and tensions and accommodations between competing interest groups and stakeholders. This chapter provides some findings on the first large-scale comparative research programme on UNESCO sites in Southeast Asia, and, among other issues, it considers how sites are being managed and how they are coping with conflicting pressures in a globalising heritage industry and in serving as symbols of national identity and prestige. In comparing sites within and beyond a particular country it is argued that we might be able to learn lessons for best practice to assist UNESCO and national governments in their planning and policies for heritage protection, conservation and tourism development.

The research interest in heritage tourism has focused primarily on the multivalent character of the concept of heritage, the development of 'discourses of the past', and the political uses and construction of heritage; these concerns overlap considerably with work on cultural invention, identity and authenticity. Apart from the comparative chapter on UNESCO sites two other chapters in the volume focus on World Heritage. And we have already drawn attention to Khoo's chapter on George Town, Penang.

Tuan Phong Ly considers in detail various issues which need to be addressed in the UNESCO World Heritage Site of the Phong Nha-Ke Bang National Park in Vietnam. When a relatively remote area in a developing country is designated as a globally important site, as in the case of this Vietnamese park, tourism inevitably becomes the primary driving force of economic growth there. However, in the case of Phong Nha-Ke Bang, the Vietnamese government has been unable to relocate all local communities in the area because of its limited budget and resources. Moreover, an increasing number of tourists prefer to experience authentic local cultures and lifestyles, and keeping local tourists in the core zones of parks may become a trend in tourism development in developing countries. Although advantageous to the improvement of the rural economy, tourism development can also result in a number of complicated issues when local communities are allowed to reside in national parks.

Another on-going concern is the much more widely used concept of commoditisation or commodification of cultural and environmental assets, which in turn is obviously closely related to the concept of authenticity and its relational character. Amnaj Khaokhrueamuang's chapter focuses on the commodification of 'rurality' in Mae Kam Pong village, Chiang Mai province, and its relationship to long-stay Japanese tourists, and proposes a conceptual model for other rural communities. The results reveal that a tourism strategy should incorporate various elements of modern 'rurality': rural recreational spaces including forest tea cultivating areas, residential and amenity areas; the development of health tourism commodities and facilities to support elderly Japanese long-stay tourists; and the provision of rural commodities and facilities such as organic food and health products which reflect the identity of the local Lanna culture.

In the chapter by Sasiwimon Khongmueang and Peter Hervik there is a further development of the concept of community-based tourism (CBT) in Mae Kam Pong this time with regard to Nordic tourists, particularly Danish visitors. The authors are concerned with the idea of building a foundation for CBT that besides providing income and helping the local economy can also contribute to less modernist and Eurocentric thinking and more cosmopolitan openness among the visiting tourists. Tourists from the Nordic countries who take part in CBT at Mae Kam Pong may arrive with significantly less Eurocentric attitudes than most other tourists, but to what extent does the CBT reproduce or counter the enduring presence of a Eurocentrism based on a perceived modern-traditional divide? In such a view the 'traditional' world is presented as timeless, outside of history and therefore authentic since it was there before 'modernity' emerged, which may be more a feature of the tourist imaginary world than a feature of local reality. Sasiwimon and Hervik argue that if CBT can counter this vision, it requires a more thorough understanding of the cultural baggage of the visiting tourists. The chapter focuses on the knowledge dynamics of predominantly Danish tourists who come to the Chiang Mai area with potential interests in enmeshing themselves in local activities, including spending time in homestays with families. Danish tourists arrive with varying degrees of prior knowledge, proficiency, openness and attitudes toward cultural difference.

Community-based tourism would also be a way forward for ethnic or cultural tourism among the hunting-gathering Mlabri or Phi Tong Luang (Spirits of the Yellow Leaves) of Northern Thailand. The chapter by Shu Nimonjiya proposes that ethnic tourism has not yet had any marked influence on the Mlabri, neither has it brought much economic benefit to them. The reason is not only that the market scale is small but also that their socio-cultural attitudes do not encourage a more positive approach to tourism and its opportunities. Nevertheless, the problems faced by a marginalised minority population in the face of more powerful and well-connected outsiders who organise tours and activities are rather more formidable obstacles than the socio-cultural attitudes of the Mlabri.

With regard to the chapters on Mae Kam Pong and on Phong Nha-Ke Bang National Park in Vietnam it is clear that we need to address both local and tourist responses to and involvement in the tourism experience, and this theme of encounters is also pursued in the chapters on ecotourism in Liled, Thailand and on homestays on the Dieng Plateau of Java. Rungrawee Jitpakdee, in her chapter on Liled, also examines, using both quantitative and qualitative data, community-based ecotourism in Surathani Province, Thailand focusing on the potential levels of community management in ecotourism, management planning, the local participation in ecotourism development and interactions between members of the local community and visitors. Rungrawee argues that the Liled community had a high level of potential attention for the development of ecotourism. According to the opinions of both Thai and foreign tourists, the Liled community managed ecotourism activities well, but the provision of souvenirs needed improvement. Ecotourism facilities, such as transportation networks within the community, parking lots and toilets also required further development. There was also a need to improve public relations, more general local awareness of conservation issues, codes of conduct, and rules and regulations for ecotourism management and monitoring. Importantly, a local community federation needed to be established for controlling and evaluating ecotourism management. The locals preferred to monitor and evaluate their activities by themselves and were reluctant for government or outside organisations to intervene and evaluate them.

Another dimension of local response to tourism is provided by Narong Sikhiram and Songsuda Poosawang. Their chapter was based on data gathered at Ban Pha Bong Village, Muang District, Mae Hong Sorn Province, Northern Thailand, close to the border with Myanmar. The Tai community there is being supported by the Thai Ministry of Public Health to develop their skills for health tourism development; currently they practise organic farming and food security based on self-sufficiency. The research focused on female residents who are involved in food preparation and management and assesses their willingness and collaboration in preparation of healthy food for tourists. Tai food is distinctive and it is highly saturated with fat and sodium, as female residents did not have a basic knowledge of nutrition and healthy food. However, as the research continued, it was found that the Tai women were eager to learn how to prepare healthier food. They acknowledged that healthy food is a key factor in maintaining good health, and that some of the main problems in their cooking, was over-reliance on such ingredients as monosodium glutamate (MSG) as the major flavouring agent. Another significant issue was minimising the cost of food with no regard for nutritional value, quality and appropriate quantity. In this action research, the researchers held workshops and seminars and along with groups of women created standardised recipes in order to improve food management and nutritional value. They were able to offer healthy indigenous menus in catering for tourists.

This current volume, engaged in a rethinking exercise, therefore aims to address a wide range of emerging conceptual and empirical issues in tourism studies (and the deconstruction of tourism studies) in order to focus on processes and developments within tourism development in Asia (and the need to de-link them from Euro-American preoccupations). Above all we have wanted to engage with locally generated research across a range of Asian countries and with recent empirical research conducted by Asian researchers.

References

Bruner, Edward M. (2005) *Culture on Tour: Ethnographies of Travel*, Chicago: Chicago University Press.

Chon, K.S. (ed.) (2000) *Tourism in Southeast Asia: A New Direction*, New York, London and Oxford: The Haworth Hospitality Press.

Cohen, Erik (1972) 'Towards a Sociology of International Tourism', *Social Research*, 39: 164-182.

—. (1979a) 'Rethinking the Sociology of Tourism', *Annals of Tourism Research,* 6: 18-35.

—. (1979b) 'A Phenomenology of Tourist Experiences', *Sociology*, 13: 179-201.

—. (1984) 'The Sociology of Tourism: Approaches, Issues and Findings', *Annual Review of Sociology*, 10: 373-392.

—. (2007) 'Authenticity in Tourism Studies: *Aprés la lutte*', *Tourism Recreation Research*, 32: 75-82.

Cohen, Erik and Scott A. Cohen (2012a) 'Current Sociological Theories and Issues in Tourism', *Annals of Tourism Research,* 39: 2177-2202.

Cohen, Erik (2012b) 'Authentication: Hot and Cool', *Annals of Tourism Research*, 39: 1295-1314.

Cochrane, Janet (ed.) (2008) *Asian Tourism: Growth and Change*, Oxford and Amsterdam: Elsevier Ltd.

Daly, Patrick and Tim Winter (eds) (2012) *Routledge Handbook of Heritage in Asia,* Routledge Handbook series, London and New York: Routledge.

Edensor, T. (2001) 'Performing Tourism, Staging Tourism', *Tourist Studies*, 1: 59-81.

—. (2007) 'Mundane Mobilities: Performances and Spaces of Tourism', *Social and Cultural Geography*, 8: 199-215.

Franklin, Adrian and Mike Crang (2001) 'Editorial: the Trouble with Tourism and Travel Theory', *Tourist Studies,* 1: 5-22.

Go, F. M. and C. L. Jenkins (eds) (1997) *Tourism and Economic Development in Asia and Australasia*, London and Washington: Cassell.

Hall, C. Michael (1997) *Tourism in the Pacific Rim: Developments, Impacts and Markets*, South Melbourne: Addison-Wesley Longman, second edition.

Hall, C. Michael, and Stephen Page (eds) (1997) *Tourism in the Pacific: Issues and Cases*, London: International Thomson Business Press.

—. (eds) (2000) *Tourism in South and Southeast Asia: Issues and Cases*, Oxford: Butterworth Heinemann.

Hannam, Kevin (2014) 'Tourism Mobilities'. In Alan A. Lew, C. Michael Hall and Alan M. Williams (eds), *The Wiley Blackwell Companion to Tourism*, Chichester: Wiley Blackwell, pp. 78-87.

Hannam, Kevin and David Knox (2010) *Understanding Tourism: a Critical Introduction*, London: Sage Publications Ltd.

Mimi Sheller and John Urry (2006) 'Editorial: Mobilities, Immobilities, Moorings', *Mobilities*, 1: 1-22.

Hatton, Michael J. (1999) *Community-based Tourism in the Asia-Pacific*, Toronto: School of Media Studies at Humber College.

Hee-Joo Han and Jae-Sub Lee (2008) 'A Study on the KBS TV Drama *Winter Sonata* and its Impact on Korea's Hallyu Tourism Development', *Journal of Travel and Tourism Marketing*, 24:115-126.

Hitchcock, Michael and Victor T. King (eds) (2003) *Tourism and Heritage in South-East Asia*, special issue of *Indonesia and the Malay World*, 31.

Hitchcock, Michael, Victor T. King and Michael J.G. Parnwell (eds) (1993) *Tourism in South-East Asia*. London: Routledge.

—. (eds) (2009) *Tourism in Southeast Asia: Challenges and New Directions*, Copenhagen: NIAS Press and Honolulu: University of Hawai'i Press.

—. (eds) (2010) *Heritage Tourism in Southeast Asia*, Copenhagen: NIAS Press and Honolulu: University of Hawai'i Press.

Inglis, Fred (2000) *The Delicious History of the Holiday*, London: Routledge.

King, Victor T. (2008) 'Tourism in Asia: a Review of the Achievements and Challenges', *Sojourn. Journal of Social Issues in Southeast Asia*, 23: 104-136.

—. (2010) Review of 'Asians on Tour: Exploring the Rise of Asian Tourism', edited by Tim Winter, Peggy Teo and T.C. Chang, A*SEASUK News*, No. 47: 18-21.

—. (2012) Review of 'Domestic Tourism in Asia: Diversity and Divergence', edited by Shalini Singh, *ASEASUK News*, No 51: 24-26.

Lew, Alan A., C. Michael Hall and Alan M. Williams (eds) (2014) *The Wiley Blackwell Companion to Tourism*, Chichester: Wiley Blackwell.

Lew, Alan. L., Lawrence Yu, John Ap and Zhang Guangrui (eds) (2003) *Tourism in China*, New York, London Oxford: The Haworth Hospitality Press.

Löfgren, O (1999) *On Holiday: a History of Vacationing*, Berkeley: University of California Press.

Logan, William (2012) 'States, Governance and the Politics of Culture: World Heritage in Asia'. In Patrick Daly and Tim Winter (eds), *Routledge Handbook of Heritage in Asia,* Routledge Handbook series, London and New York: Routledge, pp. 113-128.

MacCannell, Dean (2001) 'Tourist Agency', *Tourist Studies*, 1: 23-37.

McKercher, Bob (2002) 'Towards a Classification of Cultural Tourists', *International Journal of Tourism Research*, 4: 29-38.

Michaud, Jean and Michel Picard (eds) (2001) *Tourisme et Sociétés Locales en Asie Orientale*, special issue of *Anthropologie et Sociétés*, 25: 1-166.

Perkins, Harvey C. (2001) 'Gazing or Performing? Reflections on Urry's Tourist Gaze in the Context of Contemporary Experience in the Antipodes', *International Sociology*, 16: 185-204.

Picard, Michel and Robert E. Wood (eds) (1997) *Tourism, Ethnicity and the State in Asian and Pacific Societies*, Honolulu: University of Hawai'i Press.

Prideaux, Bruce, Dallen J. Timothy and K. S. Chon (eds) (2008) *Cultural and Heritage Tourism in Asia and the Pacific*, Oxford and New York: Routledge.

Richter, Linda K. (1989) *The Politics of Tourism in Asia*, Honolulu, University of Hawai'i Press.

Rojek, Chris (1995) *Decentring Leisure: Rethinking Leisure Theory*, London: Sage.

Rojek, Chris and John Urry (eds) (1997) *Touring Cultures*, London: Routledge.

Selwyn, Tom (1996) *The Tourist Image: Myths and Myth-making in Tourism*, Chichester: Wiley.

Sheller, Mimi (2011) 'Mobility' *Sociopedia.isa*: http://sage.pub.net/isa/resources/pdf/Mobility pdf.

Sheller, Mimi, and John Urry (eds) (2004) *Tourism Mobilities: Places to Play, Places in Play*, London and New York: Routledge.

—. (2006) 'The New Mobilities Paradigm', *Environment and Planning A*, 38: 207-226.

Sherlock, Kirsty (2001) 'Revisiting the Concept of Hosts and Guests', *Tourist Studies*, 1: 271-295.

Singh, Shalini (ed.) (2009/2011) *Domestic Tourism in Asia: Diversity and Divergence,* London: Earthscan, 2009; Singapore: ISEAS, 2011.

Smith, Valene, L. (ed.) (1979) *Hosts and Guests: the Anthropology of Tourism*, Philadelphia: University of Pennsylvania Press, second edition, 1989.

Tan Chee-Beng, Sidney C. H. Cheung and Yang Hui (eds) (2001) *Tourism, Anthropology and China*, Bangkok: White Lotus Press.

Teo, Peggy, T.C. Chang and K.C. Ho (eds) (2001) *Interconnected Worlds: Tourism in Southeast Asia*, Oxford: Elsevier Science, Pergamon.

Urry, John (1990) *The Tourist Gaze: Leisure and Travel in Contemporary Societies*, London: Sage, second edition, *The Tourist Gaze*, 2002.

—. (2000) *Sociology beyond Societies: Mobilities for the Twenty-First Century*, London: Routledge.

—. (2007) *Mobilities*, Cambridge: Polity Press.

Urry, John, and Jonas Larsen (2012) *The Tourist Gaze 3.0*, London: Sage Publications Ltd., third edition.

Van der Duim, René (2007) 'Tourismscapes: An Actor-network Perspective', *Annals of Tourism Research*, 34: 961-976.

Von Egmond, Ton (2007) *Understanding Western Tourists in Developing Countries*, Wallingford, Oxfordshire and Cambridge, MA: CAB International.

Wang, Ning (1999) 'Rethinking Authenticity in Tourism Experience', *Annals of Tourism Research*, 26:349–370.

—. (2000) *Tourism and Modernity: a Sociological Analysis*, Oxford: Pergamon Press.

Winter, Tim (2007) 'Rethinking Tourism in Asia', *Annals of Tourism Research* 34: 27-44.

—. (2009) 'Asian Tourism and the Retreat of Anglo-Western Centrism in Tourism Theory', *Current Issues in Tourism*, 12: 21-31.

Winter, Tim, and Patrick Daly (2012) 'Heritage in Asia: Converging Forces, Conflicting Values'. In Patrick Daly and Tim Winter (eds), *Routledge Handbook of Heritage in Asia,* Routledge Handbook series, London and New York: Routledge, pp. 1-35.

Winter, Tim, Peggy Teo and T.C. Chang (eds) (2007) *Asia on Tour: Exploring the Rise of Asian Tourism,* London and New York: Routledge.

Yamashita Shinji, Kadir H. Din and J.S. Eades (eds) (1997) *Tourism and Cultural Development in Asia and Oceania*, Bangi: Penerbit Universiti Kebangsaan Malaysia.

CULTURAL HERITAGE, IDENTITY AND THE POLITICS OF PERFORMANCE

UNESCO World Heritage Sites in Southeast Asia: Problems and Prospects

Victor T. King and Michael J. Hitchcock

Introductory Remarks

This critical analysis of UNESCO (United Nations Educational, Scientific and Cultural Organization)-inscribed sites in Southeast Asia has emerged from a four-year (2009-2013) cross-national, multidisciplinary comparative programme of research on selected World Heritage Sites (WHS) across the region (see King, 2015, forthcoming). This chapter focuses on three countries: Thailand, Malaysia and Indonesia, though the research also encompassed Laos, Cambodia, Vietnam and the Philippines. Among other matters, the research examines the tensions between the often competing interests and understandings of the various stakeholders involved in these globally important sites and the various pressures brought to bear on them from the stakeholders involved: local communities, national governments and their agencies, international conservation organisations and associated experts and researchers, tourists (both domestic and international) and civil society institutions. Inscription as a World Heritage Site also generates new actors, institutions and regulations (Miura, 2011a: 23), and considerable challenges for those who manage these sites (Leask and Fyall, 2006; Esposito and Gaulis, 2010; and Miura, 2011a on Angkor).

International organisations like UNESCO and the World Heritage Centre in Paris, as well as their associated bodies including the International Council on Monuments and Sites (ICOMOS), the International Union for Conservation of Nature (IUCN), and the International Centre for the Study of the Preservation and Restoration of Cultural Property (ICCROM), impose a set of conservation and protection requirements on the sites inscribed on the World Heritage List. These requirements are designed to ensure that the characteristics of the site acknowledged as of 'universal human value' (UNESCO, 1972; Francioni, 2008; and see, UNESCO, 1983, 2003, 2012) are protected, and, if appropriate, enhanced. However, protection and conservation do not always sit easily with national government interest in increasing revenue from tourism and using these sites as symbolic centres for the construction and promotion of national identity (Winter, 2007; and see Berliner and Bortolotto, 2013).

Heritage, both cultural and natural, is not handed down unchanged from one generation to another. It is subject to selection, construction, negotiation and contestation in the context of more general processes of identity formation (Hitchcock and King, 2003a, 2003b: 3-13; Harrison and Hitchcock, 2005 [2004]; Smith, 2003: 82, 103). Heritage is also a concept which is difficult to define (Herbert, 1989:10-12). In a narrow sense it is 'a legacy; a set of traditions, values, or treasured material things' (Universal Dictionary, 1987:721). In introducing the notion of interpretation, in that heritage is constructed, and given meaning and significance, we adopt a much broader conceptualisation of heritage pertaining to the arena of cultural politics (Peleggi, 1996: 432; 2002). In this latter sense heritage, presented and re-presented as something which relates to the past and which is in some way given significance as 'treasure' or 'legacy', is frequently constructed and appropriated by the state and its agents as an object worthy of political, economic and 'touristic' attention.

In post-colonial developing states this process of identity construction is an even more urgent task and the need to 'imagine' the nation leads to the selection and deployment of archaeological finds and heritage sites to present images of national resilience, unity, and innovation, often in the context of an 'imagined' golden age of endeavour and achievement (Anderson, 1991:178-185; Glover, 2003:17). The 'essence' or 'genius' of the nation is usually traced back to a glorious past and to benevolent and enlightened government when everything that is now cherished as demarcating and defining the nation was created and set in motion.

In summary then the concept of heritage refers to tangible and concrete elements of the past, as well as those aspects of culture expressed in behaviour, action and performance which are interpreted and judged to be worthy of our interest and protection. In addition to the state other domestic agents involved in the creation of meanings and understandings in relation to heritage and the past comprise local tourists and those communities which live at or in close proximity to heritage sites and those who secure their livelihood from working there (Reynolds, 1993, 1998; Paritta, 2002; Peleggi, 1996, 2002). The Thai example is particularly apt in that 'remnants of Thailand's past' have been used to construct a national identity since the foundation of Bangkok and the Chakri dynasty, and these remnants are 'excellent resources for building a politically useful heritage' (Van Esterik, 2000: 109; and see Evrard and Prasit, 2009b: 239-245).

Heritage is also contested and transformed not only by domestic agents but also by global actors, including UNESCO, and international tourists. It has therefore become a highly politicised project (Pires, 2010). UNESCO's World Heritage Committee designates World Heritage Sites as of either 'cultural' or 'natural' or 'mixed' importance, and more particularly as sites of 'outstanding universal value' (World Heritage Centre, http://whc.unesco.org/en/; and see Adams, 2003: 91-93; Hitchcock, 2004: 461-466; Long and Sweet, 2006: 445-469; Peleggi, 1996: 432; Rössler, 2006; Smith, 2003: 38, 105-116; UNESCO, 2012). Since the late 1960s heritage has been internationalised by such bodies as UNESCO which has 'helped to generate a new set of understandings of culture and built heritage' (Askew, 1996: 184). Heritage is displayed both to an international audience and to the citizenry, but, given processes of conservation and landscaping their authenticity is invariably staged to a greater or lesser extent.

The UNESCO *Convention Concerning the Protection of the World's Cultural and Natural Heritage* (1972), and the 'criteria for selection' of sites (UNESCO, 1983) are sprinkled with superlatives: 'masterpiece', '[of] human creative genius', 'unique', 'exceptional', 'outstanding'. Invariably these preoccupations stress the concepts of 'tradition' and 'continuity', expressed particularly in built heritage and material culture (International Council of Museums, http://icom.museum/; http://www.getty.edu/conservation/; and see Vines, 2005). Even though there is recognition of the importance of 'living' cultural sites, overall this emphasis on outstanding cultural (and natural) legacies tends to indulge in nostalgia for the past and in the presentation of the exotic (Kennedy and Williams, 2001; and see Berliner, 2012).

'Heritage tourism' has also proved difficult to define in that tourists as a highly differentiated category consume not just the cultural products of the past but also a range of contemporary cultural forms (Smith, 2003:29-44; Clarke, 2000:23-36; Hughes, 2000:111-122). Cultural tourism is therefore no longer seen, as it was in the past, as 'a niche form of tourism' (Smith, 2003:45). Heritage tourism therefore comprises that part of cultural tourism which, according to Richter, is 'applied by some to almost anything about the past that can be visited' (1999: 108). Tourism in this case becomes a 'history-making business' (Shaw and Williams, 2002: 203).

In summary UNESCO, though it appears to operate in a neutral, rational and logical environment based on the principles of heritage assessment and evaluation administered at the global level, is in fact deeply implicated in the politics of culture. Miura captures the dilemmas with which UNESCO has to grapple in a sequence of questions: 'what is heritage, who is the rightful owner, what can be practised and what not, what rules of ownership should be adopted, how much access to heritage [should] various actors be allowed, who is to manage heritage and how to do it [?]' (2011b: 98).

However, studying these sites in isolation tends to emphasise their uniqueness rather than that they are all subject to a set of international conventions and they are managed by observing universally determined guiding principles. In our view, the research available to date is mainly site-focused and therefore lacks any kind of coherent approach to the issues which these sites generate (Hitchcock, King and Parnwell, 1993, 2009, 2010; and Hitchcock and King, 2003). Comparative studies are rare; there is the research by Heather Black on Prambanan, Borobudur, and Ayutthaya (1997) and two relatively short chapters by Black and Geoffrey Wall on the same cases (Black and Wall, 2001; Wall and Black, 2005). Their research focuses on local involvement and meanings, the interests and engagements of local communities and the fact that local people usually have different values and perspectives with regard to these sites from international and national actors. One of the major questions they pose is 'Do local communities benefit or are they often ignored in the formulation of plans and in their detailed execution?' Their conclusion is that local people often feel separated from their heritage and disenfranchised.

In a volume providing an overview on the broader question of managing cultural resources in Southeast Asia, Miksic et al (2011; and see Miksic, 2011) point out that comparative analysis of World Heritage Sites in terms of management issues is rare. However, a recent book by Chapman (2013) provides a wide-ranging comparative examination of the history of conservation and management of monumental remains or 'ruins' across Southeast Asia, and the role and work of UNESCO, other international agencies and local institutions in this endeavour.

Black and Wall also concluded that the managerial neglect of the local dimension has tended to lose the opportunities offered to enhance the interpretation and the multidimensional character of the sites in order to make them more meaningful to tourists and to others with an interest in them. They argued that the management and understanding of the importance and place of these sites in both local and national life would be increased immeasurably if there was more attention given by heritage protection agencies to the development in partnership with local people, of a 'true atmosphere of stewardship' (Black and Wall, 2001: 134). Similar conclusions on local involvement have been reached in another comparative study which concentrates on the two World Heritage Sites in Cambodia – Angkor and Preah Vihear (Hauser-Schäublin, 2011a; 2011b). In her contribution to that book Miura observes that 'many of the traditional practices conducted by the local inhabitants in the space of Angkor were denied' (2011a: 22; and 2011c: 131) because those responsible for managing it and formulating policies saw it as belonging to the nation and the world, and not to local inhabitants (2011c: 131; 2011a: 27-31). Furthermore, the living cultures which energise a particular site are often marginalised or traditionalised, and as Miura states in relation to Angkor 'Conserving the static landscape as an ancient archaeological park may not be the only thing that tourists want to see, but more interactive and participatory tourism' (2011c: 144).

The Three Cases: Thailand, Malaysia and Indonesia

Each of the country case studies demonstrates the complex interactions between global and local processes, but in all cases the state and its agencies intervene to ensure that the country's WHS are pressed into the service of the nation. In the case of Thailand we examine Sukhothai and Ayutthaya; in Malaysia we focus on Melaka; and in Indonesia we consider Prambanan and Borobudur.

Thailand demonstrates, most especially, the vital importance of the national symbolic dimension and the significance of domestic as against international tourism. The main pressures in the Thai case appear to be generated by the domestic market in that the heritage sites are arenas of national symbolism and identity formation and, in the case of the cultural sites of Sukhothai and Ayutthaya, national religious affirmation and pilgrimage, as well as places where the wealthy Thai middle class spend leisure time in pursuit of what we might term 'Thai-ness'. Nevertheless, given the ever-increasing domestic interest in these sites visitor numbers are generating all kinds of problems in relation to the sustainability of the heritage infrastructure. Decision-making is also rendered difficult because responsibilities for the use, management and administration of the cultural sites are divided between different bodies; the Fine Arts Department has a major role (FAD, 1996), but there is also the Department of Urban Planning, the Department of Religious Affairs, various municipal authorities, and the Tourism Authority of Thailand (TAT) among others.

In the case of Melaka we find that the site is used partly to express and legitimise a Malay-Muslim political agenda and the 'reclamation' of the role of the Malays and the sultanate system in Malaysian history within a post-independence ideology of pluralism and multiculturalism. Different parts of the Melaka World Heritage Site give expression to different segments within Malaysia's plural society – in this case primarily Malay-Muslim and hybrid (*peranakan*) Chinese communities with a marginalised Eurasian element. In partial contrast to Thailand, Malaysia's historic cities are playgrounds for both local and international visitors but all of these sites have to cope with increasing tourism pressures. Melaka and George Town (Penang) are also much more subject to the Malaysian government's policy of promoting economic development through the tourism industry and encouraging the more general development of the service sector.

In Indonesia the tourism market is also substantial, but not as large as that of Thailand and Malaysia. The two WHS in Java are important in cultural, historical and archaeological terms and, though they are not directly connected in religious terms to the predominantly Muslim populations that live around them, they are important cultural and symbolic destinations for domestic tourists. Borobudur is also held in high regard by Buddhists around the world, though there is an Indonesian Buddhist population. However, it is also an important national monument as one of its cultural and historical icons, hence the substantial domestic tourism demand. Finally, it is an important local site because it is a part of the local economy. Similar points can be made about Prambanan, but here there is a different twist as there is a Hindu population in Java and there are many Balinese Hindu migrants in the region who visit the site. What is clear is that both sites are grappling with the pressures generated by increasing visitor numbers, and the tensions between the demands of conservation and protection and those of tourism development. As in Thailand the involvement of several official stakeholders in the use and management of the sites makes for problems in inter-departmental coordination and decision-making.

Thailand

Although heritage sites here are the object of the international tourist gaze (Urry, 1990), it is important to emphasise just how much they are destinations for mainly Thai urban-based middle class tourists. This is especially the case for Ayutthaya within easy reach of Bangkok for excursionists. But the catchment area for middle class tourists has expanded far beyond the Bangkok conurbation since the onset of the country's economic boom in the early 1980s, associated with the 'urbanisation' of the capital city's rural hinterland. This process of 'extended metropolitanisation' (McGee, 1991: 2008; McGee and Robinson, 1995; Ginsburg, Koppel and McGee, 1991; Forbes, 1997; Jones, 2002; Parnwell and Wongsuphasawat, 1997; Sowatree Nathalang, 1992) has brought urbanism to a region that stretches more than 100 kilometres towards the east, west and north of central Bangkok (Reynolds, 1998: 116-117). These developments have significant implications not only in terms of the volume of urban tourists visiting heritage sites in Thailand but also in relation to the ways in which domestic visitors perceive and interact with heritage sites. This domestication of tourism sites in Thailand is only one example of a much broader trend in the expansion of domestic and intra-regional tourism (Winter, Teo and Chang, 2009a, 2009b). The increase in domestic tourism is largely the product of the development of a 'new urban middle class' in Southeast Asia, as an important component of 'the new rich' (Robison and Goodman, 1996; Abdul Rahman Embong, 2001; Hsiao, 2001, 2006; Ockey, 1991; Prudhisan and Chantana, 2001).

Evrard and Prasit (2009a, 2009b) have also examined the evolution of domestic tourism in Thailand and offer insights which have some bearing on visits to World Heritage Sites there. They point out that in 2004, there were 74.8 million Thai tourists [or more accurately tourist visits/activities], compared with just 11.6 million foreign tourists (ibid: 301); yet the latter have received disproportionate attention and there is a tendency to see local tourism simply as an emulation of Western tourism (Winter, Teo and Chang, 2009a, 2009b). Evrard and Prasit find important differences in the motivation and behaviour of Thai tourists which have implications for heritage management (ibid: 302). Nevertheless, although domestic tourism in Thailand is a primarily middle class phenomenon, we should recognise that excursions are not confined to that class. Ayutthaya, for example, with its important religious meaning for the Thais, is visited frequently by those from lower and working class backgrounds as well.

At the heart of Thai domestic tourism is an implicit nationalism and an explicit nostalgia which have transformed people, places and landscapes from being things avoided, ignored or looked down upon into things attractive and curious that are worth visiting and preserving; domestic tourism attractions also importantly make a contribution to the sense of 'Thai-ness'; Ayutthaya and Sukhothai are both former Thai capitals. While foreign tourists seek the exotic and authentic Evrard and Prasit propose that 'On the whole, the improvements in communications networks, the multiplication of "local histories", the idealisation of the rural, the politics of heritage, as well as the availability of numerous magazines, journals and travel guides devoted to these subjects directly contributed to the development of leisure mobility among Thai citizens and consequently of a domestic mass tourism industry' (2009a: 312; 2009b: 244-245).

The Tourism Authority of Thailand (TAT, 2008a: 5; http://www.tat.or.th) knows precisely where to situate its World Heritage Sites. In a promotional pamphlet entitled *Paragons of World Heritage* the TAT introduces these sites with a statement which emphasises their role in giving expression to the Thai nation and their invented past (and see Winter on Angkor, 2007). Most importantly in one of the official TAT guides to Ayutthaya, the national value of the cultural sites are expressed in the words of King Bhumipol Adulyadej, appended to the back cover: 'A new building today is just the pride of the builder, but an ancient monument is the pride of the Nation. A single ancient brick alone is valuable and should be preserved. Without Sukhothai, Ayutthaya and Bangkok, Thailand would be meaningless….' (TAT, 2000).

Sukhothai and Ayutthaya are presented as 'the antecedents of the modern Thai nation-state' (Peleggi, 1996: 433). Although modernity and globalisation are acknowledged what is emphasised are the essential elements of 'Thai-ness'; there is a very strong adherence to the 'national religion', Theravada Buddhism and the monastic order (the *Sangha*). Thais are staunchly loyal to the monarchy and hold it in deep reverence; there is a set of cultural characteristics which delineate the Thai nation in language, ritual, dance, architecture, behaviour and personality, and these cultural commonalities override or at least neutralise ethnic difference and cultural dissonance. Moreover the Chakri kings established a direct connection between their dynasty and the legacy left by Sukhothai and Ayutthaya, taking some of the most important treasures from these sites to Bangkok and thereby legitimising their own rule.

However, interestingly the UNESCO status of Thailand's WHS does not seem to be promoted to the extent which one might have anticipated. In the TAT *Golden Wonderland* brochure the 'ancient wonders' section provides a brief summary of the sites. Ban Chiang, Sukhothai and Ayutthaya are referred to in relation to the historical development of the Kingdom of Thailand, and in the case of Sukhothai and Ayutthaya emphasis is placed on 'the architectural achievement of the Thais' (2008b: 16). But these sites are placed firmly in a Thai national space (Van Esterik, 2000: 120). In the 1980s the TAT began seriously to promote its 'cultural heritage', in part at least to counter the country's more racy, nightlife image, but also because it had embarked on major restoration work of its ancient monuments from the 1970s (Peleggi, 1996: 435; FAD, 1996).

What is also worth noting is that historically Thai domestic tourism began as a royal and elite project connected to the development and construction of the Thai nation-state (2009b: 243). From the mid-nineteenth century outlying sites visited by members of the elite became increasingly fixed, mapped and claimed and were incorporated into the 'Siamese geo-body' (Thongchai, 1994: 13). A nation is an imagined community (Anderson, 1991), but it is also a geographical and spatial entity, with territorial boundaries within which national landmarks, shrines and sacred places are located providing symbolic centres expressing and embodying nationhood. The national elements of this domestic tourism have been carried into the recent period of local mass tourism (Winter, Teo and Chang, 2009a: 11-14).

The case studies have revealed domestic tourism and urbanisation pressures as significant factors in intensifying the tension between economic development and the conservation of Thailand's World Heritage Sites. Thus, the expectation that WHS are arenas for the international tourist gaze has to be heavily qualified, and this has implications for the ways in which we conceptualise tourism encounters and impacts. The study has also revealed the vital importance of Bangkok as the country's dominant metropolis and extended metropolitanisation as an underlying economic, physical and cultural process, as a source of tourists and as a major influence on the use and development of these sites. Linked to this, the ways in which the appreciation, use and construction of heritage in Thailand are intertwined with the materialisation of a Thai middle class have also emerged as important themes that arguably have resonance in other parts of Southeast Asia.

The rapid growth of domestic tourism in Thailand and its steady inclusion of heritage sites as destinations have significant and distinctive implications for the management of these sites. Ayutthaya is the most 'exposed' site not only to tourism pressures but also the encroachment of urban settlement and the influx of vendors and others keen to capitalise on the site's economic potential. In attempts at controlling urban encroachment there needs to be an extension of the boundaries of the conservation area but it is unlikely that a buffer zone can be established without demolition and relocation of some existing urban areas which predictably will generate local protest and resistance. Furthermore, the increase in visitors provides a major market for local traders, whose control usually falls within the jurisdiction of the municipal authorities.

There was also a particularly urgent need for funds for emergency support and consolidation work following the serious floods of 1995, given that Ayutthaya is surrounded by water on a low-lying flood plain at the confluence of three major rivers. Anti-flood defences are now in the process of construction overseen by the Department of Public Works and the city planning authorities. Nevertheless, further disastrous floods struck Ayutthaya in October 2011during which 100 monuments were flooded, some of them remaining under at least two metres of water for a month. UNESCO has since formulated a Flood Risk Mitigation Plan (2013-14) (http://www.unescobkk.org/culture/wh/ap-sites/ayutthaya/).

There has to be negotiation over how urban development in Ayutthaya is controlled in the best interests of conservation and so that the historic areas of the city are not overwhelmed by unsightly buildings, local traders and increases in traffic flows. It is clear that in such a complex inter-departmental situation of potentially competing interests and agendas, the sheer problem of establishing and developing clear lines of responsibility and communication is a major issue. Ayutthaya presents particular management problems and it is not evident that all the mechanisms and structures are in place to enable the historical park to cope with current and anticipated pressures. There is very real tension between the municipal authorities and the site managers in terms not only of their respective visions for the site's future development but also how these heritage assets should be managed.

Sukhothai, as a less frequented heritage space, is arguably more manageable, given that it is a 450-kilometre drive away from Bangkok, or by air or rail to Phitsanulok, some 50 kilometres away; most visitors will either come on a two-day excursion which includes Sukhothai, Si

Satchanalai and Kamphaeng Phet or as individual or small group international tourists who visit for a short while and return to Bangkok or stop off there on their way to Chiang Mai and the northern hill areas. The restoration and conservation of Sukhothai and its projection as a site of benevolent government and as an essential element of Thai national identity have been subjects of considerable debate (and see Van Esterik, 2000: 111-112). Reynolds (citing Peleggi [1994]), points out that one Thai historian has claimed that the historical narratives of Sukhothai's importance are 'fictions and myths' and that its presentation to the visitor gives no clues as to the 'urban setting and planning of the past' (1998: 136). It has to be said that though the Sukhothai complexes of historical parks are awe-inspiring places to visit, and provide the visitor with a feeling of religious tranquillity, they give no positive indication of what the communities who created them and lived and worked there were like and how the ancient monuments that survive fitted into what must have been vibrant religiously-oriented farming societies focused on highly stratified urban social systems.

Despite these debates and the somewhat artificial, 'captured-in- time' presentation of Sukhothai and its associated sites, there is no doubt that they are very well maintained; tourism is controlled and there are no noticeable pressures on these sites emanating from the nearby urban areas. The distance from Bangkok has not deterred a relatively substantial number of visitors from seeing these parks and they are now firmly rooted in Thai national heritage and identity.

Malaysia

Heritage issues in the Federation of Malaysia are even more complex than in Thailand because the Malay-dominated government has deployed and transformed urban landscapes in their nation-building policies, but the established urban areas are usually home to visually prominent and demographically and economically significant Chinese and to a lesser extent Indian populations. Urban areas therefore express and embody particular sub-national ethnic identities, not only of various Chinese communities, but also increasing numbers of Malays and other Muslims, numerically smaller populations of Indians, and a whole host of mixed populations. Therefore, there is often on-going tension between the need to protect and conserve a historically and culturally important site, and the pressures exerted by the vagaries of human political, social and economic interests and values.

Malaysia like Thailand has one of the largest tourist industries in Southeast Asia, and although it has consistently promoted cultural tourism along with the usual leisure pursuits of sun, sand, sea and shopping, as well as increasingly ecotourism, at the official and popular promotional level there has been a noticeable shift in emphasis in the Malaysian Tourism Ministry's presentation of Malaysian culture and heritage (Tourism Malaysia, 2009a; and see 2009b and 2009c). In this the World Heritage Sites of George Town (Penang) and Melaka, inscribed in 2008, play a prominent part (UNESCO, 2008a, 2008b). Tourists are invited to 'come and experience the heritage of all Asia'; the promotion makes much of the different populations which have come from various parts of Asia, the Middle East and Europe to the 'crossroads' of Malaysia (Tourism Malaysia, 2009a: 2-3). The plural society of Malaysia is an ideal tourism promotional vehicle for claiming that the visitor gets an 'instant' experience of Asia. Certainly Melaka plays a part in this picture; it exemplifies 'ancient kingdoms' which through trade brought people from China, India, Persia and Arabia, and from Europe (the Portuguese, Dutch and British). Rather than Malay pre-eminence what is emphasised is ethnic and cultural variety, a 'mosaic' of cultures, multi-ethnic harmony, 'a peaceful blend', and a 'colourful spectrum' (ibid: 2-4). This also captures the UNESCO-inspired emphasis on Melaka as 'a melting pot of all the races, reflecting the diverse multiracial society that today distinguishes this country' (Schubert et al, 2004: 23). However, there is a tension here in that there is also a continuing Malay-dominated and Malay–oriented process of symbolic construction which presents Melaka as part of Malay heritage and history to the exclusion of other ethnic communities which currently reside there.

Historical Context

Much of the recent research on Melaka has focused on the central position which it occupies, as a former global port settlement, in the history and cultural symbolism of the Muslim-Malays, the Malayan Peninsula and the wider nation-state of Malaysia (Sandhu and Wheatley, 1983a, 1983b; and see 1983c: 566-567; Cartier, 2001: 193). Having been founded around the turn of the fifteenth century as a 'minor chieftainship' it grew into a major international trading emporium (Sandhu and Wheatley, 1983c: 499). With its strategically located deep water harbour and a sheltered river mouth on the Straits of Malacca, its economy came to be founded on 'the centralized collection and exchange of goods produced elsewhere' (Cho and Ward, 1983: 624). Sandhu and Wheatley pronounce that Melaka was 'one of the most famous trading emporia that the world has known, its fabled wealth a byword from Lisboa to Peking' (1983b: 50; and see I983a, 1983c: 504). More than this 'Its *raison d'être* was a network of connections both regional and extra-regional, which made it a central place among central places, the hinge point between eastern Asia and the lands to the West' (Ginsburg, 1983: 289).

In 'patrimonial' and 'galactic' style it extended its reach and authority through the island world of Southeast Asia, and in so doing the Melakan thalassocracy played a crucial formative role in the development and dissemination of Malay culture, language and literature as well as serving as a centre of Islamic learning. What is more Melaka's traditions, expressed above all in the *Sejarah Melayu* (the Malay Annals) and the *Bustanu 'l-Salatin* (Garden of the Kings) are 'without equal in the Malayo-Indonesian world, in terms of either quantity or quality' (Wake, 1983: 128). Melaka's importance was attested to by the imperialist interests of a succession of European powers. Yet the European impact on Melaka made it difficult for the newly independent Malaysian government, in its attempts to construct an indigenously-framed nation-state, to reconcile its colonial heritage with the image of a new post-colonial polity based on the achievements and aspirations of their native ancestors. The cultural and architectural expressions of Melaka's greatness as a Malay-Muslim maritime sultanate were effectively eliminated by European colonialism. The indigenous origins of the port centre and its seat of economic and political power in the Sultan's palace and the state mosque were replaced by Portuguese architectural forms, religious and civic buildings and concepts of urban landscape in an Iberian fortified, walled town (Irwin, 1983: 783; Sandhu and Wheatley, 1983c: 531).

Following Dutch succession in the seventeenth century we find communities of Dutch, Portuguese Eurasians, Chinese, Muslim Indians and Hindus, Malays, Bugis and an ethnically mixed collection of 'slaves' (Sidhu, 1983: 32). The Dutch kept broadly to the Portuguese spatial division between a European civic zone and an ethnically mixed residential zone (Sandhu and Wheatley, 1983c: 535; Wan Hashimah and Shuhana, 2005: 2). Malay residential dominance during the sultanate period was gradually displaced from its northern suburbs along the Melaka River; central Melaka is now the home primarily of Chinese, many of whom are 'Baba' or 'Peranakan'; these were traditionally hybrid communities (Clammer, 1983: 156-158). In addition, the function of Melaka as a trading emporium diminished to be replaced subsequently by a European residential, administrative and garrison town and a regional capital for the neighbouring hinterland where tin-mines and estates were located worked primarily by Chinese and Indian immigrant labourers Cartier says 'Melaka's Islamic past is missing in the cultural landscape' (ibid: 194; and see Wee, 2009: 21).

Cartier also suggests that the mobile, cosmopolitan, culturally fluid population of Melaka has been progressively re-ordered since Malaysian independence in terms of contemporary national ideologies (ibid: 194; Milner, 2008, 2010). Indeed she sees this as a major problem in presenting Melaka to a wider audience: its roots in a dynamic, open, eclectic, hybrid Euro-Asian trading enterprise has been replaced by a narrower, inward-looking, ethnically discrete nationalist agenda. The complexity of Melaka's population has been reduced on the national stage to three broad ethnic categories comprising 'Malay' (though with additional communities which are, for certain purposes, brought together as *bumiputra* [indigenous people]), 'Chinese' and 'Indian'. These politically driven issues have obvious implications for the ways in which Melaka has been presented, to some extent transformed and then deployed in nation-building.

Melaka was officially handed over to the British in 1824 by the Anglo-Dutch Treaty of London. By the 1850s it had been administratively, culturally and economically incorporated into the British Straits Settlements but in relation to Singapore and Penang it 'came to be regarded as the junior partner' (Webster, 2011: 922;b (Sandhu and Wheatley, 1983c: 518). Melaka's fate was eventually sealed following Malaysian independence when other ports, particularly Port Klang and Port Penang, were favoured in the Malaysian government's plans for economic development. As a result today the economy of Melaka does not depend on sea-borne trade. About three-quarters of the Gross Domestic Product of the state of Melaka (which is a larger territory than the metropolitan area) is derived from tourism and related service industries (Chi, 1983: 652; Osborn, 1983: 476; Lim, 1983: 719-720; Seow, 1983).

Heritage and Tourism

Yet the promotion of heritage for tourism development and the purposes of national image and identity is only part of a much wider set of constructions. The major state government guide to Melaka endorsed by the Chief Minister says 'Melaka is not just about going back in time....[there is] the new Melaka, a thriving city and business centre, that has taken its rightful place in the development of Malaysia as we know it today, particularly its business profile' (Schubert et al, 2004: 23). The roles of protection and conservation in heritage sites become uncertain when we are told that Melaka has transformed its cultural and natural treasures into economic opportunities. Reinvigorated it 'now responds to the pulse of commerce' (ibid: 25).

Interestingly the Melaka State's Tourism Promotion Division advertises a range of leisure interests and activities in its literature. In its brochure *Melaka Tourism: 12 Subsectors* it opens with 'Melaka's appeal lies in its rich and colourful past. Melaka is renowned as the place where the history of Malaysia began' (Tourism Promotion Division, 2009: 2). But the Tourism Division then moves into the presentation of a diverse tourism product: 'Today, there's a lot more to Melaka in addition to its fascinating stories, legends and historical attractions' (ibid). Overall heritage is certainly there but it is embedded in a large leisure and tourism industry and one designed to appeal to a wide range of tourists.

There is then a major tension between heritage conservation and the concern to promote economic development and large-scale infrastructural projects, including the continuing land reclamation in and around the historic port, and the construction of new mega-tourism facilities which continue to spread along the coastline in the vicinity of the old town. On balance it would seem that development rather than heritage conservation and protection is favoured. A major problem which is threatening to endanger the tourist enjoyment of the historic site is the volume of traffic, the noise and pollution and the problems it poses for pedestrians.

Melaka as a Site of Malay and Malaysian Identity

In examining the symbolic use of heritage sites we see in the case of Melaka the complexities surrounding the ways in which global heritage has, in Cartier's terms, been 'imaged'. This process of 'imaging' derives from Melaka's singular historical position and its role in the construction of the identity of a post-colonial nation-state. Melaka's importance was confirmed in the words on the plaque unveiled by the then Prime Minister Mahathir Mohamed in Melaka in 1989: translated it reads 'the historic city of Malaysia. Here is where it all began....the birth of a nation'. Indeed it was the first Prime Minister, Tunku Abdul Rahman, who made the first declaration on 20 February 1956 of the forthcoming independence of the Federation of Malaya at Padang Pahlawan in central Melaka. In Tourism Malaysia's literature and web material, Melaka is styled 'Malaysia's Historical City' (2009b: 18-19). Moreover, during the last decade, campaigns by the Melaka state government's Tourism Promotion Division emphasise the close symbolic connection between Melaka and Malaysia in the slogan 'Visit Historic Melaka Means Visit Malaysia' (Schubert et al, 2004: 22; Tourism Promotion Division, 2009).

Nevertheless, the historical domains of the fifteenth-century Malay-Muslim world were not coterminous either with the territories which the British brought together as the Straits Settlements and the Malay States and which on independence (with the exclusion of Singapore) became the Federation of Malaya on 31 August 1957, or even less with the wider territories which included the northern Borneo territories (with the exclusion of the Sultanate of Brunei) and which became the Federation of Malaysia on 16 September 1963 (Worden, 2010). European colonialism resulted in the division of the Malay world between the British domains to the north and, to the south, the Netherlands East Indies. In particular, the roots of Melaka and Malay culture in Sumatra which became incorporated into the Dutch domains (and then the Republic of Indonesia) were distanced from the Malays of the Malayan Peninsula. Melaka as a Malay sultanate which derived from the Indonesian islands to the south and which bridged the Straits of Malacca became increasingly fixed in a Malay-dominated Malaysian polity.

Another important consideration in nation-building was the identification of those elements in Malaysia's history and culture which could be brought together to constitute a national identity. This was made difficult in a new country formed from previously differently administered and historically separate units and comprising a medley of peoples and cultures. The ethnic composition of Melaka (and indeed Penang) was even more complex in that as a port it was the focus of migrations and settlement from a wide range of places, and subject to a considerable amount of cultural exchange and intermarriage. How then to unify the nation in a shared identity? This exercise was an extraordinarily difficult task. The dominant symbols, both in the pre-colonial and the British colonial period, were associated with the Malay sultans; and the senior local administration under the British system of indirect rule was primarily made up of Malays. The Malay-dominant government then chose Malay- and Muslim-centred symbols, including the institution of the sultanate and kingship, which in turn harked back to, at least in part, an 'imagined tradition' and an unbroken connection with the past, the Malay language as the national language, and Islam as the national religion; and this is where Melaka, as the state located in Malaysian territory, played an important role as the source, ancestral anchor, geographical locus and the legitimacy of the newly created Malaysian state (Chandra Muzaffar, 1983:

48-51, 63; Milner, 2008, 2010: 10-13, 24-26; Mohd Yusoff, 2004: 28; Reid, 2001: 30; Worden, 2010: 133; Zainal Abidin, 1983: 101-110)

Yet there were two particular contradictions in this post-colonial project. First, there were no material or physical remains left of a Malay-Muslim heritage in the historic core of Melaka. Secondly, the need to promote economic growth so that it could be harnessed to a redistribution strategy in favour of the indigenous population and which did not alienate the other ethnic groups required state-directed and state-promoted economic development. In the case of tourism what were favoured in the 1980s and 1990s were large-scale tourism projects and not so much the protection of heritage.

Reclaiming Malay Heritage

Since the introduction of the New Economic Policy in the early 1970s one of the major issues which faced the Malay-dominated federal government and the state government in Melaka was how to give material weight to the symbolic and historical importance of the Malay sultanate. A major development which was designed to reclaim it for the Malays and Islam was the construction in wood of what was said to be a replica of the fifteenth-century Sultan Mansur Shah's Palace opened by Prime Minister Mahathir Mohamed in July 1986 (Cartier, 2001: 198, 203; Maeda, 1998: 5). It houses a Cultural Museum whose exhibitions present a Malay- and sultanate-centred history of Melaka and Malay cultural achievements. Importantly it is a re-creation of the past, surrounded by the Historic City Memorial Garden 'in Islamic design' (Worden, 2010: 135; and Cartier, 1998a:160). More recently a Melaka Sultanate Water Mill, based on Islamic technology, was built in 2008 on the Melaka River (Tourism Promotion Division, 2009: 6).

In addition, most of the European buildings which were bequeathed the independent Malaysian state have, since the 1980s, been converted into government-funded museums which celebrate not a colonial legacy but one which serves a local agenda; the Stadthuys, opened in 1982, houses the Museum of History and Ethnography. The Museum of Literature in a building formerly occupied by the Melaka State Development Corporation celebrates the Malay history of Melaka with displays of historical documents, Malay literary genres, local Malay writers and national literary figures. The former British Clubhouse is home to the Proclamation of Independence Memorial and the Malay Governors' Collections 'have been placed in Seri Melaka, the residence of the Dutch and then the British

Governors' (Worden, 2010: 135). The Melaka Islamic Museum focuses on the historical relations between Islam and Melaka (Virtual Museum Melaka, www.virtualmuseummelaka.com). The Malay and Islamic World Museum in the former building of the British-owned Dunlop Company has served to reinforce some of the central themes of Malaysian nation-building. The Malaysia Youth Museum was designed to recognise the contribution made by young people to the building of the nation, particularly the youth branch of the United Malays National Organisation (UMNO). There is also the Melaka UMNO Museum which, through photographs, letters and other documents describes the history of the party which was founded in Melaka and its contribution to independence and nation-building. The Democratic Government Museum which occupies the old State Legislative Assembly building is designed to trace the development of parliamentary democracy in Malaysia since independence (www.virtualmuseummelaka.com).There is a Royal Malaysian Navy Museum (*Muzium T.L.D.M.*) which celebrates the history of the navy and its contribution to the nation. Cartier concludes even in the 1990s that 'In each of these museums, the state promotes national culture in the textual descriptions accompanying displays or photographs' (1998a: 161).

The obverse of this incorporation of Melaka heritage into Malay culture was the earlier attempt to remove or marginalise Chinese heritage. Cartier examined in detail the dispute over government plans formulated in 1984 to transform the site of the traditional Chinese cemetery at Bukit Cina (Chinese Hill) into a mixed-use site for offices, retail outlets and condominiums along with a cultural-historical centre, including a hotel, sports centre, cultural theatre, library, research institute, handicraft area, mosque, pagoda and temple (1993:359-360; 1997: 555-586; 2001: 199). What was startling in this redevelopment plan was the failure to give due recognition to the fact that this was a sixteenth-century cemetery and that it 'may be the oldest remaining traditional Chinese burial ground in the world' (1993: 359; Maeda, 1998: 8). In the event, a local preservation movement organised by the trustees of the Cheng Hoon Teng Temple and the cemetery, succeeded in carrying its case to the national government, the international conservation movement and to Chinese organisations within and outside Malaysia (Cartier, 1993: 362). As a result of the campaign the development project was abandoned in February 1985 (Cartier, 1997: 555-586; 1993: 361).

Melaka and Recent Tourism Development

In their edited work on Melaka published some 30 years ago, Sandhu and Wheatley argued then for the development of heritage tourism (1983a, 1983b, and see specifically 1983c: 566; and Wee, 2009). At the time they were writing, tourism, as a source of revenue and employment 'had been exploited only to a minimal degree' (1983c: 566). However, in the first stage of tourism development in the 1980s there was very little in the way of government interest in historical tourism since a considerable number of the heritage sites related primarily to a colonial past. Although there was a gradual increase in awareness of the importance and potential of heritage conservation and related tourism activities in the 1980s, it was not until the 1990s that the importance of heritage landscapes began to be incorporated into the Malaysian government's strategic planning.

The Malaysian government began to be attracted to the market potential of heritage and wider cultural tourism as another strand in its policy to expand tourism. In the case of Melaka this was crucial for generating employment (JICA, 2002: 12). But even then the shift to an interest in heritage has not precluded a strong and continuing commitment to the construction of large-scale leisure-related projects. In 1997 just before the decision to join with Penang in applying for inscription on the UNESCO World Heritage List the Chief Minister of Melaka announced the decision to proceed with four 'megaprojects' or 'leisurescapes' designed to triple the number of tourist visitors to Melaka to 4.5 million annually (Cartier, 1998a: 151). By the late 1990s urban transformations around the historic core of old Melaka were obvious: new retail outlets, shopping malls, hotels, apartments and office blocks (Maeda, 1998: 6).The result has been that in 2012 Melaka received 13.7 million arrivals, many of them from other parts of Asia (asmaliana.com; various years).

The emphasis on 'megaprojects' is also linked to the important contribution which the construction industry makes to economic development and the shift from manufacturing industry to construction, real estate and services. The official focus on 'megadevelopment' (Cartier, 2001: 201) resulted in the destruction of Melaka's original harbour and waterfront to be replaced by a large swathe of reclaimed land at Mahkota Melaka and Taman Melaka Raya on which have been constructed high rise buildings, hotels, offices, apartments, shopping malls, and a sea world amusement park (Tourism Malaysia, 2009a: 10; Schubert et al, 2004). The reclamation work continues and has had serious consequences for the ancient Portuguese community and its sea-based livelihood in that its coastal location has been transformed into an inland one and their culture marginalised (Fernandis, 2004; Sarkissian, 2000).

The tension between conservation and development is particularly acute in Melaka. Rightly or wrongly it was a prevailing view in the state government that one way to overcome the constraints on development in the historic urban core was to reclaim land and take the pressure off what is now the UNESCO WHS (Hamzah Sendut, 1983: 487). In the context of Melaka's economic development, the policy to modernise and bring commercial, retail and leisure activities onto reclaimed land makes sense, but it still has an impact on the historic core of Melaka in that it has broken the connection between the heart of old Melaka and the sea and harbour. The new build which dominates the skyline was one of the main reasons for the earlier UNESCO rejection of Melaka's submission.

Overall Melaka to a much greater and more serious degree than the sites in Thailand is threatened by all kinds of development pressures from tourism and from government economic policies to promote growth and encourage both domestic and international tourism.

Indonesia

The two major Indonesian cultural sites are Borobudur and Prambanan, but they raise issues from the perspective of the management of heritage and tourism and the balance to be struck between economic benefits on the one hand and the need for social, cultural and environmental sustainability on the other (Harrison and Hitchcock, 2005; and see Bandarin, 2005). Like many World Heritage Sites in developing countries these Javanese monumental sites have limited funds for conservation and are also complex culturally, administratively and environmentally. The Borobudur site is Mahayana Buddhist in origin while Prambanan is Hindu; they are two different kinds of structures with entirely different layouts. A further complication is that there are other temples and structures that are part of the Borobudur complex, but are not physically adjacent to it, as well as a third major site, Ratu Boku that is on the Tentative WHS List for Indonesia, which also comes under Borobudur's and Prambanan's jurisdiction. All these structures are at risk from seismic activity and eruptions from the nearby volcano of Merapi; heavy tropical rainfall also poses a threat from erosion.

These two heritage sites are highly significant structures both as national symbols and as WHS and must-see attractions for international tourists. Borobudur Temple (*Candi Borobudur*) is visited by Buddhists from other parts of the world, and by smaller numbers of Indonesian Buddhists; it is a magnificent Buddhist monument, the largest of its kind in the world dating from the eighth century CE. Also dating from the eighth century CE, the Prambanan Temple (*Candi Prambanan*) comprises a collection of magnificent towers surrounding a central temple that rises to a height of 47 metres; it remains one of the largest Hindu structures in Southeast Asia (http://whc.unesco.org/en/list/642). There still is a resident Javanese Hindu population and there are many Balinese Hindu migrants in the region; both groups revere the temple complex. In addition, aspects of Javanese Islamic culture have synthesised elements of these earlier religious traditions (Geertz, 1960). However, this latter point is controversial in that not all citizens sympathise with this view. In the final outcome the contemporary managers of these sites have to contend with large numbers of international and domestic tourists, as well as the occasional controversy relating to religious issues.

In addition to the pressures of tourism, there is another sense in which national and international interests predominate, especially in the case of Borobudur, a national symbol of the Republic of Indonesia but one which is officially promoted more as a cultural symbol rather than as a sacred religious monument (Hitchcock, King and Parnwell, 2010: 19). Borobudur continues to be a centre for national and international Buddhist pilgrimage; but it is viewed by the Indonesian authorities as primarily a cultural heritage site closely linked to the promotion of domestic and international tourism, though changes at the ministerial level in 2011 are likely to lead to the adoption of a more nuanced view.

This 'tourist gaze', adopting John Urry's well-known expression (1990), exercises its own influence over the culture that is being gazed upon and may be positive in creating a greater sense of appreciation and pride in local culture (Miksic, 2011:xiv). Alternatively, it may be negative, creating a sense of inferiority and perhaps creating an impetus to simplify local culture to make it more appealing to outside visitors. Interestingly, Miksic considers how to manage this gaze and argues that by making people aware of what it comprises will enable people to make decisions about their own culture, thereby empowering them to formulate strategies to preserve those cultural resources that they wish to conserve (ibid.).

Evolution of the Management Structure

There are clearly institutional problems with regard to heritage management in developing countries, particularly coordinating action and implementing legislation (Wiendu Nuryanti, 1996; Hall, 2000; and see Aas et al, [2005] and Devi Roza Krisnandhi Kausar et al [2011] on Borobudur). Mason (2003) also points out that problems of management can influence the kind of impact that tourism has.

It was under Suharto's long period of office (1966-98) that tourism began to develop significantly in Indonesia and Yogyakarta and Central Java were central to the planning initiatives of the period. Tourism arrivals began to rise sharply in the 1980s and by the mid-1990s tourism had become the third most important source of foreign exchange with Yogyakarta being the second most visited Indonesian destination after Bali. Of the two monuments, Borobudur is the most visited. The Asian Crisis (1997-98) and ensuing unrest in Indonesia suppressed demand for a while but by 2004 numbers were exceeding two million and by 2008 they had risen to 2,237,717 per annum (Balai Konservasi Borobudur, http://konservasiborobudur.org). The target for 2012 was 2.5 million visitors (World Heritage Site, http: //www. worldheritagesite.org/).

Despite the fact that Borobudur and Prambanan temple are religious sites, they come under the auspices of the Ministry of Tourism and Culture (as primarily national cultural sites and important tourist destinations) and not the Ministry of Religion. The Ministry of Tourism and Culture held overall authority up to the end of the 1970s but devolved the management of the two sites in 1980 to a state-owned company known as PT Taman Wisata Candi Borobudur dan Candi Prambanan. In 1991 Borobudur, which also includes the temples of Mendut and Pawon, and Prambanan succeeded in becoming World Heritage Sites. Three years later the management was also assigned responsibility for running Ratu Boko a ruined palace (*kraton*), which was submitted to UNESCO for consideration in 1995, but remains on the UNESCO Tentative List (Kausar 2010: 151). In accordance with Presidential Decree Number 1/1992, PT Taman, as it is widely known locally, has the right to charge entrance fees and retain revenues from other sources (e.g. entertainment, retail, catering) and it is subject to taxes and other contributions to the government, which, according to its Annual Report of 2005 included dividends, corporate income tax, property tax, income tax, and miscellaneous tax (e.g. on entertainment) (ibid.: 152). The parkland surrounding both temple complexes was acquired by compulsory purchase and enabled the state-owned authority to remove the markets selling food and souvenirs that clustered round the bases of both Borobudur and Prambanan. These actions conformed to UNESCO's guidelines on the introduction of 'buffer zones', which the World Heritage Centre (WHC) described as providing '…effective protection of the nominated property' (UNESCO World Heritage Centre, 2008:26) Since 1980 PT Taman has had overall responsibility for these sites, but reforms in 2010 altered this management structure, though it remains unclear that the changes will lead to a greater focus on the sites' weaknesses. There are fears that the unclear boundary arrangements could be exploited by developers to build inappropriate structures for tourism within or close to the sites.

A complicating feature of the sites' management structure is that, while PT Taman may have nominal overall responsibility for the two sites, in reality the management arrangements involve the division of each site into three zones, each with its own administration. In the case of Borobudur, responsibility for the innermost zone (zone 1) falls to the Borobudur Conservation Institute (BHCI), which answers to the Director-General of History and Archaeology under the auspices of the Ministry of Culture and Tourism. It is the surrounding park (zone 2) that comes under the state-owned authority, which is itself answerable to the Ministry of State Owned Enterprise. Another complication is that PT Taman has its headquarters near to Prambanan and does not have a high level management presence at Borobudur. A similar set of arrangements are found at Prambanan in respect of zones 1 (under the auspices of the Prambanan Conservation Institute) and zone 2 under PT Taman. But a somewhat different collection of responsibilities is found in both temples with regard to the outer areas (zone 3). Prambanan is situated in the Regency (*Kabupaten*) of Sleman and is thus part of Yogyakarta, a special administrative region (*Daerah Istimewa Yogyakarta*) comprising the city of Yogyakarta and surrounding area. In contrast, Borobudur is located in the neighbouring province of Central Java and the Regency or local government of Magelang has responsibility for this temple's outer area. In short there are two ministries, two institutes, one state-owned company and two provincial authorities (and their subsidiary arms) involved in the management of what is supposed to be a unified structure.

In view of this complexity, it is worth comparing their various functions and the expectations of these different bodies as this has a strong influence on how the sites are run on an everyday basis. Starting with zone 1, it is the institutes that have responsibility for conserving and restoring the two temple sites, as well as acting as training centres in archaeology and conservation. The institutes' mission statements are very clear in the need to support their respective World Heritage Sites. For example, Borobudur's vision comprises '…the realization of Borobudur Heritage Conservation Institute as [a] (sic) center of research and training for conservation of archaeological artefacts'. But with so many tourists visiting daily and with unclear boundary maintenance as to what is or is not off limits, the institutes struggle to fulfil their roles. Security and cleanliness remain constant headaches as visitors have to be prevented from leaving rubbish on the monument and from clambering over the sides of the temples damaging the precious reliefs. Managers complain that the budgets are insufficient to hire enough security staff and at busy times both temple complexes resemble noisy picnic sites.

The management's vision and mission in relation to the surrounding parkland present a marked contrast as the language is couched in market terms with references to such management concepts and phrases as 'professionally qualified human resources' and 'the full capacity to compete globally'. Its mission is concerned with 'cultural heritage preservation' but is also focused on the need of 'developing the tourism industry for the benefit of the community, region and nation'. A similar perspective is echoed by the managers of the third zone, the local authorities, with Magelang regarding Borobudur as a key source of regional development. This authority moreover has access to an undisclosed proportion of the entry fees for the WHS as it controls access to the two outlying temples and is thus quite closely involved in the finances of the site (Kausar, 2010: 155).

A similar perspective is apparent in Prambanan and, given its location close to the main road between two major cities (Yogyakarta and Surakarta), the commercial pressures from tourism are even more apparent. Among the most noticeable features of the site are the open-air and indoor stages with their special effects lighting gantries on the west side of the temple across the River Opak. They were built to stage the Ramayana dance drama, which was given a contemporary choreographic edge in the 1990s. During the full moon the temple itself becomes part of the stage serving as a dramatic backdrop illuminated with theatre lights.

There is, however, another contemporary twist in Prambanan, which is not so evident in Borobudur, due to the increasing presence of Hindu Balinese migrants in Yogyakarta and Central Java. Along with the Javanese Hindu community, the Balinese have drawn attention to Prambanan's religious significance and increasingly express a strong desire to perform their sacred ceremonies there. Contemporary Hindu interest in the site is comparatively new, whereas Buddhists recommenced using Borobudur as a place of worship in the 1970s. Buddhists, however, remain relatively few in number, whereas the Hindu population in Java appears to be rising and becoming more affluent and assertive. Interestingly, this religious dimension is not flagged up in the management visions and mission statements of the inner zones where the focus remains fixed on conservation and tourism development.

Physical Threats to the Sites

While the management of all WHS and the importance of devising and implementing a viable, efficient and effective management plan are central concerns for UNESCO, the sites of Borobudur and Prambanan are especially problematic because of the number and variety of both man-made and natural threats they face. The temples provide particularly tempting targets because they represent both national cultural and historical monuments for the Indonesian government and also serve as symbols of two of the country's religious minorities. They also have global recognition, and thus anyone with a grudge against either the Indonesian government or the members of another religion might be tempted to vent their frustrations by attacking these edifices, in the knowledge that actions of this kind are likely to attract significant international media interest. Thus far the temples have remained largely unscathed, though the lessons learned from an attack that took place on 21 January 1985 should not be forgotten. On this occasion bombs were placed inside the stupas on the upper part of the Borobudur temple leaving nine of them badly damaged; soon after the event the police arrested three suspects. One of them, Abdulkahir Ali Alhabsyi revealed that the attack was a response to the deaths of Muslims at the hands of the security forces in an earlier incident at Tanjung Priok; a blind cleric, Husein Ali Al Habsyie was arrested six years later for orchestrating a series of bombings from 1984 to 1985, including the Borobudur attack.

The bombings were dramatic and destructive, but thus far a one-off incident; what has concerned UNESCO a great deal more is the constant threat of vandalism by visitors. There are warning signs in both complexes telling them not to touch anything and not to climb on the statues, backed up regularly with announcements on loudspeakers. However, the number of security personnel remains limited and the instructions are seldom enforced. Sometimes the staff members in security appear quite demoralised, as if overwhelmed by the sheer volume of tourists, and stand by as the rules are flagrantly ignored. It does not help that signs posted in English are often so poorly translated from Indonesian that they appear comic and undermine their serious intent. To be fair to the site managers it is worth noting that many of the tourists who visit these sites come from highly varied backgrounds making communication with them challenging, not only from a linguistic point of view but also a cultural one, especially if one is trying to manage their experiences from the perspective of conservation. The tourists also come with profoundly different expectations ranging from seeking a fun day out on the one hand and searching for some kind of spiritual solace on the other.

While it may be difficult to communicate with these varied visitors, it is worth emphasising that there are no mechanisms at either temple for evaluating an upper limit for visitors; the visitor management systems that exist are perfunctory. For example, the use of mandatory guided tours in sensitive parts of the sites could be used to manage visitors, but guided tours are primarily offered on a voluntary basis. It is widely held among local researchers that Indonesian visitors are primarily responsible for much of the damage, but on any visit to the temples overseas visitors can also be seen scrambling over delicately carved structures and sitting for photographs on top of ancient statuary. Unfortunately, vandalism, much of it unintentional, on bas-reliefs and temple structures is a common occurrence, but it is not possible to be sure which groups are the most destructive.

Local tourists certainly seem to arrive in larger and noisier groups than international ones, but not all locally derived tourism is solely concerned with fun as there is often a mystical or spiritual dimension to Indonesian tourism. Some of the carvings and bas reliefs found in these temples are believed to have spiritual powers, something that local guides like to draw attention to. For example, if women want to look prettier then they touch the face of the statue of *Loro Jonggrang* at Prambanan and then their own faces three times (Salazar, 2009:6). Men are not encouraged by guides to do the same and instead their attentions are directed to touch the statue's breasts for good luck (ibid). As a result of this activity the parts of the statue that are most handled have become blackened through constant use, though whether these customs are seen as vandalism by the management remains a moot point. Significantly, UNESCO recognises that vandalism by visitors is very worrying, but in reality the World Heritage Committee is unable to impose sanctions to encourage a more robust approach to conservation other than the threat to withdraw its recognition, and thus far serious measures to mitigate this problem have not been implemented.

The damage caused by visitors is significant, but probably the biggest threats to both monuments are natural disasters since the temples are in an area of frequent seismic activity. Earthquakes are a serious hazard and the one that struck on 27 May 2006 registered a magnitude of 6.2 on the Richter scale. The quake caused severe damage in Central Java. There were many casualties in the nearby city of Yogyakarta. Prambanan was badly damaged with large amounts of masonry shaken to the ground. But the site reopened surprisingly quickly a few months later, though many areas remained sealed off.

In contrast Borobudur got off lightly in 2006, but was itself heavily affected by the eruption of Mount Merapi in October-November 2010. Volcanic ash from Merapi rained down on the temple complex, approximately 28 kilometres west-southwest of the volcano's crater. A layer of ash up to 2.5 centimetres deep smothered the edifice after the eruption of 3 to 5 November; it killed nearby vegetation and the custodians worried that its acidity would damage the stone carvings. The temple complex was closed between 5 and 9 November to clean up the ash and UNESCO donated US$3 million towards its rehabilitation. The clean-up took approximately six months; some 55,000 blocks of stone had to be dismantled in order to reopen the drainage system – vital to the monument's preservation – which had become clogged with slurry from a combination of ash and rain. Soil erosion is another natural problem since the earth is quite soft and can be washed away with heavy rain destabilising the temple's foundations.

Tourism Development and Local Stakeholders

There has long been the contention that local villagers around Borobudur and Prambanan are routinely ignored in plans to turn both monuments into major tourism destinations. For example, in 2003 residents and small business proprietors around Borobudur organised a series of meetings objecting to a provincial government plan to build a three-story mall complex, entitled the 'Java World'. The state-owned company was charged with turning Borobudur into a 'world class' cultural tourism destination and it would appear that serious engagement with local stakeholders was not part of its remit, though its site managers are well aware of the accusations made by local stakeholders. What makes managing sites such as Borobudur especially difficult is that it is not only local stakeholders who have an interest, but also international ones. For example, upmarket cruise ship operators such as *Swan Hellenic* which takes passengers to Borobudur often receive negative feedback from their customers following their visits complaining about being harassed by desperate traders. Such is the ubiquity of this negative feedback that planners bringing international tourists to these sites have sometimes considered excluding them from their itineraries. However, so intense is the media focus on sites like Borobudur with celebrities such as Richard Gere gracing them with their presence that removing them from a tour is not a realistic option. Upscale tourists seem to clamour for the opportunity to visit these temples and then bemoan the experience immediately after when completing the customary questionnaire, though what they recall long after the visit remains unknown.

Commercial tour operators know a great deal about the opinions of their clients, though this is rarely made available to academic researchers; however the Tripadvisor blog rankings were very enthusiastic with 625 rating a visit to Borobudur as excellent, 216 as very good and a mere 37 as average (http://www.tripadvisor.com/Attraction_Review-g297709-d32005 4-Reviews-Borobudur_Temple-Magelang_Central_Java_Java.html). In contrast there seems to be less publicly available information on the opinions of local stakeholders, though this may simply be a matter of access. One trend that seems to be emerging in Indonesia is that the views of local residents are worth canvassing, something that has occurred as part of the reform era that followed the demise of Suharto's 'New Order' regime. The point is that the relationship between the monuments and local stakeholders should no longer be seen as a stress point since there are a number of villages that have clearly benefited from tourism such as Candirejo which has had community-based tourism since 1999. The village became known for its traditional festivals and has become a centre for various activities such as walking, cycling and riding tours and traditional cooking lessons (Kausar 2010: 81). These developments also received official approval since it was the local Regent who declared the village to be worthy of local government assistance to develop community-based tourism. There is also evidence of consultations with stakeholders taking place. For example, UNESCO's portal contains a report of a meeting organised on Borobudur by the Central Java Development and Planning Agency (*BAPPEDA Jateng*) concerning road expansion and the management of the site's scenery and environment (unesco.org/geography). Also under discussion was the revitalisation of the Archaeological Museum at Borobudur, and a mission by representatives of UNESCO is specifically mentioned (ibid.). But a major outcome is that the needs of tourists prevail, which, in the case of Borobudur, has taken on elements of a theme park with fenced off areas, car parks, ticket booths, touts, security guards, loudspeakers and gardens landscaped in a contemporary fashion (Steels, 2007).

Conclusion

We commenced this chapter by asking whether the competing interests, understandings and agendas of various stakeholders in the protection and promotion of world heritage are being resolved, or capable of being resolved. Various of the case studies have revealed domestic (largely middle class) tourism, the cultural and religious needs of local populations, and urbanisation pressures and the demands of development to be significant factors in intensifying the tension between the mobilisation and promotion of heritage assets and their protection and conservation. As such our programme of research points to areas that hitherto have been neglected in mainstream heritage tourism discourse, particularly the rise of Asian tourism in Asia (Winter, Teo and Chang, 2009b). Thus, the expectation that globally designated sites are arenas for the international tourist gaze has to be heavily qualified in the ways in which we conceptualise tourism encounters and impacts.

This chapter has also revealed in the case of Thailand, the vital importance of Bangkok as the country's dominant metropolis, and extended metropolitanisation as an underlying economic, physical and cultural process, as a source of tourists and as a major influence on the use and development of these sites. The close proximity of Melaka to the extended urban area of Kuala Lumpur and the Klang Valley generates a significant level of domestic tourism and weekend visits to Melaka (though the site is also locked into international tourist circuits as well, especially from Singapore). The Javanese sites are also the subject of relatively intense domestic tourist interest surrounded as they are by the densely populated districts of Central Java.

We have already argued in the Thai case that the ways in which the appreciation, use and construction of heritage there is intertwined with the materialisation of a Thai middle class is an important theme that has resonance in other parts of Southeast Asia (King and Parnwell, 2011). However, more specifically in Thailand the growth and spatial spread of middle class tourists and excursionists, and their consumption of heritage sites can be interpreted as being linked to the search for an authentic Thai identity rooted in a past which is given expression in monumental ruins. This is less evident in our other cases, but the national symbolisation of

Melaka has had a crucial effect on the presentation and development of that site. Borobudur and Prambanan are also used as cultural and historical icons of Indonesian national identity, but in this case they cannot be deployed in the cause of the nation's Islamic identity.

The rapid growth of domestic tourism in Thailand, for example, and its steady inclusion of heritage sites have significant implications for their management. Our observations have also revealed significant variations in management issues and responses across the two sites. Ayutthaya is the most 'exposed' site not only to tourism pressures but also urban encroachment and the increasing presence of vendors. Sukhothai and its associated sites are a less frequented heritage space, and are arguably more manageable and in UNESCO terms seem to continue to embrace 'timelessness'.

More generally there are significant management challenges which require a nuanced and contextualised understanding of process, preference and impact. We are not convinced that current practice is sufficiently informed by such an understanding. Very often management approaches are guided by global 'synoptic' practices heavily geared towards international tourists. But the way sites are seen and used varies considerably between foreign and domestic tourists (Evrard and Prasit, 2009a, 2009b); they also serve as active religious and sacred sites. Given the proximity of local urban populations and the ease with which these sites can be accessed, visits to them are often more numerous and frequent which in turn has implications for the intensity of visitor pressures and the ways in which higher levels of use can be managed and controlled.

Moreover, international heritage bodies focus on the protection and conservation of 'authentic' representations of human achievements, whereas governments tend to deploy these sites for national political purposes and to generate tourist revenue. Thus an immediate policy recommendation that emerges from the research is that UNESCO must recognise these sites as 'living' cultural and 'natural' landscapes and that any management plans must incorporate domestic tourism, local perceptions, and the involvement of local communities (Hitchcock, King and Parnwell, 2010). This in turn might encourage those who promote tourism to change the way in which they present these sites to the wider world. As Teo has recently observed we must beware 'the dominance of Western knowledges and practices in tourism studies' and address the widely held assumptions that there are certain 'universalisms' in the characteristics and motivations of tourists which in fact have been derived from Western experiences (2009: 35).

In the Melaka case and its position in national ideological and identity formation, we can see that there has been a noticeable shift in emphasis during the last decade. Up to the 1990s there was an official preoccupation with the importance of the Malay-Muslim contribution to the site and its place within Malaysian national historiography, illustrated in the failure to give due credit to the multicultural character of Melaka in an earlier submission to UNESCO. Since the late 1990s, however, in the process of applying for UNESCO listing, along with George Town, and in securing inscription in 2008, the emphasis for both 'historic cities' has been on cosmopolitanism and multiculturalism, and on the bringing together of communities from across Asia and Europe. This is a much more straightforward principle to demonstrate in the streetscapes and history of George Town. Nevertheless, in Melaka's civic zone area, public agencies, particularly in the large number of state-funded museums, still tend to promote a Malay-dominated communalism and the importance of Malay culture and Islam in Malaysian history. It has been left primarily to private entrepreneurs in the commercial-residential core of Melaka to present the Chinese contribution to the site's history

In the case of Borobudur and Prambanan it is our contention that the management of tourism and conservation is challenged by a number of factors: the natural environment, the pressure for development, a lack of awareness of the negative side of the tourist gaze, and the need to manage potential religious tensions and overcome years of neglect of local community involvement in the Suharto years. The increasing interest of the Hindu community in the religious significance of Prambanan also presents challenges for its management. Resolving these challenges is further complicated by a labyrinthine form of management that disempowers managers, archaeologists, conservators, security officials, ticket sellers and guides in carrying out their tasks effectively.

There are also seven bodies, discounting their subsidiary arms, charged with managing these important edifices, each with very different perspectives and missions. These groupings have to not only deal with the problems generated by these sites, but also to engage with a complex mix of stakeholders. In addition, these management agencies have to devote time to conservation, interpretation and visitor management. The overall impression is that these important functions are handled in a haphazard way to the detriment of site sustainability and the pleasure of some visitors, at least the international ones. Merely tinkering with the superstructure of PT Taman will not have much impact on the overall management of these two sites and a clearer vision is needed which simplifies the management structure. Neither of these two sites is managed in a way that enhances their conservation.

One very important finding overall in this cross-national research programme is that the international or global dimension of UNESCO World Heritage Sites, in that they are selected on the basis of their 'universal human value', must be qualified by the important role they are assigned in the national imaginary. Perhaps most importantly many of the sites are visited by local tourists in ever increasing numbers, and often to serve religious purposes. More research needs to be undertaken on the views, interests and habits of this important category of visitors to enable a better understanding of how the sites are being used, developed and presented and how they are perceived and interpreted. For too long the international dimension of heritage has been emphasised at the expense of the local or indigenous context of these sites, and this imbalance needs to be redressed (Winter, 2009).

References

Aas, Christina, Adele Ladkin and John Fletcher (2005) 'Stakeholder Collaboration and Heritage Management', *Annals of Tourism Research*, 32: 28-48.

Abdul Rahman Embong (ed) (2001) *Southeast Asian Middle Classes: Prospects for Social Change and Democratisation*, Bangi: Penerbit Universiti Kebangsaan Malaysia, Malaysian and International Studies Series.

Adams, Kathleen M. (2003) 'The Politics of Heritage in Tana Toraja, Indonesia: Interplaying the Local and the Global', *Indonesia and the Malay World*, special issue *Tourism and Heritage in South-East Asia*, ed. Michael Hitchcock and Victor T. King, 31: 91-107.

—. (2006) *Art as Politics: Re-crafting Identities, Tourism and Power in Tana Toraja, Indonesia*, Honolulu: University of Hawai'i Press.

Anderson, Benedict R. O'G. (1991) *Imagined Communities: Reflections on the Origin and Spread of Nationalism*, London: Verso, revised edition.

Aphivan Saipradist (2005) *A Critical Analysis of Heritage Interpretation and the Development of a Guidebook for Non-Thai Cultural Tourists at Ayutthaya*, Silpakorn University: Unpublished PhD thesis.

Aphivan Saipradist and R. Staiff (2007) 'Crossing the Cultural Divide: Western Visitors and Interpretation at Ayutthaya World Heritage Site, Thailand', *Journal of Heritage Tourism*, 2: 211-224.

Asian Development Bank (2007) *Thailand: Sub-Regional Development Plan for the Tsunami Affected Andaman Region: Final Report, Volume 6: Supporting Technical Studies*, Manila: Asian Development Bank.

Askew, Marc (1996) 'The Rise of *Moradok* and the Decline of the *Yarn*: Heritage and Cultural Construction in Urban Thailand', *Sojourn. Journal of Social Issues in Southeast Asia*, 11:183-210.

Asmaliana. *Tourism Ramblings*, http://asmaliana.com/blog/tourist_arrivals_in_melaka.

Ayutthaya Provincial Administration Organization (nd) *Ayutthaya: the City of Gorgeousness*, Ayutthaya: APAO.

Balai Konservasi Borobudur, http://konservasiborobudur.org.

Bandarin, Francesco (2005) 'Foreword'. In David Harrison and Michael Hitchcock (eds), *The Politics of World Heritage: Negotiating Tourism and Conservation,* Clevedon: Channel View Publications, pp. v-vi.

Berliner, David (2010) 'Perdresa Culture: Reflexions sur les Politiques de l'Unesco à Luang Prabang (Lao PDR)', *Terrain*, 55: 4-19.

—. (2011) 'Luang Prabang, Sanctuaire Unesco et Paradis Gay', *Genre, sexualité et société*, URL: http://gss.revues.org/1888; DOI: 10.4000/gss.1888.

—. (2012) 'Multiple Nostalgias: the Fabric of Heritage in Luang Prabang (Lao PDR)', *Journal of the Royal Anthropological Institute*, 18: 769-786.

Berliner, David, and Chiara Bortolotto (2013) 'Introduction: Le Monde selon l'Unesco', *Gradhiva: Revue d'Anthropologie et d'Histoire des Arts*, 18: 4-21.

Black, Heather (1997) *Monumental Problems: Cultural Heritage and Communities in Indonesia and Thailand*, University of Waterloo: Unpublished PhD thesis.

Black, Heather, and Geoffrey Wall (2001) 'Global-local Interrelationships in UNESCO World Heritage Sites'. In Peggy Teo, T.C. Chang and K. C. Ho (eds), *Interconnected Worlds: Tourism in Southeast Asia*, Oxford: Elsevier Science, Pergamon, pp. 121-136.

Cartier, Carolyn (1993) 'Creating Historic Open Space in Melaka', *Geographical Review*, 83: 359–373.

—. (1996) 'Conserving the Built Environment and Generating Heritage Tourism in Peninsular Malaysia', *Tourism Recreation Research*, 21: 45–53.

—. (1997) 'The Dead, Place/Space, and Social Activism: Constructing the Nationscape in Historic Melaka', *Environment and Planning D: Society and Space*, 15: 555–586.

—. (1998a) 'Megadevelopments in Malaysia: from Heritage Landscapes to "Leisurescapes" in Melaka's Tourism Sector', *Singapore Journal of Tropical Geography,* 19: 151–176.

—. (1998b) 'Preserving Bukit China: a Cultural Politics of Landscape Interpretation in Melaka's Chinese Cemetery'. In E. Sinn (ed.), *The Last Half Century of the Chinese Overseas,* Hong Kong: Hong Kong University Press, pp. 65-79.

—. (2001) 'Imaging Melaka's Global Heritage'. In P. Teo, T.C. Chang and K.C. Ho (eds), *Interconnected Worlds: Tourism in Southeast Asia*, Oxford: Elsevier Science, Pergamon, pp. 193-212.

Chandra Muzaffar (1983) 'Continuity and Change in Malay Ideas of the Melakan Period'. In Kernial Singh Sandhu and Paul Wheatley (eds), *Melaka: the Transformation of a Malay Capital, c 1400-1980*, Kuala Lumpur: Oxford University Press, vol. 2, pp. 47-69.

Chapman, William, A. (2013) *Heritage of Ruins. The Ancient Sites of Southeast Asia and their Conservation*, Honolulu: University of Hawai'i Press.

Chi Sen Liang (1983) 'The Central District of Melaka Town'. In Kernial Singh Sandhu and Paul Wheatley (eds), *Melaka: the Transformation of a Malay Capital, c 1400-1980*, Kuala Lumpur: Oxford University Press, vol. 1, pp.652-707.

Cho, George and Marion W. Ward (1983) 'The Port of Melaka'. In Kernial Singh Sandhu and Paul Wheatley (eds), *Melaka: the Transformation of a Malay Capital, c 1400-1980*, Kuala Lumpur: Oxford University Press, vol. 1, pp. 623-651.

Clammer, John (1980) *Straits Chinese Society: studies in the Sociology of the Baba Communities of Malaysia and Singapore*, Singapore: Singapore University Press.

—. (1983) 'The Straits Chinese in Melaka'. In Kernial Singh Sandhu and Paul Wheatley (eds), *Melaka: the Transformation of a Malay Capital, c 1400-1980*, Kuala Lumpur: Oxford University Press, vol. 2, pp. 156-173.

Clarke, Alan (2000) 'The Power to Define: Meanings and Values in Cultural Tourism'. In Mike Robinson, Philip Long, Nigel Evans, Richard Sharpley and John Swarbrooke, (eds), *Expressions of Culture, Identity and Meaning in Tourism*, Sunderland: Centre for Travel and Tourism in association with Business Education Publishers Ltd., pp. 23-36.

Cohen, Erik (1994) 'Contemporary Tourism – Trends and Challenges: Sustainable Authenticity or Contrived Postmodernity'. In: R. Butler and D. Pearce (eds), *Change in Tourism: People, Places, Processes*, London: Routledge, pp. 12-29.

Esposito, Adèle (2011) *Siem Reap: Invention et Fabrication d'un Lieu de Tourisme aux Portes D'Angkor*, Université Paris-Est: Unpublished PhD thesis.

Esposito, Adèle, and Inès Gaulis (2010) *The Cultural Heritage of Asia and Europe: Global Challenges and Local Initiatives*, Leiden and Amsterdam: International Institute for Asian Studies and the Asia-Europe Foundation, Final Report.

Evrard, Olivier and Prasit Leepreecha (2009a) 'Monks, Monarchs and Mountain Folks: Domestic Tourism and Internal Colonialism in Northern Thailand', *Critique of Anthropology*, 29: 300-323.

—. (2009b) 'Staging the Nation, Exploring the Margins. Domestic Tourism and its Political Implications in Northern Thailand'. In Tim Winter, Peggy Teo and T.C. Chang (eds), *Asia on Tour: Exploring the Rise of Asian Tourism*, London and New York: Routledge, pp. 239-252.

Fernandis, G. (2004) 'The Portuguese Community at the Periphery: a Minority Report on the Portuguese Quest for the Bumiputra Status', *Kajian Malaysia*, 21: 285-301.

Fine Arts Department (FAD) (1996) *Ayutthaya: Historic City*, Bangkok: Samaphan Publishing Co. Ltd.

Forbes, D. (1997) 'Metropolis and Megaurban Region in Pacific Asia', *Tijdschrift voor Economische en Sociale Geografie*,88: 457–468.

Francioni, Francesco (2008) *The World Heritage Convention: an Introduction*, Oxford: Oxford University Press.

Franklin, Adrian (2004) 'Tourism as an Ordering: Towards a New Ontology', *Tourist Studies*, 4: 277-301.

Funatsu, Tsuruyo and Kazuhiro Kagoya (2003) 'The Middle Classes in Thailand: the Rise of the Urban Intellectual Elite and their Social Consciousness', *The Developing Economies*, special issue, 41: 243-263.

Geertz, Clifford (1960) *The Religion of Java*, Chicago: Chicago University Press.

Getty Conservation Institute,http://www.getty.edu/conservation/

Ginsburg, Norton (1983) 'The Changing Meaning of Modernization in Southeast Asia'. In Kernial Singh Sandhu and Paul Wheatley (eds), *Melaka: the Transformation of a Malay Capital, c 1400-1980*, Kuala Lumpur: Oxford University Press, vol. 2, pp. 285-298.

Ginsburg, N., B. Koppel and T.G. McGee (1991) *The Extended Metropolis: Settlement Transition in Asia*, Honolulu: University of Hawai'i Press.

Glover, Ian C. (2003) 'National and Political Uses of Archaeology in South-East Asia', *Indonesia and the Malay World*, special issue *Tourism and Heritage in South-East Asia*, Michael Hitchcock and Victor T. King (eds), 31: 16-30.

Gozzoli, Robert (2011) *Ayutthaya. Past, Present and Future of a Heritage City. Final Report*, Bangkok: Siam University.

Hall, C. Michael (2000) *Tourism Planning: Policies, Planning, Relationships*, Harlow: Prentice Hall.

Hamzah Sendut (1983) 'The Future of Melaka Town'. In Kernial Singh Sandhu and Paul Wheatley (eds), *Melaka: the Transformation of a Malay Capital, c 1400-1980*, Kuala Lumpur: Oxford University Press, vol. 2, pp. 479-492.

Harrison, David and Michael Hitchcock (eds) (2005) *The Politics of World Heritage: Negotiating Tourism and Conservation*, Clevedon: Channel View Publications; also as a special issue of *Current Issues in Tourism*, 7: 281-466, 2004.

Hauser-Schäublin, Brigitta (ed.) (2011a) *World Heritage Angkor and Beyond: Circumstances and Implications of UNESCO Listings in Cambodia*, Göttingen: Universitätsverlag Göttingen, Göttingen Studies in Cultural Property, vol. 2.

—. (2011b) 'Preah Vihear. From Object of Colonial Desire to a Contested World Heritage Site'. In Brigitta Hauser-Schäublin, (ed.), *World Heritage Angkor and Beyond: Circumstances and Implications of UNESCO Listings in Cambodia*, Göttingen: Universitätsverlag Göttingen, Göttingen Studies in Cultural Property, vol. 2, pp. 33-56.

Herbert, David T. (1989) 'Leisure Trends and the Heritage Market'. In David T. Herbert, Richard C. Prentice and Colin J. Thomas, (eds), *Heritage Sites: Strategies for Marketing and Development*, Aldershot: Avebury, pp. 12-14.

Hitchcock, Michael (2004) 'Afterword'. In David Harrison and Michael Hitchcock, (eds), *The Politics of World Heritage: Negotiating Tourism and Conservation*, special issue of *Current Issues in Tourism*, 7: 461-466 (and see Harrison and Hitchcock, 2005).

Hitchcock, Michael, and Victor T. King (eds) (2003a) *Tourism and Heritage in South-East Asia*, *Indonesia and the Malay World*, special issue, Abingdon: Carfax Publishing, 31.

—. (2003b) 'Discourses with the Past: Tourism and Heritage in South-East Asia', *Indonesia and the Malay World*, special issue *Tourism and*

Heritage in South-East Asia, Michael Hitchcock and Victor T. King (eds), 31: 3-15.

Hitchcock, Michael, Victor T. King and Michael Parnwell (eds) (1993) *Tourism in South-East Asia,* London: Routledge.

—. (2009) *Tourism in Southeast Asia: Challenges and New Directions,* Copenhagen: NIAS Press and Honolulu, University of Hawai'i Press.

—. (2010) *Heritage Tourism in Southeast Asia*, Copenhagen: NIAS Press and Honolulu, University of Hawai'i Press.

Hsiao, Hsin-Huang Michael (ed.) (2001) *Exploration of the Middle Classes in Southeast Asia*, Taipei: Program for Southeast Asian Area Studies, Academia Sinica.

—. (ed.) (2006) *The Changing Faces of the Middle Classes in Asia-Pacific*, Taipei: Center for Asia-Pacific Studies, Academia Sinica.

Hughes, Howard L. (2000) 'The Elusive Cultural Tourist'. In Mike Robinson, Philip Long, Nigel Evans, Richard Sharpley and John Swarbrooke, (eds), *Expressions of Culture, Identity and Meaning in Tourism*, Sunderland: Centre for Travel and Tourism in association with Business Education Publishers Ltd., pp.111-122.

ICOMOS (1986) *ICOMOS 1964-1984*, Naples: International Council of Monuments and Sites.

International Council of Museums, http://icom.museum/.

Irwin, Graham W. (1983) 'Melaka Fort'. In Kernial Singh Sandhu and Paul Wheatley (eds), *Melaka: the Transformation of a Malay Capital, c 1400-1980*, Kuala Lumpur: Oxford University Press, vol. 1, pp.782-805.

Jaruwan Daengbuppha, Nigel Hemmington and Keith Wilkes (2006) 'Using Grounded Theory to Model Visitor Experiences at Heritage Sites: Methodological and Practical Issues', *Qualitative Market Research: An International Journal*, 9: 367-388.

Jenkins, Gwynn (2008) *Contested Space: Cultural Heritage and Identity Reconstructions. Conservation Strategies within a Developing Asian City*, Zurich: Lit Verlag GmbH and Co. KG Wien and Berlin: Lit Verlag Dr. W. Hopf, Freiburger Sozialanthropologische Studien.

—. (2010) 'Interpreters of Space, Place and Cultural Practice: Processes of Change through Tourism, Conservation, and Development in George Town, Penang, Malaysia'. In Michael Hitchcock, Victor T. King and Michael Parnwell (eds), *Heritage Tourism in Southeast Asia*, Copenhagen: NIAS Press, pp.147-172.

Japanese International Cooperation Agency (JICA) (2002) *The Study on the Improvement and Conservation of Historical Urban Environment in the Historical City of Melaka. Summary of Report*, Tokyo: JFY (included in the Malaysian State Party Nomination Dossier).

Johnson, Mark (2001) 'Renovating Hue (Vietnam): Authenticating Destruction, Reconstructing Authenticity'. In R. Layton, P. Stone and J. Thomas (eds), *Destruction and Conservation of Cultural Property*, London: Routledge, pp. 75-92.

—. (2010) 'Aspiring to the "Tourist Gaze": Selling the Past, Longing for the Future in Hue'. In Michael Hitchcock, Victor T. King and Michael Parnwell (eds), *Heritage Tourism in Southeast Asia*, Copenhagen: NIAS Press and Honolulu: University of Hawai'i Press, pp. 173-201.

Jones, David (2010) *Garden and Landscape Heritage: a Crisis of Tangible and Intangible Comprehension and Curatorship*, Asian Studies Association of Australia, 18th Biennial Conference.

Jones, Gavin W. (2002) 'Southeast Asian Urbanization and the Growth of Mega-Urban Regions', *Journal of Population Research*, 19: 119-136.

Kausar Devi Roza Krisnandhi (2010) *Socio-Economic Impacts of Tourism on a World Heritage Site: A Study of Rural Borobudur, Indonesia*, Nagoya University: unpublished PhD thesis.

—. (2011) 'Socio-economic Impacts of Heritage Tourism on its Locality: a Case Study of Borobudur Temple Compounds World Heritage Site', *Forum of International Development*, 40: 131-150.

Kausar Devi Roza Krisnandhi, Yoshiaki Nishikawa and Yoshihiko Nishimura (2011) 'How Could Management of Borobudur World Heritage Site be Enhanced for Improving Tourism Impacts for the Community: a Preliminary Comparison with Angkor World Heritage Site, *Forum of International Development*, 40: 31-42.

Kennedy, Laurel B. and Mary Rose Williams (2001) 'The Past without the Pain – the Manufacture of Nostalgia in Vietnam's Tourist Industry'. In Hue-Tam Ho Tai, (ed.), *The Country of Memory: Remaking the Past in Late Socialist Vietnam*, Berkeley: University of California Press, pp. 135-163.

Keyes, Charles F. (1987) *Thailand: Buddhist Kingdom as Modern Nation-state*, Boulder and London: Westview Press.

Khoo Su Nin (2007) *Streets of George Town, Penang: an Illustrated Guide to Penang's City Streets and Historic Attractions*, Penang: Phoenix Press, fourth edition.

King, Victor T. (2012) *UNESCO IN Melaka: Cultural Politics, Identities and Tourism in a World Heritage Site*, Leeds East Asia Papers, New Series No. 4, 2012, e-series.

—. (2015) *UNESCO in Southeast Asia: World Heritage Sites in Comparative Perspective*, forthcoming.

King, Victor T. and Michael Parnwell (2010) *World Heritage Sites in Thailand: a Comparative and Critical Appraisal*, Leeds East Asia Papers, New Series No. 1, e-series.

—. (2011) 'World Heritage Sites and Domestic Tourism in Thailand: Social Change and Management Implications', *South East Asia Research*, 19: 381-420.

Leask, Anna and Alan Fyall (eds) (2006) *Managing World Heritage Sites*, London: Butterworth-Heinemann.

Lim Heng Kow (1983) 'The Suburban Fringe'. In Kernial Singh Sandhu and Paul Wheatley (eds), *Melaka: the Transformation of a Malay Capital, c 1400-1980*, Kuala Lumpur: Oxford University Press, vol. 1, pp.708-738.

Long, Colin (2003) 'Feudalism in the Service of the Revolution: Reclaiming Heritage in Hue', *Critical Asian Studies*, 35: 535-558.

Long, Colin, and Jonathan Sweet (2006) 'Globalization, Nationalism and World Heritage: Interpreting Luang Prabang', *Southeast Asia Research*, 14: 445-469.

McGaskill, Don, Prasit Leepreecha and He Shaoying (2008) *Living in a Globalized World: Ethnic Minorities in the Greater Mekong Subregion*, Chiang Mai: Mekong Press.

McGee, T.G. (1991) 'The Emergence of Desakota Regions in Asia: Expanding a Hypothesis'. In N. Ginsburg, B. Koppell and T.G. McGee (eds), *The Extended Metropolis. Settlement Transition in Asia*, Honolulu: University of Hawai'i Press, pp. 3–25.

—. (2008) 'Managing the Rural-Urban Transformation in East Asia in the 21st Century', *Sustainability Science*, 3: 155-167.

McGee, T.G. and I.M. Robinson (1995) *The Mega-Urban Regions of Southeast Asia*, Vancouver: UBC Press.

Maeda, Narifumi (1998) *Touristic Impressions of Social Transformation in Melaka* (www.emp.com.my/touristic.pdf).

Malaysian State Party (2008) *Historic Cities of the Straits of Malacca: Melaka and George Town. Nomination Dossier* (http://whc.unesco-org/en/list/1223/documents/ (including *Conservation Management Plan for the Historic City of Melaka*).

Mason, Peter (2003) *Tourism Impacts, Planning and Management*, Oxford: Elsevier Butterworth-Heinemann.

Miksic, John N. (2011) 'Introduction'. In John N. Miksic, Geok Yian Goh and Sue O'Connor (eds), *Rethinking Cultural Resource Management in Southeast Asia: Preservation, Development and Neglect*, London: Anthem Press, pp. xiii-xxi.

Miksic, John N, Geok Yian Goh and Sue O'Connor (eds) (2011) *Cultural*

Resource Management in Southeast Asia: Preservation, Development and Neglect, London, New York and Delhi: Anthem Press, Anthem Southeast Asian Studies.

Milner, Anthony (2008) *The Malays*, Oxford: Wiley-Blackwell.

—. (2010) *Race or Civilization: the Localizing of 'The Malays'*, Bangi: Institute of Malaysian and International Studies (IKMAS), Universiti Kebangsaan Malaysia.

Miura, Keiko (2004) C*ontested Heritage: People of Angkor*, University of London, School of Oriental and African Studies: Unpublished PhD thesis.

—. (2010) 'World Heritage Sites in Southeast Asia: Angkor and Beyond'. In Michael Hitchcock, Victor T. King and Michael Parnwell (eds), *Heritage Tourism in Southeast Asia*, Copenhagen: NIAS Press and Honolulu: University of Hawai'i Press, pp. 103-129.

—. (2011a) 'World Heritage Making in Angkor: Global, Regional, National and Local Actors, Interplays and Implications'. In Brigitta Hauser-Schäublin (ed.), *World Heritage Angkor and Beyond: Circumstances and Implications of UNESCO Listings in Cambodia*, Göttingen: Universitätsverlag Göttingen, Göttingen Studies in Cultural Property, vol. 2, pp. 9-31.

—. (2011b) 'From Property to Heritage: Different Notions, Rules of Ownership and Practices of New and Old Actors in the Angkor World Heritage Sites'. In Brigitta Hauser-Schäublin (ed.), *World Heritage Angkor and Beyond: Circumstances and Implications of UNESCO Listings in Cambodia*, Göttingen: Universitätsverlag Göttingen, Göttingen Studies in Cultural Property, vol. 2, pp. 97-120.

—. (2011c) 'Sustainable Development in Angkor: Conservation Regime of the Old Villagescape and Development'. In Brigitta Hauser-Schäublin (ed.), *World Heritage Angkor and Beyond: Circumstances and Implications of UNESCO Listings in Cambodia*, Göttingen: Universitätsverlag Göttingen, Göttingen Studies in Cultural Property, vol. 2, pp. 121-144.

Morris, Rosalind (2000) *In the Place or Origins: Modernity and its Mediums in Northern Thailand*, Durham, NC: Duke University Press.

Nagaoka, Masanori (2011) *Revitalization of Borobudur: Heritage Tourism Promotion and Local Community Empowerment in Cultural Industries*, Paris: ICOMOS, openarchive.icomos.org, series 3.

Ockey, James (1999) 'Creating the Thai Middle Class'. In Michael Pinches (ed.), *Culture and Privilege in Capitalist Asia*, London and New York: Routledge, pp. 230-250.

Office of Environmental Policy and Planning (OEPP) (nda) *The World's*

Historical Heritage. The Ancient City of Ayutthaya and Associated Cities, Bangkok: OEPP in cooperation with the National Science Museum, Ministry of Science Technology and Environment (brochure).

—. (ndb) *The World's Historical Heritage. Historic Town of Sukhothai and Associated Cities*, Bangkok: OEPP in cooperation with the National Science Museum, Ministry of Science Technology and Environment (brochure).

Osborn, James (1983) 'Melaka in Malaysian National Development'. In Kernial Singh Sandhu and Paul Wheatley (eds), *Melaka: the Transformation of a Malay Capital, c 1400-1980*, Kuala Lumpur: Oxford University Press, vol. 2, pp.449-478.

Oxford Business Group (2013) 'Thailand Visitor Arrivals, 2012', http://www. oxfordbusinessgroup.com/.

Paritta Chalermpow Koanantakool (2002) 'Thai Middle-class Practice and Consumption of Traditional Dance: "Thai-ness" and High Art'. In C. J. W-L. Wee (ed.), *Local Cultures and the 'New Asia': the State, Culture, and Capitalism in Southeast Asia*, Singapore: Institute of Southeast Asian Studies, pp. 217-241.

Parnwell, Michael J.G. (2010) 'Tourism and Natural Heritage Management in Vietnam and Thailand'. In Michael Hitchcock, Victor T. King and Michael J.G. Parnwell (eds), *Heritage Tourism in Southeast Asia*, Copenhagen: NIAS Press and Honolulu: University of Hawai'i Press, pp. 236-263.

Parnwell, Michael J.G. and Luxmon Wongsuphasawat (1997) 'Between the Global and the Local: Extended Metropolitanisation and Industrial Location Decision Making in Thailand', *Third World Planning Review*, 19**:** 119–138.

Peleggi, Maurizio (1994) *National Heritage and Nationalist Narrative in Contemporary Thailand: an Essay on Culture and Politics*, Canberra, Australian National University: Unpublished MA Dissertation.

—. (1996) 'National Heritage and Global Tourism in Thailand', *Annals of Tourism Research*, 23: 432-448.

—. (2002) *The Politics of Ruins and the Business of Nostalgia*, Bangkok: White Lotus.

Pires, Ema (2010) 'Reading Emptiness: on Tourism, Appropriation and Contested Spaces', *iNtergraph: Journal of Dialogic Anthropology*, 3, 1 (www.intergraphjournal.com).

Prudhisan Jumbala and Chantana Banpasirichote (2001) 'Thai Middle Classes: Between Class Ambiguity and Democratic Propensity'. In Hsin-Huang Michael Hsiao (ed.), *Exploration of the Middle Classes in*

Southeast Asia, Taipei: Program for Southeast Asian Area Studies, Academia Sinica, pp.381-413.

Reid, Anthony (2001) 'Understanding *Melayu* (Malay) as a Source of Diverse Modern Identities', *Journal of Southeast Asian Studies*, 32: 295-313.

Reynolds, Craig, J. (ed.) (1993) *National Identity and its Defenders: Thailand, 1939-1989*, Chiang Mai: Silkwork Books.

—. (1998) 'Globalization and Cultural Nationalism in Modern Thailand'. In Joel S. Kahn, (ed.), *Southeast Asian Identities: Culture and the Politics of Representation in Indonesia, Malaysia, Singapore, and Thailand*, Singapore and London: Institute of Southeast Asian Studies, pp. 115-145.

—. (2006) *Seditious Histories: Contesting Thai and Southeast Asian Pasts*, Singapore: University of Washington Press.

Richter, Linda K. (1989) *The Politics of Tourism in Asia*, Honolulu: University of Hawaii Press (chapter on 'The Philippines: the Politicization of Tourism', pp. 51-81).

—. (1999) 'The Politics of Heritage Tourism Development: Emerging Issues for the New Millennium'. In Douglas G. Pearce and Richard W. Butler, (eds), *Contemporary Issues in Tourism Development*, London and New York in association with the International Academy for the Study of Tourism: Routledge, pp. 108-126.

Robison, Richard and David S.G. Goodman (eds) (1996) *The New Rich in Asia. Mobile Phones, McDonalds and Middle-class Revolution*, London and New York: Routledge.

Rössler, Mechtild (2006) 'World Heritage Landscapes: a UNESCO Flagship Programme, 1992-2006', *Landscape Research*, 31: 333-353.

Salazar, Noel B. (2009) 'The World's, Asia's, Indonesia's, or Ours? Heritage Interpretation and Appropriation in Times of Change', Asia Research Institute, National University of Singapore: Conference Paper – Heritage in Asia: Converging Forces and Conflicting Values, January 2009.

Sandhu, Kernial Singh (1983a) 'Chinese Colonization in Melaka'. In Kernial Singh Sandhu and Paul Wheatley (eds), *Melaka: the Transformation of a Malay Capital, c 1400-1980*, Kuala Lumpur: Oxford University Press, vol. 2, pp. 93-136.

—. (1983b) 'Indian Settlement in Melaka'. In Kernial Singh Sandhu and Paul Wheatley (eds), *Melaka: the Transformation of a Malay Capital, c 1400-1980*, Kuala Lumpur: Oxford University Press, vol. 2, pp. 174-211.

Sandhu, Kernial Singh and Paul Wheatley (eds) (1983a) *Melaka: the Transformation of a Malay Capital, c 1400-1980*, Kuala Lumpur: Oxford University Press, 2 vols.

—. (1983b) 'The Historical Context'. In Kernial Singh Sandhu and Paul Wheatley (eds), *Melaka: the Transformation of a Malay Capital, c 1400-1980*, Kuala Lumpur: Oxford University Press, vol. 1, pp. 3-69.

—. (1983c) 'From Capital to Municipality'. In Kernial Singh Sandhu and Paul Wheatley (eds), *Melaka: the Transformation of a Malay Capital, c 1400-1980*, Kuala Lumpur: Oxford University Press, vol. 2, pp. 495-597.

Sarkissian, Margaret (2000) *D'Albuquerque's Children: Performing Tradition in Malaysia's Portuguese Settlement*, Chicago: Chicago University Press.

Schubert, Datuk Dr Paddy et al (eds) (2004) *The Guide to Melaka, Malaysia. Essential Information for Business and Pleasure in the Heart of South-East Asia*, Melaka: Melaka State Government.

Seow, E.J. (1983) 'Melakan Architecture'. In Kernial Singh Sandhu and Paul Wheatley (eds), *Melaka: the Transformation of a Malay Capital, c 1400-1980*, Kuala Lumpur: Oxford University Press, vol. 1, pp.770-781.

Shaw, Gareth and Allan M. Williams (2002) *Critical Issues in Tourism: a Geographical Perspective*, Oxford: Blackwell, second edition.

Sidhu, Manjit S. (1983) 'An Introduction to Ethnic Segregation in Melaka Town'. In Kernial Singh Sandhu and Paul Wheatley (eds), *Melaka: the Transformation of a Malay Capital, c 1400-1980*, Kuala Lumpur: Oxford University Press, vol. 2, pp. 30-46.

Smith, Melanie K. (2003) *Issues in Cultural Tourism Studies*, London and New York: Routledge.

Sowatree Nathalang (1999) *Rangsit in Transition: Urbanisation and Cultural Adaptation in Central Thailand*, synthesis of PhD thesis submitted to the Postgraduate School of Anthropology, Macquarie University, Sydney.

Steels, Stephanie (2007) *On Being Indonesian: Heritage Tourism at Borobudur Temple*, University of Leeds: Unpublished MA dissertation.

Taylor, Ken (2003) 'Cultural Landscape as Open Air Museum: Borobudur World Heritage Site and its Setting', *Humanities Research*, 10: 51-62.

Teo, Peggy (2009) 'Knowledge Order in Asia'. In Tim Winter, Peggy Teo and T.C. Chang (eds), *Asia on Tour: Exploring the Rise of Asian Tourism*, London and New York: Routledge, pp.34-51.

Thongchai Winichakul (1994) *Siam Mapped: A History of the Geo-body of*

a Nation, Honolulu: University of Hawaii Press.
Tjoa-Bonatz, Dorothea Mai Lin (1998) 'Shophouses in Colonial Penang', *Journal of the Malaysian Branch of the Royal Asiatic Society*, LXX: 122-156.
—. (2000) 'Penang's Historic City Centre', *Journal of the Malaysian Branch of the Royal Asiatic Society*, LXXIII: 53-69.
Tourism Authority of Thailand [TAT] (2000) *Ayutthaya 1350-1767: Historical City Park,* Bangkok: Damsutha Press.
—. (2007) *Ayutthaya*, Bangkok: Promotional Material Production Division, Marketing Services Department, TAT Central Region Office: Region 6.
—. (2008a) *Paragons of World Heritage*, Bangkok: Promotional Material Production Division, Marketing Services Department.
—. (2008b) *Golden Wonderland*, Bangkok: Promotional Material Production Division, Marketing Services Department.
Tourism Malaysia (2009a) *Heritage and Crafts*, Kuala Lumpur: Ministry of Tourism.
—. (2009b) *History. Heritage. Recreation. Feel the Thrill! Southern Region*, Kuala Lumpur: Ministry of Tourism.
—. (2009c) *Malaysia Travel Guide*, Kuala Lumpur: Ministry of Tourism.
—. http://www.tat.or.th
Tourism Promotion Division (2009) *Melaka Tourism: 12 Subsectors*, Ayer Keroh: Melaka State Tourism Division.
Tripadvisor, http://www.tripadvisor.com/Attraction_Review-g297709-d320054-Reviews-Borobudur_Temple-Magelang_Central_Java_Java.html
Turnbull, C.M. (1983) 'Melaka under British Colonial Rule'. In Kernial Singh Sandhu and Paul Wheatley (eds), *Melaka: the Transformation of a Malay Capital, c 1400-1980*, Kuala Lumpur: Oxford University Press, vol. 1, pp. 242-296.
UNESCO (1972) *Convention Concerning the Protection of the World's Cultural and Natural Heritage, Geneva*: United Nations Educational, Scientific and Cultural Organisation.
—. (1983) *Convention and Recommendations of UNESCO Concerning the Protection of the Cultural Heritage*, Geneva: United Nations Educational, Scientific and Cultural Organisation.
—. (2004) *Tourism and Heritage Site Management in the World Heritage Site of Luang Prabang Lao PDR*, Bangkok: UNESCO.
—. (2008a) *Melaka and George Town (Malaysia) No 1223*, World Heritage Convention, Advisory Body Evaluation, http://whc.unesco.org/en/list/1223/documents/

—. (2008b) *Decision-32COM 8B.25*, World Heritage Centre, http://whc.unesco.org/en/sessions/32COM/

—. (2011). http://portal.unesco.org/geography/en/ev.phpURL_ID12950&URL_DO=DO_TOPI (1st September 2011).

—. (2012) *World Heritage Sites: a Complete Guide to 936 UNESCO World Heritage Sites,* Willowdale, Ontario and New York: Firefly Books, UNESCO Publishing.

—. unesco.org/geography

UNESCO, Bangkok, http://www.unescobkk.org/culture/wh/ap-sites/ayutthaya/

UNESCO World Heritage Centre, http://www.whc.unesco.org/

—. http://whc.unesco.org/en/list/592

—. http://whc.unesco.org/en/list/642

Universal Dictionary (1987) London: The Reader's Digest Association.

UNWTO (2013) 'Malaysia Country Report, Malaysia Visitor Arrivals, 2012', UNWTO 25th CAP-CSA, Hyderabad, Conference on Sustainable Tourism Development, April 2013.

Urry, John (1990) *The Tourist Gaze: Leisure and Travel in Contemporary Society*, London: Sage.

Van Esterik, Penny (2000) *Materializing Thailand*, Oxford and New York: Berg.

Vines, Elizabeth (2005) *Streetwise Asia: a Practical Guide for the Conservation and Revitalization of Heritage Cities and Towns in Asia*, Bangkok: UNESCO and The World Bank.

Virtual Museum Melaka, www.virtualmuseummelaka.com

Vu, Jo and Quynh-Du Ton-That (2012) 'World Heritage Listing and Implications for Tourism – the Case of Hue, Vietnam'. In Murut Kasimoglu and Handan Aydin (eds), *Strategies for Tourism Industry – Micro and Macro Perspectives*, InTech, www.intechopen.com, pp. 233-240.

Wake, C.H. (1983) 'Melaka in the Fifteenth Century: Malay Historical Traditions and the Politics of Islamization'. In Kernial Singh Sandhu and Paul Wheatley (eds), *Melaka: the Transformation of a Malay Capital, c 1400-1980*, Kuala Lumpur: Oxford University Press, vol. 1, pp. 128-161.

Wall, Geoffrey and Heather Black (2005) 'Commentary. Global Heritage and Local Problems: Some Examples from Indonesia'. In David Harrison and Michael Hitchcock (eds), *The Politics of World Heritage: Negotiating Tourism and Conservation*, Clevedon: Channel View Publications, Current Themes in Tourism, pp. 156-159.

Wan Hashimah Wan Ismail and Shuhana Shamsuddin (2005) *The Old Shophouses as Part of Malaysian Urban Heritage: the Current Dilemma*, 8th International Conference of the Asian Planning Schools Association, 11-14th September, 2005 (http://www.vintagemalaysia.com/files/pdf).

Webster, Anthony (2011) 'The Development of British Commercial and Political Networks in the Straits Settlements 1800 to 1868: the Rise of a Colonial and Regional Economic Identity?' *Modern Asian Studies*, 45: 899-929.

Wee, Bonny (2009) *Malacca: a World Heritage Site*, Kuala Lumpur: Purple Productions and PR Consultants (M) Sdn Bhd.

Wiendu Nuryanti (1996) 'Heritage and Postmodern Tourism', *Annals of Tourism Research*, 32: 249-260.

Winter, Tim (2003) 'Tomb Raiding Angkor: a Clash of Cultures, *Indonesia and the Malay World*, special issue *Tourism and Heritage in South-East Asia*, Michael Hitchcock and Victor T. King (eds), 31: 58-68.

—. (2004) 'Cultural Heritage and Tourism in Angkor, Cambodia: Developing a Theoretical Dialogue', *Historical Environment*, 17: 3-8 (and as *Cultural Heritage and Tourism at Angkor, Cambodia: Developing a Theoretical Dialogue*, Institute for Culture and Society, pre-print journal articles, 2004).

—. (2005) 'Landscape, Memory and Heritage: New Year Celebrations at Angkor, Cambodia'. In David Harrison and Michael Hitchcock (eds), *The Politics of World Heritage: Negotiating Tourism and Conservation*, Clevedon: Channel View Publications, Current Themes in Tourism, pp. 50-65 (and special issue of *Current Issues in Tourism*, 7, pp. 330-345).

—. (2007) *Post-Conflict Heritage, Postcolonial Tourism: Culture, Politics and Development at Angkor*, London and New York: Routledge.

—. (2009) 'Conclusion: Recasting Tourism Theory towards an Asian Future'. In Tim Winter, Peggy Teo and T.C. Chang (eds), *Asia on Tour: Exploring the Rise of Asian Tourism*, London and New York: Routledge, pp. 315-325.

Winter, Tim, Peggy Teo and T.C. Chang (2009a) 'Introduction: Rethinking Tourism in Asia'. In Tim Winter, Peggy Teo and T.C. Chang (eds), *Asia on Tour: Exploring the Rise of Asian Tourism*, London and New York: Routledge, pp. 1-18.

—. (2009b) *Asia on Tour: Exploring the Rise of Asian Tourism*, London and New York: Routledge.

Worden, Nigel (2001) 'Where it all began: the Representation of Malaysian Heritage in Melaka', *International Journal of Heritage Studies,* 7:199-218.

—. (2003) National Identity and Heritage Tourism in Melaka, *Indonesia and the Malay World*, special issue *Tourism and Heritage in South-East Asia*, Michael Hitchcock and Victor T. King (eds), 31: 31-41.

—. (2010) 'National Identity and Heritage Tourism in Melaka'. In Michael Hitchcock, Victor T. King and Michael Parnwell (eds), *Heritage Tourism in Southeast Asia*, Copenhagen: NIAS Press and Honolulu: University of Hawai'i Press, pp. 130-146.

World Heritage Site, http: //www. worldheritagesite.org/

Zainal Abidin bin Abdul Wahid, Datuk (1983) 'Power and Authority in the Melaka Sultanate: the Traditional View'. In Kernial Singh Sandhu and Paul Wheatley (eds), *Melaka: the Transformation of a Malay Capital, c 1400-1980*, Kuala Lumpur: Oxford University Press, vol. 1, pp. 101-112.

Tourists' Perceptions of Authenticity: The Case of Heritage Experiences in Hong Kong

Thi Hong Hai Nguyen
and Catherine Cheung

Introduction

Heritage tourism is one of the most notable and widespread types of tourism, in terms of visitors and attractions, drawing hundreds of millions of visitors every year (Timothy and Boyd, 2006). In the urban tourist destination of Hong Kong, heritage tourism is only a secondary or tertiary tourist attraction. Nevertheless, there is a growing concern for developing heritage tourism. The idea of heritage in Hong Kong has been established since the 1980s in recognising the process by which the former Chinese fishing village was transformed from the mid-nineteenth century into a metropolitan city (Cheung, 1999). Recently, heritage was identified as one of the key options in order to pursue a long-term strategy for tourism development (Ho and McKercher, 2004; Hong Kong Planning Department, 2012).

Due to the rapid transformation of Hong Kong since the 1980s, together with the strong commodification of tourist assets, heritage sites in the city have been reconstructed on various levels. In a study of cultural attractions in Hong Kong, the curators and managers of these assets, not only showed no objections towards commodification, but also acknowledged commodification as an essential means to manage increasing visitor numbers (McKercher, Ho and du Cros, 2004). However, it is commonly suggested that the process of commoditising cultural and heritage assets for tourism purposes results in a loss of authenticity (Cohen, 1988; Finn, 2009; Goulding, 2000; Greenwood, 1977; Halewood and Hannam, 2001; MacCannell, 1973; Shepherd, 2002; Watson and Kopachevsky, 1994).

The topic of authenticity and the tourist search for authentic experiences have been the subjects of a heated debate since the 1960s. A number of studies have indicated that tourists have different preferences related to authenticity. Hence, they seek different types of authentic experiences (Chhabra, Healy and Sills, 2003; Chhabra, 2010; Moscardo and Pearce, 1999; Pearce and Moscardo, 1986; Silver, 1993; Waitt, 2000). The three major views of authenticity discussed in the literature are objectivism, constructivism and existentialism (Chhabra, 2012; Reisinger and Steiner, 2006; Wang, 1999). From the management and marketing point of view, it is essential that we should comprehend how tourists understand the concept of authenticity and to recognise whether they acknowledge the authenticity claimed for a site or event (Kolar and Zabkar, 2010; Xie and Wall, 2002).

In developing the theme of authenticity we believe that in the context of Hong Kong heritage tourism it is a vital topic for investigation. Thus, the purpose of this study is to examine tourist perceptions of authenticity with regard to Hong Kong heritage tourism experiences and the factors that affect these perceptions.

Review of Literature

Authenticity in Tourism

The concept of authenticity is claimed to have been originally used in a museum context (Trilling, 1972, cited in Wang, 1999); it was then extended to various tourism products and is currently commonly used as an important marketing and selling point. In a tourism context, authenticity refers specifically to traditional culture and origin, relating to a sense of realness, genuineness and uniqueness (Sharpley, 1994) and to issues of identity (Lanfant, 1995; MacDonald, 1997; Picard, 1997). Authenticity is also defined as being associated with the presentation of the past in an accurate manner (Timothy and Boyd, 2003).

The literature demonstrates divergent opinions on perceiving authenticity. Generally there are two research directions concerning the meaning of authenticity. Some scholars consider authenticity as intrinsic to the objects so designated, whilst others suggest that authenticity lies in tourist perceptions or experiences (Timothy, 2011). Wang (1999) contended that the concept of authenticity should be divided into separate issues, which are often confused: *tourist experiences* and *toured objects*. This idea arose from the previous concepts of 'real world' and 'real self' proposed by

Handler and Saxton (1988); and 'authenticity as knowledge' ('cool' authenticity) and 'authenticity as feeling' ('hot' authenticity) by Selwyn (1996) (as cited in Wang, 1999). According to Wang (1999), it is not correct to conclude that the 'authenticity as feeling' from the 'real self" has emerged from 'authenticity as knowledge' or from the 'real world'. The 'real self' can have no relationship with the 'real world'. Nonetheless, one could experience authenticity either by knowledge/real world or feeling/real self or both. In other words, objects and tourist perceptions are both used to perceive authenticity, yet one can be stronger than the other. Indeed, the concept of authenticity is often considered to be negotiable (Cohen, 1988), and therefore different perspectives of authenticity exist. The three most widely discussed and acknowledged are 'objective', 'constructed' and 'existential' authenticity.

Objectivist and constructivist approaches are the two conventional conceptions of authenticity. Objective authenticity is based on 'pseudo-events' as described by Boorstin and 'staged authenticity' as examined by MacCannell (Wang, 1999). This museum-linked view refers to the pure, original, genuine version of the objects (Chhabra, 2012; Wang, 1999). The objectivists contend that authenticity is an obvious feature of sites and objects and that it can be measured by certain criteria (Reisinger and Steiner, 2006). When tourists search for authenticity in this sense, then an inauthentic experience results from an inauthentic object (Rickly-Boyd, 2012). This conceptualisation of authenticity, however, is based on knowledge of the object and falls within the arena of experts, intellectuals and members of the elite and is not applicable to mass tourists (Wang, 1999). Reisinger and Steiner (2006) even suggest abandoning the concept of objective authenticity because they believe there is no common ground for its existence and meaning. Nonetheless, an empirical study of student perceptions of authenticity by Chhabra (2010) revealed that the demand for objective authenticity does exist and continues to prevail.

Meanwhile, constructivists see the 'real world' as the result of interpretations and constructions (Schwandt, 1994). A constructivist approach therefore addresses the complex and constructed nature of authenticity within the context of the influence of capitalism and commercialisation (Britton, 1991; Chhabra, 2012; Finn, 2009; Goulding, 2000; Wang, 1999). The constructivist approach implies that the object is comprehended by tourist interpretations and their knowledge of it; and that the authenticity of the object is constructed by perspectives, beliefs, and expectations. Wang (1999) has summarised the common elements of this school of thought as follows: (1) the refusal to accept the notion of absolute authenticity; (2) the premise that origins and traditions are invented according to certain contexts; (3) the view that authenticity is a pluralistic concept, dependent on tourist perspectives and interpretations; (4) the position that authenticity is associated with stereotypes and the expectations of the societies from which tourists derive; and, (5) the claim that the authenticity of objects can emerge over time even if its origins are artificial. Subsequently, it is argued that tourists indeed search for authenticity. However, they do not search for objective authenticity but rather symbolic authenticity, which results from the process of social construction (Wang, 1999).

These conventional concepts of authenticity which are influenced by objectivist and constructivist approaches are directly relevant and important for several types of tourism connected with the past, such as cultural, heritage, historical and ethnic tourism (Wang, 1999). However, they are claimed to be 'too simple' for explicating contemporary tourism (Urry, 1990; and Britton, 1991). Some modes of travel are believed to be inappropriate for using the conventional concept of authenticity, such as visiting friends and relatives, beach holidays, nature-based tourism, shopping tourism, sports tourism, and so on. Using another perception of the concept, Wang (1999) has proposed the notion of existential authenticity. In fact, many other scholars have questioned the conventional concepts of authenticity which are mainly associated with 'toured objects' (Wang, 1999).

Existential authenticity advocates subjective versions of authenticity which might be irrelevant to the realness of the 'toured objects' (Chhabra, 2012). It denotes one's state of mind and perceptions, existential state of being, and self-discovery (ibid). Accordingly, tourists are mostly searching for their authentic selves by travelling, and experiencing activities and 'toured objects' (Wang, 1999). The 'toured object' is irrelevant or less relevant in informing an authentic experience as it is only a medium through which one finds existential authenticity. Although this perception of authenticity is claimed to explain authenticity for certain types of tourism (nature, beach, cruising, visiting friends and relatives), it may also be applicable to cultural and heritage tourism, particularly in that tourists do not necessarily visit cultural and heritage sites because of the sites themselves but for other reasons, i.e. convenience or accompanying their friends or family.

Tourist Perceptions of Authenticity

The topic of tourists and their search for authentic places and experiences has been the subject of discussion in tourism studies since the 1960s (Timothy, 2011). Principally, there are two contrasting points of view, namely (1) tourists are not concerned about the authenticity of the places they visit, and (2) tourists really look for authentic experiences and places. One of the earliest ideas of authenticity presented by Boorstin in 1961 contended that tourists are not concerned about the authenticity of the places they visit or the experiences they have, but their purposes for travelling are mainly for fun and entertainment (as cited in Timothy, 2011). Boorstin also argued that touristic places are often inauthentic and fabricated for tourists; and that tourists actually seek this kind of inauthentic experience. Urry (1990) claimed that tourists even prefer spurious places which give them unreal experiences and do not require mindfulness, thoughtfulness or effort even if they are able to recognise real or unreal heritage places.

MacCannell indicated that tourists in fact looked for authenticity but they were not able to identify it. He then proposed the concept of ‘staged authenticity’, where everything is set up for the consumption of tourists (MacCannell, 1973). The terms ‘front stage’ and ‘back stage’ are used to clarify the concept of ‘staged authenticity’. The ‘front stage’ where tourists often visit, is disposed to present local cultures to tourists, while real local life is at the ‘back stage’ (Timothy, 2011). Tourists therefore only experience the ‘performed’ or ‘staged culture’.

From these seminal discussions of authenticity, many other scholars have contributed to these debates. For example, Moscardo and Pearce (1986) concluded from their research on Australian historic theme parks that authenticity is important for tourist choices to visit places and that authenticity is often promoted as a part of the visitors’ experiences. Herbert (1995) was particularly interested in authenticity when discussing issues of heritage as ‘literary place’. He argued that ‘some visitors, though probably a small minority, are extremely interested in the authenticity of the site and are likely to be disappointed if things are not “real”’ (ibid: 45). Timothy (2011) has also proposed that tourists might not be looking for fabricated experiences in that they are in fact blinded by previous stereotypes or false images. In this case, tourist perception of what is authentic is actually not a real and authentic experience, because what they think they are searching for is in fact not genuine.

In sum, the importance of authenticity differs among different types of tourists. There are tourists who search for authentic places and have a desire for authentic experiences; whilst others are not concerned about authenticity and simply wish to experience fun and relax. Different levels of authenticity can be identified in the 'toured object', ranging from the genuine to the totally fabricated. Subsequently, tourists may perceive authenticity in their own ways and from their own perspectives.

In fact, a considerable amount of research has been undertaken on the theme of authenticity from the tourist perspective through empirical studies (see Budruk, White, Wodrich and van Riper, 2008; Chhabra, 2010; Chhabra, Healy and Sills, 2003; Cole, 2007; Kolar and Zabkar, 2010; McIntosh and Prentice, 1999; Moscardo and Pearce, 1986; Reisinger and Steiner, 2006; Robinson and Clifford, 2012; Waitt, 2000; Waller and Lea, 1998). Some of these studies indicate that tourists have different preferences related to authenticity and seek different types of authentic experiences (Chhabra, 2010; Moscardo and Pearce, 1999; Silver, 1993; Waitt, 2000). Authenticity is therefore seen as a negotiable concept (Cohen, 1988).

Indeed, people perceive authenticity differently and, sometimes even ambiguously. This means that an object could be judged as inauthentic by experts or elites, but be perceived as authentic by some tourists. Therefore, from the management and marketing standpoint, it is crucial to understand authenticity from tourist perceptions (Kolar and Zabkar, 2010; Xie and Wall, 2002). Especially when various perceptions towards authenticity are defined, an investigation of these points of view is essential.

The three prominent views indicated above present different tourist perceptions towards authenticity. In a heritage tourism context, tourists vary from what might be termed 'serious' to 'accidental' tourists, and their heritage experiences range from enjoying their real self to learning from the real world. Previous studies have shown that a range of perceptions of authenticity are associated with certain visitor characteristics such as age, stage of career, tourism style (Littrell, Anderson and Brown, 1993), gender, place of residence, stage of lifecycle (Waitt, 2000), education, mode of travel (Chang, Wall and Chang, 2008), visitor motivation, place identity, educational attainment, and previous experiences (Budruk, White, Wodrich, van Riper, 2008). In addition, perceived authenticity should be understood as linking tourist motivation to future behaviour (Kolar and Zabkar, 2010). Perceived authenticity is also an important factor in tourist satisfaction, enjoyment and loyalty (Chhabra, 2010; Kolar and Zabkar, 2010; Pearce and Moscardo, 1986; Waller and Lea, 1998).

Study Sites

Hong Kong is commonly known as an urban tourism destination, which offers a spectacular skyline view, diverse shopping and recreational facilities, and a special mixture of Chinese and British culture. This cosmopolitan metropolis attracts millions of visitors a year, and in 2011 recorded almost 42 million tourists (Hong Kong Tourism Board, 2012). Recently, the Hong Kong Government has paid more attention to widening the range of tourist experiences and to diversifying tourist attractions in order to attract new visitors, keeping them staying longer and encouraging repeat visits (Hong Kong Planning Department, 2012). The focus for long-term tourism development is on ecotourism and cultural tourism (Hong Kong Planning Department, 2012). In cultural tourism, special attention is given to arts, culture and heritage attractions (Hong Kong Planning Department, 2012).

In Hong Kong, the concept of heritage has been developed from the 1980s with an emphasis on Hong Kong's Chinese culture and history (Cheung, 1999). But the British colonial period has also left Hong Kong with special Western features. It is the fusion of Chinese and Western cultures, the traditional and the modern, which gives Hong Kong a distinct image of 'East meets West'. Although heritage tourism has never been a primary tourist attraction of Hong Kong, the local government has put great efforts into expanding this type of tourism to local as well as foreign tourists. Different heritage trails have been established and promoted since 1993, of which the Ping Shan Heritage Trail in the New Territories was the first. Also, the Lung Yeuk Tau Heritage Trail and the Central and Western Heritage Trail with three different routes present the special Chinese and British features of Hong Kong. These trails have been well-visited by both local and international visitors (Hong Kong Planning Department, 2012). Recently, a large-scale exhibition entitled 'Hong Kong Heritage Tourism Expo - Access Heritage' was held from December 2010 to November 2011 in different places, promoting six specially designed heritage tour routes (Commissioner for Heritage's Office, 2013).

There are a total of 101 declared monuments and more than one thousand historic buildings in Hong Kong (Antiquities and Monuments Office, 2013), including a wide range of Chinese tangible and intangible heritage (such as temples, festivals and villages) and British colonial heritage/historic buildings. Nonetheless, only a few of these heritage sites are able to attract tourists. A study by McKercher, Ho and du Cros (2004) indicated more than half out of nearly 100 declared monuments and museums promoted by the Hong Kong Tourism Board recorded no visitors at all.

In this study, in order to achieve the proposed objectives of investigating tourist perceptions, the chosen heritage attractions should not only have cultural and/or historical value but also a significant number of visitors. From the review of literature and our own visits to sites, six different heritage attractions were chosen for this study (see Table 1). The primary data of the study were mainly collected by semi-structured interviews. This approach provided the opportunity to obtain relevant information on the main topics of interest, but also enabled the respondents to express their thoughts and stories spontaneously. It is particularly appropriate in a study in which the perceptions of tourists are investigated. Accordingly, a list of open-ended questions was prepared in advance to gather information about tourist motivation in visiting the sites, their awareness of the sites, their satisfaction with the visits, and most importantly, their perceptions towards the authenticity of heritage experiences. Also, new or follow-up issues were brought up during the interviews on a case-by-case basis and the order of the questions was flexible.

Table 1: Description of the Heritage Attractions

Name	Description
Wong Tai Sin Temple	Home to three religions: Taoism, Buddhism and Confucianism. This is one of the most famous temples in Hong Kong and an important religious centre where local worshippers pray for good fortune. It has also become a very popular tourist attraction with shops and fortune-teller services.
Ten Thousand Buddhas Monastery	This is a Buddhist temple, located on a hill in the Pai Tau Village, Sha Tin. There are about 13,000 statues of the Buddha, spreading from the gates at the bottom of the hill up to the main temple.

Man Mo Temple	Built in 1847, the temple is dedicated to two gods, Man Cheong, the God of Literature and Kwan Yu, the God of Martial Arts. This temple is located in the busy Central District of Hong Kong Island. It is a popular and esteemed religious site for locals.
Ping Shan Heritage Trail	Introduced in December 1993, this is the first heritage trail in Hong Kong. The district of Ping Shan has a long history with the Tang clan first residing there in the twelfth century. This one kilometre trail includes numerous traditional Chinese buildings such as pagodas, ancestral halls, study halls and temples.
Po Lin Monastery	The monastery was founded in 1906 and is now one of Hong Kong's most important Buddhist sanctuaries. It is located in a popular cultural tourist complex, together with the Tian Tan Buddha (Big Buddha) and the Ngong Ping village on Lantau Island.
Museum of Heritage	The museum is located in Sha Tin. It provides a wide selection of exhibitions and activities with a mix of history, culture and arts of early Hong Kong and the nearby South China region.

A total number of 21 interviews were carried out in April and May 2013, mostly through face-to-face dialogues at six different heritage sites in Hong Kong. Table 2 presents the basic demographic characteristics of the respondents and the heritage sites where the interviews took place, as well as the main subjects of the interviews. The respondents were inbound tourists to Hong Kong, including seven short-haul tourists from Asian countries and 14 long-haul tourists from non-Asian countries. Their ages ranged from 21 to 52 years. Respondents visited Hong Kong for various reasons, from convenience (such as language, safety, close to China, and so on) to visiting friends and relatives, business and vacation.

Together with interviews, the physical settings of the heritage sites were also observed regarding the matters of authenticity, commodification and tourist activities.

Table 2: Respondents' Information

Interviewee	Nationality	Gender	Age	Heritage site
#1	China	Female	21	Wong Tai Sin Temple
#2	Netherlands	Female	22	Man Mo Temple
#3	Italy	Male	29	Big Buddha and Po Lin Monastery
#4	China	Male	35	Wong Tai Sin Temple
#5	Finland	Female	31	Ten Thousand Buddhas Monastery and Po Lin Monastery
#6	China	Male	42	Po Lin Monastery
#7	Poland	Female	25	Wong Tai Sin Temple
#8	Spain	Male	29	Wong Tai Sin Temple
#9	Spain	Male	28	Po Lin Monastery
#10	China	Male	34	Po Lin Monastery
#11	France	Female	52	Ten Thousand Buddhas Monastery and Man Mo Temple
#12	Russia	Female	24	Ten Thousand Buddhas Monastery
#13	Poland	Female	26	Ten Thousand Buddhas Monastery and Ping Shan Heritage Trail
#14	Poland	Male	26	Ten Thousand Buddhas Monastery and Ping Shan Heritage Trail

#15	Vietnam	Female	28	Museum of History
#16	Vietnam	Male	30	Po Lin Monastery
#17	Canada	Female	25	Ten Thousand Buddhas Monastery
#18	Canada	Female	25	Ten Thousand Buddhas Monastery
#19	France	Male	27	Ten Thousand Buddhas Monastery
#20	France	Female	27	Ten Thousand Buddhas Monastery
#21	Vietnam	Female	26	Man Mo Temple and Wong Tai Sin Temple

Findings

Tourist Visits to Hong Kong Heritage Attractions

Half of the non-Asian respondents followed the recommendation from guidebooks to visit these heritage attractions. This fact confirms the important role of guidebooks in the tourist decision-making process (Lew, 1991), especially for long-haul tourists who are not so familiar with the destination. For most Asian tourists, religion was the primary or secondary purpose of the visits as almost all surveyed attractions are religious sites. Word-of-mouth, specifically recommendations from friends and relatives, was also an important reason for the respondents when choosing the attractions. Nevertheless, almost all respondents claimed their heritage interests extend from travelling in general to the visit to Hong Kong in particular. Hence, the ultimate reason for visiting these attractions has been found to be acquiring knowledge about Hong Kong and learning about the local cultures and customs.

Even for a Chinese tourist who was not new to Hong Kong, the contemporary local customs appeared to be interesting: *'I like to experience what local people experience. I want to see, I want to do what they do'*. Since Hong Kong is overwhelmed with modern architecture and lifestyle, heritage and its atmosphere which present *'another side of the city'* was another point of interest for many respondents. For example, tourists stated that: *'Now you just see high buildings, it's new and it's impersonal. It doesn't give me the feeling about the people, it's just large and concrete. Heritage is completely different, the atmosphere and everything around. For me, I feel more comfortable with this kind of surrounding'*. Or: *'I try to understand how life was in the old days [in Hong Kong], how people worked ... Because now it is so different, huge buildings, modern life'*. For the sites that are located in suburban or mountain areas (Po Lin Monastery/the Big Buddha, Ten Thousand Buddhas Monastery), escaping from the city was also an important reason for the visits.

Many of the long-haul tourists were first time visitors to Hong Kong, some were even first time visitors to Asia. Therefore, their knowledge about Hong Kong and Chinese culture was limited. The main source of information about the sites for most respondents was a guidebook. The information they had, however, was rather superficial, in that it mainly related to where to go and what to see. For instance, tourists said *'I only heard that it is a nice place to go'* or *'I saw few pictures, I saw it was big enough to have something interesting'*. On the other hand, there were tourists who not only had read about the history of the heritage sites but also had previous experiences about Asia as well as Chinese culture. It is the difference between these two groups that has resulted in different perspectives towards heritage experiences.

With the purpose of learning about local cultures and customs, tourists spent around two or three hours at the attractions, mainly for sightseeing and taking photographs. Only some short-haul tourists, who came also for religious purposes, spent some more time praying for good fortune. However, there were tourists who had the chance to interact with locals and this was found to make their visits more exciting. A tourist shared her story: *'We went in, we saw people praying. I was wondering what people were doing. So I asked a person how it worked with the candles, praying and stuff. He told me you had to offer something and you prayed for something good. Then we walk around, I burned a candle as well. And that was really nice'*.

In general, the respondents had a positive impression of the visited sites, especially towards their appearance and structural design. All respondents appreciated the aesthetic aspect of the heritage attractions in Hong Kong.

The words '*beautiful*' and '*impressive*' were mentioned frequently when tourists were asked about their impression of the visited sites.

Tourist Perceptions of Authenticity

Tourists were asked to assess the authenticity of their heritage experiences in the surveyed sites. Experiences in three studied sites (Man Mo Temple, Ten Thousand Buddhas Monastery and Ping Shan Heritage Trail) were perceived as rather authentic. Experiences in the other three attractions (Wong Tai Sin Temple, Po Lin Monastery, and Museum of History) were not so authentic according to the respondents' perceptions. In order to understand the reasons behind this, tourists' explanations of their assessments were analysed and classified into 'enhancers' and 'diminishers' of perceived authenticity. 'Enhancers' of authenticity are understood as elements that increase the perceived authenticity of the heritage experiences, whereas, 'diminishers' are factors that lessen the perceived authenticity of heritage experiences.

'Enhancers' of Perceived Authenticity

Table 3 shows eight categories of perceived authenticity 'enhancers' which are arranged in the order of frequency of occurrence. The first two categories (appearance of the site and the presence of local culture) were the most common reasons for tourists having stronger perceptions of authenticity.

Table 3: 'Enhancers' of Perceived Authenticity

Categories	Properties
Appearance	Age (i.e. old) Ruin/ Desolation Original/ no modification
Local culture/custom	Presence of monks/religious practitioners Presence of local people Used by locals for original purposes

	Interactions with locals
Novelty	Lack of knowledge about the site Different culture, custom Discovery
Senses	Smell of incense Sound of praying
Location	Local residential surroundings Historic/original location
Accessibility	Necessity to make an effort to access the site
Atmosphere	Spirituality
Authority	Government involvement

According to most respondents, the site appeared to be authentic if it looked old or even in ruins. Heritage is typically understood as the legacy from the past, hence logically, it should have the appearance of age. Authenticity was also found to have the meaning of 'original', with no perceived modifications. The presence of local culture and custom which is represented by local residents is another essential factor of authenticity. As stated by the respondents, it was the presence of the monks in the monasteries and the locals who were praying in the temples that made their experiences authentic. Moreover, a tourist claimed to have an extremely authentic temple experience when she was instructed by a local worshipper.

Another visitor said: *'When I went to Taiwan, I have a local friend there and I think it's more authentic when I went for lunch with her and then see really old cultural attractions. It is a really authentic thing to do'*. Hence, the interactions with locals are also found to increase tourists' perceived authenticity.

The third factor we discovered which made tourists' perceived authenticity higher is novelty. When tourists had either no or a limited knowledge of the site, they tended to show a higher level of perceived authenticity. Tourists, when encountering different cultures which are new to them, are usually unable to recognise what is real and what is fake. When they are impressed about what is presented then they accordingly consider it to be real and in consequence then have what they consider to be authentic experiences.

Tourists also used their senses when evaluating their experiences. Therefore, the presence of certain sounds or smells could enhance their heritage experiences and increase their perceived authenticity. Many tourists were fascinated to hear the sound of prayers and to smell the incense at the temples and monasteries. The presence of assets stimulating the senses was subsequently found to increase perceived authenticity. The opposite was found to be disappointing. A tourist commented: *'It was pretty, nice to look at, but I think I miss the smell. When I think of a temple, there is a smell in my mind'.*

In addition to original appearance, original or historical locations were mentioned as an element of authenticity. For some attractions, tourists perceived them as more authentic if they were located in a residential area and surrounded by local residents. An example was the heritage trail in Ping Shan, as the trail goes through the village lined with ancestral halls, temples, and study halls. The respondents were extremely satisfied with their related authentic experiences. On this trail, various details made tourists feel like they were having the most authentic Hong Kong heritage village experience. For example, the heritage site was found to be *'incorporated with other buildings [residents, houses], it's something different from a usual heritage, with fences and guards. It is still in use for daily lives'*. So tourists could *'see how people spend their time with family, gathering and praying together'*.

Necessity of efforts to get access to the sites, and the spiritual atmosphere were also noted as possible enhancers of perceived authenticity. One tourist who had *'suffered'* climbing up a hill when visiting the Ten Thousand Buddhas Monastery, believed this effort contributed to her authentic experience. She said that *'it is so difficult to come here. I don't think people would have built this kind of temple if it was not in the old times'.*

As most of the surveyed attractions were religious sites, also the spiritual atmosphere prevailed in the sites as an essential element of authenticity. Lastly and most interestingly, a tourist from China believed that the involvement of the authorities in the construction of the heritage site made it authentic. It is rather uncommon to see that, even if the site is known to be constructed, it is still considered as authentic. However, in this case, it might be the trust in the authority of the government that determines the perception of authenticity.

'Diminishers' of Perceived Authenticity

The five categories of authenticity 'diminishers' are summarised in Table 4.

Table 4: 'Diminishers' of perceived authenticity

Categories	Properties
Commodification/ Tourist facilities	Construction for tourism purposes Overcrowding Shops, restaurants Attraction park/*Disneyfication* Commercialisation
Physical setting	Artificial elements Modern elements New/freshly built appearance Presence of certain building material (i.e. concrete)
Over-management	Over-maintenance (i.e. too well-maintained) Over-cleanliness (i.e. too clean) Professional staff

Previous experiences	Comparison with previous experiences/knowledge
Surroundings	Modern surroundings Unrelated surroundings (i.e. non-religious)

When an assessment of non-authenticity occurred, one topic which was always repeated was commodification. The presence of shops, restaurants and other tourist facilities was found to reduce the authenticity of a heritage experience. The case of a tourist visiting Po Lin Monastery is an example: *'When I was at the Big Buddha and the Monastery, I saw tourists, shops, Starbucks... That is the main reason that makes me feel it is not authentic... When this kind of attraction is surrounded by shops and touristic facilities it takes away the authenticity'*. The high density of these tourist facilities also creates the image of a tourism-purpose-built attraction, hence it can destroy the authentic heritage experience. Also with the case of Po Lin Monastery and its tourism complex, a tourist stated: *'You walk through the place and you see that everything is for tourists. It feels like it was built for tourists'*.

In the case of the Wong Tai Sin Temple, the commercialised elements were also a significant 'diminisher'. A tourist commented: *'The biggest impression in Wong Tai Sin that I have is that there was a big area for fortune tellers. It was too organised on a large scale. They made a separate area for fortune tellers, it looks so professional. It lost the feeling of fortune tellers or a temple. It seems like a business, too commercialised'*.

Nonetheless, the presence of tourists seemed not to be an issue when the number was moderate. Indeed, the respondents were tourists themselves, hence obviously they accepted their existence. But when there were too many tourists, the overcrowding tended to weaken the authentic experiences.

In addition to the commodification factors, the physical setting or appearance of the heritage sites was another essential focus when assessing authenticity. When old is authentic, as discussed in the 'enhancers', understandably, new/modern/fresh is considered as inauthentic. A tourist when seeing the zodiac statues in Wong Tai Sin Temple stated that: *'From my perspective, it seems all pretty fresh. That's why I don't have an authentic feeling'*. The relatively new appearance also made tourists suspicious about the real purpose of the heritage site. A tourist commented on the statues of the Ten Thousand Buddhas Monastery: *'It does look a little bit new, maybe it has been developed for tourists'*.

Also, the obvious appearance of concrete in a temple construction was found to decrease perceived authenticity. Artificial elements added to the heritage sites were disappointing for tourists and reduced their authentic experience. According to a tourist who was visiting Wong Tai Sin Temple, the temple itself was acknowledged as real and original. Yet the artificial elements such as sculptures and decorations, commercial shops, and a modern logo gave her an inauthentic experience of the temple visit.

The third 'diminisher' is related to the management system of the heritage sites. Commonly, the better the management system, the better the service quality and the tourist experience. However, in the case of over-management, such as a site being too well-maintained and too clean with professional staff then these factors reduced the perceived authenticity. This finding can be associated with the previous positive concept of authenticity that heritage sites should be old or ruined. Therefore, when they are perceived as too nice and too clean, then they are not authentic heritage sites. In the Wong Tai Sin Temple, a tourist said: *'In these kinds of places in China, you see monks or religious persons in the surroundings. But here, there are security people or other people who are working here. There is the guy who removes the ashes with gloves and an orange t-shirt. It's just so strict, organised, planned'*.

While lack of information could increase perceived authenticity, as discussed in the 'enhancer' factors, possession of knowledge from previous experiences or reading potentially diminishes perceived authenticity. Respondents compared their visits to their previous experiences, ultimately being more demanding with the current experiences. Many tourists reflected on their experiences in other heritage attractions in Asia such as in China, Malaysia, and Thailand. For example, a tourist commented: *'I have been to a really large temple before in Penang, Malaysia. My feelings or impressions of the temple there and here are really different. I really felt inspired by the atmosphere in the other temple. Penang was really spiritual. It's different from here. The feeling that I had is different. I could feel in the air that it is different. For me, here it is just a touristic site'*. Or: *'I went to Thailand a few months ago and comparing this to places in Thailand, it just doesn't feel like an ancient ruin or anything similar'*.

Lastly, modern surroundings were indicated as a 'diminisher' of perceived authenticity. As heritage experiences were investigated, modern elements including the surroundings were contended to damage the genuineness of the experience. Moreover, in the case of religious sites, the presence of non-religious surroundings made the experiences less authentic. This factor together with the over-management issue was particularly emphasised in the case of Hong Kong, where modern elements are dominant and the management system is precise and stringent.

The Significance of Authenticity

As we have stated in relation to previous literature, authenticity plays different roles among different tourists or tourists have different preferences related to authenticity. This study has presented similar findings, in the sense that authenticity was not always a concern for all tourists. In any case a number of tourists were of the view that authenticity was of importance and said that they were really looking for authentic experiences. One tourist stated that: *'It [authenticity] is important for me, I want to have an authentic experience. I really work hard to find it, I will not leave the place until I get my authentic experience'*. Meanwhile, for tourists who travel for the purpose of fun and relaxation, having an authentic experience or not is a minor issue. For instance, there were such comments as: *'It doesn't need to be authentic to be enjoyed'* or *'Although we know it's not authentic, it's just something to see. We are on vacation, so it is not very bad'*. Others considered aesthetics and novelty as more important than authenticity. With a similar outcome, a study by Mkono (2013) indicates that for African tourists, aesthetics and artistry are more meaningful criteria than authenticity in evaluating cultural performances. Interestingly, some respondents were found to tolerate modifications of the site. Tourists acknowledge that due to the original building material, *'this kind of temple has to be reconstructed by copying the original. So, I don't expect a 100 per cent original'*. However, they expected to see the original idea, the impression of history, or the right value, and the right message conveyed in their experiences.

Conclusion

The aim of this study was to scrutinise tourist perceptions of authenticity towards Hong Kong heritage tourism experiences and the factors that affect their perceptions. The findings indicated the existence of a heritage tourism demand among tourists visiting Hong Kong. However, most heritage experiences were rather superficial, typically based on sightseeing for long-haul tourists and religious reasons for short-haul tourists. Tourists were found to be quite impressed by architecture or the aesthetic aspects of Hong Kong heritage attractions.

Regarding the perceived authenticity of these experiences, half were not considered as authentic. However, most of the respondents were overall satisfied with their visits. This study also indicates that authenticity is not always a concern for all tourists, as aesthetics, novelty or relaxation was of major interest for some. Having said this authenticity is still found to be an essential component of heritage experiences for certain groups of tourists.

The results of this study also suggest different 'enhancers' and 'diminishers' of perceived authenticity. The 'enhancers' include the old appearance of the sites, the presence of local culture, the lack of information, the presence of certain senses, the original location, the necessity of making an effort to access a site, the spiritual atmosphere, and the kind of government involvement. The common 'diminishers' were found to be commodification or the existence of tourist facilities, the modern/new elements in physical settings, over-management, previous experience and modern surroundings. Among these factors, appearance or physical settings of the attractions are found to be important when assessing authenticity. In addition, the involvement of local residents and religious practitioners tends to have positive impacts on tourists' authentic experiences. The excessive involvement of the authorities in terms of modifying and maintaining the attractions was found potentially to damage the authenticity of the attractions. Knowing that tourists would need certain facilities and comfort, development has to be done with care as too much of this effort would destroy the authentic image of heritage assets. Subsequently, finding a balance is essential. A division into zones as is commonly found in ecotourism or World Heritage Sites could be an idea for dealing with this issue. This preliminary mapping of 'enhancers' and 'diminishers' of perceived authenticity in heritage tourism experiences also needs to be further developed and confirmed in other contexts, especially in destinations where heritage tourism is a major attraction. It would subsequently be helpful for the government and other authorities to improve the management of heritage sites and enhance positive tourist experiences.

References

Antiquities and Monuments Office (2013) 'Main', retrieved from http://www.amo.gov.hk/en/main.php, page consulted 20/08/2013.

Britton, S. (1991) 'Tourism, Capital, and Place: Towards a Critical Geography of Tourism', *Environment and Planning D: Society and Space*, 9: 451-478.

Budruk, M., D.D. White, J.A. Wodrich and C.J. van Riper (2008) 'Connecting Visitors to People and Place: Visitors' Perceptions of Authenticity at Canyon de Chelly National Monument, Arizona'. *Journal of Heritage Tourism*, 3: 185-202.

Chang, J., G. Wall and C. L. Chang (2008) 'Perception of the Authenticity of Atayal Woven Handicrafts in Wulai, Taiwan', *Journal of Hospitality and Leisure Marketing,* 16: 385-409.

Cheung, S.C.H. (1999) 'The Meanings of a Heritage Trail in Hong Kong', *Annals of Tourism Research*, 26: 570-588.

Chhabra, D. (2010) 'Back to the Past: a Sub-segment of Generation Y's Perceptions of Authenticity', *Journal of Sustainable Tourism*, 18: 793–809.

—. (2012). 'Authenticity of the Objectively Authentic', *Annals of Tourism Research*, 39: 499-502.

Chhabra, D., R. Healy and E. Sills (2003) 'Staged Authenticity and Heritage Tourism', *Annals of Tourism Research*, 30: 702–719.

Cohen, E. (1988) 'Authenticity and Commoditization in Tourism', *Annals of Tourism Research,* 15: 371-186.

Cole, S. (2007) 'Beyond Authenticity and Commodification', *Annals of Tourism Research*, 34: 943-960.

Commissioner for Heritage's Office (2013) *Events and Promotions: Hong Kong Heritage Tourism Expo - Access Heritage.* Retrieved 12 August 2013, from http://www.heritage.gov.hk/en/whatsnew/events_20.htm

Finn, J. (2009) 'Contesting Culture: a Case study of Commodification in Cuban Music', *GeoJournal,* 74: 191–200.

Goulding, C. (2000) 'The Commodification of the Past, Postmodern Pastiche, and the Search for Authentic Experiences at Contemporary Heritage Attractions', *European Journal of Marketing*, 34, 835-853.

Greenwood, D. J. (1977) 'Culture by the Pound: an Anthropological Perspective on Tourism as Cultural Commoditization'. In V. L. Smith (ed.), *Hosts and Guests: the Anthropology of Tourism*, Philadelphia: University of Pennsylvania Press, pp. 129-138.

Halewood, C. and K. Hannam (2001) 'Viking Heritage Tourism: Authenticity and Commodification', *Annals of Tourism Research*, 28: 565-580.

Herbert, D. T. (1995) 'Heritage as Literary Place'. In D. T. Herbert (ed.), *Heritage, Tourism and the Society*, London: Mansell Publishing Limited, pp. 32-48.

Ho, P. S. Y. and B. McKercher (2004) 'Managing Heritage Resources as Tourism Products', *Asia Pacific Journal of Tourism Research*, 9: 255-266.

Hong Kong Planning Department (2012) *Hong Kong 2030: Planning Vision and Strategy,* Hong Kong: Strategic Planning Section, Hong Kong Planning Department.

Hong Kong Tourism Board (2012) *A Statistical Review of Hong Kong Tourism 2011*, Hong Kong: Research, Hong Kong Tourism Board.

Kolar, T. and V. Zabkar (2010) 'A Consumer-based Model of Authenticity: an Oxymoron or the Foundation of Cultural Heritage Marketing', *Tourism Management*, 31: 652–664.

Lanfant, M. F. (1995) 'International Tourism, Internationalization and the Challenge to Identity'. In M. F. Lanfant, J. Allcock and E. Bruner (eds), *International Tourism: Identity and Change*, London: Sage, pp. 24-43.

Lew, A. A. (1991) 'Place Representation in Tourist Guidebooks: an Example from Singapore', *Singapore Journal of Tropical Geography,* 12: 124–137.

Littrell, M. A., L.F. Anderson and P.J. Brown (1993) 'What Makes a Craft Souvenir Authentic?' *Annals of Tourism Research*, 20: 197-215.

MacCannell, D. (1973) 'Staged Authenticity: Arrangements of Social Space in Tourist Settings', *American Journal of Sociology*, 79: 589-603.

MacDonald, S. (1997) 'A People's Story: Heritage, Identity and Authenticity'. In C. Rojek and J. Urry, (eds), *Touring Cultures*, London: Routledge, pp. 155-176.

McIntosh, R. W. and R.C. Prentice (1999) 'Affirming Authenticity: Consuming Cultural Heritage', *Annals of Tourism Research,* 26: 589-612.

McKercher, B., P.S.Y. Ho, and H. du Cros (2004) 'Attributes of Popular Cultural Attractions in Hong Kong', *Annals of Tourism Research*, 31: 393–407.

Mkono, M. (2013) 'African and Western Tourists: Object Authenticity Quest', *Annals of Tourism Research*, 41: 195-214.

Moscardo, G. M. and P.L. Pearce (1986) 'Historic Theme Parks: An Australian Experience in Authenticity', *Annals of Tourism Research*, 13: 467-479.

Moscardo, G. M. and P.L. Pearce (1999) 'Understanding Ethnic Tourists', *Annals of Tourism Research*, 26: 416-434.

Pearce, P. L. and G.M. Moscardo (1986) 'The Concept of Authenticity in Tourist Experiences', *The Australian and New Zealand Journal of Sociology*, 22: 121-132.

Picard, M. (1997) 'Cultural Tourism, Nation-building, and Regional Culture: the Making of a Balinese Identity'. In M. Picard and R.E., Wood (eds), *Tourism, Ethnicity, and the State in Asian and Pacific Societies*, Honolulu: University of Hawai'i Press, pp. 181-214.

Reisinger, Y. and C.J. Steiner (2006) 'Reconceptualizing Object Authenticity', *Annals of Tourism Research*, 33: 65–86.

Rickly-Boyd, J. M. (2012) 'Through the Magic of Authentic Reproduction': Tourists' Perceptions of Authenticity in a Pioneer Village', *Journal of Heritage Tourism*, 7: 127-144.

Robinson, R. N. S. and C. Clifford (2012) 'Authenticity and Festival Foodservice Experiences', *Annals of Tourism Research*, 39: 571-600.

Schwandt, T. A. (1998). 'Constructivist, Interpretivist Approaches to Human Inquiry'. In N. K. Denzin and W. S., Lincoln (eds), *The Landscape of Qualitative Research: Theories and Issues,* Thousand Oaks: Sage Publications, pp. 189-213.

Sharpley, R. (1994) *Tourism, Tourists and Society*, Huntingdon: ELM Publications.

Shepherd, R. (2002) 'Commodification, Culture and Tourism', *Tourist Studies*, 2: 183-201.

Silver, I. (1993) 'Marketing Authenticity in Third World Countries', *Annals of Tourism Research*, 20: 302-318.

Timothy, D. J. (2011) *Cultural Heritage and Tourism: an Introduction*, Bristol: Channel View Publications.

Timothy, D. J. and S. W. Boyd (2003) *Heritage Tourism*, Harlow: Prentice Hall.

—. (2006) 'Heritage Tourism in the 21st Century: Valued Traditions and New Perspectives', *Journal of Heritage Tourism*, 1: 1-14.

Urry, John (1990) *The Tourist Gaze: Leisure and Travel in Contemporary Societies*, London: Sage Publications.

Waitt, G. (2000) 'Consuming Heritage: Perceived Historical Authenticity', *Annals of Tourism Research*, 27: 835–862.

Waller, J. and S.E.G. Lea (1998) 'Seeking the Real Spain? Authenticity in Motivation', *Annals of Tourism Research*, 26: 110–129.

Wang, N. (1999) 'Rethinking Authenticity in Tourism Experience', *Annals of Tourism Research*, 26: 349–370.

Watson, H. and J. Kopachevsky (1994) 'Interpretations of Tourism as Commodity', *Annals of Tourism Research,* 20: 643-660.

Xie, P. F. and G. Wall (2002) 'Visitors' Perceptions of Authenticity at Cultural Attractions in Hainan, China', *International Journal of Tourism Research*, 4: 353–366.

EDIBLE CULTURE AND INEDIBLE CULTURE: ETHNIC TOURISM OF THE MLABRI IN NORTHERN THAILAND

SHU NIMONJIYA

Introduction

Thailand is one of the most successful countries in the tourism industry in Southeast Asia. In 2004, it attracted approximately 12 million visitors, earned THB 384,360 million and employed approximately three million people directly and indirectly (Pradech, 2007: 41). The tourism industry certainly has played an important role in the economic and social development of this country since 1976 when the first National Tourism Development Plan was begun. A region depends on the kinds of potential resources for tourism business there are, and in the case of Northern Thailand, ethnic diversity is one of the resources. In fact, according to statistics collated by the Tourism Authority of Thailand (TAT), ethnic tourism generated THB 62,203 million for Northern Thailand in 2003 (TAT, 2004).

In Northern Thailand, there are many ethnic groups which are ethnically, culturally and linguistically different from the Thai. They also differ from each other, but they have been officially lumped together as *chaokhao* ('hill tribes') [1] since the late 1950s because the Thai government problematised their existence in the context of nation-building (Pinkaew, 2003; Chayan, 2005). As Thailand was exposed to geopolitical threats due to the political unrest of neighbouring countries such as Burma and Laos after the end of the Second World War, the hill tribes, living in the border area, were regarded as a 'dangerous element' which posed a great threat to national security. For that reason, the government began to intervene in the

[1] The word 'hill tribes' is as an official term which refers to 10 ethnic groups in total: Karen, Hmong, Yao, Akha, Lisu, Lahu, Khamu, Lua, H'tin, and Mlabri.

hill areas in the name of development through assimilation and integration policies into Thai society to solve the so-called *panhachaokhao* ('hill tribe problems') (Wanat, 1989)[2]. In this process, the socio-economic situation of the hill tribes was dramatically changed, and they have increasingly been involved in ethnic tourism as a tourist attraction since the 1970s. As Cohen indicates, ethnic tourism in Northern Thailand has developed commercially with the lowland political, economic, and cultural influences on them rapidly intensifying (Cohen, 1996a: 64).

Today, the hill tribes attract many domestic and foreign tourists, while the Thai government had not predicted that Western tourists, especially young tourists, had already been attracted to Northern Thailand when the country was not yet involved in ethnic tourism (Prasit, 1997: 272)[3]. In fact, only counting foreign tourists, over 100,000 people participated in ethnic tourism each year during the late 1980s and early 1990s (Dearden and Harron, 1992). Thus, ethnic tourism, also known as 'trekking', has attracted the interest of researchers, and many studies, both empirical and theoretical, have been accumulated adopting various perspectives and approaches. For example, Cohen who has researched various tourism forms in Thailand since the 1970s and has been in the forefront of this field of studies, has discussed, among other matters, the image of the hill tribes in the context of tourism, interaction between tourists and the hill tribes, the role of tour guides, and the impacts of tourism on ethnic minorities (1973; 1996a; cf. Cohen, 1984). Moreover, Dearden has considered the sustainability and impacts of ethnic tourism (1991; 1996); Ishii has examined the effects of ethnic tourism on hill tribe diversity and hierarchy, its economic influence on the division of labour and the power dynamics of gender relations within communities through a case study of the Akha (2007; 2012).

However, these studies have mainly focused on the well-known hill tribes such as the Karen, Hmong, Yao, Akha, Lahu and Lisu, who are

---

[2] According to Khachatphai who presided at the National Security Council, the problems that the Thai government realised were: 1) opium cultivation, 2) destruction of forests and water resources, 3) border insecurity, 4) socio-economic development, 5) ethnic minority problems such as a lack of patriotism and susceptibility to communist influence (Khachatphai, 1995: 126-130).

[3] Surprisingly, such young Western tourists hired private guides to visit the hill tribes in remote areas because of their strong desire for 'authentic experiences' (Cohen, 1996a: 38).

traditionally known as farmers practising swidden cultivation, while there are other less well known ethnic groups, such as the Khamu, Lua, H'tin and Mlabri. This chapter focuses on ethnic tourism among the Mlabri, who are the only hunter-gatherers among the hill tribes and therefore occupy a unique position in tourism in Northern Thailand; the Mlabri have also not been the subject of detailed research. As Cohen states, the interest in the study of hunter-gatherer tourism in Thailand lies, not in their popularity as attractions, or in the number of tourists who visit them, but in their particularity as the potential 'Other' (Cohen, 1996b: 230)[4]. Indeed, he has already discussed hunter-gatherer tourism in Thailand, including among the Mlabri, but his study was not based on empirical research but on a literature review. Thus, the first purpose of this chapter is to build on his pioneer work and to reveal the current situation of Mlabri tourism through an ethnographic case study.

In addition, this chapter attempts to consider the current impact of ethnic tourism on Mlabri social and cultural life. Since the publication of Valene Smith's collection of essays entitled *Hosts and Guests* (1977), the impact of ethnic tourism on minority populations has become a significant issue (Hinch and Butler, 1996; Cohen, 1988; Wood, 1997). In this issue, there are two tendencies in general: stressing either the negative impacts or the positive ones. The former, which is preferred by sociologists and anthropologists, regards tourism as a process of cultural destruction and economic exploitation, but the latter, in contrast, preferred by economists, regards it as a means for cultural revitalisation and economic benefit (UNESCO, 1976). Indeed, it appears that many sociologists and anthropologists take a negative viewpoint in that ethnic tourism brings a significant socio-cultural impact in return for relatively few benefits, because this issue is closely linked to the sensitive matter of the commoditisation of ethnicity and culture. For example, in the case of ethnic tourism in Northern Thailand, Prasit stresses the negative impacts, such as destruction of natural and cultural resources, and social problems as by-products of tourism, though he also refers to the positive impacts, such as an increasing understanding of local cultures and additional income for local communities (1997). However, it is feared that such a viewpoint is biased in that it regards ethnic tourism as a threat to the

[4] In Thailand, there are only two ethnic groups which have traditionally lived as hunter-gatherers, the Mlabri (Phi Tong Lueang) and Mani (Sakai), and there is an ethnic group which has traditionally lived as sea nomads, the Moken.

people's traditional way of life, or a case of the 'noble savage syndrome', a concept that Cohen borrows from Boissevain (Cohen, 1996a: 114), and at the same time, as Wood points out perceptively, the adoption of a normative cost-benefit framework that questions whether impacts are 'good' or 'bad' is too simple to address the complex realities of tourism processes and consequences (Wood, 1993: 49).

Thus, we should attempt to describe the actual situation and assess the impact of ethnic tourism while avoiding falling into the normative cost-benefit framework because issues of equality and the scale and extent of tourism depend strongly on the social, political and economic conditions of the particular ethnic group in question (Toyota, 1996), and as a matter of course, the actual situation varies in each case (Cohen, 1996a: 113-144). Furthermore, ethnic tourism certainly has the great potential to affect a minority ethnic group, but it does not always have to be actualised. It is in fact very probable that the impact of tourism on some ethnic groups remains at an extremely low level, as we shall see in the case of the Mlabri, neither has it brought much economic benefit to them. Why is this so? Well it turns on the complex relationship between tourism and culture and in the Mlabri case not only is the scale of the tourism market small but their socio-cultural attitudes inhibit tourism development and their participation in it, and, in this regard ethnic tourism does not bring much in the way of economic benefits to them.

The Mlabri in Thailand

The Mlabri (/mlaʔ/briʔ/)[5], also known as *Phi Tong Lueang* ('Spirits of the Yellow Leaves') are an ethnic group and one of the Northern Thailand hill tribes. The word *mlaʔ* means 'human beings', and indicates the Mlabri themselves, and *briʔ* means 'forest' in their own language which belongs to the Khmuic branch within the Mon-Khmer language group of the Austro-Asiatic linguistic family. Their population is very small. According to a population census on the hill tribes in 2002, the overall population was 923,257, constituting 1.45 per cent of the total national population of Thailand, but the population of the Mlabri was 282, constituting only 0.03 per cent of the total hill tribes population (Thailand, Krom Phattana Sangkhomlae Sawatdikan, 2002). There are about 400 Mlabri individuals

[5] They do not call themselves *mlaʔbriʔ* (= forest people), a term coined by outsiders, but simply *mlaʔ* ('human beings'), their own term for themselves.

in Thailand today[6], and it can be said that they are one of the smallest ethnic groups in the world. In addition, it is believed that the Mlabri migrated into Thailand from Laos in the early twentieth century, and this opinion is supported not only by the government but also by some scholars (Bernatzik, 1951: 131; Boeles, 1963: 153; Trier, 2008: 28). However, the Thai government did not have a strict control system of the border area at that time, and there is a description of the Mlabri in an old article written by a member of the Thai elite in 1886 (cited in Thongchai Winichakul, 2000: 46). In short, the Mlabri have probably lived in Thailand since at least before the early twentieth century. Finally, it is very important to discuss ethnic tourism among the Mlabri in that a recent genetic study analysed Mlabri mtDNA and concluded that they were recently found about 500 to 800 years ago, from a very small number of individuals who engaged in agriculture (Oota et al, 2005). The result supported the position that the Mlabri are not 'continuous foragers' but 'respecialised foragers' (Endicott, 1979).

While they have traditionally lived in the forests as the only nomadic hunter-gatherers in Northern Thailand, they have gradually relinquished their traditional way of life based on hunting-gathering due to the substantial deforestation that has occurred in Northern Thailand from the end of the Second World War. As a natural resource that the Mlabri depended on the forest has dramatically decreased, and the Mlabri have had to increase their economic dependence on other hill tribes, especially the Hmong, by working as wage labourers (Chanan, 1992)[7]. However, unlike other hill tribes, the Mlabri were ignored by the Thai government for many years intentionally because the government thought that they were not involved in the major hill tribe problems such as opium cultivation and communist insurgency, and therefore did not pose a threat to the state (Nimonjiya, 2014). Thus, it is during the mid-1980s when the

---

[6] The Mlabri live not only in Thailand but also in Laos (Chazée, 2001) and Burma (The Lahu National Development Organization, 2005). The population in Laos and Burma is not certain. In the case of Laos, Chazée estimated that there were about 20 individuals in 2000 (2001), but Schliesinger estimated that there were 40 individuals in the same year (2003).

[7] In fact, while the total forest area of Thailand was 53 per cent in 1953, it decreased to less than 30 per cent by the 1980s. Moreover, the forest area of Northern Thailand decreased dramatically from 68 per cent in 1961 to 60 per cent in 1976, and only two years later in 1978, it dropped to 56 per cent (Thongchai Caruppat, 1998).

civil war terminated that the government finally began to pay attention to the Mlabri and to intervene in their affairs in the name of development. On the other hand, an American missionary who was sent by a large evangelical Christian mission organisation based in the USA, *The New Tribes Mission*, began missionary work and development projects among the Mlabri from the early 1980s, and his efforts bore fruit in terms of the establishment of a settlement, Ban Huai Hom (Rongkwang district, Phrae province). After that through state-led development projects, Ban Huai Yuak was established as an annex of the same named village of the Hmong in 1999. After the official visit to Ban Huai Yuak of HRH Princess Sirindhorn in 2007, the royal project on behalf of the Mlabri was started, and as a result, new settlements were founded: Ban Tha Wa (Song District, Phrae Province), Phu Fa Development Center (Bo Kluea District, Nan Province), and Ban Huai Luu (Muang District, Nan Province). Thus, there are now five permanent settlements in total in Nan and Phrae Provinces (Figure 1). Among the settlements, Ban Huai Hom, Ban Huai Yuak, and Phu Fa Development Center are opened for tourists, but this chapter will mainly focus on ethnic tourism in Ban Huai Yuak because not only does it comprise the largest population, about 200 individuals, but also it receives the most tourists. The data used in this paper were collected in Ban Huai Yuak from January to December 2013.

Image of the Mlabri in the Context of Tourism

In Thailand, there is a strong dichotomy between *muang* (city) and *pa* (forest), and the hill tribes have traditionally been pushed into the latter category (Thongchai Winichakul, 2000). From the lowland Thai point of view, *muang* is a political domain and implies 'civilised' or 'socialised', but on the other hand, *pa* is a chaotic domain and implies 'uncivilised' or 'unsocialised'. However, this negative image of *pa* is easily switched to a positive image in the context of ethnic tourism. In fact, as Cohen indicates, the image of the hill tribes which attracts many foreign tourists presents them as primitive, exotic, natural and so on (Cohen, 1996a: 43-48), and the image of the Mlabri in the context of ethnic tourism is no exception.

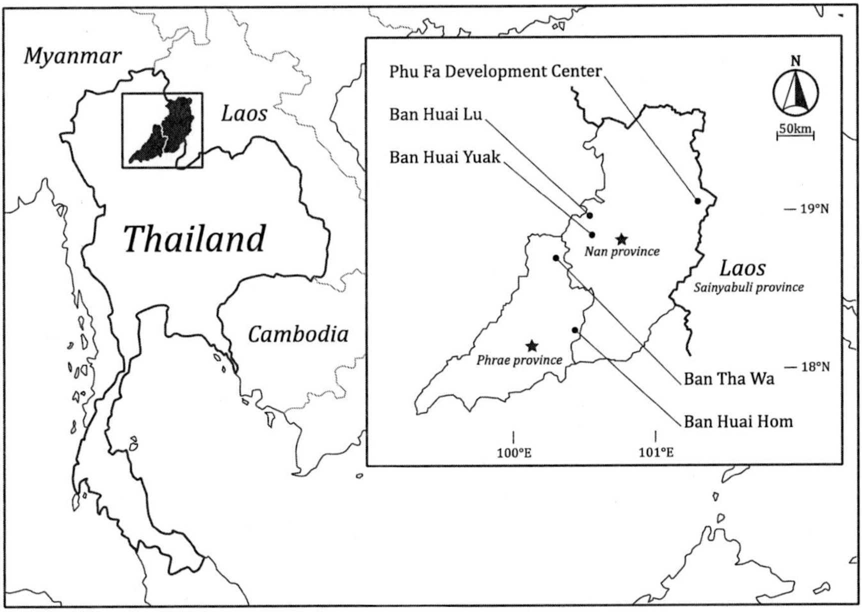

Figure 1. Mlabri Settlements in Nan and Phrae Provinces

The Mlabri are traditionally referred to as *Phi Tong Lueang* ('Spirits of the Yellow Leaves') among the lowland Thai and Lao, and they were considered as 'spirits' because they had rarely been seen directly. In the past, when they sensed outsiders approaching their living space, they ran away to the deep forest. Thus, outsiders called the Mlabri 'spirits' because they could find some evidence that something was there but could not obtain any conclusive evidence of the presence of human beings. The Mlabri were also called *Phi Pa* (forest spirits) or *Khon Pa* (forest people), and these names clearly reflected the dichotomy. However, it is important to stress that the Mlabri are not mere people who belong to *pa* because they are regarded as the most primitive people, who still remain in the first stage of human history due to their traditional mode of subsistence. They are not 'pure' hunter-gatherers after all, though the dominant external viewpoint is still based on the concept of cultural evolutionism and the Mlabri are seen as representatives of this early period of human development.

The touristic discourses that reflect such images of the Mlabri are too numerous to mention. For example, in an advertisement of 1988, *Unknown Thailand,* it states 'Discover it with us! 'Phi Tong Luang' . . . or 'Forest People' is the name of a tribal folk, inhabiting the jungle of Nan province . . . Five times a week from Bangkok. You can visit this tribe in the North of Thailand!' (*Reisen in Thailand* 1988, quoted in Cohen 1996a: 225), and in a tourism advertisement at a well-known hotel in Nan City, Dhevaraj Hotel, with a picture of almost-naked Mlabri men, women, and children, 'Visit the Phi Tong Lueang, one of the most primitive tribes of Thailand'(quoted in *Bangkok Post* 1990a). Furthermore, the discourse is still being reproduced. In a Thai travel magazine, it is stated that 'the yellow leaves community at Ban Huai Yuak is the most primitive tribe, which does not know even how to weave textiles and make pottery, in Thailand. The yellow leaves tribe retains its life in harmony with nature and maintains hunting-gathering with a nomadic life. In visiting the yellow leaves at Ban Huai Yuak, you may touch the tribe's lifestyle which is the most difficult to find in Thailand because the yellow leaves tribe usually does not make a permanent living place' (*Trips Magazine*, 2011: 118, translated by the author). In addition, it was written in a Thai tourist guidebook featuring Nan province, 'An anthropologist refers to the yellow leaves people as the most primitive society in Thailand . . . They do not make a permanent living place and also do not know agriculture and keeping livestock which are a characteristic of human society before developing [as] an agricultural society, or it may be said that they are people of the Stone Age . . . Studying their culture is equivalent to learning the progress of human history' (Thiaothua Thai baikap 'Nai Rop Ru', 2004: 97-98, translated by the author).

In the context of tourism, the hill tribes are often represented as 'primitive' and the Mlabri are also forced to share the same image. However, as Cohen argues the Mlabri are presented and viewed by tourists more as 'nature people' than other hill tribes (Cohen, 1996b: 251). There is an obvious difference in the representation between the Mlabri as hunter-gatherers and the other hill tribes as farmers. In short, due to their traditional mode of subsistence, the Mlabri are regarded as a remnant of the Stone Age. Surprisingly, even the government authorities also follow this discourse; for example, it is written in an official leaflet of Nan province, *10 Wonderful Cultures of Nan*, 'Mlabri or Thong Luang, our relatives from the pre-historic age still maintain their lineage' (translated by the author).

Expansion of Mlabri Tourism

In the mid-1980s when the Mlabri could not live without their dependence on other hill tribes, especially the Hmong, due to large-scale deforestation in Northern Thailand (Delang, 2002), the government finally began to pay attention to the Mlabri because the hill tribe problems, such as opium cultivation and communist insurgency, were settled by the end of the civil war. As Northern Thailand, especially Nan Province which was one of the main battlefields, regained peace, the media (newspapers, TV and film) began to be interested in and featured the Mlabri. In particular, a Thai movie which was shot in 1985, *Tawan Im Chaeng* ('The Grinning Sun'), caught the public's imagination, and the Mlabri became a must-see tourist attraction. Thus, Mlabri tourism has gradually developed in Nan and Phrae provinces.

In Phrae Province, Mlabri tourism was promoted by an American missionary, Eugene Robert Long or Bunyuen Suksaneh. He and his family arrived in Thailand in 1978 and began to work for the Mlabri in 1981 (*Bangkok Post*, 1990b). Through the 1980s, he had accepted domestic and foreign tourists at Ban Huai Hom because he thought that 'occasional visits by foreign and Thai tourists [would] help the Mlabri learn about people in the world beyond the hills of Nan and Phrae' (*Bangkok Post*, 1990c) and, probably, that tourism enables the Mlabri to get money and food. The then touring system was the village tour. Tourists visited the settlement and hiked up the hill to the Mlabri houses to take pictures of and with the Mlabri men who wore G-strings and the Mlabri women who were bare-breasted, and they saw the sacrificing of a pig (ibid). Mlabri tourism at Ban Huai Hom, however, did not last for long. According to my interview research in Ban Huai Hom, the American missionary told me that he was ready to accept tourists at any time, but there were no tourists because there were obstacles such as traffic and security problems. Incidentally, a Thai research team from Maejo University in Chiang Mai carried out research and development work for agro-tourism in Ban Huai Hom in 2010, and they wrote that they were successful in establishing the Association of Mlabri Culture for which the missionary acted as the adviser in their report (Yaiying and Thirawong, 2010). Their project, however, has come to a deadlock because their work was not sustainable. In any case, Mlabri tourism in Phrae Province is no longer carried out.

On the other hand, Mlabri tourism was also carried out in Nan Province around the same time (cf. *Bangkok Post*, 1990a; 1990d). According to an article in the *Bangkok Post*, there was a tour that was arranged by the

Singha tour agency (1990a). The contents of this tour comprised visiting the Mlabri, who lived in a forest in Naluang sub-district about 40 kilometres from the city, enjoying the demonstration of a pig sacrifice and tree-climbing. To join in this tour, tourists had to book at least three days in advance because the Mlabri still lived a nomadic life in the forest, and the cost was about THB 1,000 per person for a small group of less than five people. It is interesting that even a local Thai police officer was also involved in this tour as a middleman, who provided convenience and protection for tourists and made preparations for them, while he had no direct access to the Mlabri: when a tour group was scheduled to arrive, he just informed other hill tribes such as the Hmong and Lua, who usually employed the Mlabri in their fields, to bring the Mlabri for tourist visits (*Bangkok Post*, 1990b).

Mlabri tourism was begun more systematically in the mid-1990s. A then chief of Ban Luang District in Nan Province decided to establish the 'Yellow Leaves Development and Preservation Center' to the north of Ban Phi in 1994 and gathered the Mlabri, who lived within the district, to develop and preserve their community and culture. On the other hand, some local tour companies also began to develop Mlabri tourism to the south of Ban Phi which was about one kilometre from the Center. However, the project at Ban Phi began to meet problems, and at that point the Governor of Nan Province decided that a tourism development plan should be carried out from 1995 to 2002. In this plan, there were six projects in total, and the Center to the north of Ban Phi was chosen as one of the projects. The objective was to gather the Mlabri, who were scattered in Nan Province, and to get them to settle down in a permanent place as a tourist attraction. In 1997, the authorities thus requested the missionary to cooperate with them because he had experience of working with the Mlabri. However, in the same year, the project had a serious problem because of dissension between the missionary who worked to the north of Ban Phi and the local tour companies which worked to the south of Ban Phi. The missionary criticised the companies in that they forced the Mlabri to perform their traditional way of life for tourists, while the Mlabri no longer lived like that; on the other hand, the local tour companies criticised the missionary in that they argued that he had damaged their traditional way of life by implementing the development project. This 'North-South' problem, however, also tended towards an accusation that the missionary and the Mlabri caused environmental degradation. In fact, in 1998, the local Thai farmers of Ban Phi demanded that the Mlabri and the Center left from there because they thought that the Mlabri polluted the river with trash and destroyed the forest by hunting-gathering. The government authorities were compelled to close the Center, and the Mlabri, who were expelled from there, scattered to other places, such as Ban Huai Hom in Phrae Province, Ban Tha Wa (a village of the Tai Yuan in Phrae Province), and Ban Huai Yuak (a village of the Hmong, in Nan Province).

Ethnic Tourism in Ban Huai Yuak

After the failure of the Center at Ban Phi, the authorities tried to find other places to develop the Mlabri in a permanent place, and Ban Huai Yuak (Wiang Sa district, Nan Province) was finally chosen as one of the suitable places in 1999 because the Mlabri, about 90 individuals, had lived in and around there as wage labourers for the Hmong. While Ban Huai Yuak was originally a village of the Hmong, a settlement of the Mlabri was established near that village.

As a means of self-sufficient development, the authorities started development and welfare projects, such as education, public health, occupational training including cash crop cultivation and livestock keeping and so on, and ethnic tourism was also introduced as one of the self-sufficient developments in this context. In particular, the Hill Tribe Development and Social Welfare Center of Nan Province (it was renamed the Social Development Center) has played an important role. In fact, the address and phone number of the Center are listed in a Thai tourist guidebook, and it is written, 'If you contact the Center in advance, they will prepare a show that reproduces the traditional life in the forest' (Thiaothua Thai baikap 'Nai Rop Ru' 2004: 97-98; translated by the author). In addition, there is a road sign between Ban Luang and Nan City, indicating the 'Tong Lueang Community' in Thai and English with a star mark which expresses a tourist attraction[8]. However, there is no mutual agreement between the Mlabri and the authorities on tourism. In fact, one day I pointed at the road sign and asked a Mlabri man, 'Do you know what it says? He answered, 'I don't know because I can't read Thai'. This indicates that Mlabri tourism in Ban Huai Yuak is supported officially without the agreement of the Mlabri.

---

[8] Prasit writes that 'the road to such remote villages such as Nam Phiang Din of the Karen long neck village in Mae Hon Song and the Huai Yuak Mlabri village in Nan would not have been paved if the villages were not tourist sites' (2008: 228), but the road to Ban Huai Yuak was paved for the official visit of Princess Sirindhorn.

As a matter of fact, while there are not many tourists who visit Ban Huai Yuak through the Center recently, they can be divided into two categories: domestic and foreign, and this categorisation also reflects their kinds of visit. Most domestic tourists visit Ban Huai Yuak by themselves, whilst most foreign tourists visit by using tour packages offered by tour companies. However, the tour companies are not only in Nan City but also in other cities such as Bangkok and Chiang Mai. Sometimes, the distant tour companies arrange the tour by themselves, but a few also undertake the tours in cooperation with a local tour agent in Nan City: they bring foreign tourists to Nan in their own cars from other cities, but they also provide a tour guide and cars from the local company. On the other hand, it should be noted that tour agents are not only official tour companies but also members of other hill tribes, especially the Hmong of Ban Huai Yuak. A few Hmong men, for example, engaged in Mlabri tourism as middlemen, and interestingly, a Hmong man has his own website to contact foreign tourists.

The tour system can be divided into two types by location and activity: the village tour and the jungle tour. The village tour comprises visiting and walking through Ban Huai Yuak, and taking souvenir pictures of and with the Mlabri; on the other hand, the jungle tour engages tourists with the forest and cultural presentations.

(1) The Village Tour: tourists visit Ban Huai Yuak in a tour company car from Nan City. Then they give the Mlabri some gifts, such as fat pork, candy, snacks, fruits, and so on, and take souvenir pictures of and with the Mlabri old men who wear G-strings. After that, tourists move to Mlabri houses made of bamboo and wood, and see staged cultural and everyday events, such as cooking in bamboo containers, lighting a fire with a flint and steel and so on, while listening to explanations of Mlabri life and culture by a tour guide (Figure 2).

(2) The Jungle Tour: tourists are taken to the entrance of a forest in a tour company car. They walk along a small forest trail to a place where the Mlabri are standing by. When they find the Mlabri, they place gifts, such as rice, pork, fish, and so on, on banana leaves in front of the Mlabri's traditional windscreens. After that, a tour guide begins to say something about the Mlabri, and then the Mlabri stage some presentations, such as killing a pig, cooking in bamboo containers, lighting a fire with a flint and steel and eating pork in windscreens (Figure 3).

Figure 2. The Village Tour (photographed by the author 1 July, 2013)

Figure 3. The Jungle Tour (photographed by the author 16 January, 2013)

The village tour is simple and the most successful in the tour system. In fact, during my fieldwork, I observed the village tour 102 times, but it was only 12 times that I observed the jungle tour. While the Mlabri are usually not in Ban Huai Yuak because they go to work in the fields, the old men and children are there. The tour company always comes to Ban Huai Yuak on the spur of the moment, and the old men take off their clothes and don their G-strings for the tourists when they hear the sound of a tourist car. They know that they receive food or money if they wear their G-strings for the visitors, but they do not appear to be very active participants in tourism; it is a very simple act to appear as tourists expect them to appear and do what tourists expect them to do. On the other hand, the jungle tour is more elaborate; it is advertised as the 'discovery of the primitive', unlike the village tour that is presented as 'seeing of the primitive'. In order to succeed in the jungle tour, the tour company has to organise the Mlabri as a polished tourist attraction in advance.

In the case of a tour company in Nan City, after having secured a reservation, they contacted the Hmong of Ban Huai Yuak on the previous day and informed them of how many tourists would arrive and at what time they would be participating in the jungle tour. After that, the Hmong went to inform the Mlabri at early morning on the day of the visit, took the Mlabri to the forest in their own car and then instructed them to build windscreens in a place at a distance from a small forest trail. The Hmong also prepared a small pig and tied it to a tree as if the Mlabri had hunted it a little while ago and then marked trees along the trail with a knife to inform the tour guide where the Mlabri were to be found. Tourists, however, are not allowed to walk the Mlabri trail. They are directed by the tour guide to another trail that is overgrown with weeds to let tourists witness a 'great historical moment'. Incidentally, the tour guide may be Thai or a Western guide because the translator will be changed according to the nationalities of the tourists. In any case most of the knowledge of the guides on the Mlabri is taken from the internet. A Thai tour guide told me, 'It is not so difficult to explain about the Mlabri because their lifestyle is very simple. So, it is quite enough just to get the information with net surfing'.

While about 100,000 tourists visited Nan City in 2013, according to my own data collected from January to December 2013, there were not so many tourists who participated in Mlabri tourism, only 920 tourists (Table

1)[9]. Thai tourists accounted for 48 per cent of all visitors, and Western tourists who are the only people who participate in the jungle tour accounted for 29 per cent, but the most remarkable tourist phenomenon is that members of the Hmong, a neighbouring hill tribe, accounted for 17 per cent of visitors. The Mlabri are therefore a tourist attraction for other hill tribes as well. Besides, it is very interesting to note that even American-based Hmong visit Ban Huai Yuak for tourism purposes. According to my interview research, it seems that the Mlabri are well-known among the American Hmong, and one Hmong woman from America told me, 'I've had a very strong interest in them since I was a child because I have heard some stories about them from my grandpa'. Incidentally, the greatest number of tourists tends to be concentrated in the hot season and the dry season, but the number of Western tourists tends to be concentrated in the high tourist season, from January to April and from October to December (Figure 4).

Table 1. Details of Tourists

	NUMBER	RATE	FROM	TOUR SYSTEM
Thai	444	48	from all provinces	the Village Tour
Westerner	268	29	American, French, German, Belgian, etc.	the Village Tour the Jungle Tour
the Hmong	154	17	the Thai Hmong, the American Hmong	the Village Tour
Other	54	6	Buddhist priest, Asian, etc.	the Village Tour
TOTAL	920	100		

[9] However, it should be noted that the village tour by domestic tourists is very different from the village tour that is planned for foreign tourists, and at the same time, it is necessary to identify domestic visitors (Thai, Buddhist priests and Hmong) because they do not always visit Ban Huai Yuak for tourism purposes. In Thailand, Buddhists donate money or various goods to make merit (and perform good deeds, *thambun*). Thus the boundary between domestic tourism and *thambun* is unclear. In addition, Christian groups (domestic and foreign) also occasionally visit Ban Huai Yuak to donate. Nonetheless, visitors can be identified as tourists because they are also eager to take souvenir pictures of and with the Mlabri, which is motivated by a desire to interact with the Mlabri as an exotic object, regardless of the prime purpose.

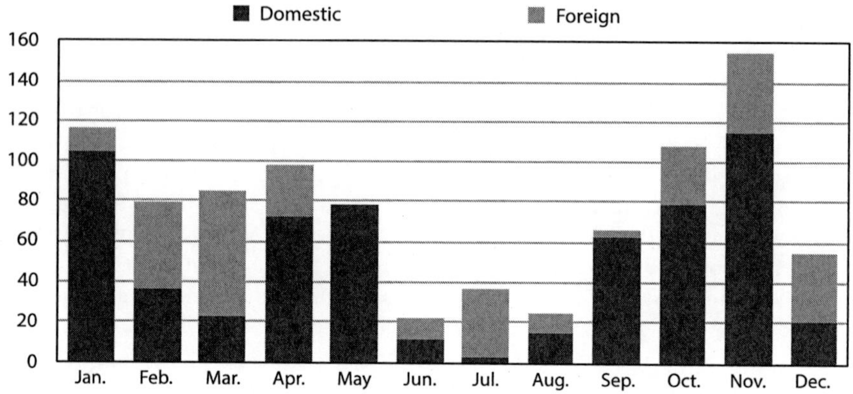

Figure 4. Seasonal Change of the Number of Tourists

Economic Benefits of Ethnic Tourism

Not all ethnic tourism brings economic benefits to the local communities. While there is not much difference between the benefits of the village tour and the jungle tour, the difference appears to depend on how much pork is required in the respective tours. In the case of the village tour by foreign tourists, the Mlabri can get pork, usually about two to three kilogrammes, but it is normally fat pork that is sold very cheaply, about THB 50 per 1 kilogramme, at the market in the city. On the other hand, in the case of the jungle tour, the Mlabri can get a very small pig, about 10 to 15 kilogrammes in weight, which is prepared by the tour company for the pig show as an eye-catching attraction. The other important benefit is money. Tour guides sometimes give the Mlabri money as a wage, about THB 20 to 40 per person, and tourists also sometimes give them donations, about THB 20 to 40 per person because the tour guide explains that the Mlabri are very poor. Interestingly, the narrative by tour guides is different in the village tour and the jungle tour. In the case of the village tour, it is emphasised that the Mlabri are socio-economically disadvantaged people who were driven from their forests by outside forces, and for that reason, tourists sometimes donate money to them. However, in the case of the jungle tour, tourists simply give something for the Mlabri to eat because tour guides explain that the Mlabri still remain in the forest where they do not need money. This difference indicates very clearly that the Mlabri are represented and presented by others, and that their interaction with tourists depends on the tour system and the tour guides.

In any case, it has to be said that the benefits from tourism that the Mlabri can derive is minimal. In the case of a tour company in Nan City, three packages are prepared from one day to three days. In all tour packages, tourists can visit the villages of H'tin, Yao, Hmong, and Mlabri, and the tour company gets THB 3,200 or more per one village tour; for example, in the case of a one-day village tour, two tourists pay THB 1,600 per person, and if there are three tourists, they pay THB 1,200 per person. According to my interview research for the tour company, the fee includes lunch, fruits, drinking water, transportation, and an English-speaking Thai guide, but the actual expenditure of one tourist is about THB 400. Thus, the profit of the tour company is about THB 2,400 per one tour or more, and it can be expected that the net profit of the tour company is about THB 1,500 per one tour after having paid the wages of the driver, guide and Mlabri. Calculated roughly the benefit to the Mlabri is about THB 200, which is 7.5 percent of the tour company's returns. However, it is not that all the Mlabri enjoy the benefits; usually only two to five adults can get something from a visit and some children can get something to eat, but it seems that tourism does not have any noticeable influence on their social life, and the reason for this is not related to the fact that the market scale is very small.

The Impact of Ethnic Tourism

The controversy about the impact of ethnic tourism on local communities frequently tends to evaluate whether it has positive or negative effects on what is usually referred to as 'traditional' culture, and research on Mlabri tourism is no exception to this. In general, it appears that the government authorities prefer to take the positive position, but other constituencies such as newspaper reporters and academic researchers prefer to take the negative position. In fact, the then chairman of the Ad-Hoc Committee to Promote Tourism of Phrae Province stressed that not all tourism involves exploitation and presented the case for its advantages in that tourism can provide economic opportunities for the Mlabri, in that they can maintain their traditional skills through selling handcrafts and to learn about the outside world through meeting Western or Thai visitors (*Bangkok Post*, 1990d). On the other hand, a newspaper reporter described Mlabri tourism as 'exploitation' and the tourist experience as a 'human zoo', and Professor Kwangsuan Atipote of Chulalongkorn University also described it as 'inhuman' (*Bangkok Post*, 1990b).

If we think about Mlabri tourism from the perspective of the economic benefits to the local communities, then it cannot be denied that Mlabri tourism has a dimension of 'exploitation'. One of the reasons why this has happened to the detriment of local communities is probably that there is no agency which has the authority to control all the stakeholders. As the Tourism Authority of Thailand (TAT) of Chiang Mai stated, 'We do not have the authority to control tour operators, neither can we take any legal action against them. The most we can do is to educate them and hope they cooperate' (ibid). Nevertheless, the negative opinions about ethnic tourism are superficial because this form of tourism does not seem to have any noticeable influence on the Mlabri. Specifically, ethnic tourism does not bring much in the way of economic benefits to the Mlabri due to its very small market scale; also the socio-cultural attitudes of the Mlabri themselves also mitigate against any exploitative tendencies of ethnic tourism.

There are many people who visit Ban Huai Yuak every year, but Mlabri attitudes to them do not change regardless of who they are. In addition, for the Mlabri, their purpose is also not a matter of concern. When someone visits Ban Huai Yuak, the Mlabri, regardless of whether they are adults or children, keep a distance from them and watch what they are doing, either through trepidation or curiosity. It seems to indicate that, for the Mlabri, the visitors are neither more nor less than outsiders. Without exception, the Mlabri refer to outsiders as *kwʌr*[10], and it depends on their powerful emic dichotomy, *mlaʔ/kwʌr*. When someone visits Ban Huai Yuak, the Mlabri just say '*kwʌrʔaleh*' ('the outsiders are coming'), even if they know who they are. Furthermore, it is very remarkable that they just talk about what *mlaʔ* did and what *kwʌr* did without using any personal names, when they talk about what happened to the Mlabri. In brief, *kwʌr* is *kwʌr,* and this concept does not have further meaning in their perception. Probably there is a reason for the Mlabri being extremely afraid of outsiders because they have memories, in that they have been raped or killed by outsiders (see, for example, Bernatzik, 1951; Boeles, 1963; Trier, 2008). Therefore, they say '*mlaʔhakmlaʔ, kwʌr hak kwʌr*' ('we are with us, they are with them') and they never try to have any close and active relationships with outsiders. Such a passive attitude is fundamental in their daily life, and it

[10] It can be said that *mlaʔ* means 'human beings' and *kwʌr* means 'monkey', but *kwʌr* is referred to as a particular kind of monkey, a *macaque*, which is seen as especially aggressive, and it seems to reflect their memory of the fear of outsiders.

has not changed up to the present. In short, regardless of the visitors' purposes, they are only outsiders and are not an object to cause any concern for the Mlabri.

However, it is very interesting to note that the Mlabri do not organise themselves for any positive project. In other words, they have a strong sense of belonging to the Mlabri as an ethnic group, but paradoxically they are tied very loosely to each other. Due to their socio-cultural attitudes, they have never tried to negotiate with the tourism middlemen to correct the economic disparity generated by tourism neither do they attempt to maximise the benefits from tourism because they do not naturally unite to achieve a common purpose, coupled with the fact that they are afraid of outsiders. In addition, the Mlabri do not have a recognised leader who can manage the affairs of the community. If anything happens they will talk with each other, but nobody can make a decision, and the final decision is left to all those involved in the discussion. They must respect the opinions of each other. Conversely, the parson who likes to force an opinion or decision on others is disliked. As an old man told me, 'It is better to think alone and do it alone'.

Moreover this attitude is also related to another aspect of Mlabri perspectives on tourism, to deny the risk and possibilities of ethnic tourism and to adopt a flexible attitude to it. For example, a Mlabri man said to me that he preferred not to become involved in ethnic tourism or to derive benefits from it because he thought that it was a form of 'prostitution', but he has never forbade his wife from participating in it. He stated '*kalam do mòy*' ('it is up to her'), when I asked him for the reason. In short, the matter whether his wife participated in it as a tourist attraction is very personal, and he conveyed his thoughts that he could not force her to stop her involvement, even though it was unbearable for him. Furthermore, it is interesting to note that such an attitude is not only found among the Mlabri, but also accepted by the Mlabri in relation to outsiders: for the Mlabri it is up to tourists whether they come to watch them as part of a tourism experience. The Mlabri do not derive significant benefits from ethnic tourism; clearly they are exploited by tour companies and middlemen; yet the Mlabri maintain a certain social and cultural distance from the effects of tourism.

Conclusion

In the context of ethnic tourism as a business, 'culture' is usually classified into two sorts: well-sold and ill-sold, or 'edible' and 'inedible'. In general, the former is chosen and commoditised, and the latter is excluded from the process. However, it may be said that the former does not always bring benefits to ethnic minorities because it is possible that well-sold or 'edible' culture that the middlemen wish to promote is 'inedible' for the people who are the subjects of the tourist encounter. Conversely, it is possible that ill-sold or 'inedible' culture for the tourism middlemen is 'edible'for the people. In the case of Mlabri tourism, the 'edible' culture which the middlemen wish to promote is the G-string, the bamboo pipe used for cooking and so on, but it is interesting to note that these are only 'useful' things for the Mlabri. For example, a Mlabri old man told me once, 'Why did we wear G-strings? Why did we use a bamboo pipe to cook? We did these things because they were comfortable for our lives in the forest. But now, the situation is changed. Why do we wear T-shirts today? Why do we use a steel pot today? We do these because they are more comfortable now!' On the other hand, the 'inedible' culture for the middlemen such as socio-cultural attitudes is 'edible' for the Mlabri because it is necessary for them to live as the Mlabri among the Mlabri. A Mlabri young man told me, 'The "culture" which the outsiders think about is different from the "culture" which we think about. Our culture is the way of life itself'. In short, 'edible' culture to eat is not always 'edible' to live, and vice versa. However, it is also true that Mlabri socio-cultural attitudes are a main cause of why they cannot gain more economic benefits from tourism; it is not that they cannot make the effort but that they do not want to do it. Of course, if the market scale becomes bigger, it is possible that ethnic tourism will give them more influence because the Mlabri are opportunists. If there is a chance in front of them, then they will try to catch it immediately, but they will not do it, if it has the possibility of disturbing their social relationships, because they do not live just to eat.

However, I am not arguing that Mlabri ethnic tourism should maintain its present condition. At least, intervention by the government authorities is clearly necessary to rectify the current unequal treatment of the Mlabri. It is obvious that it is difficult to introduce community-based tourism immediately due to Mlabri socio-cultural attitudes about the outside world and the role of their culture within it, but it is possible to correct the economic inequity between the Mlabri and the tourism middlemen; and the government authorities in particular should intervene because they have the responsibility for having recommended ethnic tourism among the

Mlabri positively. Furthermore, ethnic tourism certainly raises a serious problem about ethnic identity among the younger generation in particular. In fact, some of them, who are educated and have awareness of citizenship, have begun to become aware of their lowly social status in Thai society through their daily lives and their experience as a tourist attraction. Indeed, the older generation must make a living by themselves, and it cannot be denied that ethnic tourism provides an important income for them. But, as a young man told me, 'I'm awfully ashamed because the old men throw off their clothes immediately when they hear the sound of a tourist car'; there is a serious problem concerning Mlabri ethnic identity between the older and the younger generation. Nevertheless, the question of how this problem has an influence on their way of life and their ethnic identity in the future still remains an important subject for further study.

References

Bangkok Post (1990a) 'Phi Tong Luang: a Culture for Sale', 31 August.

—. (1990b) 'Among the Yellow Leaves', 19 April.

—. (1990c) 'Tourists and Tribesmen', 6 December.

—. (1990d) 'A Tiny Nomadic Forest Tribe that Faces Extinction', 16 April.

—. (1990e) 'The Benefits of Tourism', 12 October.

Bernatzik, H. A. (1951) *The Spirit of the Yellow Leaves*, London: Robert Hale Ltd.

Boeles, J.J. (1963) 'Second Expedition to the Mrabri ("Khon Pa") of North Thailand', *Journal of the Siam Society*, 51: 133-178.

Chanan Vongvipak (1992) 'Economic and Social Change among the Mlabri'. In S. Pookajorn and Staff (eds), *The Phi Tong Lueng (Mlabri): A Hunter-Gatherer Group in Thailand*, Bangkok: Odeon Store Printing House, pp. 92-103.

Chayan Vaddhanaphuti (2005) 'The Thai State and Ethnic Minorities: From Assimilation to Selective Integration'. In K. Snitwongse and M. S. Thompson (eds), *Ethnic Conflicts in Southeast Asia*, Singapore: Institute of Southeast Asian Studies, pp. 151-166.

Chazée, L. (2001) *The Mlabri in Laos: A World under the Canopy*, Bangkok: White Lotus Press.

Cohen, E. (1973) 'Nomads from Affluence: Notes on the Phenomenon of Drifter Tourism', *International Journal of Comparative Sociology* 14: 89-103.

—. (1984) 'The Sociology of Tourism: Approaches, Issues, and Findings', *Annual Review of Sociology*, 10: 373-392.

—. (1988) 'Authenticity and Commoditization in Tourism', *Annals of Tourism Research*, 15: 371-386.

—. (1996a) *Thai Tourism: Hill Tribes, Islands and Open-Ended Prostitution*, Bangkok: White Lotus.

—. (1996b) 'Hunter-Gatherer Tourism in Thailand'. In R. Butler and T. Hinch (eds), *Tourism and Indigenous Peoples*, International Thomson Business Press: London, pp. 227-254.

Dearden, P. (1991) 'Tourism and Sustainable Development in Northern Thailand', *Geographical Review* 81: 400-413.

—. (1996) 'Trekking in Northern Thailand: Impact, Distribution and Evolution over Time'. In M. Parnwell (ed.), *Uneven Development in Thailand*, Avebury: Athenaeum Press, pp. 204-225.

Dearden, P., and S. Harron (1992) 'Tourism and the Hill Tribes of Thailand'. In B. Weiler and M. Hall (eds), *Special-Interest Tourism*, London: Bellhaven Press, pp. 95-104.

Delang, C. O. (2002) 'Deforestation in Northern Thailand: The Result of Hmong Farming Practices or Thai Development Strategies?', *Society and Natural Resources,* 15: 483-501.

Endicott, K.M. (1979) *Batek Negrito Religion: the World-view and Rituals of a Hunting and Gathering People of Peninsular Malaysia,* Oxford: Oxford University Press.

Hinch, T. and Butler, R. (1996) 'Indigenous Tourism: A Common Ground for Discussion'. In R. Butler and T. Hinch (eds), *Tourism and Indigenous Peoples*, London: International Thomson Business Press, pp.3-19.

Ishii, K. (2007) 'Creating Diversity: Ethnic Tourism and Hill Tribes of Northern Thailand', *Ritsumei kandaigaku Jinbun kagakuken kyujyo Kiyou*, 89: 37-55.

—. (2012) 'The Impact of Ethnic Tourism on Hill Tribes in Northern Thailand', *Annals of Tourism Research*, 39: 290-310.

Khachatphai Burutsaphat (1995) *Chao Khao*, Bangkok: Samnakphim Phraephitthaya.

Nimonjiya, S. (2014) 'Another History of Chao Khao: The Mlabri in Northern Thailand', *Aséanie*, in press.

Oota, H. et al (2005) 'Recent Origin and Cultural Reversion of a Hunter-Gatherer Group', *PLoS Biology* 3: 536-542.

Pinkaew Laungaramsri (2003) 'Ethnicity and the Politics of Ethnic Classification in Thailand'. In C. Mackerras (ed.), *Ethnicity in Asia*, Routledge: London and New York, pp. 157-173.

Pradech Phayakvichien (2007) 'Thailand's Tourism Development: Past, Present and Future'. In Mingsarn Kaosaard (ed.), *Mekong Tourism:*

Blessings for All?, Chiang Mai: Social Research Institute, Chiang Mai University, pp. 41-59.

Prasit Leepreecha (1997) 'Jungle Tours: A Government Policy in Need of Review'. In D. McCaskill, and K. Kampe (eds), *Development or Domestication? Indigenous Peoples of Southeast Asia*, Chiang Mai: Silkworm Books, pp. 268-288.

—. (2008) 'The Politics of Ethnic Tourism in Northern Thailand'. In A. Adam and M. Kaosaard (eds), *Mekong Tourism: Competitiveness and Opportunities*, Chiang Mai: Social Research Institute, Chiang Mai University, pp. 223-245.

Schliesinger, J. (2003) *Mountain People of Laos Vol. 2: Profile of Austro-Asiatic-Speaking Peoples*, Bangkok: White Lotus.

Smith, V. L. (ed.) (1977) *Hosts and Guests: The Anthropology of Tourism*, Philadelphia: University of Pennsylvania Press.

TAT (Tourism Authority of Thailand) (2004) *Raingan Khrongkan Samruat Sathiti Kanthongthiawnai Prathet Thai, pi pho so 2546*, Bangkok: Tourism Authority of Thailand (in Thai).

Thailand, Krom Phattana Sangkhomlae Sawatdikan (2002).*Thamniap Chumchon bon Phunthi Sung: 20 Canwatnai Phrathet Thai Pho. So. 2545.*

The Lahu National Development Organization (2005) 'No Place Left for the Spirits of Yellow Leaves: Intensive Logging Leaves Few Options for the Mlabri People", *Undercurrents* 1: 16- 18.

Thiaothua Thaibaikap 'Nai Rop Ru' (2004) 'Nan', *Thiaothua Thai baikap 'Nai Rop Ru'*, Bangkok: Sarakadi Press.

Thongchai Caruppat (1998) *Sathanagan Pamaikhong Prathet Thai naichwangrayawera 37 pi (Pho. So 2504-2541).* Bangkok: Krom Pamai.

Thongchai Winichakul (2000) 'The Others Within: Travel and Ethno-Special Differentiation of Siamese Subjects 1885-1910'. In A. Turton (ed.), *Civility and Savagery: Social Identity in Tai States*, Richmond: Curzon, pp. 38-62.

Toyota, M. (1996) 'The Effect of Tourism Development on an Akha Community: a Chiang Rai Village Case Study'. In M. Parnwell (ed.), *Uneven Development in Thailand*, Avebury: Athenaeum Press, pp. 226-240.

Trier, J. (2008) *Invoking the Spirits: Fieldwork on the Material and Spiritual Life of the Hunter-gatherers Mlabri in Northern Thailand,* Aarhus: Aarhus University Press.

Trips Magazine (2011) 'Nan', *Trips Magazine*, vol.15, no. 181, Bangkok: World Trip Co., Ltd.

UNESCO (1976) 'The Effects of Tourism on Socio-Cultural Values', *Annals of Tourism Research*, 4: 74-105.

Yaiying, A. and K. Thirawong (2010) *Research and Development Potential Tourism Resource for Supporting Agro-tourism in Mlabri Community Rongkwang District, Phrae province*, Chiang Mai: Maejo University (in Thai).

Wanat Bhruksasri (1989) 'Government Policy: Highland Ethnic Groups'. In J. MacKinnon and B. Vienne (eds.), *Hill Tribes Today: Problems in Change*, Bangkok: White Lotus, pp. 5-31.

Wood, R. (1993) 'Tourism, Culture and the Sociology of Development'. In M. Hitchcock, V.T. King, and M.J.G. Parnwell (eds), *Tourism in South-East Asia*, London and New York: Routledge, pp. 48-70.

—. (1997) 'Tourism and the State'. In M. Picard and R. Wood (eds), *Tourism, Ethnicity, and the State in Asian and Pacific Societies*, Honolulu: University of Hawaii Press, pp. 1-34.

FIESTA AND TOURISM: EXPLORING THE ROLE OF A SOCIO-CULTURAL ACTIVITY TOWARDS THE DEVELOPMENT OF LOCAL TOURISM IN THE PROVINCE OF BOHOL, PHILIPPINES

MAE CLAIRE G. JABINES

Introduction

The island-province of Bohol is located in the Central Visayas Region of the Republic of the Philippines. It is the tenth largest island in the country with a land area of 4,117.26 square kilometres (1,589.68 square miles). It has a population of 1.2 million according to the latest Census of the National Statistics Office. The island is a known tourist destination of the country showcasing its famous beaches, rich wild and marine life and the famous chocolate hills (See Figure 1).

Aside from the attractions, people flock to Bohol to celebrate a socio-cultural activity and that is the fiesta. The province is known to celebrate fiesta for the whole month of May. People congregate in Bohol to join the festivities and practices of the fiestas bringing along their friends and families. There is an increase of arrival rates at ports and terminals of local tourists and visitors as the fiesta season starts. The motivation of the Boholanos to celebrate fiesta is considerable.

Fiestas are celebrations in honour of a saint, particularly the patron saint of a town. This is usually accompanied by rituals, traditions, merry-making and festivities. Fiestas are common to predominantly Catholic countries. The Philippines, as a former colony of Spain, widely celebrates fiestas based upon the church calendar signifying the feast days of saints. However, the practice of celebrating fiesta is not solely Spanish in origin. Prior to the arrival of the Spaniards, the natives (pre-colonial Filipinos) were practising such celebrations. During the harvest season, festivities were held to symbolise an act of paying tribute and appreciation to their gods (*anitos*). The people offered their prime harvest, the best of their livestock and even their first-born to their gods. They practised the spilling of blood of their prime livestock like chickens, pigs, or carabao as a sign of gratitude for the good harvests that they had had in the previous seasons (Luspo, 2005). When the Spanish colonisers arrived they saw the significance of festivities in encouraging the natives to convert to Christianity as well as pacifying the inhabitants to settle into the mission or relocation towns (*reduccion*). The colonisers fused the pre-colonial practices with Christian practices, thus creating what we refer to now as fiesta.

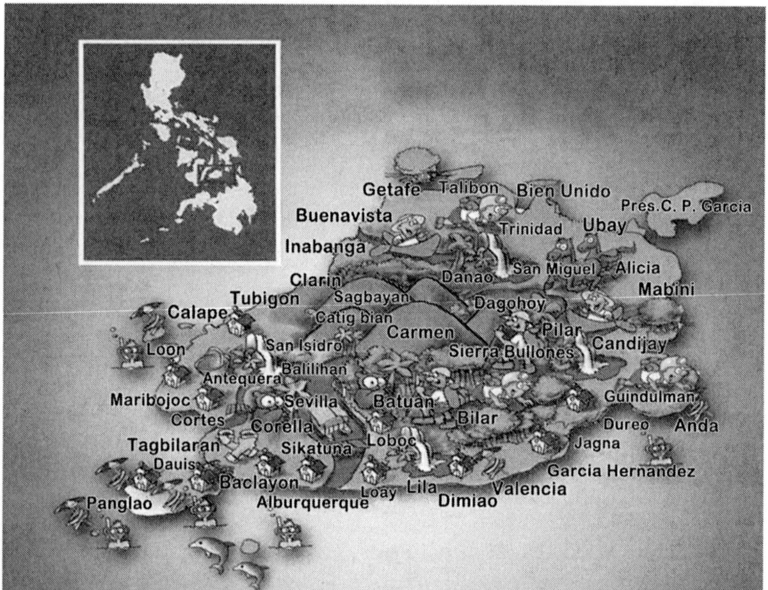

Figure 1. Map of Bohol.
Source: Bohol Environment Management Office (BEMO), 2006

The celebration of fiestas proved to be a good venue for witnessing different Filipino cultural activities as well as providing social and economic opportunities. Every church has its rituals practised by devotees of a patron saint; jobless people can peddle candles, scapulars and other religious items; and almost every house in a town is fully occupied because of visiting relatives. Excitement and anticipation capture people as the fiesta is approaching.

Fiestas do not just happen in a flash; they are planned, organised, prepared, executed and financed (Roces, 1980). Fiestas are more of a communal rather an individual activity. The lifeblood of a fiesta is the collective effort and support of the community. This collective effort and support depends very much on the kinship ties of the people, which encompass all forms of relationship (Hollsteiner, 1979).

The celebrations of fiestas around the towns of Bohol in the month of May are an annual socio-cultural spectacle. Boholanos coming from different parts of the world always have the urgency to come home and celebrate fiestas bringing their family and friends. There is an increased passage of people going to the island by air, sea and land. Terminals get busy with inbound and outbound passengers. Beyond this annual scene there is a need to investigate why people in this province had the need to celebrate fiesta? What are the other spill-over effects of fiesta? How can a socio-cultural activity significantly contribute to the development of local tourism?

This chapter presents a descriptive exposition of how a socio-cultural activity like fiesta contributes to the development of local tourism in the province of Bohol. It explores the different images of fiestas, spiritual and socio-cultural, which illustrate the ways in which the Boholanos celebrate them. Specifically, it examines the significance of fiesta celebrations; the ways in which fiestas affect the lives of Boholanos, spiritually and socially, and lastly, how the fiesta phenomenon re-enacts the traditions and culture which have catalysed the development of local tourism. It establishes that socio-cultural and economic practices and the promotion of tourism are spill-over effects of the spiritual practices observed during the event.

The author hopes that by presenting the fiesta culture of Bohol, we may understand how fiestas commence a meaningful and in-depth celebration anchored on the great conviction of a certain group of people. Likewise, in retrieving, rewriting and reliving a local culture, it is hoped to contribute to the development of the literature on fiestas and to a comprehensive local history of Bohol as well as understanding the role of fiesta in the development of local tourism.

The scope and the locale of the study cover six towns and one city in Bohol. The province has 47 towns and one city. The sites were purposely identified through their geographical location, three coastal towns and three interior towns. The coastal sites comprise Tagbilaran City, Maribojoc, Candijay and Talibon while the interior sites cover the municipalities of San

Miguel, Loboc and Bilar. The sites were classified into interior-coastal in order to determine whether there is a significant difference in the practices in fiesta celebration. All of the fiestas were held in the month of May. Most of the sites have a fixed schedule of fiesta celebrations except for Talibon, which is a moving schedule falling always on the last Saturday of May. This exemplifies that there is an alternative way of fiesta scheduling not on the basis of a fixed date but on a moving date depending on the order of days.

Aside from the towns, other sites like transport terminals, ports, hotels and some commercial centres were observed to explore the impact of fiestas on the economic and tourism development of the province.

The study employs ethnographic methods and can be classified as descriptive and interpretative; descriptive as the researcher gathered essential details for the topic; and interpretative as the researcher has determined the significance of what was observed in the identified sites. Participant observation, focus group discussion (FGD) and interviews with key informants were the data gathering techniques applied in the study.

There is some literature available on fiestas. Alejandro Roces' *Fiesta* (1980) traces the beginnings of fiestas in the country. He describes how Filipinos fused the celebration as a combination of pre-Hispanic rituals and those of the Catholic Church. According to Roces, fiestas do not just happen; they involve a great deal of planning, organising, mobilising and financing. He further proposes that fiestas are more of a communal rather than an individual activity. The limitation of this literature for the study of Bohol fiestas is that the study focuses more on Luzon festivities. There is a need to explore other provinces with a fiesta culture. Again, as a photo-based book, it provides minimal textual content for readers to further understand the concept and practice of fiesta.

An article by Simplicio Apalisok in his book, *Bohol without Tears, volume 3* (1999) examined how fiestas came to be celebrated in Bohol through the fusion of pre-Hispanic and Catholic practices. He related the traditional practice of veneration of the patron saint before other fiesta activities. He examined the different challenges that Boholanos underwent when a national law attempted to halt the celebration of fiesta. He further stipulated that fiesta is part and parcel of the lives of the Boholanos.

Finally, according to the article by Dr Jes B. Tirol, 'Fiestas in Bohol: its Economic, Social and Cultural Significance' (2007), some aspects of the fiesta are not based on religious principles but they have nevertheless been integrated into religious practices over time. He suggests that fiesta celebrations are basically social in their significance in that Boholanos return to the province every year for social gatherings and family reunions. In my interviews with Dr Tirol in 2004 and 2005 respectively, he made the proposal in his article that there might be a rescheduling of the May fiestas of Bohol to once a week throughout the whole year. For him, this is a practical and economic proposal. However, this statement was met with objections from the Church and other local historians.

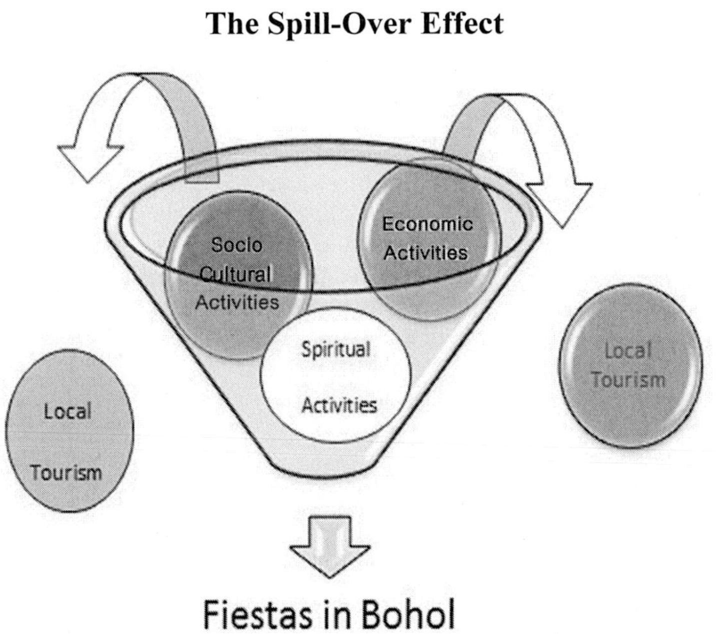

Figure 2. The Spill-Over Effect

The chapter focuses on the notion that fiestas in Bohol are deeply rooted in the spiritual and socio-cultural beliefs and practices of the Boholanos. Being the core foundation, it has fused together the social and economic activities of the people. The rituals and practices are generated from an immense belief in and veneration of the patron saint. Social gatherings and physical preparations are held in honour of the feast of the saints. Thus, without the feast of the saints, there would be no other celebrations or activities facilitated in the community. However, in the process of carrying out the celebrations, there have been spill-over effects in the development of local tourism in the area. The influx of people to the island to celebrate the fiesta putting into practice their religious beliefs and being reunited with their families have given an important impetus to the development of local tourism. In other words a spiritual and socio-cultural activity like fiesta, which is not directed primarily to tourism, can contribute importantly to a domestic or local tourism industry.

Discussion

The Boholano Concept of Fiesta Celebrations

Local Boholano historians have recognised that fiestas were practised in the early communities of Bohol prior to the Spanish colonisation. The people, back then, held rituals in offering their prime crops and livestock as symbols of gratitude to their gods for successful harvests (Luspo, 2005). When the Spaniards came they saw these ritual celebrations which were integrated into the agricultural year as a channel for pacification and encouraging the natives to convert to Christianity. It made the natives feel comfortable in their new religion as they could identify and incorporate similar practices from their pre-Christian culture. Since then, the fiesta has become a central and crucial part of Boholano life. It illustrates a perfect fusion of pagan beliefs and practices mixed with Christian faith and beliefs (Luspo, 2005).

> The celebration of fiesta is a perfect marriage between local tradition and western tradition because the natives found meaning in it. This is why it developed by itself, if it was otherwise imposed, maybe it would have taken a different character (Luspo, 2005).

> Fiesta has been practiced before Christianity came to the Philippines. It was practised to extend gratefulness to blessings received and to appease the upset gods (Dagohoy, 2005).

> The fiesta is not religious. The Spaniards only used it for their religious activity. Fiesta is a social gathering for whatever reason like death, birthday… (Tirol, 2005).

Almost all the fiestas in Bohol are celebrated in the month of May. It should be understood that the celebration of fiestas is connected to the harvest season and the rearing of livestock and in general to the whole pattern of agricultural activity. The month of May is termed by local historians as ‘Himabuyan’, the time of year when pigs and agricultural products come to the full term of their growth (Tirol, 2007).

> The month of May is pig season. This is the time when pigs come to their full term and it is also a conducive time for harvesting crops. So, it's easy to have a feast in the month of May… (Tirol, 2007).

The patron saints of the towns which celebrate fiestas in May are themselves related to agriculture. Take the case of Saint Isidore (San Isidro), the patron saint of farmers and rural communities; five towns celebrate a fiesta on 15 May in his honour. Aside from Bilar, there are the towns of Tubigon, Busao of Maribojoc, Trinidad and Tabuan of Garcia Hernandez. On the same day, the Boholanos have a choice of which towns to visit depending on where they live or are staying and the time and the distance required to reach the town. The other saint related to agriculture and labour or workers is Saint Joseph, whose feast is celebrated by three towns particularly in Tagbilaran City (1 May), Candijay (19 May) and Nahawan Clarin (30 May) (Trota-Jose, 2001:111).

There are varied views of Boholanos pertaining to fiesta celebrations. The most dominant view manifested in the interviews and focus group discussions (FGDs) is that a fiesta is more of a spiritual than a social activity. The respondents identified the importance of the devotion to the patron saint. As devotees to a particular saint, they also fulfill their *pana-ad* (promise or vow) of undertaking special activities or duties in honour of the saint or just being home in time for the feast of their saint. Fiesta for Boholanos is a venue and celebration or thanksgiving for the blessings that they received in the previous year. Paying homage to the patron saint is the eminent reason why Boholanos from other parts of the country and abroad come home to celebrate the feast of their patron saint (Luspo, 2005). The social gathering and the feast of the table comes second to the devotion of the people (Biliran, 2005).

> It is instilled in ourselves that we have to go home. It is not for the reunion but for the Patron. We go home because of the Patron and to avoid any karma from the Patron. That's why everyone who is away from the town has the urgent desire to go home. So the effect is the gathering of relatives having the same goal of paying homage to the Patron, then the reunion happened (Luspo, 2005).

However, for non-Catholic Boholanos, they view the fiesta as a purely a social event. The fiesta for them is a social celebration of life, success, reunions and acquaintances. According to Dr Jes Tirol, 'Fiesta is a social celebration for Boholanos. A social event where there are people celebrating for the arrival, gathering and success. It is supposed to be separate from the religious side' (Tirol, 2005). Dr Tirol was open in suggesting for fiestas to be distributed equally in the 12 months of the year and not be solely concentrated in the month of May. This will help those people living in poverty have a full meal every time there is a fiesta. This suggestion was opposed by other respondents. One cannot just simply alter and redistribute fiesta dates because they are founded on the date of death of a saint and it has been part of the tradition. Altering it to give way to social benefits would eventually destroy the tradition and essence of fiesta celebrations (Luspo, 2005).

Beliefs and Practices in the Fiesta

The Spiritual Dimension

For most Boholanos, spiritual devotion is the foundation of the practices and beliefs in a fiesta celebration, while the social and economic activities are secondary. Fiesta is an avenue of expressing gratitude for all the blessings received as well as asking petitions and intentions. People usually participated in a Novena for nine days and in the Pontifical Mass on the day of the fiesta. For devotees, the high mass (Pontifical Mass) is a necessity to complete their Novena for nine days (Torralba, 2005). The devotees of a patron saint do not only include the locals but there are also pilgrims from other towns. During the fiesta season, one can see bus-loads of pilgrims in the church grounds. Most pilgrims offered prayers and attended mass and kissed the statue of the patron saint.

Pana-ad

The practice of *pana-ad* or vows fuels the spiritual devotion of the locals to their patron saint. The word *pana-ad* means promise or vow to be fulfilled by a devotee to his or her patron saint especially during the festivities of the saint. Once fulfilled, the devotee and his or her family will receive blessings or indulgence from their patron saint. The acts of *pana-ad* range from simply completing the Novena, attending the Pontifical Mass to perform charitable acts, volunteering in church activities, pledging donations to help in cleaning the church and assisting in the floral arrangements of the altar and *caro* (carriage) of the patron saint. For some people, the mere presence in the church during the feast of their saint is already a fulfilled *pana-ad*.

> If you fulfill your *pana-ad*, you will achieve spiritual fulfillment. There is a sense of responsibility to express gratitude for all the blessings you receive and to pay homage to your patron saint (Monreal, 2009).

The practice of *pana-ad* is one of the reasons why people especially Boholanos insist in going home to their towns for every fiesta no matter how far they have to travel. The urgency of going home cuts across social strata. Balikbayans (Filipinos residing abroad) working as nurses, accountants, engineers, seamen, caregivers and domestic helpers plan their trip home months before the fiesta. The main priority is to pay homage to their patron saint but on the sideline they attend family gatherings and reunions.

The practice of *pana-ad* has fuelled the influx of pilgrims and local tourists during fiesta. Bus-loads of pilgrims and local tourists come from other towns and flock to the churches to pay homage to the patron. For them, this is a way of showing gratitude and devotion to their patron which has helped them in times of need. Some thank the patron for healing their ailments, others for the success of their children (i.e. passing exams, finding work) and for good health and family relations. Most pilgrims participate in the dancing in front of the carriage of the patron, which is usually done after the Pontifical Mass up to a day or two into the fiesta. Among the sites studied, Maribojoc, Tagbilaran and Loboc had a huge number of pilgrims during their fiesta.

Procession

Participation in the procession after the completion of the nine days *misa novena* is an activity in which people with *pana-ad*, pilgrims, devotees and church-goers partake. The procession usually takes place on the eve of the fiesta. The patron is placed on a *caro* or carriage, which is positioned last in line. It goes around the *poblacion*, or the plaza with the accompaniment of a brass band. The procession commences with fireworks in the grounds of the church. In some areas, the church has created mechanisms to prevent the crowd from harvesting the flowers in the carriage of the patron saint. Some people, especially cock-fighters or *sabungero*s, considered the flowers from the *caro* an amulet for their rooster in a cock-fighting tournament.

> The *sabungeros* are the first ones to get the flowers from the *caro*. That's why the *caro* is already bare when it enters the church. They make use of the flowers as amulets inserted in the bladed armour of their rooster during cockfights (Ampusta, 2005).

There are some towns that innovate in their processions. Aside from the customary land-based processions, fluvial processions are conducted along the waters of the towns which hold the fiestas. In Maribojoc and Loboc, fluvial processions are held in the surrounding coastal waters and along the river, respectively. The people will either join the procession riding in their own *bangka* or *baroto* or simply light candles along the procession route.

Basao or Bong Bolibong Kingking.

The *Basao* also known as *Bong Bolibong Kingking* is a unique and interesting practice in a fiesta in Bohol. The *Basao* refers to the practice of dancing in front of the *caro* (carriage) of a patron saint with the accompaniment of percussion instruments like gongs and drums. There is a variety of dance steps in other places but one thing is common, the dancers usually touch a part of their body that has an ailment. They believe that dancing in front of an image will heal their afflictions. Some carry and offer their infants while in front of the patron saint's statue. Others wave their handkerchiefs or hold up candles to the statue of the saint. *Basao* is usually done after the Pontifical Mass until the next two days. There are varied terms for the dance. People in coastal areas such as Maribojoc and Tagbilaran call it *Basao* while interior towns like Loboc and Bilar call it *Bong Bolibong Kingking.*

Basao depicts the pre-Hispanic practice of natives dancing in front of their gods. The Catholic priests adopted this practice and replaced the natives' gods with the Catholic saints. They allowed the use of pagan music and the rituals and eventually fused it into western Catholicism. The Spanish church authorities tolerated this practice.

> The rhythm used is pre-Hispanic. The instruments used are pre-Hispanic and it's like they just changed the object of devotion. At first, it was the *anitos* (as objects of devotion) then when the Spaniards came, it was replaced by statues. They (the Spanish) allowed the use of pagan music, pagan ritual and allowed it to be inculcated into Western Catholicism. The Spanish authorities tolerated the practice. That's why it's really a perfect fusion of the church to be using Western religious instrumentalities but the ritual is pre-Hispanic (Luspo, 2005).

The Socio-cultural Aspect

After fulfilling the obligations as devotees in the church, the people are preoccupied with socio-cultural activities. On the macro-level there are the town-based activities organised by the Church and the Local Government Unit (LGU). As the Church facilitates the Novena for nine-days, the LGU and other socio-civic organisations sponsor nightly activities such as variety shows, dramas, singing contests, disco and ballroom dancing and coronation night. The coronation night cuts across ages in that there is a coronation for children (Little Princess and Prince), for teenagers and even for matrons. The disco usually takes place on the night of Vesper or *Bisperas* (eve of the fiesta) and on the day of the fiesta or *Katumanan*. One can see the unity and cooperation of the two major institutions of a town. There is no competition between the Church and the LGU as each of them had scheduled activities for the fiesta.

> A fiesta is not complete without nightly social activities. It goes with the beginning of the novena until the day of the fiesta. There was already a coronation before until today. It involves children and older people in the coronation night. There are discos, basketball league, variety show and drama (Racho, 2005).

The fiestas in Bohol are celebrated for two days but for some it extends to three days. The town gets crowded on the eve of the fiesta or Vesper or *Bisperas* and then continues on the actual fiesta day *Katumanan*. Others have three days of celebration which start on the day before the eve of the fiesta or *Ante Bisperas* up to the day of the fiesta celebration. There are other people who continue the fiesta the day after or *Liwas*.

> Mostly, visitors go to a fiesta during *Bisperas* (eve of the fiesta) because there are times that they have to work the following day. But there are many who prefer to go to a fiesta on the *Katumanan* (fiesta day) and even the day after (*Liwas*). The food served comprises the left-overs from the fiesta (Calipusan, 2005).

Family Gatherings and Reunions

On the micro-level, family gatherings are widespread in a town celebrating a fiesta. There is an anecdote about Bohol that the island is sinking under several inches of fiesta attendance during the month of May because all Boholanos are going home for their town fiesta (Ampusta, 2005). Another anecdote states that Boholanos are always given visas abroad as the Embassy there is assured that they will not overstay in a foreign country because they will always go home for fiesta (Racho, 2005). As it is a tradition for Boholanos to pay homage to their patron saint in the fiesta, they also participate in family reunions held annually. The large arrival of Boholanos in the port of Tagbilaran starts in the last days of April signifying the beginning of the fiesta season. The port and airport gets busy two to three days before a fiesta, and Boholanos usually bring along *pasalubongs* (gifts), additional food such as cakes or pastries, fruits, cans of biscuits, utensils and appliances.

Family reunions usually take place a day after the fiesta although informal gatherings are evident during vespers and the day of the fiesta. Most reunions are done on a family basis with the name of the family patriarch printed boldly on the uniformed coloured shirts of the members of the family. These activities facilitate the renewal and remembering of family ties especially when there are relatives who are first timers in the reunions. Visiting the beaches and tourist spots follows after the day of fellowship. There are some families that have their annual itinerary of local tourist sites to showcase to their relatives during the reunion season.

Balikbayan (returning) relatives also sponsor prizes and activities. In affluent families, some of their activities include outreach programmes like free clinics and giving bundles of joy to the indigent families in their community. The constant factor during reunions is the singing through *videoke*, which brings entertainment to the family and their visitors. Older family members reconnect and recall their amusing and memorable experiences while the young ones share their hobbies and interests. Having all the members of their family together during the fiesta is another celebration for a Boholano family. Thus, celebrating the fiesta of a patron saint and the return of family members brings about the *Fiesta de la Mesa*.

> Celebrating fiesta is fun because of family members coming home. Aside from the devotion of the Saints, it brings the family together. Relatives living in faraway places always make an effort of coming home. But there are those who cannot go home, they just celebrate the fiesta in their place (Tabel, 2005).

Festivals

The facilitation of organised festivals started in the late 1980s in Bohol. Although there were towns that had their traditional festivals these were not organised around particular themes and events nor did they encourage tourism. The Sandugo Festival (Blood Compact) was the first major festival of the province. It was facilitated by the provincial government. However, it was not a religious-based festival as it was based on a historical event on sealing the friendship between a local chieftain and a Spanish conquistador. The festival gained less support for Boholanos as it was not rooted in their religious faith. It was in the late 1990s and early 2000s when festivals anchored to the feasts of the saints and patrons came into existence. The festivals were centred on the lives of the saints, the miracles performed and the struggles their specific patrons underwent. The festivals were mostly a joint collaboration between the church and the local government. Even families with returning relatives from abroad also gave sponsorship to the event. Socio-civic organisations usually provided the committees for organising the festivals. The event comprised street dancing and a dance demonstration in an open field. In Maribojoc, the town annually held the Enting-Enting Festival in honour of their patron saint, St Vincent Ferrer. It showcased dance presentations of the various organisations highlighting the miracles the saint performed. In the town of San Miguel, the festival dwells on the duel between St. Michael the Archangel and Lucifer. The townsfolk presented different versions of the duel.

There are certain features of the festivals which can be observed in the towns of Bohol: most of the festivals are religious in character; the dances of *Basao* or *Bong Bolibong Kingking* are performed in front of the statue of the saint; and the festivals require the joint collaboration of the church and the local government with the support of socio-civic organisations.

Fiesta Cuisine

The food served during fiestas is mostly Spanish inspired. Most of the food has sauces like *menudo*, *afritada* and *caldereta*. There is also a cuisine mostly preferred by Boholanos like *hamonada* and *humba*. Some dishes are fried such as crispy *pata*, fried chicken, *lumpia* and breaded pork chop. For those who can afford it there may *belechon* (roasted pig) on the table. Pigs, chickens and goats are commonly offered in festivals. One would be amazed to hear the chorus wailing of pigs from different parts of the neighborhood as early as 4 am on a fiesta day. The social status of the owner of the house does not matter in giving a feast. No matter how small one's income compared to the next-door neighbour, the household still offers you food. Most households believe that celebrating a feast on the table in honour of a saint may bring more blessings to the family in the coming year.

> If it is an obligation of the people to go home every fiesta for the patron, it is also needed to put food (fiesta food) on the table no matter how small or big in quantity. It is a thanksgiving celebration to the patron. If one cannot do it, there will be no blessings in the coming year for the family (Monreal, 2009).

Celebrating a fiesta and providing food for guests is not easy. Some households, particularly poorer ones, begin their preparations a year before the fiesta. They arrange an economic plan to acquire major ingredients needed for a fiesta. Other households hire cooks, those to wash up and servers during the fiesta. Families brag about their traditional recipes with their visitors. Fiesta visitors also have their preferred food on the table such as *humba* (softened pork meat cooked with soy sauce, vinegar, seasoning, *tausi* and banana flowers) especially the one that floats in oil. There is no significant difference between the cuisine of the coastal towns and the interior towns in Bohol. A slight difference can be seen in their preference for a particular meat. The interior towns have *carabao* meat added to their main recipe, served in soup or in dry meat form locally called *kusahos* while in the coastal areas, the households already add seafood like crab, fish and shrimps. Other than that, everything is just the same.

> There is no significant difference between the celebration of coastal and interior towns. In the manner of slicing the meat, interior towns have bigger chunks compared to the coastal. They [interior] slaughtered *carabao* and cook either in soup or *kusahos* but in coastal areas they have seafood on their tables (Luspo, 2005).

> I have a friend who always has two pigs for fiesta celebration; one for the food on the table and the other for 'Bring House' for their visitors (Calipusan, 2005).

Bring House

Another practice that encourages the development of social relations among Boholanos in the fiesta season is the custom of 'Bring House' or taking home fiesta food. The visitors, aside from eating sumptuous meals, are given packed fiesta food to take home for family members who could not attend. For most households, it is a standard operating procedure (SOP) to pack viands, desserts, and pastries in plastic bags for their visitors. Fiesta-goers commonly call the take home 'BH' (Bring House). In affluent homes, the owners have a separate pig roasted and divided among visitors for 'Bring House'. In middle income families, they usually pack delicacies i.e. *putosuman* (rice cakes) and *torta* (omelette) for their visitors. The practice of 'Bring House' cuts across social strata in Bohol. As time passes by, new terms for 'Bring House' emerged to keep up with new trends i.e. 'Cellpon' or 'Cellophane Puno', which means filled plastic cellophane and 'Laptup' or 'Lapaw Tupperware', which refers to a plastic container filled to the rim. The practice of bringing home fiesta food illustrates collective generosity and the hospitality of the hosts to their visitors.

> In preparation for the fiesta, it is a must to have excess from your estimated number of guests so that you can give them take home fiesta food. It does not matter how small as long as one was able to send a 'bring house'. We always prepare cellophane in case our visitors like to bring house a certain viand (Calipusan, 2005).

> In the town of Candijay, there are several people, who went from one house to another but they will not necessarily eat when asked but they prefer to have 'bring house' for their kin or relatives left at home (Ampusta, 2005).

Balos-Balos

The *Balos-Balos* practice compliments the 'Bring House' practice. The practice embodies reciprocity in the lives of the fiesta-goers in Bohol. To demonstrate, family B visits family A in another town having a fiesta and brings back 'BH'. When the time comes for family A to visit family B, the latter would also do the same for their visitors. Usually the visiting family would stay in the host family for one to two days during the fiesta celebration. This custom is widely practiced in some interior towns. It is common to hear it said among people, *Kung himistahonka, daghan sad mamistasainyoha* (If you are a regular fiesta-goer, it is expected that many people will visit your house during your town's fiesta).

Open House

The 'Open House" practice promotes a distinct type of Boholano hospitality. The family hosting a banquet during a fiesta welcomes visitors and total strangers. The house is open to all who want to partake in the feast. 'In May, people in Bohol are never hungry' *(*Tirol, 2005). This practice is widely observed by Boholano households. The practice is considered by families as a way of sharing their blessings and a means of expressing their gratitude to their patron saint. For fiesta visitors, there is no limit to how many households you can visit as long you can compartmentalise your stomach. There is a certain Boholano way of entering into an unfamiliar household during fiesta as explained in this quotation:

> If you are a visitor before entering a house, you are expected to greet in the traditional way, which is being indirect and never, never ask of what you want directly…That's the way to do it, especially when you are still

> outside, never go inside directly. You look for familiar persons in the house or trace your family relations with the host (Luspo, 2005).

The Economic Dimension

During the fiesta season, it is a practice among Boholano households to have a part of their house repaired, extended or repainted. Changes are done to accommodate visitors during the fiesta. No matter how big or small the house, its owners would see to it that there would be changes undertaken either permanently by extension or repainting, or temporary by having new curtains or blinds or new furniture. Others buy new appliances to be used during the fiesta. The celebration of fiesta has contributed significantly to the economy of Bohol. People spend their money to celebrate the fiesta no matter how large or meager their income. It has inspired Boholanos to work hard and save for the year in time for the coming fiesta. It is a common sight in major stores in the city to see boxes of grocery items, hardware, kitchen utensils and rolls of curtains in the advent of a fiesta, 'Though some would declare that times are hard yet the manner of spending is still consistent during fiesta season' (Biliran, 2005).

Tampa-Tampa

The *Tampa-Tampa* system is a mechanism that Boholanos have initiated to reduce expenses in fiesta preparation. The word *tampa* means contribution. This mechanism involves several households in the community contributing small amounts for 12 months for a certain item to be used during the fiesta. The *Tampa-Tampa* would cover contributions for soft drinks, meat (*carabao*, pork or beef) and rice (Biliran, 2005). This communal economic activity usually starts a month after the fiesta and will commence well before the next fiesta. Through the *Tampa-Tampa*, Boholanos from different social classes can avail themselves of items to meet their needs in the next fiesta. This scheme reduces the burden on the households as the commodities will be distributed in time for the fiesta.

> The *Tampa-Tampa* scheme is a big help because it could put food on the fiesta table. You can join a Tampa for meat or for soft drinks or even for rice. The expenses will be lessened because there is a monthly contribution. That's why we will just add the seasoning and fruit salad expenses during fiesta (Biliran, 2005).

For those not engaged in *Tampa-Tampa*, they opted to avail themselves of the credit scheme offered by big stores in the capital of the province. The stores offer a two-payment scheme for one month for grocery items and a six-payment scheme or three months for dry goods or department store items like curtains, utensils and appliances. This provides a reasonable payment system for the consumers.

Remittances and Demands

The Boholanos stationed in other areas of the country and outside of the Philippines would save a part of their salary for the fiesta celebrations and for the renovation or extension of their house. It is noticeable if the house has many visitors during the fiesta, if there is a long table and wide *sala* (large room or reception area) and patio that could accommodate visitors. Another anecdote would relay how a Boholano working as a house help in Manila allocates her meager salary in preparation for the fiesta and for the house renovation (see quotation below). There is an increase in economic activity in Bohol during the month of May. One indication that a residence is having a fiesta is the hanging of new curtains. Indeed, there are demands on curtain materials and seamstresses to sew it. Aside from curtain demand, pork meat or literally pigs are in demand. There was a time that pigs were in shortage. Many flock to different places to find hog-raisers selling their livestock. Another noticeable element is the transactions in hardware for construction materials, which is eventually used in the extension or repair of a part of the house prior to fiesta.

> Just like someone employed as a maid in Manila who sent money to her mother with instructions on how to divide the amount for hollow blocks, for the *tampa* and for consumption. Everybody is like that, whether rich or poor, they always allocate for fiesta (Dagohoy, 2005).

The *Sabong* (Cock-fight Tournaments)

The *Sabungeros* (Cock-fighters) also have their time in the fiesta season because of cock-fighting derby tournaments. Prizes for winners are huge during special occasions such as the fiesta. Tournaments start two days before the fiesta. 'Whenever there is a cock-fight, there is always an economic opportunity for people'. There are people peddling food, others are hired as *Manari-ay* (person in-charge of putting blades on the rooster's legs) while true blue cock-fighters gamble for their chances of winning the cash prize.

Other Economic Opportunities

There are small-scale businesses that have emerged from the celebrations of fiestas. There are households engaged in raising pigs for roasting while others bake pastries like botarts, pies, tortas as desserts in the fiesta banquet. Some would work as cooks, washers, cleaners and landscape gardeners. There are people who peddled candles, scapulars, balloons, toys and images of the saint from one town to another during the fiesta season. One particular occupation during the fiesta which becomes a family activity is cooking. There are families in Bohol whose job is to cook in different fiestas. They have clients in various towns and always they have booked schedules already.

> We are used to this work to cook every fiesta. The dishes that we cook are fiesta food. I am in-charge in the cooking and seasoning while my husband is in-charge of the chopping and slicing of meat while one of my daughters is into slicing the different spices and seasoning and the other one is washing the dishes. Aside from getting our income from this job, we also have our *pana-ad* (pledge) of cooking good food for the fiesta (Pablita Inting).

Table 1.Summary of Fiesta Activities per Category

Spiritual	Socio-cultural	Economic
• *pana-ad* • Procession • *Bong Bolibong Kingking* (dancing in reverence to the patron saint)	• Family Reunions • Festivals • Fiesta Cuisine • Bring House • *Balos-Balos* (reciprocity) • Open House	• *Tampa-Tampa* (contribution) • Remittances and Demands • Cock-fight

The Fiesta and Local Tourism Cycle

The celebration of fiesta has been a part of the Boholano way of life. Throughout the year, Boholanos reside in different places due to the demands of their working life but when the fiesta season approaches, these people shift automatically to fiesta mode. This trend cuts across social classes and professions. For those away from Bohol, there is an urgency to go home for fiesta.

For local residents, they basically engage in the activities facilitated by the two major institutions in the community, the church and the family (household). The activities complement each other. There is a specific time for church preparations with the joint effort of the different religious and socio-civic organisations. There is a time for household preparations and community preparation with the supervision of the Local Government Unit (LGU). The Boholanos are used to budgeting their time for the church, community and household fiesta preparation. Activities during the fiesta are considered as a cycle and are grouped into pre-fiesta (Vespers or *Bisperas*), the fiesta proper (*Katumanan*) and the post-fiesta activities (*Liwas*).

> It's natural for the people to be engaged in the activities of the church and the household. It's always a cycle. The rest of the year, people worked hard either in the country or outside. But when it comes to fiesta season in Bohol, they really will go home to celebrate fiesta. Mostly for spiritual and social reasons (Monreal, 2009).

The cycle of celebrating fiesta can be validated in the number of arrivals at the points of entry of the province. The increase of arrivals starts in the month of April which signifies that the fiesta season is about to begin (Cabarrus, 2013). The Bohol Tourism Office (BTO) constantly monitors tourist arrivals at the sea and airports of the capital of the province. Table 2 shows the consistent increase in the number of domestic arrivals in the months of April to May, which coincides with the fiesta season. Furthermore, Figure 3 shows the trend of local and domestic arrivals in the province from 2009 to 2012. The high concentration of arrivals falls during the fiesta season (April-May). However, there is also a significant increase during the Christmas season but not as significant as during the fiesta season.

As for the foreign arrivals, they increase from December to February. Most foreigners spend their vacation or visit the province during the winter months in their home country. According to Ms Jo Cabarrus, the Provincial Tourism Officer, westerners prefer to visit tropical countries from late November to February to escape the cold temperature of their place (see Table 3) This signifies that there is a cycle of arrivals in the province. From April to May, domestic arrivals peak for fiesta season while December through to February constitute peak months for foreign arrivals. This means the domestic arrivals during the fiesta season are an indicator of the urgent need for the locals to go home to their towns to celebrate and partake in the different socio-cultural activities.

Table 2. Domestic Arrivals at Sea and Air Ports 2006-2012

Month	Year						
	2006	2007	2008	2009	2010	2011	2012
January	21,934	28,581	36,738	20,194	20,334	25,289	59,166
February	16,326	31,739	32,515	18,816	24,170	22,185	68,898
March	20,880	40,611	35,182	26,378	31,464	29,871	54,261
April	27,443	32,650	36,862	39,144	42,165	33,442	88,562
May	33,194	55,582	55,814	45,820	42,743	34,589	88,467
June	24,075	38,444	36,176	29,105	21,798	32,253	49,002
July	25,091	39,109	37,034	23,089	20,626	33,667	5,083
August	30,113	21,713	29,814	27,495	20,698	24,784	10,300
September	27,600	30,547	28,541	22,973	34,744	27,239	13,303
October	29,083	26,873	22,561	26,388	33,172	35,991	16,643
November	28,831	27,111	18,908	20,251	42,713	39,655	15,768
December	30,314	36,657	18,882	25,202	43,834	44,245	16,612
Total	314,884	409,617	389,027	324,855	378,461	383,210	486,065

Source: Bohol Tourism Office, 2013

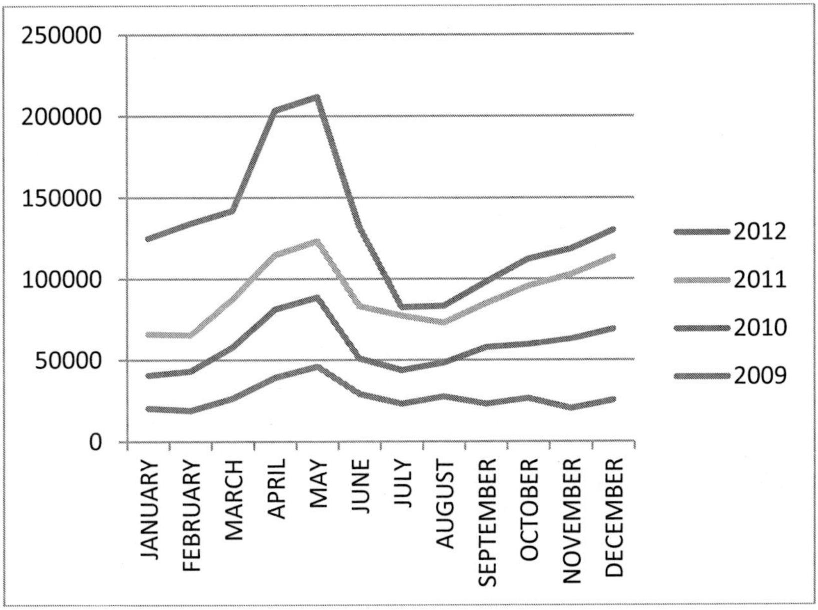

Figure 2. Trend of Domestic Arrivals in the Province from 2009-2012
Source: Bohol Tourism Office, 2013

Contribution to the Development of Local Tourism

Fiesta, as a socio-cultural activity significantly contributes to the development of local tourism. It basically promotes the five 'As' of the Tourism Supply Chain (Cabarrus, 2013). The five 'As' of tourism comprise Arrival, Access, Accommodation, Attraction and Activities. The people involved in the fiesta, the locals and their visitors have unconsciously contributed to the development of local tourism. The facilitation of family get-togethers during the fiesta season has indirectly contributed to the tourism supply chain (Monreal, 2013).

Table 3. Foreign Arrivals at Sea and Air Ports, 2006-2012

Month	Year						
	2006	2007	2008	2009	2010	2011	2012
January	8,729	11,216	18,114	14,575	12,279	15,838	19,172
February	8,302	11,508	21,791	11,426	18,603	14,059	17,169
March	9,533	10,770	18,058	11,011	11,615	14,245	13,259
April	8,587	10,307	15,125	11,199	9,687	11,956	17,555
May	9,196	6,520	10,282	10,044	10,198	13,652	13,041
June	7,426	8,230	14,629	8,106	14,825	14,487	10,340
July	8,476	8,649	17,700	10,530	15,732	14,174	3,839
August	8,905	8,793	15,424	14,438	23,066	9,809	14,692
September	7,627	9,890	12,893	10,404	11,526	9,993	11,159
October	8,175	10,913	12,857	12,831	9,124	15,658	11,202
November	8,894	10,581	9,565	9,697	6,680	11,165	10,523
December	9,296	14,817	11,709	12,065	10,265	11,509	13,598
Total =	103,146	122,194	178,147	136,326	153,600	156,545	155,549

Source: Bohol Tourism Office, 2013

On Arrivals

There is an increase in ticket sales for sea, air and land travel to the province. This specifically refers to domestic arrivals. There is also an increase in the arrangements for pre-arrival particularly for online ticket purchases and reservations. People returning home prefer to book in advance to get cheaper ticket prices. Table 2 shows the increase in domestic arrivals during the fiesta season.

On Access

Indirectly, the fiesta celebrations influenced the repair of roads leading to the towns. Repairs to the roads with potholes are evident in towns whose feast dates are near. With the influx of visitors returning to their home towns, the local government authorities established local tourism offices to highlight new local sites for the returning locals to explore. Different means of transportation are organised in every town. Visitors exploring sites can choose to rent a motorcycle, or hire a local motorcycle service, tricycle, *tricykad* (bicycle with sidecar), motorvan or bus (Monreal, 2013).

Due to the concentration of people, locals and Boholano tourists, during fiesta season, it indirectly contributed to the development and institutionalisation of the Tourist Police in 2008 (Office of the Governor, 2012). The police were deployed in ten towns of the province. The institution conducts mobile and foot patrols for crime prevention; the setting up of check points in tourist crowded areas and the provision of intelligence reports.

On Accommodation

The influx of domestic visitors has contributed to the development and establishment of accommodation in the province. Traditionally, returning locals (*balikbayan*) would just stay in the homes of their relatives not minding the space that they had to share with the rest of their family. More recently visiting family members, after spending time with their relatives, prefer to go to local resorts and hotels to unwind. There has been a significant increase in the amount of accommodation in the province. In the 1990s, there were less than fifty accommodation establishments registered like pension houses. Now, it has increased to 137 establishments (Office of the Governor, 2012).

In some towns, there are some households that have developed homestays. This was made possible because there are government agencies that provide training and capability-building activities to locals wanting to move into the homestay accommodation business (Roslinda, 2011). Homestays provide accommodation to returning locals who cannot be accommodated by their relatives as their houses are fully booked with other relatives. The accommodation is accessible to the visitors because it is located in the vicinity of their town.

On Attraction and Activities

Local Government Units (LGUs) have taken the opportunity to showcase and promote local attractions to local visitors during the fiesta season. Fiesta visitors will always look for new sights and attractions to be explored with their families after the fiesta. Local tourism officers have eventually developed brochures and other information materials about the towns and the sites to be visited. Local leaders together with church officials have also developed social activities during the fiesta season, which involve different sectors of the community. Various activities which range from the usual nightly social events such as the coronation of the fiesta king and queen, discos, bingo nights, beauty pageants to physical activities like marathons, small boat races, dragon boat races, fluvial processions to traditional activities like contests in weaving nipah leaves for roofing and local wine-drinking contests. These activities which are part of the local cultural and religious practices during fiestas are also considered to be vital visitor attractions and tourist activities (Monreal, 2013).

Synthesis and Conclusion

The fiesta culture of Bohol has come a long way from a ritualistic celebration of pre-Hispanic culture to its fusion into the Catholic religion. It has become a part of the lives of the Boholanos as it can be viewed and practised in different ways: spiritual, social and economic. The crucial element is the spiritual one, comprising the people's devotion to a patron. The urgent need of the Boholanos to come home and fulfill a *pana-ad* or vow/pledge to their patron saint readily explains how they value the practice. It depicts the priority of their spiritual obligation of paying homage to the patron before anything else. The dancing in front of the *caro* in *Bong Bolibong Kingking* manifests the fusion of pre-Hispanic practices and Catholicism. The procession depicts the sacrifice of the devotees. The social aspect like the feast, reunions and other social activities and practices comes into the scene as a derivative of the spiritual celebration.

As people come together for the fiesta, it strengthens the social ties among the Boholanos. The fiesta displays the generosity and the hospitality of the people. It is both a feast (referring to festivities and food) and a feast of the Catholic mass (referring to the homage to patron saints). For the people, the fiesta is never an economic liability. Spending and feasting is a way of sharing their blessings.

In the process of exploring the fiesta, it serves as a catalyst in the development of local tourism. Through the varied socio-cultural activities generated during the fiesta season, it has indirectly contributed to the tourism industry. Clearly, the socio-cultural and economic activities of the celebration spill-over to enable the further growth of local tourism. The institution of the fiesta has interwoven all elements in the society creating a tapestry of culture and tradition and an arena for domestic tourism development.

References

Agoncillo, T. (1990) *History of the Filipino People*, Quezon City: Garotech Publishing.

Apalisok, S. (1992) *Bohol without Tears: Volume 2: Bohol's 47 Towns and 1 City*, Surigao City: Surigao BB Press.

—. (1999) *Bohol without Tears: Land of the Country's Most Battered People. Volume 3: Bohol's Prehispanic Past to the Present*, Surigao City: Surigao BB Press.

Blair, E. and R. James *The Philippine Islands, 1493-1898. Vol. XIII., 1604-1605*, e-book by Project Guttenberg, retrieved from http://www.gutenberg.net, page consulted 10/6/2005.

Chirino, P. (1604) *Relacion De las Islas Filipinas*, e-book by Project Gutenberg, retrieved from http://www.gutenberg.net, page consulted 15/06/ 2005.

Hollsteiner, M. R. (ed.) (1979) *Society, Culture and the Filipino: A Textbook of Readings in Anthropology and Society*, Quezon City: Institute of Philippine Culture: Ateneo de Manila University Press.

Jabines, M.C. (2012) 'Spiritual and Socio-cultural Practices of Bohol Fiestas', *NEXUS*, 17: 80-96.

Office of the Governor (2012) *Bohol Economic Factbook*, Tagbilaran: Bohol Investment Promotion Center.

Provincial Planning and Development Office (PPDO) (2000) *The Bohol Provincial Profile*, Tagbilaran, Bohol.

Roces, A. R. (1980) *Fiestas*, Manila: PCPM Vera-Reyes Inc. Pictures.

Scott, W. H. (1994) *The Barangay: 16th Century Culture and Society*, Quezon City: Ateneo de Manila University Press.

Tirol, Jes B. (1998) 'Boholano Social and Cultural Traits', *Bohol Chronicle*, February 15.

—. (2007) *Fiestas in Bohol: its Economic, Social and Cultural Significance*, A Lecture presented during the Oral History National Conference, Silliman University, Dumaguete City, 5 December, 2007.

Trota-Jose, Regalado (2001) *Visita Iglesia Bohol: A Guide to Historic Churches*, Manila: National Commission on Culture and Arts (NCCA)

Personal Interviews

Ampusta, Nellie. Resident and People's Organization Organizer.Poblacion, Candijay, Bohol, May 19, 2005 (on the Fiesta Practices of Candijay, Bohol).

Boncales, Antonio. Resident, San Miguel, Bohol. May 9, 2005 (on Fiesta Practices of San Miguel, Bohol).

Biliran, Marcelino. Parish Priest. Holy Cross Parish, Maribojoc Bohol. May 3, 2005 (on the Significance and Practices of Fiesta Celebration).

Calipusan, Bennie. Business Sector and Socio-civic Leader.Bilar, Bohol. May 14, 2005 (on Socio-economic Activities during Fiesta).

Cabarrus, Josephine. Provincial Tourism Officer and Officer in Charge, Bohol Tourism Office. August 8, 2013 (on Contribution of Fiesta to Local Tourism).

Dagohoy, Adolf. Diocesan Priest. Talibon Parish, Talibon , Bohol. May 26, 2005 (on Fiesta Practices of Talibon, Bohol).

Inting, Pablita. Seasoned Cook in Fiestas. Tagbilaran City, Bohol. May 1, 2005 (on Fiesta Cuisine and Traditional Occupation as Cook).

Jabines, Mary Annie. Municipal Eco-tourism Heritage and Culture Officer, Municipality of Maribojoc, Bohol. August 6, 2013 (on Impact of Fiesta on Tourism).

Luspo, Marianito. Director, Office of Culture and Development (OCAD). Holy Name University.Tagbilaran City, Bohol. February 22, 2005 (on History of Fiesta and its Significance to Boholanos).

Luspo, Marianito. Director, Office of Culture and Development (OCAD). Holy Name University.

Tagbilaran City, Bohol. June 5, 2007 (on Data Validation of Fiesta Research and Additional Norms and Practices in Fiesta Celebration).

Monreal, Reigh. Culture and Arts Advocate and Heritage and Tourism Officer. Loon, Bohol. May 22, 2009 (on Traditional Fiesta Practices).

Monreal, Reigh. President, Bohol Association of Tourism Officers. August 7, 2013 (on Effects of Fiesta on Local Tourism).

Racho, Primitiva. Socio-civic and Religious Organization Leader. Holy Cross Parish, Maribojoc, Bohol. May 7, 2005 (on Preparatory Activities and Practices of Fiesta).

Roslinda, Emilia. Executive Director. PROCESS Bohol Inc. November 2011 (on Proliferation of Homestays).

Tabel, Felicidad. Socio-civic Leader. Tagbilaran City. May 1, 2005. (on Traditional Preparations and Practices of Fiesta).

Tirol, Jes. Director, Research and Development Office. University of Bohol, Tagbilaran City. May 11, 2005 (on History of Fiesta and its Practices and Implications).

Tirol, Jes. Director, Research and Development Office. University of Bohol, Tagbilaran City, June 6, 2007 (On the Practice of Fiesta).

Torralba, Milan Ted. Diocesan Chancellor and Diocesan Heritage Consultant. St. Joseph Cathedral. Tagbilaran City. May 13, 2005 (On the Religious Significance of Fiesta).

TOURISM AND POLITICAL AGENDAS IN THE DUM HUA PROCESSION IN THE SONGKRAN FESTIVAL

PLOYSRI PORANANOND

Introduction

Extensive academic studies have focused on festivals and their political motivation. Carnivals were especially driven by political considerations from the start. What makes a carnival stand out is the manner in which it has been used by both the subordinated groups against government authorities, often to make their cause heard, and the ruling class to suppress the reality of a divided society through the portrayal of a united country of diverse people.

The Songkran Festival in Chiang Mai is similar to a carnival, due to the fact that its performance is politically driven. The Songkran Festival was first known to people in Bangkok through the promotion of train travel to Chiang Mai. Consequently, Songkran has become synonymous with the culture and has been promoted to the rank of a tourist attraction for Thai national tourists.

The political agenda of provincial government officials is also obvious in the invention of a procession called Dum Hua by using traditional Lanna culture. Although the political agendas behind the procession have evolved during the last fifty years since it was introduced, they have always been a part of the procession.

Political Roles and Meanings of Festival Performances

Several scholars agree that the carnival is a form of festive activity related to political actions or agendas (Cohen, 1982; Bakhtin, 1984; Gilmore 1998; Guss, 2000). In other words, a festival in the form of a carnival was used as a time-space event for the subordinate class to express an oppositional consciousness (Cohen, 1982; Gilmore, 1998). Bakhtin, a Russian theorist, views the carnival as the outcome of social conflict and as a revolutionary event (1984). He asserts that the logic of the carnival relates to the confrontation of oppositions. Similarly, Guss (2000) argues that the carnival comprises a process of masking and unmasking, or the way people hide themselves under masks by presenting their oppositional thoughts through forms of mimicry, parody and satire. A carnival, in this way, is seen as a means to express class, race and gender oppositions, a symbol of social reversal, or a time when the world is turned upside-down (Bakhtin, 1984). For instance, the Caracas Carnival in Venezuela has long been a site of active and even violent contestation. It was the first festival in Venezuela in which students demonstrated their political agendas to resist the ruling class during the dictatorship regime (Guss, 2000). Cohen (1982) recognises the Notting Hill Carnival as a symbol of the struggle of minority groups in British society. Thus, the political function of the Notting Hill Carnival is to serve as a 'medium for expressing and organizing protest' (ibid: 34). Indeed, the Notting Hill Carnival was planned by locals under pressures due to the housing problems in this area and amid violent confrontation with police. Accordingly, the early performances in the Notting Hill Carnival expressed resistance to the British authorities (ibid).

Similarly, Nurse (1999) points out that many carnivals in post-colonial countries are related to political actions. The Trinidad Carnival in the post-slavery period was used by the local black people to instigate a riot against the colonial authorities. The carnivals in Latin America and the Caribbean have also evolved in connection with political conflicts. As a result, Rio's carnival in Brazil, the carnivals of Santiago de Cuba, and the Barranquilla carnival in Columbia are the reflection of social forces. Nurse (1999) adds that in some societies, such as Brazil, the expression of African ancestral identity subverted the official Catholic institutions. In this way, the carnival is seen as politics masquerading behind cultural forms or rituals of resistance.

As discussed above, the carnival is also conceived as a ritual practice, which provides a means of political-symbolic communication to its participants. Thus, carnivals can be seen as rituals of reversal, of conflict and of rebellion. According to Gilmore, the ritual of rebellion is a 'ritual that allows for institutionalized protest, and in complex ways renews the unity of the system' (1998: 30). In this way, carnivals enable the poor to renew their rebellion against the political order and the restrictions of the social order. It is a time of permission, a time when people expect to provoke and to challenge something. The carnival is also understood as a ritual of conflict when tensions between segments of society are revealed (Campbell, 1988; Nurse, 1999). There is agreement between scholars that where social groups are in conflict and 'where no higher mechanism can provide mediation, ritualism provides a safe outlet for the expression of potential conflict' (Gilmore, 1998: 31).

In contrast to carnivals, several festivals celebrate the institutionalised components of the nation-state. In some countries, festivals are used by nationalists to develop a sense of one's own nationality in an infant democratic nation. In this way, performances express the unity of people in the country (Guss, 2000). According to Marschall (2006), festivals in this sense are invented as a venue for nurturing the melting pot of a country's cultural diversity and to create the new national symbol of the 'rainbow nation', or a nation with different cultural groups.

Specific devices have been employed by the subordinate class to reflect their political ideas and agendas in carnivals. Bakhtin (1984) considers the creation, by ordinary people, of carnival lyrics as tools to 'praise' and 'abuse' the elites and authorities. Accordingly, carnival lyrics and carnival songs can be used for humour, or to admire someone or something. Nevertheless, in addition, the lyrics can easily be swayed to satirise, insult, openly criticise or incite against the ruling class (Cohen, 1982). With a similar view, Gilmore (1998) points out that the successful lyrics of carnival songs must have the essential 'spice' as an ingredient. This can be in terms of provocative and sexually suggestive lyrics, while some people may favour more violent forms of expression via 'verbal attack or verbal abuse' (ibid: 24). Thus, lyrics became 'symbolic violence' and 'the verbal aggression of public insult' (ibid: 14, 24). It comes as no surprise, then, that carnivals were seen as vulgar and violent by the middle class and immoral by the high priests (Turner, 1987), and that in some societies, authorities tried to ban this kind of celebration (Nurse, 1999) and managed to do so during periods of dictatorship (Gilmore, 1998). On the other hand, carnival lyrics are also seen as messages that people in the same society use to 'define themselves to themselves' (Geertz, 1983: 58). In other words, they reflect how people experience and perceive their society (Gilmore, 1998). Therefore, the deep secrets in society can be exhibited through the messages of these oral productions. The carnival, in this sense, can be seen as a festivity of the lower working class, in which they can express their point of view to the world. Accordingly, the carnival is a political ritual for these people. In addition to lyrics, costumes in carnivals can also be employed as devices against dictatorship. Thus, people use the carnival to express their 'ritual of rebellion' by performing as comedians, soldiers or pirates in fancy costumes to satirise the dictators (Gilmore, 1998).

By contrast, festival celebrations in some societies are controlled by churches, authority groups or the state (DaMatta, 1991; Guss, 2000). Nurse (1999: 665) considers that actually, 'carnivals were set up exclusively by dominant groups to allow subordinate groups to play at rebellion'. In this view, the dominant or ruling class uses the carnival as a 'safety-valve', so 'letting the steam off', or releasing political tensions, social conflicts, or stress in society (Nurse, 1999: 666; see also Gilmore, 1998), in other words, to allow people to play the fool.

Political Development of Chiang Mai

Chiang Mai, a city situated in northern Thailand, has always been a desirable place to visit for Thai people as it is perceived as a historic place with a unique culture. Indeed, Chiang Mai has a long history which dates back over 700 years. As a former capital of the Lanna Kingdom, Chiang Mai has been embedded within the unique Lanna culture for generations.

Chiang Mai was ruled by the traditional rulers for hundreds of years before it was annexed as part of Thailand in the reign of King Chulalongkorn (1868-1910). It was founded as an independent state and the capital of the Lanna Kingdom in 1296. Initially, the traditional rulers who were respected as kings ruled Chiang Mai; furthermore, the surrounding states were governed by the ruler's families or noblemen, while the other lands controlled by Chiang Mai had their own rulers. These controlled areas were the lands of the Tai people in the Shan State and Keng Tung in Burma, Xishuangbanna in Southern China, and the land of the Lue people in Burma (Ongsakul, 2001).

Chiang Mai was ruled by Burma for 216 years from 1558 to 1774 before it came under the control of Siam (Ongsakul, 2001). During the period of Burmese rule, the Kings and Queens of Burma were appointed to rule Chiang Mai (Na-Chiang Mai, 1996). Later, King Taksin of Siam helped to free Chiang Mai from the control of Burma, and Chiang Mai came under the control of Siam (ibid). The relationship between Chiang Mai and Bangkok became closer than that of a controlled land when Princess Dararusamee, the daughter of Chiang Mai's ruler Phra Chao Inthawitchyanond, became the consort of King Chulalongkorn (Charoenmuang, 1999). Pitpreecha (1999) has claimed that Princess Dararusamee was a 'political hostage' of Siam to guarantee the allegiance of Chiang Mai to Siam. This can be viewed as a very astutely arranged marriage within Siam because, at that time, Burma was a British colony and traditionally Chiang Mai had a closer economic and political relationship with Burma than with Siam.

In the same period, during the late nineteenth century, the logging industry owned by the British in Chiang Mai became involved in the conflict between Chiang Mai and Siam, since traditionally there was no clear borderline between the states. This traditional practice could not be accepted by the modern management of the logging companies because they needed the correct borders to be drawn for the permission to access forests from the ruling family, since all forests in the North were owned by the royal family. As a result, some forest areas, offered for concessions by the ruling family, overlapped and some of the employees of these companies, who were protected by British law, were harmed by the ruling family. These problems brought about conflicts between the ruling family and the British-owned companies which ultimately asked the Siamese government to manage the problems for them, as at the time Chiang Mai was under the control of Siam (Charoenmuang, 1999; Ongsakul, 2001).

The conflicts between the ruling family and the British logging companies affected the course of modernity in Chiang Mai. Firstly, it forced the Siamese government to sign the first 'Chiang Mai Treaty' with the British government in India in 1874. One result of this was that Siamese officials were sent from Bangkok to oversee the ruler of Chiang Mai and to ensure that he followed the treaty. However, the first treaty did not stop the conflicts in the logging business; thus, the second 'Chiang Mai Treaty' was signed in 1884. Consequently, an international court was established in Chiang Mai to manage the conflicts among the different parties involved in logging. Finally, a western lawyer was sent to Chiang Mai to try to impose legal order on the situation (Chanwitan, 1996). Out of this conflict came the establishment of a British Consulate and a Department of Forestry in Chiang Mai. During the reign of King Chulalongkorn a modern map of Siam was drawn up and clear borderlines delineated between different areas of the region. This did much to quell the logging disputes.

It is claimed that the involvement of Siam in the conflict between the ruler of Chiang Mai and the British-owned companies is one factor that forced

Siam to reform its political system, with the result that Chiang Mai was included as part of Siam (Charoenmuang, 1999). Because of this the lands in the name of the Lanna Kingdom disappeared through a new form of political arrangement, introduced late in King Chulalongkorn's reign. The reformation of the Siamese political system affected the traditional political system of Chiang Mai when the first Siamese official was sent to help the ruler govern the city in 1874. The ruler of Chiang Mai lost much of his power and many of his benefits to Siam. For instance all forests in Chiang Mai which were owned by the ruler under the traditional system came to be owned by Siam (Ongsakul, 2001). In the beginning, Siamese noblemen were sent to control the Northern region, including Chiang Mai, a political strategy of Siam to decrease the traditional power of the ruler of Chiang Mai. However, it was also seen as the strategy that could decrease British control over the city.

The new political system of Siam had a greater impact on Chiang Mai after a brother of King Chulalongkorn was sent to rule the city as a court official of Siam. The 'Payap Precinct' was first established in 1885 by the Siamese government as the 'regional government' and Chiang Mai and some cities in the north were ruled as 'a special governance area'. At the same time, the old form of traditional authority by the ruler still existed, but the new form of governance was grafted on top of this rule and the traditional ruler of Chiang Mai did not hold any power in the governance system. After the Thai revolution, the monarchical system changed to become a democracy in 1932. The centralisation system, which emerged in the reign of King Chulalongkorn, affected Chiang Mai, a former capital of the Lanna Kingdom, as it was annexed as part of Siam and eventually became a province of Thailand.

Songkran Festival and Tourism Promotion

Songkran is a traditional festival to celebrate the Lanna New Year (Rungruangsri, 1997). It is thought that the word *Songkran* is derived from the Pali word *Sankhara,* which refers to the passing of the sun from Pisces to Aries (Payomyong, 1976). Songkran is the most significant of the traditional Lanna ritual practices. At present, the term Lanna people refers to the people who live in the northern provinces of Thailand (Ongsakul, 2001). The activities of Songkran in Chiang Mai are thought to be unique to Lanna culture.

For the Lanna people, the three days of traditional Songkran (April 13-15) carry both a religious and a more secularly located significance relating to recreation and enjoyment for local people and a break from normal life. In the past the Songkran was an occasion for communal celebration and an opportunity for young people to meet publicly. Moreover, it was a time for young people to pay respect to their elders and to ask for forgiveness for any inappropriate things they may have done during the previous year. In response to this form of confession, elders would bless the youngsters and wish them good luck and good health through the New Year. Such activities would thus assist in strengthening social relations, reinforcing traditional social cohesion and hierarchies (Payomyong, 1976; Rungruangsri, 1997).

Chiang Mai became the destination for visitors from Bangkok and other provinces who liked to join the Songkran in Chiang Mai. There were many factors that affected the influx of Thai tourists to Chiang Mai during Songkran in the 1950s to 1960s for instance; the promotion of train travel for Songkran in Chiang Mai (Asanachinta, 1992) through the reduction of the train fare (Chutima, 2000, interview). At the same time, the image of Chiang Mai was invented as the land of beautiful women and the orchid by the elite class and local media for tourism promotion (Rattana, 2000) This affected the demand of the Thai people at that time who wanted to visit Chiang Mai at least once in their lifetime.

Tourism promotion of Chiang Mai, together with transportation development, enhanced the popularity of Songkran, especially for Thai tourists. The construction of the highway from Bangkok to Chiang Mai, begun during the Sarit regime (1959-1963) and completed in 1967, led to an increase in the number of tourists coming from Bangkok for Songkran. Tourism promotion of Chiang Mai as a tourist centre of the North in 1977, the economic boom and tourism boom in Thailand during the 1980s to 1990s, and government policy to promote Songkran in Chiang Mai as ‘Mega Songkran 2004’ can be viewed as additional factors in increasing the numbers of tourists in Songkran.

Political Agendas and the Invention of the Dum Hua Procession in Songkran in 1964

The Dum Hua procession emerged in Songkran on the afternoon of April 15, 1964. The major purpose of the invention of this procession by the provincial officials (Chaiyanam, 1985) was to pay respect to Mr.

Nirandorn Chaiyanam, the Governor of Chiang Mai at that time. The procession paraded from the provincial government office to the residence of the governor on the bank of the Ping River near Nawarat Bridge (*Khon Muang*, April 13, 1965: 4). Traditionally, the Dum Hua is a practice of the local people during Songkran to pay respect to their elders and to ask for forgiveness for inappropriate words or impolite behaviour during the previous year. Furthermore, groups of local people came to pay respect to the traditional rulers during Songkran. This marked the first time that the local people had to pay respect to the city governor, who had been appointed by the central government in Bangkok as the highest ranking official in Chiang Mai. It is arguable that the invention of the Dum Hua procession had a political purpose in re-orienting the respect of the local people from their traditional ruler towards the provincial governor as the representative of the Thai central government. This phenomenon can be seen as an attempt by Thai officials to decrease the power of the traditional ruler in Chiang Mai, with Songkran providing a suitable time and space to express this political agenda.

Continuity, Decoration and Increasing Groups in the Dum Hua Procession

After the establishment of the Dum Hua procession in 1964, groups of participants in the procession increased over time. In the first Dum Hua procession, only the provincial officials and people in the heart of the city participated (*Khon Muang,* April 13, 1965: 4). Later, more groups of people, such as teachers from all districts, heads of sub-districts and the heads of the villages, were authorised to participate in this procession by the provincial government via the district government offices (*Khon Muang*, April 12, 1966: 4). Essentially, all of the participants in the Dum Hua procession in this period were local people.

Later on, the Dum Hua procession became more decorative. In 1970, an artificial elephant and three pairs of artificial oxen were added (*Khon Muang*, April 15, 1970: 4). In 1977, it was reported that 'tourists from other provinces were amazed that the "Dum Hua" procession was decorated by small beautiful processions and exotic performances that one cannot see anywhere else in Thailand' (*Thai News*, April 17, 1977: 1). The first one was a convoy of police jeeps and motorcycles, followed by a troop of men carrying flags, a group of men in army costumes, and groups of traditional drummers and dancers. This expresses the change in the pattern and practices in the Dum Hua procession in Songkran.

Figure 1: The Dum Hua procession in 1983
Source: *Raming* (1983), April 16: 9

More groups of people participated in the Dum Hua procession. In 1977, groups of officials from all districts in Chiang Mai, including government departments, organisations, associations and private businesses, joined in the Dum Hua procession (*Thai News*, April 11, 1977: 6). Furthermore, the numbers of women participating in the procession increased. Thus, beautiful women who won the beauty contests were assigned to hold the signs of the small processions and, in 1977, there were 34 groups of people who participated. It was said that 'the visitors would be stunned by these beautiful parades which they could not see anywhere else' (*Thai News*, April 17, 1977: 1). In 1980, more groups from the government and private sectors began to participate in the 'Dum Hua' procession. It was reported in the local newspaper that

> [B]esides the government sections in the city and in all districts, private businesses, companies and state enterprise were informed to bring their employees to participate in the Dum Hua procession. This increased the number of participants in the procession [...]. This makes the procession look very grand compared to the past [...] (*Raming*, April 3, 1977: 3).

In 1984, all government agencies and divisions, plus all Thai, Chinese, Indian merchants and foreign businessmen in Chiang Mai, cooperated to conduct the small groups of processions and floats which were decorated with fruits and vegetables in the Dum Hua procession (*Raming*, April 7,

1984: 3). Again, this indicates the continually increasing numbers of groups of participants and the increasing use of decoration in the Dum Hua procession.

The number of participants in the Dum Hua procession increased considerably during the 1990s. In 1990, the numbers of traditional dancers increased to 100, with 90 dancers from the nine sub-districts in the city and ten from the Office of the Muang District (*Thai News*, April 12, 1990: 7). Furthermore, thousands of local people were spectators of the procession along the roads in the city (*Chiang Mai News*, April 16, 1995: 4). Groups of government officials also increased in the procession. In 1995, the deputy governors and the other provincial officials led the procession, followed by groups of officials from the municipality, including the city mayor and the municipal councillors. In 1997, there were three vice-governors of Chiang Mai and their wives leading the procession, followed by groups of officials from 24 districts, as well as groups of other government sectors and groups from the private sectors (*Thai News*, April 15, 1997: 15). Later, more groups of people participated. These included: groups of private businesses in Chiang Mai; the Association of Hotels in the North; people from every district in Chiang Mai; staff from media and all channels of television; and newspaper reporters (*Chiang Mai News*, April 19, 1995: 4). It can be seen that the increasing number of groups of people in the 1990s comprised both government officials and private sector groups. However, these were regarded as local groups.

In the 2000s, other groups participated in the Dum Hua procession. People from remote rural areas and the hill-tribe groups were invited to join with the authorisation of the provincial government (Hongladalom, 2004, interview). Later, additional groups of hill-tribe people were brought in to join the procession in Songkran in order to promote tourism in the city.

In 2003, there were 35 groups of people with 15,000 participants in the procession from the Ta Pae Gate to the governor's residence on the bank of the Ping River (*Thai News*, April 15, 2003: 2). In 2004, 50 groups of participants paraded. Furthermore, there were groups of business companies from Bangkok and foreign groups in the procession in 2004.

Figure 2: A parade of the Lahu tribe in the Dum Hua procession in 2004
Source: Ploysri Porananond

Figure 3: A parade of the Hmong tribe in the Dum Hua procession in 2004
Source: Ploysri Porananond

Figure 4: Groups of municipal officials and their wives in the Dum Hua Procession in 2003
Source: *Thai News* (2003), April 12: 1

Figure 5: Performance of a tribal group to express their identity in the Dum Hua procession in 2006
Source: Ploysri Porananond

Tourism can be viewed as a factor in the elaboration of decorations and the increasing number of groups of people in the Dum Hua procession. To respond to the tourism policy of the government, more groups of local people were asked to join by the local authorities. In this way, the Dum Hua procession was more elaborately decorated and colourful to make it attractive to tourists in Songkran.

Discussion

Studies of scholars acknowledge that carnivals can be viewed as devices for political action or agendas (Cohen, 1982; Bakhtin, 1984; Gilmore 1998; Guss, 2000). There are various understandings of the political function of carnivals in the past. For instance, it is argued that they were used as a weapon in the political struggle against class domination but also against restrictions of social order (Campbell, 1988; Gilmore, 1998; Nurse, 1999), and that carnivals were the outcome of social conflict or revolution (Bakhtin, 1984). Carnivals, in this sense, are viewed as 'ritual practices' which provide a means of political symbolic communication to participants. In this way, they can be seen as rituals of reversal, of conflict and of rebellion, 'where no higher mechanism can provide mediation, ritualism provides a safe outlet for the expression of potential conflict' (Gilmore, 1998: 31).

The invention of the Dum Hua procession in Songkran in 1964 can be viewed as the use of this procession as a tool for political purposes of the organising group. It can be regarded as the use of a traditional practice of the Lanna people for political advantage by the ruling class in Chiang Mai and the Thai government in Bangkok.

The political history of Chiang Mai and Siam can be linked to the invention of the Dum Hua procession. It was established to pay respect to the governor who was sent by the central government in Bangkok to govern Chiang Mai and hence the political history, and the processes by which Chiang Mai became part of Thailand, should be considered. It can be argued that without the city's involvement with the imperial power via the British-owned logging businesses, Chiang Mai would not have been included as part of Thailand. The conflicts between the British-owned logging businesses and the traditional ruler of Chiang Mai regarding access to concession forests forced the Siamese government to sign a 'Chiang Mai Treaty' with the British government in India in 1874 and again in 1884. The situation caused Siam to pay more attention to Chiang

Mai, which Charoenmuang (1999) views as one factor in forcing Siam to reform its political system, with the result that Chiang Mai was included as part of Siam. In relation to the first 'Chiang Mai Treaty', Siamese officials were sent from Bangkok to oversee the ruler of Chiang Mai and to ensure that the ruler followed the treaty. After Chiang Mai became part of Thailand, government officials, such as the governor, were sent from the central government in Bangkok to rule Chiang Mai.

The invention of the Dum Hua procession in 1964 demonstrates how the Thai government in Bangkok took a political decision to reduce the power of the traditional ruler and to re-orientate the respect of local people in Chiang Mai towards the governor. In this sense, to employ the term 'Dum Hua' (pay respect) in this practice can be viewed as politically motivated. Again, following the theories put forward by Greenwood (1989) and DaMatta (1991), who view festival processions as ritual practices, the Dum Hua procession can be viewed as a ritual practice of the Thai government, with a hidden political agenda. It presented the symbols that the local people, in terms of the government officials and several local groups, used in order to pay respect to the city governor as the highest ranking official in the city, or in another symbol, the new ruler of Chiang Mai. In terms of 'rites of conspicuous display', the present discussion follows Falassi (1987: 4), although the Dum Hua procession expressed respect for the governor from groups of local people, it also mimicked political symbolic signs and in doing so, decreased traditional power and respect in Chiang Mai. In this way, Songkran was first used for political purposes by the Thai government via the government officials. In other words, the Dum Hua was invented to present the unity of groups of people in the same society. This demonstrates how the festival was employed by the authorities to control local people in the festival location (Guss, 2000). Furthermore, political advantage was exercised by the participation in Songkran.

The participation of local government officials in the Songkran Dum Hua procession can be viewed as a political practice. Campbell (1988), Cohen (1982) and Greenwood (1989) all suggest that festival performances can be used by different groups of people to express themselves. In this way, the participation (as the procession leaders) of the officials can be seen as a means for them to express their authority or power to the crowd in Songkran. According to DaMatta (1991), festival performance spaces are occupied differently and a hierarchical space is prepared in festivals for elites or authorities, which DaMatta calls a 'high platform'. In this sense, spaces where these local high ranking officials are contained, at the head of processions, can be judged as the 'high platform'. These spaces are arranged for these authorities separately from other spaces in the processions used by commoners, who tend to be followers in the processions. In this way, participation in the procession has assisted in creating political images of the local high ranking officials in Chiang Mai as the authority class. In other words, spaces in the Dum Hua procession were used and arranged differently by the local authority group for political purposes, where heads of districts and the other high-ranking officials in the district led the parades while local people from villages and the hill tribes were merely the followers.

It is observed that the Dum Hua procession in Songkran, which was invented in 1964 to serve the political purposes of the ruling group in the city, continued to be used to express the power of government officials at provincial and district levels. As Burr (2006) and Hughes (2006) suggest, the original aims of festivals -- especially carnivals in several societies as protests or expressions of resistance – are changed. The use of the Dum Hua procession changed the original political aims. The procession invented in 1964 as a symbol to decrease traditional power over Chiang Mai was thus transformed into spaces in which to present the authority and power of the new political elite in the local society. In other words, the Dum Hua procession may not simply serve as a means to pay respect to the governor, but to publicly serve the political aims of those in power.

If one accepts the views of Turner (1969, 1982), the organisation and participation in the Dum Hua procession can be regarded as reflections of the 'lived-in-world'; the reality of how these different social class groups are organised may be reflected in the organisation of the participants in the processions. The high-ranking officials at the provincial head office in the city of Chiang Mai used government authority over the head of district officials to ask for their cooperation in encouraging local people to join in the Dum Hua procession. Then, district officials asked the lower level officials for similar cooperation (Hongladarom, 2004, interview). This process of encouraging local people to join in the procession can be considered as a political exercise of those in power over those local people who are powerless. The organisation and participation in the procession can also reflect the reality of different social classes (in terms of economic and political power) living in the local society of Chiang Mai.

The participation in the Dum Hua procession of minority groups can also be considered in political terms. Although in the 2000s, the hill tribe groups may have been forced to join in the procession through the authority of government officials, it may in fact be the case, as Campbell (1988), Cohen (1982) and Greenwood (1989) suggest in other contexts, that these minority groups actually used this opportunity for their political advantage, to express themselves through their traditional costumes and cultural performances in public. In this way, Dum Hua becomes a time and space for them to transform their negative identities into positive ones, as marked by the government in the past, among the crowds and media in Songkran (Leepreecha, 2003; Luangaramsri, 2003; Bunyasaranai, 2003). As Guss (2000) suggests, the cultural identities of many ethnic groups in festival performances can present cultural diversity in the society where the festivals are located. The participation and presentation in the procession of the hill tribe groups have contributed to their new images, but also to their recognition by Thai society as people belonging to the same national community. In summary, the Songkran Dum Hua procession provides space for unseen groups in the society to be seen in public.

DaMatta (1991) finds that the tail-end of processions, which provide platforms for the lower class, always appeared as unstructured spaces – in other words, spaces without a master or authoritative order. Thus, these spaces were used by the commoners or working class groups for 'play', with musical performance and dance. These enjoyable spaces in processions can be viewed as spaces of 'rite without a master' (DaMatta, 1991). They can be regarded as 'liminal' spaces, in Turner's terms (1969), or spaces for drinking, dancing, and freedom from order in comparison with spaces at the head of processions, which are more ordered as hierarchical spaces. The tail-end of small parades in the Dum Hua procession in Songkran were the loose spaces where the powerless groups of people used to play in a drunken style of dancing with their traditional musical instruments. These separated head and tail spaces can reflect the reality of local society in Chiang Mai, in terms of social classes, class identities and behavioural presentation.

Conclusion

The political agenda to decrease the power of the traditional ruler of Chiang Mai, a former capital of the Lanna Kingdom, is discussed in the invention of the Dum Hua procession in 1964. The political development of Thailand or Siam before 1939 can be viewed as a factor in explaining the politicisation of a festival. The conflicts between the traditional rulers of Chiang Mai and the British companies in the logging industry is considered to be the driving force in Siam gaining control over Chiang Mai. As a result, Chiang Mai became incorporated as a province of Thailand.

This study examines the invention of the Dum Hua procession organised by the provincial officials during the Songkran Festival in Chiang Mai in 1964. This invention of tradition was motivated by a political agenda to decrease the power of the traditional ruler of Chiang Mai. The traditional practices of Lanna culture, including the Dum Hua, were used as a political tool to achieve this goal. Although the early political aims of the procession have disappeared from the present Dum Hua procession, political motives have never been absent. Groups of participants in the present procession also continue using their participation for political purposes, and in turn the politics of festival has also served to encourage tourism.

References

Asanachinta, P. (1992) 'Roles of the local people in promoting the tourism industry'. In: *Memorial book distributed in the royal conferring cremation of Professor Colonel Phoon Phon Asanachinta*, Chiang Mai, 1 February, pp. 345-351 (in Thai)

Bakhtin, M. (1984) *Rabelais and His World* (Helene Iswolsky trans.), Bloomington and Indianapolis: Indiana University Press.

Bunyasaranai, P. (2003) 'Akha Tribe: The image construction as dirty and undeveloped but attractive'. In Pinkaew Luangaramsri (ed.) Identity, Races and Marginality. Bangkok: Anthropology Centre.

Burr, A. (2006) 'The Freedom of the slaves to walk the streets': celebration, spontaneity and revelry versus logistics at Notting Hill Carnival. In D. Picard and M. Robinson (eds.) *Festivals, Tourism and Social Change*, Clevedon: Channel View Publication pp. 84-98

Campbell, S. (1988) 'Carnival, Calypso and Class Struggle in Nineteenth Century Trinidad', *History Workshop*, 26:1-27.

Chaiyanam, N (1985) *Publication distributed at the royal supported cremation for Nirandorn Chaiyanam*, Bangkok: Press for Local Part, Department of Local Administration.

Chanwitan, P. (1996) *Lanna Thai in the Reign of King Chulalongkorn*, Bangkok: Karan Printing (in Thai).

Charoenmuang, T. (1999) *A Hundred Years of the Siam and Lanna Relationship 1899 to 1999*. Chiang Mai: The Project to Study Local Politics, Faculty of Social Science, Chiang Mai University (in Thai).

Cohen, A. (1982) 'A Polyethnic London Carnival as a Contested Cultural Performance', *Ethnic and Racial Studies*, 5: 23-41.

—. (1993) *Masquerade Politics: Explorations in the Structure of Urban Cultural Movements,* Oxford: Berg.

DaMatta, R. (1991) *Carnivals, Rogues, and Heroes: an Interpretation of the Brazilian Dilemma,* Notre Dame: University of Notre Dame Press.

Falssi, A. (ed.) (1987) *Time out of Time: Essays on the Festival*, Albuquerque: University of New Mexico Press.

Geertz, Clifford (1983) *Local Knowledge: Further Essays in Interpretative Anthropology*, New York: Basic Books.

Gilmore, D. D. (1998) *Carnival and Culture: Sex, Symbol and Status in Spain*, New Haven and London: Yale University Press.

Greenwood, D. J. (1989) 'Culture by the Pound: An Anthropological Perspective on Tourism as Cultural Commodization'. In Valene Smith (ed.), *Hosts and Guests: The Anthropology of Tourism*, University of Pennsylvania Press, Philadelphia (second revised edition), pp. 171-186.

Guss, D. M. (2000) *The Festive State: Race, Ethnicity, and Nationalism as Cultural Performance,* Berkeley: University of California Press.

Hughes, L. H. (2006) 'Gay and Lesbian Festivals: Tourism in the Change from Politics to Party'. In D. Picard and M. Robinson (eds), *Festivals, Tourism and Social Change: Remaking Worlds*. Clevedon: Channel View, pp.238 – 254.

Laungaramsri, Pinkaew (ed.), (2003) *Identity, Races and Marginality,* Bangkok: Anthropology Centre (in Thai).

Leepreecha, P. (2003) 'Clan Identity of the Hmong among Modernisation'. In Pinkaew Laungaramsri (ed.), *Identity, Races and Marginality,* Bangkok: Anthropology Centre (in Thai).

Marschall, S. (2006) 'Creating the "Rainbow Nation": the National Women's Art Festival in Durban, South Africa'. In D. Picard and M. Robinson (eds), *Festivals, Tourism and Social Change: Remaking Worlds*, Clevedon: Channel View, pp. 152-171.

Na-Chiang Mai, W. (1996) *The Rulers of Chiang Mai*, Bangkok: Amarin Printing and Publishing (in Thai).

Nurse, K. (1999) 'Globalization and Trinidad Carnival: Diaspora, Hybridity and Identity in Global Culture', *Cultural Studies*, 13: 661-690.

Ongsakul, S. (2001) *History of the Lanna*, Bangkok: Amarin Printing and Publishing (in Thai).
Payomyong, M. (1976) *Lanna Traditions within Twelve Months*, Chiang Mai: Sor Sapkarnpim (in Thai).
Pitpreecha, J. (1999) *A Man Called Louis*. Bangkok: Prapuntsarn (in Thai).
Ratana, P. (2000) *Image of the northern women from the 25th to 26th Buddhist century*, Master's Thesis, Chiang Mai University. (in Thai)
Rungruangsri, U. (1997) 'Songkran Lanna: Traditional New Year', *Traditional New Year Festivals in Five Countries: a Comparative Cultural Study,* Chiang Mai University: Public and Affairs Division, Department of Information, and Center for the Promotion of Arts and Culture, Ministry of Foreign Affairs.
Turner, V. W. (1969) *The Ritual Process: Structure and Anti-structure*, Chicago: Aldine Pub. Co.
—. (ed.) (1982) *Celebration: Studies in Festivity and Ritual*, Washington, D.C: Smithsonian Institution Press.
—. (1987) 'Carnival, Ritual, and Play in Rio de Janeiro'. In Alessandro Falassi (ed.), *Time Out of Time: Essays on the Festival*, Albuquerque: University of New Mexico Press, pp. 74-90.

Local Newspapers

KhonMuang, April 13, 1965: 4
KhonMuang, April 12, 1966: 4
KhonMuang, April 15, 1970: 4
Raming, April 3, 1977: 3
Thai News, April 17, 1977: 1
Raming, April 7, 1984: 3
Thai News, April 12, 1990: 7
Chiang Mai News, April 16, 1995: 4
Chiang Mai News, April 19, 1995: 4
Thai News, April 15, 1997: 15
Thai News, April 15, 2003: 2

Photographs

Raming, April 16, 1983: 9
Thai News, April 12, 2003: 1

TOURISM ENCOUNTERS, COMMODITISATION AND LOCAL RESPONSES

The Commodification of 'Rurality' in Mae Kam Pong Village for Japanese Long-stay Tourism in Chiang Mai

Amnaj Khaokhrueamuang

Introduction

Trends in global tourism indicate that long-stay tourism is a growing market segment that comprises an ever-increasing elderly population whose primary need is to maintain their health (Schröder and Widmann, 2007). In Thailand, Japanese long-stay has been considered a tourism niche market since the late 1990s, after receiving international retirees and promoting health and medical tourism (Ono, 2008), including long-stay travel projects for tourist cities (Ugotreviews, 2013). In recent years, the number of long-stay Japanese has increased, especially in Chiang Mai, which has embraced no fewer than 3,000 (*Bangkok Post*, 2011; Krailearg, 2011; Chamchan and Soparat, 2012), and the trend has grown since the Great East Japan Earthquake and tsunami in March 2011 (*TTRweekly*, 2012). Chiang Mai, as one of five pilot provinces (Hongsranagon, 2005) and the hub of medical and health tourism for long-stay tourists since 2003, has advocated this opportunity to private sector companies that operate commodities and services such as Japanese restaurants, hospitals, apartments, and condominiums. Nevertheless, Chiang Mai still lacks interactions between Japanese long-stay residents and local communities, most of which require cooperation with suburban villages (ibid).

To respond to their needs and support the government's policy, rural communities in Chiang Mai should consider the tremendous opportunities which are offered by the long-stay market. Scholars have investigated this phenomenon from many perspectives, including the factors that influence long-stay choices of places to visit (Chamchan and Soparat, 2012), the economic and societal impact of long-stay residents (Korkietpitak and Pinyaphund, 2009), needs and level of satisfaction in Chiang Mai city (Srivatananukulkit and Srivatananukulkit, 2004), and advice to governmental organisations regarding planning and development (Hongsranagon, 2005).

Relatively few scholars have explored the surrounding rural communities to help facilitate their activities in line with the development of rural tourism. Thus, this chapter aims to propose strategic planning guidelines and a conceptual model to create the conditions for the commodification of 'rurality' in the neighbourhood of Chiang Mai to support Japanese long-stay tourism.

Mae Kam Pong, a small upland village near Chiang Mai, is an example. It is a famous community-based tourism village that has experience with the Japanese. In 2000, tourism in the village commenced formally when a pilot group of 15 Japanese students lived and volunteered in the village for about one week (Rabibhadana and Jatuworapruk, 2007). They built a village pavilion named 'Sala Ruam Jai Kagoshima' to commemorate their visit and encourage cooperation between the Japanese and Thais. In recent years, the government sector has promoted such exchanges. For instance, the 'Japan Long Stay Camp' organised by the Office of Chiang Mai Public Health hosted 30 Japanese long-stay residents and 30 urban dwellers engaging in cultural and health care exchange activities in Mae Kam Pong village in 2009. It is likely that Mae Kam Pong village has the potential to engage Japanese long-stay residents; moreover, it is possible to re-create the village to forge strong relationships among Japanese long-stay residents, urban dwellers and rural villagers.

To promote rural tourism activities in the village, creating tourism commodities and activities in response to the target group's needs, is crucial to bridge the gap between Japanese long-stay residents in urban areas and rural indigenous people. In terms of rural tourism, the commodification of 'rurality' is important for discussions about urban-rural relationships (Tabayashi, 2010), such as the interaction of Japanese long-stay residents in the city of Chiang Mai who desire tourism activities in rural communities. This chapter therefore, examines the existing rural commodification in Mae Kam Pong, the acceptance of villagers towards creating rural resources to target and engage Japanese long-stay residents, and the expectation of Japanese long-stay residents towards tourism commodities and village activities. The results from the study are discussed. Tourism strategy guidelines and a conceptual model of rural commodification for Japanese long-stay tourism in other rural villages are proposed.

Conceptual Framework of Rural Commodification for Japanese Long-stay Tourism

'Rural tourism', which is a term used generally to refer to visits to places outside metropolitan areas is characterised by features related to 'rurality' (Melsen, 2012). The notion of 'rurality' is associated with the characteristics of rural spaces, areas where rural communities exist and rural activities occur (Kikuchi, 2010). 'Rurality', the experiencing of rural areas as a motivation for rural tourism (Hájek, 2002), includes various recreational activities such as farm-based holidays, special-interest holidays, nature-based and ecotourism holidays, cultural-based and community-based tourism, adventure, sport and health tourism, educational travel, and food tourism (Melsen, 2012).

Such recreational activities are generated by 'commodifying rurality', which is exemplified by rural resources that are bought and sold through tourism activities; real estate investments by outsiders; and buying, selling, and promoting rural products by publicising a rural landscape image (Tabayashi, 2010). The commodification of 'rurality' in this chapter, therefore, is the process of creating and making rural tourism commodities and activities generated from rural communities, rural spaces, and rural activities, including rural products and facilities. This supposes that the rural lifestyle has become a commodity to satisfy urban fantasies and hence a desirable place to live.

For urban dwellers, increased travel in rural areas is promoted by 'nostalgia' and 'escapism'. Nostalgia is a strong motivation for tourists choosing destinations, so many seek the rural experience to reconnect with the past, perceived simple life, or their 'roots'. However, it is no different from escaping from globalisation; in other words, tourists wish to escape from the stress or monotony of ordinary urban daily life (George et al., 2009). In the case of Japanese long-stay residents in the city of Chiang Mai, the nostalgia can push them towards rural areas, for the rural landscapes of Chiang Mai are similar to those of Japan. Accordingly, the commodification of 'rurality' for this group is a major challenge given its ambiguity and the necessary cooperation between rural communities and urban associations.

Hence, the process of rural commodification for this niche market is advocated by both organisers in urban and local rural communities based on their own systems. Generally, urban associations utilise urban spaces to produce urban commodities and activities to attract Japanese long-stay residents living in the city. Those Japanese residents who desire a temporary escape will become tourists who visit rural communities and consume rural commodities and activities generated from 'rurality' instead. The commodification of 'rurality', therefore, involves collaborative relationships between organisers in the urban and rural systems. For instance, the local government sets the policy to promote rural tourism for this group through tour operator services or through the cooperation of any support organisations such as educational institutes, NGOs, and Japanese associations. While rural communities develop the quality of tourism commodities, activities and services to reinforce this policy.

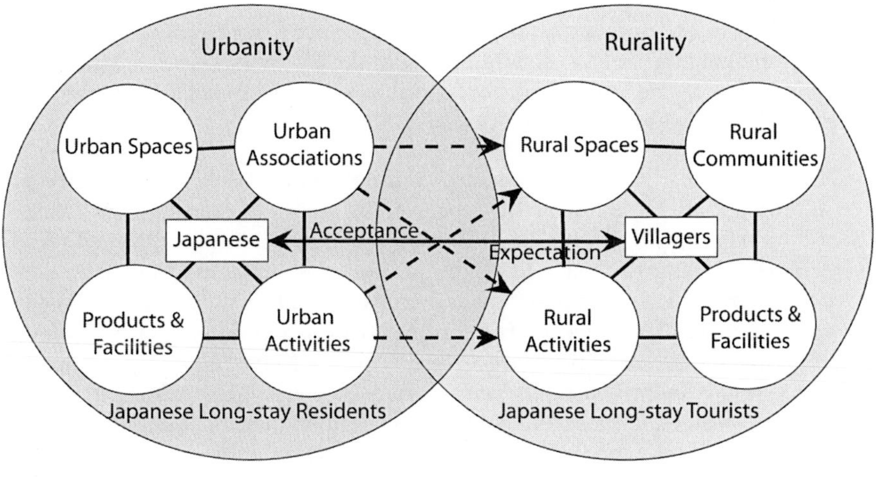

Figure 1. The relationships between urbanity and rurality as a conceptual framework of rural commodification for Japanese long-stay tourism
Source: the author.

As explained above, the conceptual framework for this advocacy emerged from such relationships between urbanity and 'rurality', as shown in Figure 1, though the villagers' acceptance of the ideas to create rural tourism commodities and activities related to this target group's expectations should be considered.

Japanese Long-Stay Tourism in Thailand

Long-stay tourism is an alternative tourism focusing on staying and experiencing life in a particular destination, known in Japanese as 'rongusutei' (Ono, 2008). The Long Stay Foundation (2013) defines Japanese long-stay tourism as 'leisurely stay abroad to live in a place for a longer period, learning the culture and living style of that country, and to promote international friendship through contributing to the society while keeping a residence in Japan'. In other words, it is the second home for the Japanese. It is not migration, nor is it a permanent residence in a foreign country because they eventually return to their home in Japan. According to a survey by the Long Stay Foundation in Japan, Thailand is one of the top-ten favourite countries for Japanese long-stay tourism. As of 2013, the country ranks second after Malaysia. The reason is that Malaysia has granted a visa stay of up to 10 years, while Thailand's non-migrant visa is permitted for a year (*TTRweekly*, 2012).

The history of Japanese long-stay tourism dates back to the 'Silver Columbia Plan 92' launched by the former Ministry of International Trade and Industry (MITI) in 1986. The project promoted Japanese retirees residing overseas and aimed to build Japanese villages; however, the project was rejected domestically and internationally via claims that Japan was exporting its elderly. The project was, therefore, reformed and proposed not as 'migration' but as a new style of leisure activity, namely 'Long Stay' which focused on people from 20 to 50 years of age - such as seasonal visitors, artists, and volunteers - rather than the retired elderly (Ono, 2008; Korkietpitak and Pinyaphund, 2009).

However, Japanese retirees are the target group of many destination countries, such as Malaysia and Thailand, which have been receiving foreign retirees since the late 1990s (Hongsranagon, 2005; Ono, 2008). The Tourism Authority of Thailand (TAT) has officially promoted and developed long-stay tourism since 2001 through the campaign 'Long Stay in Thailand' which supports Japanese long-stay tourism as well as medical and health tourism. The project defines long-stay tourism in Thailand as overseas visitors who temporarily spend their leisure time in Thailand for over one month without the desire to earn an income but who intend to enjoy a good quality of life with locals at a low cost. From this definition, long-stay tourists are categorised into four groups: tourists who come to maintain health, healthy retirees, students, and athletes (Chamchan and Soparat, 2012). For Japanese long-stay tourists, healthy retirees have been heavily promoted as the main target group since the initial project was implemented in five pilot tourist cities (i.e. Chiang Mai, Sukhothai, Hua Hin and Cha-am, Kanchanaburi, and Nong Kai) (Korkietpitak and Pinyaphund, 2009).

Of these, Chiang Mai is the favourite destination due to the low cost of living, friendliness and generosity of the locals, unique culture, diverse food, and appeal of the tourist attractions and range of recreational activities (Chamchan and Soparat, 2012). Most Japanese long-stay residents in Chiang Mai are retired males with a higher education (Hongsranagon, 2005; Srivatannukulkit and Srivatannukulkit, 2004) who prefer staying in a single house or condominium in the city. They are pleased by the natural beauty of the land, bank services, accommodation, golf facilities, and access to medication (Srivatannukulkit and Srivatannukulkit, 2004), the quality of which is high (Fukahori et al., 2011).

Mae Kam Pong Village as a Case Study

Mae Kam Pong village is situated in Huay Keaw sub-district, Mae On district, Chiang Mai province, 50 kilometres east of Chiang Mai city (Figure 2). The village is not far from other famous tourist attractions such as Muang On cave, San Kamphaeng and Chae Son hot springs, and Bo Sang, a village well known for its hand-made umbrellas. It is a part of Mae On national reserve forest on Pee Pun Nam mountain range, about 1,300 metres above sea level. Villages adjacent to Mae Kam Pong are Mae Lai to the north, Mae Ruam to the south, Tarn Thong to the west, and Pa Miang in Chae Son National Park in Lampang province to the east. The community was formed more than 100 years ago by immigrants from Doi Saket district searching the land for forest tea cultivation and then was officially established in 1914. As of 2011, the village has a total population of 386 persons. The majority of the working population is currently engaged in fermented tea production, locally called *miang* (a Thai northern-style chewing snack made of forest tea leaves). It is a unique product because it is now rarely seen. Since the decline of its consumption in recent generations, coffee has been grown with forest tea for additional revenue

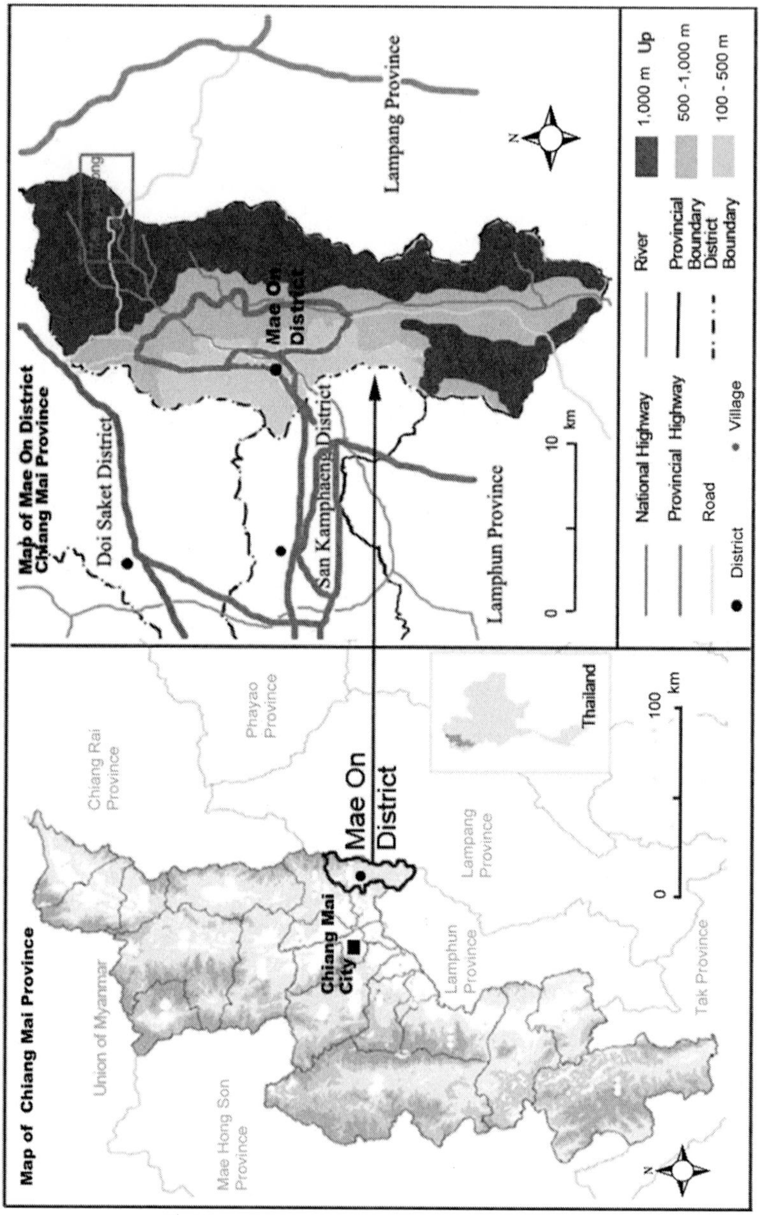

Figure 2. The location of Mae Kam Pong village

Methodology

This study used both qualitative and quantitative methods. The qualitative methods included interviews of key informants (i.e. a village headman, occupational group members, and the staff of a travel agent) and a field observation to examine the existing rural commodification in Mae Kam Pong village, specifically its rural land use and tourism management. The quantitative method employed two sets of questionnaires to examine the prospective rural commodification. The first questionnaire was administered to a sample group of 68 family households (out of 132) from 6 community groups from Mae Kam Pong village to survey the villagers' acceptance of the ideas for creating rural resources to target Japanese long-stay residents. The second questionnaire was a survey of Japanese long-stay residents' expectations toward tourism commodities by a convenience sampling group of 61 Japanese long-stay residents in the city of Chiang Mai. The study took place from December 2011 to February 2012. The data collected during the interview and field observation were segmented and de-contextualised. The data from questionnaires were analysed and presented in terms of frequency and percentage. The results were discussed within the conceptual framework to propose tourism strategy guidelines and a conceptual model of rural commodification for Japanese long-stay tourism in rural villages.

The Existing Rural Commodification in Mae Kam Pong Village

The commodification of 'rurality' in Mae Kam Pong village is formed from four elements: rural spaces, rural communities, rural activities, and rural products and facilities. Rural spaces occupy 622 hectares that are categorised into three types of land use: residential area, agro-forest area, and forest area.

Residential area

This area can be seen from the western to the eastern foothills where houses and other amenities are scattered along the narrow landscaped valley with the stream passing through. The village was further divided into six village groups with 132 households: Pang Nok (30 households), Pang Klang (19 households), Pang Khon (19 households), Pang Thon (15 households), Pang Nai 1 (13households), and Pang Nai 2 (36 households) (Figure 3).

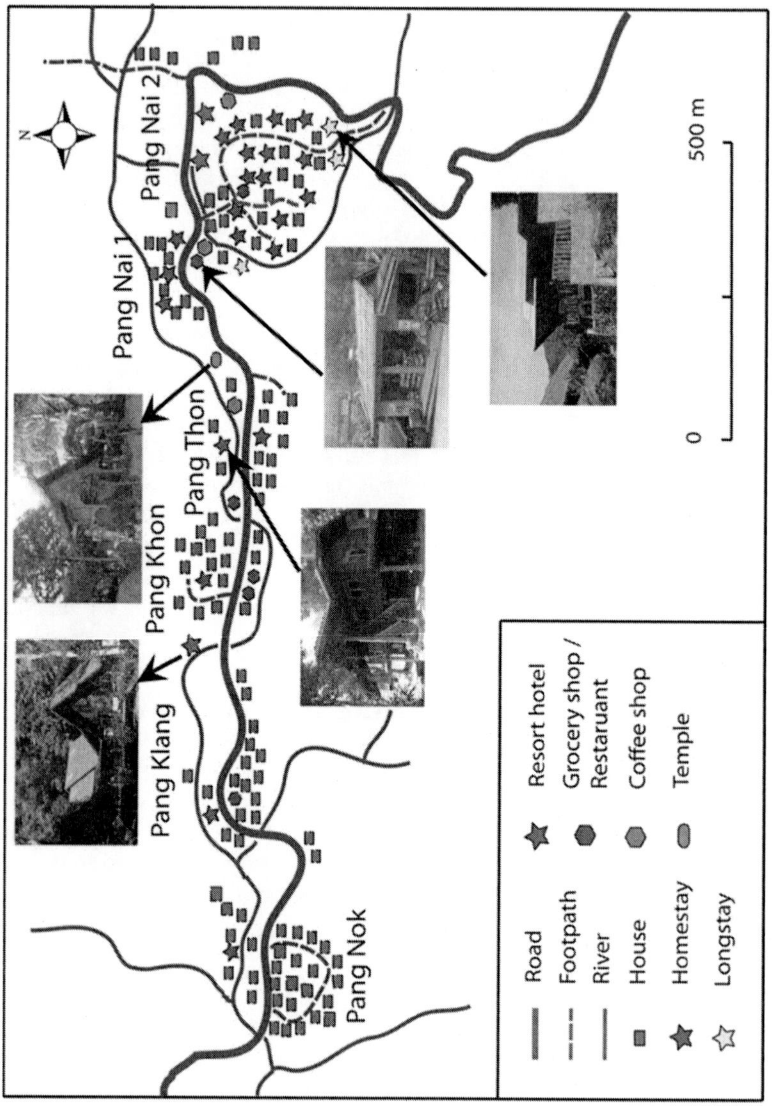

Figure 3. The settlement of houses and other amenities in the residential area
Source: field survey, December 2011

Those gentrified as homestays have been increasing. In recent years, 22 households have participated in the project that commenced in 2001 with 7 homestays. Besides the increase in homestays, the tendency to construct other accommodation is also on the rise (i.e. resort hotels and rental houses for longer stays). In addition, services and facilities, such as restaurants and coffee shops, have been developed. This circumstance manifests the crucial phenomenon of the commodification of the settlement landscape influenced by rural tourism in this village area.

Agro-forest area

This is the village's most distinctive land use area where the forest tea and coffee cultivation provides an important landscape for rural tourism. Due to the historical settlement of the village, forest tea has been traditionally grown for more than a century, and it remains a major crop in the agricultural area. In fact, it has been cultivated alongside Arabica coffee, herbal medicines, and the stunning natural forest, so it is considered agroforestry (Figure 4). Much of the forest tea is used to produce *miang*, a fermented forest tea that local people chew as a snack after dinner, or when they feel tired. To produce *miang*, only the tips of the tea leaves are picked to allow sunlight to reach the old leaves, enabling the farmers to harvest year-round. Producing fermented forest tea from cultivation to harvesting and processing is a special knowledge, a local wisdom of Mae Kam Pong, which has been accumulated and passed on for many generations. Although the forest tea leaves are available year-round, those harvested in winter are small, yellowish-green, and poorer in quality. Therefore, the farmers will harvest the seeds of coffee instead during this period. The Arabica coffee that is cultivated with the forest tea can be harvested once per year from the end of November to January after planting for two years. The cultivation of coffee has been promoted to generate more income and value for the agricultural land use area for a decade. Accordingly, agricultural land is utilised almost year-round, which implies that tourism activities, such as harvesting forest tea or coffee can occur every season.

Figure 4. Forest tea and coffee add value to the agricultural landscape for rural tourism.
Source: taken by the author, December 2011.

Forest area

This area covers the indigenous forest and the community forest called *pa chum chon* which is a habitat of diverse species of flora and fauna. The distinctive flora comprise cherry blossoms, locally called *Thai sakura* or *Nang Phraya Sue Krong*, which can be found on the high mountain near Doi Mon Lan, the village's highest point (1,700 m.) where a pine forest was reforested as a large campsite for ecotourism. Here, the community set aside 3.2 hectares for a herbal garden, so many species of local medicinal plants have been added to this herbal forest with the indigenous herbs. Besides forest conservation, the watershed is well preserved. Because of the Mae Kam Pong waterfall streams abound, enabling the village to produce hydro-electricity and pure drinking water, serving as a major tourist attraction (Figure 5). Consequently, the forest area generates biodiversity and non-timber forest products (for example, hydro-electricity, drinking water and herbs), boosting tourism.

Figure 5. Major attractions of the forest area
Source: taken by the author, December 2011.

Besides the rural spaces, rural communities including rural activities and rural products play a significant role in creating new tourism resources. They are managed within the framework of 'Community-Based Sustainable Ecotourism' in which two types of tourism are promoted: ecotourism and community-based tourism. Ecotourism management directly concerns nature-based tourism and overlaps with culture-based tourism. Nature-based tourism management primarily involves the commodification of rural activities in agricultural and forest areas; for instance, managing walking trails in forest tea cultivating areas and community forests and cooperating with Fight of the Gibbon, the foreign company using the abandoned forest tea plantation area for a zip-line canopy walk (an activity in which patrons hang from a zip-line as they glide over the top of the jungle). Culture-based tourism is also part of the process of the commodification of rural communities and cultural activities including homestays, and forest tea cultivating and producing, Lanna traditional music and performance, cuisine and herbal medicine, and traditional massage.

However, both nature-based and culture-based tourism reinforce the sustainable management of the community-based tourism committee, which manages the benefits from tourism allocated to the village. The income from tourism is operated through a village cooperative in which members get dividends as benefits. The engaged members are seven occupational groups that provide rural tourism products and facilities: homestays, tea pillow making, tea and coffee, tour guides, massages, herbals, and music and performances. These rural resources are commodified and sold as one of three tour programmes:

Programme 1 (*One-Day Tour)* offers the waterfall visit, short trekking in the forest and the forest tea cultivation area with local guides, and participation in the occupational groups such as tea pillow making. In this programme, both domestic and international tourists who visit without prior inquiry are targeted. Domestic tourists are mostly walk-in visitors, whilst the international tourists are mostly westerners who purchase the package from travel agents.

Programme 2 (Homestay) offers two main tour packages by making a reservation in advance directly through the village's officer or indirectly through tour agencies, one-night accommodation, and two-nights' accommodation with meals and cultural activities at night. In addition, the programme offers the Lanna cultural performances by local musicians and student performers and the welcome ceremony called *Bai Sri Sukhwan*. The programme's main activities include sightseeing in the agro-forest area, a waterfall visit, short or long trekking in the community forest with local guides, tree planting, participation in occupational groups, and participation in homestays. This programme targets allocentric tourists, both domestic and international, who want to stay overnight to learn and participate in rural-based activities.

Programme 3 (Study Tour) targets domestic tourists who make a reservation in advance through the village. These tourists include students, educators, private and government organisations, and other villagers who are interested in any special interests, such as forest tea or coffee cultivation and production, hydro-electric power plants, homestays and tourism management. The programme lasts one day or longer. In the case of an overnight stay, the cultural activities (i.e. Lanna cultural performances and welcome ceremony) are also available upon request. The price of this programme depends on the numbers of visitors and activities available. As previously mentioned, all tour programmes are linked with roadside attractions and walk trails, as shown in Figure 6.

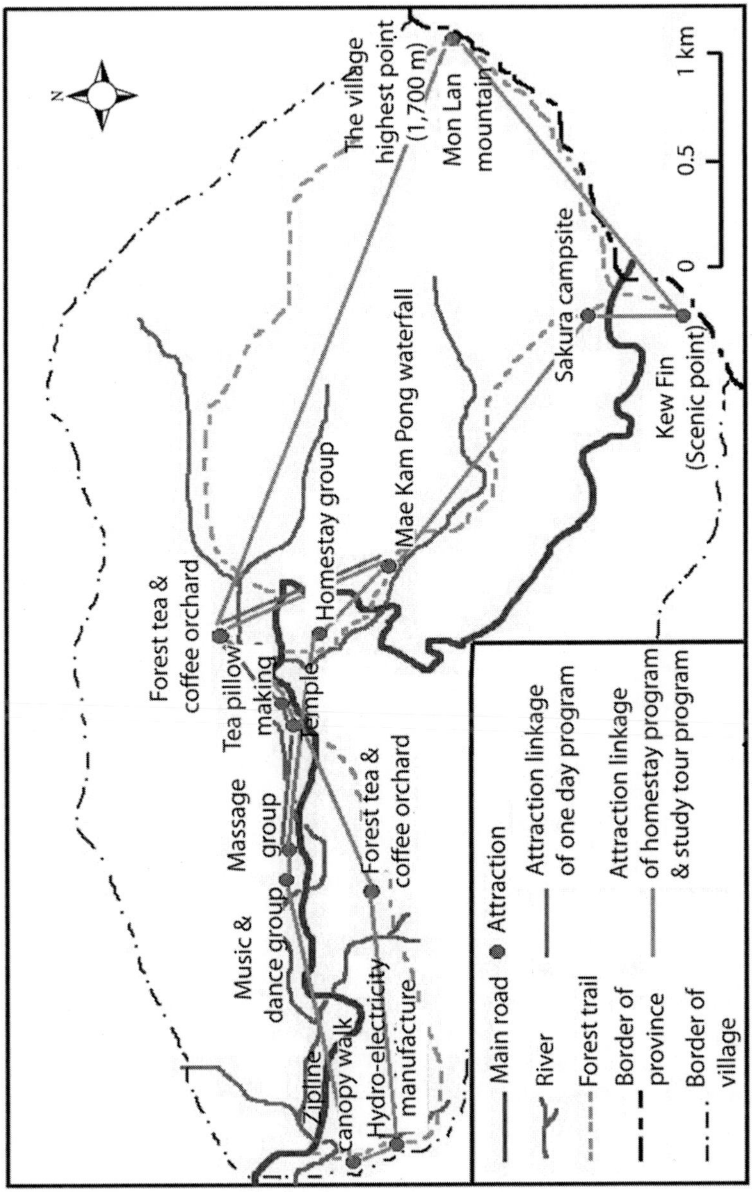

Figure 6. Tour programme attractions

Prospective Rural Commodification for Japanese Long-stay Tourism

The commodification of 'rurality' for Japanese long-stay tourism was examined in two sets of questionnaires, (a) villagers' acceptance of the ideas to create rural resources that target and facilitate Japanese long-stay residents, and (b) Japanese long-stay residents' expectations regarding tourism commodities in the village.

Villagers' acceptance of the ideas to create rural resources that target and facilitate Japanese long-stay residents

According to the questionnaire survey administered to 68 family households, half of the respondents (51.5%) were male. The average age was 31 to 60 years old (60.0%). The average gross annual income was 36,000 to 120,000 baht (74.1%), mostly derived from coffee cultivating (37.1%) and forest tea cultivating and tourism (32.3%). More than half of the respondents (61.8%) did not know that Japanese long-stay residents prefer staying in Chiang Mai city. However, most of them (91.2%) welcome Japanese long-stay residents in their village.

Given the ideas to create rural resources for this target group, the commodification of rural spaces was mostly accepted. They included the promotion of the forest tea cultivating area (95.6%), the standardisation of the health service centre (85.3%), the publicity for the community forest with the season of cherry blossoms (83.8%), and the facilitation of long-term staying by providing rental houses (42.6%), respectively. However, the villagers (42.6%) did not agree to improve the homestays to meet the needs of Japanese long-stay tourists (Table 1).

The commodification of rural communities, products, and activities was accepted. The promotion of hiking to the Sakura campsite and Mon Lan Mountain was the most acceptable (95.5%). Promoting health care therapy with forest tea and local herbs was the second most acceptable (91.2%). Developing various kinds of forest tea and coffee products was the third most acceptable, as well as providing organic food in homestays (86.7%). Last, coordinating the volunteer activities of Japanese long-stay tourists was also acceptable (85.2%) (Table 2).

Table 1. Frequency and percentage of villagers' acceptance of rural space commodification

Rural space issues	Acceptance Frequency (%)			Total
	Disagree	**Agree**	**Not sure**	
1. Homestays should be improved for the needs of Japanese long-stay tourists	29 (42.6)	20 (29.5)	19 (27.9)	68 (100)
2. Rental houses should be provided to facilitate long-term staying	17(25.0)	29 (42.6)	22 (32.4)	68 (100)
3.Health service centre should be standardised	2 (3.0)	58 (85.3)	8 (11.7)	68 (100)
4.Forest tea cultivating area should be heavily promoted	2 (3.0)	65 (95.5)	1 (1.5)	68 (100)
5. Community forest should be publicised during the season of cherry blossoms	1 (1.5)	57 (83.8)	10 (14.7)	68 (100)

Table 2. Frequency and percentage of villagers' acceptance of the commodification of rural communities, products, and activities

Rural communities, products and activity issues	Acceptance Frequency (%)			Total
	Disagree	Agree	Not sure	
1. Forest tea and coffee should be developed in various kinds of products	2 (3.0)	59 (86.7)	7 (10.3)	68 (100)
2. Health care therapy by forest tea and local herbs should be used as a tactic to promote health tourism	1 (1.5)	62 (91.2)	5 (7.3)	68 (100)
3. Organic food should be provided in homestays	1 (1.5)	59 (86.7)	8 (11.8)	68 (100)
4. Volunteer activities of Japanese long stay tourists (e.g. Japanese guide, Japanese teaching) should be facilitated and cooperated in by villagers.	2 (3.0)	58 (85.2)	8 (11.8)	68 (100)
5. Hiking to the Sakura campsite and Mon Lan mountain should be promoted	2 (3.0)	65 (95.5)	1 (1.5)	68 (100)

Japanese long-stay residents' expectations regarding tourism commodities in the village

The survey was carried out by a convenience sampling group of 61 Japanese long-stay residents in the city of Chiang Mai. Respondents were categorised into three groups: retirees, exchange students, and workers. More than half were male (59.02%) and retirees (47.5%), staying in the city of Chiang Mai for fewer than six months (39.3%). The reason for their stay was to relax after retirement (45.9%). Most of them (85.2%) did not know Mae Kam Pong village and had never visited this village (90.2%). However, more than half (67.2%) wanted to visit Mae Kam Pong village.

A survey of their interests in rural activities that primarily focused on nature-based activities reveal that Japanese long-stay residents desired seeing the cherry blossoms *Thai sakura* near Mon Lan Mountain (37.7%);

hiking on nature trails (34.4%); and participating in adventure activities in the forest (32.8%). For culture-based activities, most of them (41.0%) wanted to learn new ways of life by interacting with indigenous people; staying overnight at a homestay; and participating with hosts, such as cooking (29.5%), and dining during the Lanna performances by indigenous people (22.9%), respectively. Based on health and wellness activities, they preferred relaxing in hot springs close to the village (41.0%); enjoying the spa or traditional massage with herbal therapy (32.8%); and walking in the village or community forest (29.5%), respectively (Table 3).

Table 3. Frequency and percentage of interest in rural activities

Nature-based activities	Frequency	%
1. Learning community forestry management	10	16.4
2.Taking the adventure activities in the forest such as a zip-line canopy	20	32.8
3.Visiting the Mae Kam Pong waterfall	12	19.7
4. Harvesting the forest tea	17	27.9
5. Bird watching	10	16.4
6.Wildlife viewing	15	24.6
7. Hiking on nature trails	21	34.4
8.Watching the cherry blossoms *Thai sakura* near Mon Lan mountain	23	37.7
9.Watching the Mae Kam Pong flower	17	27.9

Culture-based activities	Frequency	%
1.Learning the producing of *miang* (forest tea) for chewing gum products	12	19.7
2. Learning handicraft making such as tea pillows	12	19.7
3.Visiting the temple, respecting the Buddha image and making merit	11	18.0
4.Staying overnight at a homestay and participating with hosts such as cooking	18	29.5
5.Dining during the Lanna performances by indigenous people	14	22.9
6.Learning the way of life by interacting with indigenous people	25	41.0
7.Doing volunteer activities such as teaching Japanese or being interpreters	6	9.8

Health and wellness activities	Frequency	%
1.Learning about the local herbs for health maintenance	9	14.7
2.Taking the spa or traditional massage with herbal therapy	20	32.8
3. Doing meditation in a peaceful mode	11	18.0
4. Having meals with organic food such as a menu from *miang*	15	24.6
5. Enjoy drinking local forest tea with beautiful nature	16	26.2
6. Walking in the village or community forest	18	29.5
7. Relaxing in hot springs close to the village	25	41.0

Concerning rural products and facilities, patrons needed tourism information provided in Japanese (45.9%), Japanese tour guides (37.7%), and hot water in the homestay (34.4%), respectively (Table 4).

Table 4. Frequency and percentage of needs regarding rural products and facilities

Needs	Frequency	%
1. Japanese tour guides	23	37.7
2. Tourist information provided in Japanese	28	45.9
3. Service and warm welcome	20	32.8
4. Hot water in the homestay	21	34.4
5. Local organic products such as tea, coffee and herbs	15	24.6
6. Staying in resort hotels near or in the village	11	18.0
7. Others (i.e. accommodation in the hot spring areas)	2	3.3

Considerations for Planning Tourism Strategies: Discussion

According to recent trends in global tourism, as noted earlier in this chapter, long-stay tourism has been growing in the senior market segment due to the greater number of elderly tourists or pensioner tourists who desire to maintain their health (Schröder and Widmann, 2007). This trend is evident from the questionnaire survey results which indicated that most of the respondents were Japanese retired males who stay to relax. This finding coincides with the studies of Hongsranagon (2005) and Srivatannukulkit and Srivatannukulkit (2004) which indicate that most Japanese long-stay residents in Chiang Mai were retired males who had completed higher education. Therefore, the commodification of 'rurality' for facilitating Japanese long-stay residents in Chiang Mai should target healthy retirees.

According to this suggestion, the results from the survey on prospective rural commodification should be considered along with the villagers' accepted ideas and Japanese long-stay residents' expectations. The most accepted ideas were promoting the forest tea cultivating area and hiking to the Sakura campsite and Mon Lan Mountain. These ideas are related to Japanese long-stay residents' expectations that they mostly preferred seeing the cherry blossoms and learning a new way of life. 'Nostalgia' or 'escapism' are the primary reasons, conforming with the notion of George et al. (2009) and the personality of 'midcentric tourists' and 'allocentric tourists' described by Plog (cited by McKercher and De Cros, 2002).

Promoting the forest tea cultivating area supports the need to learn diverse ways of life, particularly forest tea cultivation, producing and consuming fermented forest tea (*miang*). In Japan, tea consumption is a delicacy, particularly the 'tea ceremony' which is the traditional style of welcoming guests. In fact, serving tea in houses or restaurants is a Japanese custom. Similarly, in northern Thailand, the consumption of *miang* as a snack or for chewing is part of the traditional lifestyle, though this practice has declined recently. Similarities and differences, such as the consumption of tea, therefore, can be a cultural allure influenced by nostalgia.

As mentioned in the conceptual framework, George et al. (2009) note that nostalgia is a strong motivation for tourists to seek the rural experience to reconnect with their past or to recall the places they lived. This should be considered when promoting hiking to the Sakura campsite and Mon Lan Mountain to observe the cherry blossoms. For the Japanese, watching *Thai sakura* in Mae Kam Pong village elicits nostalgia. In Japanese society, watching the cherry blossoms or *sakura* is a spring pastime, what the Japanese called *hanami*, which is a glorious time to reflect and refresh, evoking memories of their hometowns. This is apparent in terms of the word *furusato* which means hometown. Indeed, although in reality one's hometown may be quite different, the Japanese identify with *furusato* overseas as places that portray wholesome, natural, and traditional aspects of Japan (Surman, 2009). Watching cherry blossoms in Thailand's rural areas, therefore, evokes a myriad of feelings associated with the Japanese hometown.

In terms of nostalgia, according to Swarbrooke and Horner (2007), elderly Japanese tourists want the familiar when on holiday, which supposes that Japanese long-stay residents can be categorised as 'midcentric tourists'. Plog (cited by McKercher and Du Cros, 2002) states that 'midcentric tourists' travel primarily for relaxation, pleasure, or for escape, and they want to get out of their comfort zones only to the extent that it does not interfere with their ability to enjoy their vacation. Take, for example, the need to relax in hot springs close to the village. Hot spring bathing, what the Japanese call *onsen*, is a favourite rural tourism activity for elderly people in Japan. Relaxing in hot springs near the village, then, attracts this target group that wishes to escape from the city.

However, if we consider their interests in learning a new way of life by interacting with indigenous people, it can be assumed that some Japanese long-stay residents act as 'allocentric tourists' who comprise community-minded people. Plog (cited by McKercher and Du Cros, 2002) explains that these tourists are interested in experiencing as much change and strangeness as possible to sharpen their worldview, whether for educational or cultural reasons, or for learning and greater appreciation. Ryan (2005) argues that they prefer to stay overnight in the communities of indigenous people. Accordingly this involves learning a new way of life by interacting with indigenous people which parallels with Japanese long-stay residents who can be categorised as allocentric tourists.

For these reasons, the tourism strategy for this target group should include creating the theme of nostalgia and rural heritage that can attract the interests of both 'midcentric' and 'allocentric tourists' in terms of 'cultural comparison'. Based on this idea, the existing rural commodification is also necessary for strengthening new commodities generated. For example, the forest area encourages hiking and viewing cherry blossoms, activities that have never been promoted. In addition, occupational groups are provided as a way to learn a new way of life. Thus, the existing tourism commodities cannot be ignored when identifying a strategy. Figure 7 shows the evaluation of both existing and prospective rural commodities.

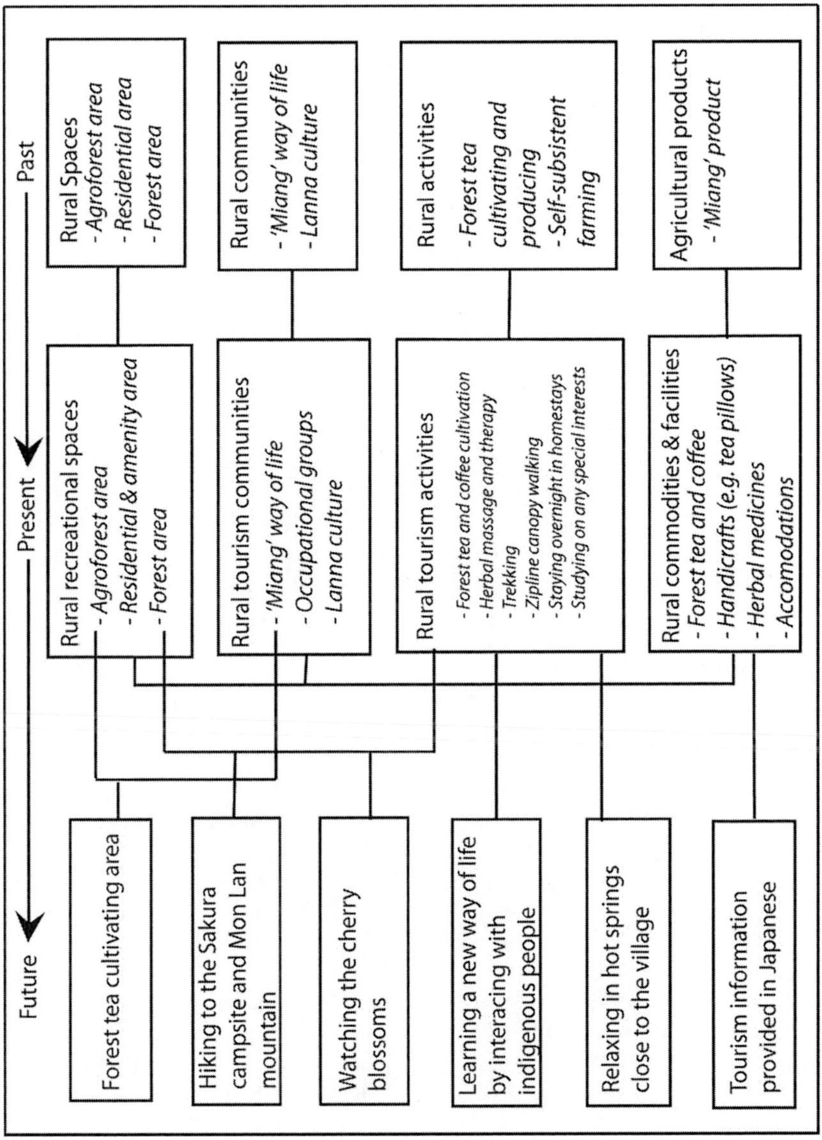

Figure 7. Issues related to existing and prospective rural commodification

As shown in Figure 7, existing and prospective rural commodities are mostly generated from the past. This evolution implies that the basis of generating new resources results from a 'traditional rurality' in which commodification is not introduced. The 'traditional rurality' is associated with the authentic rural aspects: rural spaces, rural communities, rural activities, and agricultural products. When urbanism develops and tourism begins, it changes to a 'modern rurality' influenced by the commodification of 'rurality' as a playground of urban dwellers. Thus, rural spaces have been modified as rural recreational spaces, and rural communities have become rural tourism communities that produce a variety of rural tourism activities, and tourism commodities and facilities. However, the commodification of 'rurality' to serve the needs of Japanese long-stay tourists will eventually affect 'modern rurality'.

Focusing on 'modern rurality', strategic planning should begin with a SWOT (strengths, weaknesses, opportunities, threats) analysis, which involves considering factors that are likely to make the implementation a success or a failure, and should examine both the internal and external organisation (Briggs, 2001). In the case of Mae Kampong, the SWOT analysis can be discussed as follows:

Strengths – the cultural identity of forest tea cultivation and local participation in tourism management to improve economic status, which highlights its rural land use as a featured, community-based ecotourism village; ***Weaknesses*** – lacks quality production and facilitation of forest tea and other local vegetation in supporting health tourism in various optional tourism products; ***Opportunities*** – the reputation of the village in attracting Japanese long-stay residents, due to the proximity to Chiang Mai city and major tourist attractions such as hot springs and golf courses; ***Threats*** – the potential to develop amenities in the residential areas is limited in scale (e.g. accommodation and parking).

From a SWOT analysis in planning the village's strategy, the strengths, weaknesses, and opportunities to identify the action plan or establish the projects, and the threats must be considered in order to monitor the problems. The action plans or new projects based on elderly Japanese long-stay tourists should focus on promoting health tourism. It should produce various health tourism products. Examples might include transforming organic food products from forest tea, coffee, or other local vegetables; developing herbal products used for hot springs or spas; and linking a health tour programme with other attractions around the village, such as hot springs and golf courses.

Besides health tourism, which should be emphasised in the action plan or programme, long-stay tourism should also be heavily emphasised as a tourism policy for monitoring the problems that may arise from threats to the space for amenity development. Ideally, long-stay tourism in Mae Kampong, which is evident judging by its increasing number of resort hotels and rental houses in recent years, should be monitored by the local community. Regulations should be established to control this phenomenon, including oversight for the expansion of residential space to the agricultural area or forest area, or for other uses, such as shops, restaurants, and parking lots. In addition, amenity development, particularly in the construction of accommodation to support Japanese long-stay tourists, should be culturally and environmentally friendly via eco-lodges, for example.

As the discussion and suggestions have shown, ways to target Japanese long-stay tourists can be proposed within the elements of 'modern rurality' associated with rural recreational spaces, rural tourism communities, rural tourism activities, and tourism commodities and facilities (Figure 8). For rural recreational spaces, the forest tea cultivating area and forest area generate two rural tourism activities: hiking to the Sakura campsite and Mon Lan Mountain and viewing the cherry blossoms. The village's festival or tourism events during the cool season when flowers bloom, *Thai sakura* or *Nang Phraya Sue Krong*, for example should be heavily promoted and advertised. Whilst the residential and amenity area should re-create learning a new way of life, including support services on a hot spring tour programme and tourism information provided in Japanese. Meanwhile, six rural communities of the village, by occupation, produce various rural tourism commodities such as commoditised agricultural products for elderly Japanese long-stay tourists. It should emphasise organic food and health products that reflect the identity of the Lanna culture and the *miang* way of life, such as organic forest tea salad, locally called *Yam Bai Miang*.

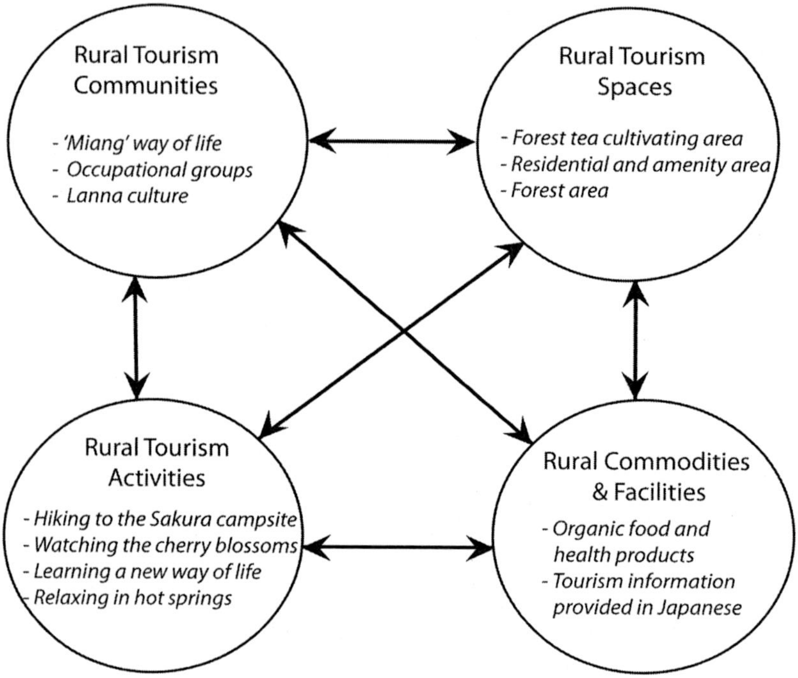

Figure 8. The commodification of modern rurality for Japanese long-stay tourism in Mae Kam Pong village

However, these ideas cannot be implemented without strengthening the relationship between 'urbanity' and 'rurality', which is necessary to advocate this framework. As Kitano (2010) stresses, in order to sustain a position as a stable commodity, various factors must be considered. These include not only obvious factors such as the quality of the cultural landscape or products, but also marketing, advertising, and the consciousness and capacity of local government and community. Accordingly, it is very important that rural communities interact with urban associations and are supported by urban and local organisations. For instance, the Tambon (sub-district) Administration Organisation (TAO) supports budgets for developing this project; the university or NGOs provide academic support, such as Japanese interpretation and training; the tour operators promote marketing and advertising; urban dwellers contribute to rural development; and Japanese associations in Chiang Mai cooperate with urban dwellers to create exchange activities with locals such as homestays or volunteer programmes in rural communities.

Such examples of implementation could bridge the gap between rural and urban residents. Many elderly Japanese long-stay residents enjoy doing volunteer work, an activity that can be promoted as Japanese volunteer tourism, a contribution from which the villagers will benefit, particularly the activities concerning natural conservation. This suggestion is in line with Kikuchi's (2010) notion that urban residents participating in natural conservation efforts will enjoy rural recreation, understand the natural environment, and satisfy their inner yearning for a sense of belonging. Thus, one major challenge in the commodification of 'rurality' for Japanese long-stay tourism in Mae Kam Pong village is not only a focus on planning a marketing strategy, but also on restructuring rural communities in which the partnership between rural and urban organisations eventually leads to the sustainability of rural development. This is the virtual meaning of 'commoditised rurality', a notion exemplified in Tabayashi's (2010) study that points out the essentials of rural commodification and how to mutually connect various small-scale, scattered tourism resources, what new tourism resources should be promoted, and how educational and experiential tourism should be incorporated.

Conceptual Model of Rural Commodification for Japanese Long-stay Tourism: Conclusion

The guidelines resulting from this research suggest that the policies monitoring Japanese long-stay tourism in Mae Kam Pong village might result in the re-creation of 'rurality' by rural tourism uniting rural and urban residents. Thus, the commodification of 'rurality' for this target group is not only a focus on marketing to generate more income, but also a focus on restructuring rural communities through the cooperation of urban and rural organisations. Restructuring 'rurality', commoditised by urbanisation and tourism, has been consolidated from the four elements of 'modern rurality': rural recreational spaces, rural tourism communities, rural tourism activities, and rural commodities and facilities.

However, 'modern rurality' cannot emerge and exist unless it is modified from the elements of 'traditional rurality' and supporting factors. Generally, rural spaces changed into rural recreational spaces, and rural communities turned into rural tourism communities, whilst, rural activities concerning agriculture have been transformed as rural tourism activities are not limited to agricultural activities. They also influence the re-creation of rural commodities and facilities. In addition, the commodification of 'rurality' for Japanese long-stay tourism is supported by rural-urban organisations such as tour operators, urban dwellers, villagers, and Japanese long-stay residents in Chiang Mai city. In sum, the conceptual model can serve as a framework for other rural communities, as shown in Figure 9.

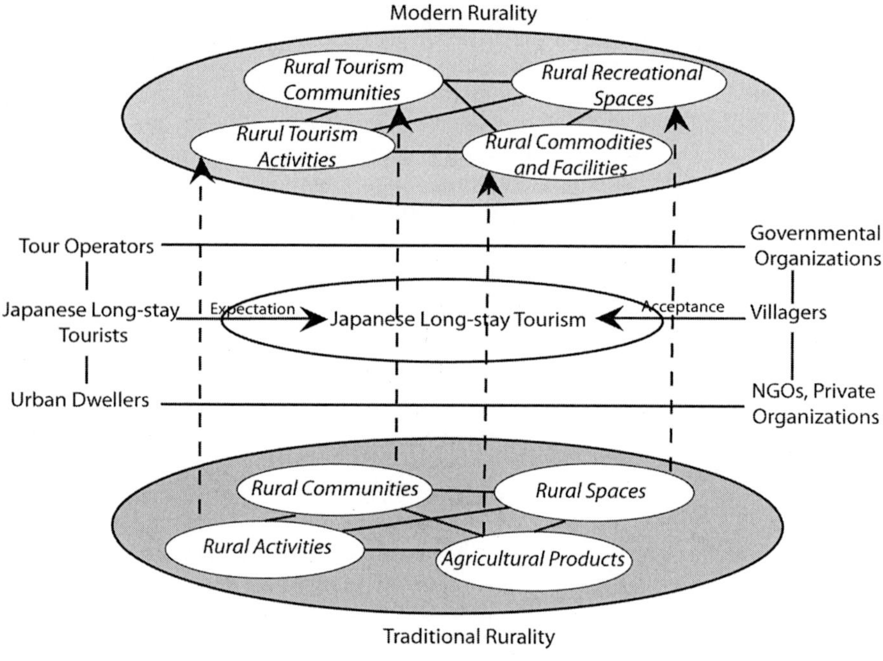

Figure 9. The conceptual model of rural commodification for Japanese long-stay tourism

Acknowledgements

This research was supported by the Asian Human Resources Fund from the Tokyo Metropolitan University, Japan. The author is deeply indebted to Professor Dr. Kikuchi Toshio of Tokyo Metropolitan University for his invaluable advice on this chapter. Special appreciation goes to all villagers of Mae Kampong village, and Japanese long-stay residents whose generous assistance made this research possible.

References

Bangkok Post (2011) 'Chiang Mai Hopes for a Long-Stay Life Preserver', *Bangkok Post*, April 20.

Briggs, S. (2001) *Successful Tourism Marketing,* London: Kogan Page Limited (second edition).

Chamchan, C. and O. Soparat (2012) 'Long-stay of the Japanese in Chiang Mai: Analysis of the Determining Factors in the Pre- and Post-period of the Visit', *Japanese Studies Journal,* 29: 16-34 (in Thai with English abstract).

Fukahori, H., Y. Baba, F. Hioki, S. Monkong, P. Intarasombat and P. Malathum (2011) 'Healthcare Services for Japanese Elderly Long-staying in Thailand from the Perspective of the Patient and Healthcare Providers: a Survey Study', retrieved from http://www.ncbi.nlm.nih.gov/pubmed, page consulted 11/05/2011.

George, E.W., H. Mair and D.G. Reid (2009) *Rural Tourism Development: Localism and Cultural Change,* Bristol: Channel View Publications.

Hájek, T. (2002) 'The Development Potential of Czech Rural Areas and Rural Tourism', *Zemeldelská Ekonomika*, 48: 559-562.

Hongsranagon, P. (2005) 'Advisory Facilities for Long-stay Japanese Senior Travelers in Chiangmai', *MANUSYA: Journal of Humanities*, 8: 58-66.

Kikuchi, T. (2010) 'The Commodification of Rurality and its Sustainability in the Jike Area, Yokohama City, the Tokyo Metropolitan Fringe', *Geographical Review of Japan Series B,* 82: 1-14.

Kitano, S. (2010) 'Preserving ruralities? Green tourism in the globalization urban world', *Encounters*, 1:35-54.

Korkietpitak, W. and D. Pinyaphund (2009) 'Notes on the Effects of Japanese Long Stay on Thai Economy and Society', *Japanese Studies Journal*, 26: 54-70.

Krailerg, N. (2011) 'Chiang Mai Hosted a Seminar on the Potential of Long Stay Tourist Development in the Upper Northern', retrieved from http://www.chiangmaipost.net/a46-seminar-on-the-potential-of-long-stay-held-in-chiang-mai, page consulted 21/11/2011.

McKercher, B. and H. Du Cros (2002) *Cultural Tourism: the Partnership between Tourism and Cultural Heritage Management,* New York: The Haworth Hospitality Press.

Melsen, L. (2012) 'Rural Tourism'. In P. Robinson (ed.), *Tourism: The Key Concept*s, Abingdon: Routledge, pp. 173-175.

Ono, M. (2008) 'Long-stay Tourism and International Retirement Migration: Japanese Retirees in Malaysia', *Senri Ethnological Reports,*

77:151-162.

Rabibhadana, A. and T. Jatuworapruk (2007) 'Impact of Tourism upon Local Communities: Changes in an Urban Slum Area and a Rural Village in Chiang Mai'. In M. Kaosaard (ed.), *Mekong Tourism: Blessing for All?* Bangkok: White Lotus, pp. 62-81.

Ryan, C. (2005) 'Introduction: Tourist-Host Nexus-Research Considerations'. In C. Ryan and M. Aicken (eds) *Indigenous Tourism: The Commodification and Management of Culture*, Oxford: Elsevier, pp.1-14.

Schröder, A. and T, Widmann (2007) 'Mega Trends and their Impact on the Tourism Industry'. In R. Conrady and M. Buck (eds), *Trends and Issues in Global Tourism 2007*, Berlin: Springer Berlin Heidelberg, pp. 3-16.

Srivatananukulkit, J. and S. Srivatananukulkit (2004) *Needs and Satisfaction Survey of Long Stay Foreigners in Chiang Mai,* Social Research Institute, Chiang Mai University.

Surman, B. (2009) 'The Search for the Real Thing: Japanese Tourism to Britain'. In Guichard-Anguis, S. and O. Moon (eds), *Japanese Tourism and Travel Culture*, London and New York: Routledge, pp. 193-202.

Swarbrooke, J. and S. Horner (2007) *Consumer Behavior in Tourism*, Oxford: Elsevier (second edition).

Tabayashi, A. (2010) 'Regional Development owing to the Commodification of Rural Spaces in Japan', *Geographical Review of Japan Series B*, 82: 1-23.

The Long Stay Foundation (2013) 'Countries that Wish to Stay, Generation Raking by Long Stay Foundation 2013' retrieved from http://www.longstay.or.jp/upload/photo1/703.pdf, page consulted 29/06/2013.

TTRweekly (2012) 'Hotels Eye Japanese Long-stay', retrieved from http://www.ttrweekly.com/site/2012/04/hotels-eye-japanese-long-stay/, page consulted 22/08/2013.

Ugotreviews (2013) 'Chiang Mai Long Stay' retrieved from http://www.ugotreviews.hubpage.com/hub/Chiang-Mai-Long-Stay, page consulted 23/06/2013

THE KNOWLEDGE DYNAMICS OF DANISH TOURISTS IN MAE KAM PONG COMMUNITY-BASED TOURISM

SASIWIMON KHONGMUEANG AND PETER HERVIK

Introduction

Kasper, a Danish tourist explains:

> Engaging in community based tourism wasn't my major purpose for visiting Chiang Mai. But it was offered as part of a package tour. I primarily wanted to see the Suthep Temple. I find that community based tourism is artificial not traditional. Why do I have to pay to see these products of mass tourism? The local residents just want to make money from the Western tourists (Kasper, 28, in Chiang Mai).

Since Kasper found community-based tourism (CBT) artificial, he decided instead to go on his own to what he saw as a 'real', 'traditional' village, which did not charge him to enter and accordingly had not destroyed the real values and meanings of the everyday lives of villagers.

For Kasper, paying is a sign that a 'village visit' has become a commodity and this commoditisation of culture is even the negation of culture and the coming into modernity. Therefore paying is a constraint to his quest for reaching the 'authentic' (non-commercial) life of local 'traditional' villages. Kasper's reasoning is by no means unique, but widely known throughout the tourist literature (see for instance Hervik, 2002).

Kasper's case illustrates one of the dilemmas of CBT tourism. The number of tourists worldwide visiting through this form of tourism has increased dramatically, resulting in the further commoditisation of culture where representations of 'culture' have been reified into a commercial product for tourism exclusively. Such a process risks degrading the cultural identity of the host community in such a way that it loses the kind of local authenticity tourists pursue. The dilemma continues as a vicious circle when transformations of local culture require a still better structuring of the tourist experience of authenticity, for instance, by avoiding entry fees and the overt presence of modern technologies. Yet, we argue in this chapter, that the dynamics of this quest for authenticity may not lie in local commodification, but with tourists in their home countries, where tourism is, on the one hand, a derived label for types of travel that are on the face of it both associated with 'inauthentic' experiences, but, on the other hand, also part of modernist society's endless quest for 'authentic' experiences, as MacCannell has convincingly argued (1999).

The presence of Nordic tourists visiting Thailand and Thai CBT shows at least a positive degree of cosmopolitanism rather than mere hedonism, such as the desire to 'learn about different cultures' and local ways of living by participating in local cultural practices and 'being local' with local inhabitants. Nevertheless, those tourists may still hold strong modernist thoughts and be motivated in their travels with a deeper search for the 'authenticity' of ways of living not associated with tourism, preferably, outside tourism and tourist areas. In this view, being a tourist is being a modernist, and the object of the tourist is by definition traditional. Or, events need to be structured in a way that they do not show features of mass tourism too openly, i.e., paying for interaction with local people. Therefore, the Thai CBT is currently faced with the question of whether it should maintain an increased commoditisation of local culture to meet the growing demand or attempt to reconsider and even address tourists' modernistic knowledge through hands-on cultural practices in order to reach an authenticity that is based on a more equal interaction, dialogue and recognition. The broader version of this dilemma is one that is concerned with how to reconcile increased economic growth with sustainable development.

The aim of this chapter is to analyse the conditions for how CBT in Thailand through a more dynamic use of knowledge about Nordic tourists can simultaneously attract more participants in CBT providing income and helping the local economy and contributing to less modernistic thinking and more cosmopolitanism among the visiting tourists. The study draws on Khongmueang's doctoral research project, particularly an analysis of the questions to 100 Nordic tourists visiting Thailand and Thai CBT, particularly Mae Kam Pong.[1]

CBT was heavily promoted in 1998 to accommodate visitors' desires to encounter and experience local Thai culture and ways of living in short intervals. In this way it was meant to be an alternative to mass tourism. The idea was initially crafted out of the concept of 'homestay', where tourists spent time with local host families, including homestays, in order to have more personalised interaction between native hosts and foreign guests. According to Thailand's CBT Network Coordination Center (CBT-N-CC) the overall objectives of CBT has first of all been to enable local residents to develop community-based capacity and skills in the management of local natural resources and access to 'local culture'; secondly, to simultaneously generate income from tourism and distribute it equally to low income families in impoverished areas of rural Thailand.

Mae Kam Pong CBT offers various types of tourist activities grounded in visiting natural attractions, assessing local 'culture', village tours, trekking, mountain camping, homestays, learning to cook Thai food, public ceremonies and shows, music shows and the ritual welcoming and 'spirit cultivating' ceremony called *Bai Srisukwan*.[2]

Nordic tourists in Thailand

Recent statistics reveal a slight increase of tourists from the four largest Nordic countries from 2011 to 2012, which seems to continue into 2013 (Table 1).

---

[1] The questionnaire and interviews are part of Khongmueang's PhD research project carried out at Aalborg University. They were conducted in the spring and winter of 2012 in the Aalborg area in northern Denmark and in Chiang Mai, Thailand and were supplemented by qualitative interviews and participant observation, which contributed to her study of the constraints and enablers of enhanced Danish tourist participation in Thai CBT. Respondents were predominantly Danish, Swedish and Norwegian tourists to Thailand, who answered questions about demographic profiles; general knowledge and attitudes about Thailand; knowledge and attitudes attained from participation in the Mae Kam Pong CBT; as well as suggestions and comments.

[2] http://communitybasedtourism.wordpress.com/cbtcommunity/northern-thailand/mae-kam-pong/.

Table 1: Nordic tourist arrivals to Thailand in 2011-2012 and from January-August 2013

Country of Nationality	2011	2012	2013 (Jan-Aug)
	Number	**Number**	**Number**
Denmark	164.096	167.499	117.112
Norway	136.931	148.796	107.061
Sweden	373.856	364.681	253.504
Finland	157.046	154.919	102.232

Source: adapted from Ministry of Tourism and Sports, Thailand, 2013

The numbers also indicate that tourism has fully recovered from the drastic decline of tourists that followed after the devastating tsunami in 2004.

However, these numbers do not provide us with the popular motivation for travelling or the cultural baggage tourists bring with them to Thailand. This is where we turned to Khongmueang's data. The findings of the questionnaire answered by 100 Danish, Nordic and European tourists to Thailand revealed, not surprisingly, that tourists first of all think about Thailand's attractive natural resources, its landscape, as well as warm and pleasant weather. Secondly, Thailand is an ancient and culture-rich country. More specifically tourists' general attitudes to Chiang Mai are that it is a beautiful city, with friendly people, plenty of old and beautiful temples, and with Western amenities.

Although, Thailand is one of the most popular tourist destinations among Western visitors, the negative images of Thailand are also a major constraint namely the conflict between Muslim groups and the Thai state in Pattani, Yala and Narathiwat; arbitrary accusations for carrying drugs; the general reputation of Thai police and Thai prisons; worries of natural disasters originating from the tsunami in the southern coastal area in Thailand; and finally sex tourism including the image of Thailand as a safe haven for paedophiles.

These first associations must of course be supplemented by more in-depth tourist knowledge and more directly how tourists relate to locals. In the following discussion we focus on popular Danish – Thai knowledge and personal relations as a source of knowledge.

Danish knowledge about Thai people

Images of Thai female immigrants in Denmark

According to the questionnaire findings the perception of Thai female immigrants in Denmark encompasses unskilled labour, hospitality, friendliness and the involvement in prostitution. The images of Thai women residing in Denmark and in other western countries have been particularly negative in their strong association with prostitution. Many Danish people associate Thailand with sex tourism and prostitution. As a consequence, this perception serves to frame the negative stereotypical attitudes towards Thai women in general. This negative stereotype can be transformed into prejudice as well as discrimination, which it is difficult to change or to remove as long as the sex industry in Bangkok and the mass tourist areas is so strong. Some Thai women have been involved in massage, prostitution, or both leading further to degrading the overall image of Thai women who are living in Denmark for other positive purposes such as for study, for legal work, visiting friends and relatives, travelling and so on.

Inter-racial Marriage

What Danish people know about Thailand and Thai culture is perhaps most clearly embodied in inter-racial marriage relationship between Thai female immigrants and Danish men. Inter-racial marriages make up a site of interpersonal interaction and transcultural encounter, which may serve one primary site for intensive cross-cultural learning and negotiation across different positions of power. The reverse case of Danish women marrying Thai men and more generally between Nordic women and Thai men are the exception to the rule. In this chapter we deal only with the dominant Nordic men-Thai women relations.

The numbers of Thai females in Danish inter-racial marriage have been fairly steady within the last decade adding up to slightly less than 4000 (Table 2).

Table 2: Numbers of intermarriage between Thai female immigrants with Danish men by year

Year	Numbers
1999	283
2000	287
2001	319
2002	215
2003	130
2004	173
2005	190
2006	199
2007	315
2008	400
2009	361
2010	393
2011	187
2012	227

Source: adapted from Statistics Denmark, 2013

Two decades ago a number of lowly educated Thai women from rural areas of Thailand began to migrate to Denmark in order to get married to Danish men. According to Plambech (2008) most Thai women, who came to Denmark through transnational marriage arrangements held the hope that marriage would lead to an improvement in the quality of their lives and enable them to send remittances to their family back home. Spanger suggests that the stereotypical perception of Thai female residents as connected with prostitution in Denmark is the result of Thai women migrants who work in the sex and prostitution industry (2010). However, the strength of the sex image of Bangkok does play a crucial role as well. In addition popular perceptions of mixed marriages being associated with prostitution feed the negative image as well (we shall return to this later).

Table 3: The average age of Danish men and Thai female immigrants involved in inter-racial marriages in the year 2007-2011

Age of male/female / Year/No. of couples	2007	2008	2009	2010	2011
Age of male 50-54					
Age of spouse					
30-34	7	9	7	8	8
35-39	15	10	12	19	7
40-44	10	9	10	11	11
Age of male 55-59					
Age of spouse					
30-34	4	6	5	6	1
35-39	9	12	11	8	2
40-44	5	8	7	8	4
Age of male 60-64					
Age of spouse					
30-34	2	6	2	5	0
35-39	1	5	4	5	3
40-44	5	10	2	7	0

Source: adapted from Statistics Denmark, 2013

Most Thai female immigrants in mixed marriages have found work such as cleaning, massaging or in Thai food stands, restaurants or working as housewives. When they first come to Denmark, they can neither speak Danish nor English. For newcomers like these women, it is compulsory for them to study the Danish language. Thus, they go to the language school slowly enabling them to speak more and more in Danish with their husbands, with whom they were living from day one of their entrance into Denmark. Their husbands generally speak little English and know only a few words and phrases in Thai. Moreover, as Plambech has shown, most of these men come from rural areas, where they are fairly isolated and find it difficult to find a life partner (2008) (see also Spanger, 2010). The asymmetric relation between these mixed marriage partners is obviously seen through the big gap in age differences between the Danish men and the Thai female immigrants.

The majority of Danish-Thai couples reveal that Danish men are much older than their Thai wives, which forms part of a pattern also noted by Erik Cohen (2003). The pragmatic character of intermarriage is revealed by the marriage contract, which must be signed before returning to Denmark with the new partner. There is little time for the couple to get acquainted before they make out their contract. The relationship, we conclude therefore, is not so much a love relation serving as a start of a new nuclear family, although of course it can develop into a romantic love relationship. The age of the Thai women in a mixed marriage is usually early 30s to mid-40s, which is 10 to 15 years older than observed by Cohen (ibid). Most of them had been married before they came to Denmark and have children with their Thai ex-husbands. In many cases they will try to arrange for their children to come to Denmark at some point, when they are settled and have their own independent income.

The common trajectory is that of a Danish man in his 50s or 60s who travels to Thailand, pays a middle man to broker a relationship, or uses advertisements, finds a spouse, works out her legal papers, pays for her travel to Denmark, and covers her expenses in her new country.

The general perception is that Asian women are exotic, erotic, dedicated, caring, and hard-working housewives. For the Thai women the Danish males in Thailand are associated with wealth, the Western world and are thus considered able to enhance their social status and even provide wealth. In other words, for the Danish man she seems to be living up to the classic ideals of a male-dominated marriage relationship.

With the lack of common language as a means of communication problems frequently arise when expectations and ideals are not made explicit from the beginning of the relationship. The Danish husband may find her much more demanding, more independent than he expected, which is further unfolded, if she becomes economically independent by entering the labour market or acquiring her own business. She may find him less willing to support her economically than expected and too demanding, when it comes to household chores (see also Christian Groes-Green Interview, Denmark Radio 20 January 2011, http://www.youtube.com/watch?v=CkXwL4ZOM5o (23 September 2013).

These issues are illustrated in the following case. Suda is a Thai woman who has lived in Denmark for nearly 20 years and now runs a Thai food stand. She is married to an elderly Danish man and explains:

> Whenever we go to a party with our Thai-Danish friends, the food has to be prepared separately. The Danish husbands eat their food and we [the Thai wives] eat our food. They speak Danish and we speak Thai. That does not ruin our relationship. (Suda, 43, Thai-Dane intermarried couple in Denmark)

Suda's statement bears witness to a separation of social spheres and language areas that have continued after years of living in Denmark. Like most other Thai-Danish couples, daily food also consists of one meal for the husband and another for the Thai wife. When Suda's husband brings home fish from his leisure time fishing, she cooks separate dishes. His parents have taught her to cook Danish food, so she can cook for her husband. This is what he prefers, when he has a choice. In Suda's case having separate jobs further underscores the compartmentalisation of their lives, where he spends most of his time working as an engineer in Norway.

When Suda's husband goes to visit her family and relatives in her hometown in northern Thailand, she finds that he will eat some Thai dishes. Moreover, he prefers staying with Suda's family rather than staying in a hotel. During these visits he enjoys using a few Thai words like *sawasdee krub* ('hello' in Thai) and *kob khun krub* ('thank you' in Thai) and thus further conveys a cosmopolitan image. The example illustrates a more general trend among Danish men in this kind of mixed-marriage. They see themselves as cosmopolitan, and express this in food choice, lodging, language and visiting in Thailand, under circumstances where they are off work and alone among Thais, whereas given the cosmopolitan choice and the power to decide in Denmark, they prefer the traditional mode of marriage and expect the Thai wife to comply.

Most of the Danish males who married Thai female immigrants do hold a cosmopolitan openness to Thai culture, even if this is a simplified and adjusted version of cosmopolitanism that covers only a small slice of Thai culture: eating Thai food, speaking a little bit of the Thai language and sojourning locally with the families of their wives in Thailand. Here in Denmark they practice the old-fashioned gender relations with an authoritarian, working, husband and his wife who is perhaps doing wage labour and in charge of housework including cooking. This difference between the outreach for cosmopolitanism in Thailand and the reliance on old fashioned gender roles in Denmark exposes the superficiality of cultural interest in cosmopolitan practices.

Again, one of the Danish female tourists to Thailand expressed her view of Danish-Thai marriage relations as a form of prostitution, a view she shares with many others.

> How come that they [Thai women] got married and lived with a man without knowing or being accustomed to them before. I just wonder what the difference is between this marriage and [a] sexual relationship within the sex industry (Susanne, 47, Danish tourist).

When Susanne offered her opinion on what she called 'mail-order-brides' she associates them with prostitution. She admits that she may have a biased view of Thai female immigrants to Denmark, who have married with older Danish men, but she sees them as if they were 'digging for gold'. In Susanne's perception of the mixed-marriage the sexual pleasantness overrides that of a 'love marriage' relationship. She believes that the primary reason for Thai immigrants in Denmark in mixed-marriages is intimately tied to economic objectives, which are reachable through the formation of intimate relationships with men, who at first are strangers to them. To her, a real intimate relationship needs time to be established and consistently developed.

The profoundly different background and age gap does also lead to conflict. The following case of Kwanjai shows an unsuccessful inter-racial intimacy relationship between a Thai woman and Danish man in Denmark.

> Our marriage did not derive from love. We know each other via the dating advertisement. I decided to get married with a Danish man, because I needed the marital status to live in Denmark legally. He didn't treat me as a wife as someone who cares and is concerned in a mutual relationship. I work fulltime during the day and took over all the household chores as well (Kwanjai, 52, Thai-Dane couple in Denmark).

Kwanjai comes from the rural north-eastern part of Thailand. She used to do farm work for her own family, which is a low-income job in Thailand. Due to her hard life in Thailand, Kwanjai decided to marry with an unknown Danish man through a dating agent and migrate to Denmark. Her first job in Denmark was cleaning but because of a health problem, she changed and began to run a Thai massage parlour with the financial support of Lasse (her Danish husband). Unfortunately, her relationship with the Danish husband did not go well. She has realised that her husband treated her as nothing but a 'sexual object', as a 'sex slave' and 'paid servant'. When Lasse lost his job tensions arose drastically; fighting broke out; and in the end they got divorced. Fortunately, Kwanjai had obtained a certificate for training in caring for the elderly, and could take up a job as an attendant for the elderly at a residential home. Recently, she has begun to plan her return to her Thai hometown, where she wants to run a laundry business with her sister.

In Kwanjai's rendition of her marriage this did not arise out of love but from the mediation of a commercial matchmaker. Lasse paid to marry her and brought her to Denmark. She explained that paying to marry a Thai woman and bringing her to Europe entitles him to be the ultimate source of authority as head of the family even according to traditional Danish male values. This unequal gender relation implies a European male superiority, which plays a larger role than affection.

The relationship between the Danish husband and his Thai wife contains much more than a difference of age and money. According to Erik Cohen's depiction of the dynamics of intermarriage between Western men and their transnational Thai spouses it suggests that the respective partners usually have vastly different backgrounds. On the one side he finds obvious marks of intersecting characteristics, such as 'race, ethnicity, language, culture, and religion' and on the other incidental, unmarked ones: 'age, class, education, and rural versus urban origins' (Cohen 2003:68). Cohen also finds that since the foreign husbands are responsible for financial obligations, which accommodate their Thai wives' standard of living as well as more social recognition, they have superior positions in this asymmetric relationship (ibid).

Moreover, the European husband's traditional conception of his ultimate power in the relationship is based not only on his financial capability but also on a modernist, Eurocentric ideology that sees itself as superior to the traditional non-Western society. According to this view northern Thai people are approached as any non-Western people, in a way Cathy Lutz and Jane Collins have described, more generally, as being perceived as exotic, idealised, naturalised and sexualised in a process where they are taken out of all but a single historical narrative; and they are sexualised (1993:89). This relates to a historical evolutionary narrative with only two worlds, the traditional and the modern, one with civilisation and history, and the other without history (Wolf, 1982). In popular representations people in the traditional world can be slowly eased into the modern Western world through the pedagogical push of Westerners, who do not cause problems or conflict in the process (Hervik, 1999:172; and 2003). Obviously, the modern versus traditional dichotomy is a gross simplification (Finnström, 1997; Comaroff and Comaroff, 1992), yet this popular way of thinking prevails among the European tourists visiting Thailand. But it is also present in the tourism advertisement that attempts to lure people into visiting, in what could perhaps be coined as a 'time-stood-still' genre that hammers out modernism's meeting with traditionality. Here are some local examples:

> Just 45 min drive to the unique village of Mae Kampong where time has stood still. Once a poppy growing area and a bastion of hill tribes, it is now home to a small community of forest dwellers who cultivate tea and coffee plantations. Experience the culture of the local people with a soft eco trek and visit stunning Kampong falls where you can relax in the cool fresh water
> http://www.northernsmiletravel.com/optional%20trip%20(full%20day).html

> If you are looking for a place where time stood still and the environment is clean and beautiful, than this is one place you must stop and stay
> http://www.tripadvisor.com.sg/Hotel_Review-g4419177-d3864878-Reviews-TAd_Marine_Resort-Pulau_Tinggi_Johor.html

> 2012-11-25 Thailand Day 07, Time stood still in Chiang Mai 2012-11-25 Thailand Day 07, Time stood still in Chiang Mai
> http://www.flickr.com/photos/qsimple/8343929566/

In the conversations with Kwanjai, she revealed that Lasse represented himself as a kind of hero, who 'rescued' her from the unfortunate 'primitive' life in rural Thailand, through the marriage arrangement and this effort in fact makes him proud of himself.[3]

In the light of difficulties in finding a proper marriage partner in Denmark, whether these difficulties are connected to the isolated life in rural areas for men working many hours a week, or for frustrations mounting from prior experiences with Danish women, these Danish men, who travel to Thailand, are keenly aware of their superiority in relation to these women. They use their wealth and agency to leave Europe to find a Thai female who can become their spouse. In this transformation of status ascribed to the Thai female, she leaves behind simple, rural, poor conditions of living for a highly modern, affluent, European country in which the Danish man

[3] Lasse was not interviewed for this project.

and his family are experts. This awareness of position is accompanied by a cosmopolitan outreach, where they are doing 'good things' for a Thai woman and her family, despite the fact that the project they have engaged in can be, and is being seen, as Susanne's interpretation and Kwanjai's story confirm, as buying access to a wife, who is then a provider of sex, labour, care, and sometimes even love.

Nobue Suzuki (2004) has also studied the motivations for intermarriage between Japanese men and Filipina women. She found that in the men's image of themselves in the relationship they were on the side of the western world and the so-called 'First World' with well-developed economies and civilised countries. The 'Third World Woman' and non-Western countries (like the Philippines) suggest the images of women with poor education from rural families. This reveals a discourse of what she calls the twin stereotypes of the 'First World Man' and the 'Third World Woman' based on her desire to get away from poverty and his contribution to this project.

Gayatri Spivak has coined the phrase 'White men are saving brown women from brown men' (1988), which is now used to capture these narratives of justification more generally. The original quotation refers to the year 1829, when the British colonialists abolished the ritual practice of Hindu widows sacrificing themselves by ascending the funeral pyre of their deceased husband. It is a formulation of a structured belief of White supremacy and White power as superior to brown people in the Europe-Asia context. That is to say, Spivak is trying to use a shorthand formulation for capturing the relation of the white British colonialists, the (brown) Hindu women, and her (brown, suppressive) husband. 'White men are saving brown women from brown men' has been used more specifically in the contribution to the context of inter-racial marriage of Thai females and Danish males which implies the encouragement of European superiority by rescuing women from their poverty.

Nordic tourist encounters with Mae Kam Pong CBT

The hands-on cultural practices through Mae Kam Pong CBT are an arena where people meet in a cross-cultural encounter, exchange knowledge, and share experiences. Potentially, this arena can facilitate the generation of new knowledge and transformation of Eurocentric modernist views held by Nordic tourists that may reduce the asymmetric gap between Europeans and Thai people.

Based on the questionnaire findings 48 respondents learn about a different culture and norms, making friends with local Thai people, and gaining new local cultural knowledge as the positive outcome of the hands-on community practices in Mae Kam Pong. This is not to say that many friendships emerge or that new idiosyncratic local knowledge is really learned, but these are the prevailing reasons given. In contrast to these stand 52 respondents who were not interested in CBT. These tourists claimed that they felt their appearance in the eyes of local residents would be that of strangers or aliens, and they would be uncomfortable with staying locally due to the lack of familiar amenities and unhealthy private living conditions.

Claus is one of the Danish tourists visiting Thailand and encountered community-based tourism. He explained:

> Visiting [a] rural village seems like travelling by a time-machine which takes me back to the very old and laggard days where there was no electricity, no water supply, no internet access (Claus, 30, Danish tourist in Chiang Mai)

However, rather than talking with Thai people he met or referring to acquired local wisdom or stories, he employed the term 'time-machine' with his reasoning that 'the very old and laggard days where there was no electricity, no water supply, no internet access' reveals his opposition of ways of life in the past to modern life styles.

Northern Thailand, objectively speaking, is neither backward nor underdeveloped in the sense of being a 'traditional society' without 'modern' technology. There is television, internet, gas stations, Seven-Elevens, and so-called Western amenities to comfort the visitors and please everyone else as well. There is even a profit-oriented community-based tourism enterprise using communication technologies and social media for example, mobile phones, Skype, Facebook, Blogs, and Twitter. Being traditional is not an objective feature of Northern Thailand in that like most other places across the globe the traditional aspects of social life are moulded together with modern aspects. The point in this chapter is however, not that Claus, and many like him, are right or wrong, but people engaged at various levels of organising CBT should know better how the stereotypical modernistic perception of visiting tourists is used in making sense of local people, events, and landscapes.

Torben is a Danish tourist with individualistic values at odds with superstitious practices in Northern Thailand such as the *Bai Srisukwan* ceremony.

> I believe in myself, what I have done and what I am doing. If I am doing the good thing, then the consequence will turn out to be positive accordingly. My destiny depends on my own actions. Superstitious things cannot steer my future! Do *you* pray to God when you need the rain? This ritual welcoming ceremony [*Bai Srisukwan*] is just an irrational and superstitious practice. Spirits seem to me to be an intangible entity (Torben, 25, Danish tourist in Chiang Mai).

After having enjoyed the nature of the Southern islands and doing white-water rafting and snorkeling, Torben had joined a village tour and tried out a homestay with a Chiang Mai family through a community-based tourism programme. However, he explained he was not really interested in Thai culture and norms. Uncomfortable with a traditional Thai setup such as a bedroom with the fly screens makes him feel like 'an animal in a zoo'. He admitted that he preferred the modern convenient life in Denmark rather than the simple conditions he found in Thailand. Being middle class and a rationalist not really interested in local ways of seeing things, Torben was quick to categorise ritual practices and beliefs as irrational and superstitious. He did not feel comfortable when the sacred rituals are carried out by locals. He went on to argue that it is incredible that people believe in ritual practices such as *Bai Srisukwan* and how by people praying this could encourage one's soul and promote spiritual well-being. The soul and spirit of a human being comprise an abstract and intangible belief, which sounded nonsense to him.

Torben's views – again by no means unique – nicely illustrate a European idea of modernity with its belief in scientific advancement, technological progress and rationality as opposed to the 'traditional', here represented by the folklore of the Mae Kam Pong villagers which relies heavily on transcendent and folk religious beliefs. Yet, if Torben was like most other Danes, in late December he would bring a 1.5 to 2 metre-tall fir tree into his living room. On 24 December each year he is likely to join family members in a circle walking around the adorned tree illuminated by living candles, while singing psalms and old Christmas songs more or less worshipping the tree. Through 'modernist' ideas this practice too would show the irrational character of a 'local' set of cultural practices. This example suggests that Torben's home space, here the modern world, is perceived as a different social space. He approaches the two spaces through two different filters of perception rather than objectively describing features within these spaces.

The statements by Claus, Torben, and Kasper in this chapter on the artificiality of CBT, where they had to pay to enter a village, reveal a modernist way of thinking. They may appear as cosmopolitans, but they are not reaching beyond modernism's quest for 'the traditional'. Instead, they are projecting modernity onto the Thai social space and the ways of living in that space. For Claus the experience of northern Thailand lives up perfectly to being a traditional society and it reminds him of modernity's past, while for Kasper it reveals that commodification is encroaching upon the traditional space making it up to the tourists' own creative genius to find the traditional, away from the experiences of mass tourism. And finally for Torben, the dominance of spiritual beliefs combined with a lack of interest in Thai culture generates an experience of almost 'too much' primitivism and non-modernity. The three examples, which are illustrations of common streams of thinking, approach a 'cultural Other' or 'society' that may be best understood from within the confines of 'Western culture' and modernist thinking. This discourse of the 'Other' also reflects a dominant asymmetric relation of power in tourism.

Grethe shares her experience of cross-cultural encounters in CBT, which is different for its apparent larger degree of cosmopolitanism and for bringing her two children along. Her favourite thing to do is to visit local villages on the outskirts of urban areas, spend the time observing residents' ways of life, talk with them and try to live locally.

> Embarking [on] CBT is a vantage point to instill my kids to gain social skills and life experiences outside the classroom. In my opinion, I think engaging in the CBT by interacting with local community residents through cooking, eating, giving hands to pick up tea leaves, giving food to the monks can benefit especially my kids in the future. This is my way of teaching them to learn from people of different culture[s], to learn how to give and share. Because in the future they will have to work with many people who may come from different parts of the world (Grethe, 38, Danish tourist in Chiang Mai).

Grethe's expectation from engaging in CBT is to seize the opportunity for interactions with local families, in order to gain new experiences such as preparing and making Thai food, experience living a simpler kind of life, escape from technologies like social media, and a stressful life. She also wanted to explore what the villagers conventionally do for a living apart from the income from homestays and CBT activities. During the stay,

Grethe and her children took part in several activities and local practices. During the day time, they did village touring, seeing how local workers picked *miang* (tea) and visited the nearby temple. They went to a waterfall in the village and spent a few hours there. In the evening, Grethe and her children helped the host family to make a potpourri of local northern Thai foods, including *Kaeng Hung Lay* (pork curry), *Kaeng Ho* (mixed vegetable curry) and *Nam Prik Num* (green chili sauce), and had dinner with the host family and made up the easy bed.

Grethe's wish for her two children to learn about a different cultural and social environment makes her seek a contact point between traditional ways of life in the Thai CBT and her modern world views. Her approach to the CBT underscores her cosmopolitan view and open-mindedness as a person who is open to learning from people from elsewhere, particularly her intention for having her kids take part in local and simple lives, which she anticipates will benefit her children's prospective careers in the increasingly globalised world. The value she seems to place on the experience is the ability to recognise the skills and views of these other people as well as people able to efficiently take part in dialogue and activities.

The story of Jens discloses the acknowledgement of modernist ideas of Western intellectual superiority.

> I have been travelling a lot in my life; enjoy different kinds of tourist stuff. My preliminary purpose of visiting rural and local village[s] in Thailand is to meet local native[s] and experience their comfortable lifestyles. Apart from this, I also want to use my knowledge and professional skills to build a better standard of life for locals. Once, I first arrived there, I realised that probably my background in construction can help local village[s] to develop their basic infrastructure such as building a water reservoir and a public place, where people could relax and hang out with others. I will be a volunteer to help them (Jens,63, Swedish tourist in Chiang Mai).

Jens is an engineer and has visited Thailand on more than ten occasions. He loves to stay away from his busy chaotic life in Sweden. For the CBT, he likes the idea of making use of local ways of doing things, seeing traditional folk dances and experiencing local music performances even though they are part of package tours. However, Jens believes strongly in his educational and professional knowledge and skills, which to him are based on his Western intellectual superiority. He believes that his educational background and his work experiences in Sweden have given him superior intellectual capital next to the local wisdom in Thailand. In other words the advanced technological skills are seen as being based on an advanced intellectual capability.

Grethe's and Jens' engagement in the CBT reflect the characteristics of open-mindedness and willingness to benefit from experiencing different cultural practices. They both express modernist perspectives and know they are crossing cultural and class boundaries, while their cosmopolitanism is a humanist kind that allows constructive social interaction across differences. Incidentally, this may be facilitated in Grethe's case, since – all things considered – it may be easier for local people to interact with a mother and her two children than it is with single men. Grethe points out that CBT allows her children to become accustomed to people of diverse cultural backgrounds and provide cross-cultural competency in their future career paths. Jens believes that the residences used for CBT and its infrastructural setting need to be developed by the introduction of Western intellectual insights. In this manner, the CBT is a playground for him to exercise his superior technological views against traditional local wisdom.

Concluding remarks

How should northern Thai community-based tourism (CBT) act on the stories of Kasper, Claus, Torben, Susanne, Grethe and Jens? Should the CBT try to meet their demands and accommodate their wishes that fall so clearly within a European modernist ethos? In this regard is it keeping modern symbols and payments for experiencing local cultural practices at arms' length from the tourists, so the experience of authenticity and traditional life is restored? In such an approach CBT will acknowledge its inferior position in relationship to the powerful economic and cultural position of European tourists and even, we argue, reproducing these crude world views, or should CBT seek to learn more about what kinds of knowledge and positioning European tourists bring with them into the encounter with CBT, and *then* see how CBT can creatively challenge these views? Would it even be possible for CBT to facilitate a transformation of the experience of authenticity as traditionalism and highly structured forms of performances for tourists to an authenticity that is linked to the quality of Thai-tourist interactions in the CBT, which of course is where Thai generosity comes in as a bonus? Therefore, the hands-on cultural practices and activities and close collaboration offered by Mae Kam Pong CBT could be deployed as the operational tools for countering and challenging the Eurocentric bias of modern European tourists.

References

Cohen, E. (2003) 'Transnational Marriage in Thailand: the Dynamics of Extreme Heterogamy'. In K. Sung Chon, T. Bauer, and B. McKercher (eds), *Sex and Tourism: Journeys of Romance, Love and Lust*, London and New York: Routledge, pp. 57-67.

Comaroff, J. and J. Comaroff (1992) *Ethnography and the Historical Imagination*, Boulder, Co: Westview Press.

Finnström, S. (1997) 'Postcoloniality and the Postcolony: Theories of the Global and the Local', retrieved from http://www.postcolonialweb.org/poldiscourse/finnstrom/finnstrom2.html, page consulted 29/09/2013.

Groos, C. (2011) retrieved from http://www.youtube.com/watch?v=CkXwL4ZOM5o, page consulted 29/09/2013.

Hervik, P. (1998) 'The Mysterious Maya of National Geographic', *Journal of Latin American Anthropology*, 4: 166-197.

—. (2002) *Mediernes muslimer. En antropologisk undersøgelse af mediernes dækning af religioner i Danmark',* Copenhagen: The Board for Ethnic Equality.

—. (2003) *Mayan People Within and Beyond Boundaries. Social Categories and Lived Identity in Yucatan*, Amsterdam: Harwood Academic Publishers, and New York and London: Routledge, Studies in Anthropology and History, Volume 25, originally published in 1999, revised paperback edition.

Lutz, C.A. and J. I. Collins (1993) *Reading National Geographic*, Chicago: University of Chicago Press.

MacCannell, D. (1976) *The Tourist: a New Theory of the Leisure Class*, New York: Shocken.

Nobue, S. (2004) 'Inside the Home: Power and Negotiation in Filipina-Japanese Marriages', *Women's Studies*, 33: 481-506.

Plambech, S. (2008) 'From Thailand with Love: Transnational Marriage Migration in the Global Care Economy. Anti-Trafficking, Human Rights, and Social Justice' *Wagadu*, 5: 32-48.

Spanger, M. (2010) *Destabilising Sex Work and Intimacy? Gender Performances of Female Thai Migrants Selling Sex in Denmark*, Roskilde University, Department of Society and Globalization: PhD Thesis.

Spivak, G.C. (1988) 'Can the Subaltern Speak?' In C. Nelson, and L. Grossberg (eds), *Marxism and the Interpretation of Culture,* Urbana: University of Illinois Press, pp. 217-313.

Wolf, E. R. (1982) *Europe and the People without History*, Berkeley: University of California Press.

http://www.tourism .go.th, page consulted 29/09/2013

http://www.statbank.dk/vie4, page consulted 29/09/2013

http://www.northernsmiletravel.com/optional%20trip%20(full%20day).html, page consulted 29/09/2013

http://www.tripadvisor.com.sg/Hotel_Review-g4419177-d3864878-Reviews-TAd_Marine_Resort-Pulau_Tinggi_Johor.html, page consulted 29/09/2013

http://www.flickr.com/photos/qsimple/8343929566/, page consulted 29/09/2013

HOMESTAYS IN DIENG PLATEAU: COMMUNITY RESPONSES TOWARDS TOURISM DEVELOPMENT IN DIENG PLATEAU-BANJARNEGARA, CENTRAL JAVA

DESTHA TITI RAHARJANA

Introduction

This chapter elaborates one type of tourism business, which has grown in the Dieng Plateau, a mountain-based tourist destination in Central Java Province. Located in Wonosobo and Banjarnegara District, the Dieng Plateau has been a tourist destination since the Dutch colonial era (Sukatno, 2004; Thohir, 2007). Over 2,000 metres above sea level, Dieng is known as the 'Place of the palace of the gods' (Sukatno, 2004; Sonjaya, 2005). Hindu relics and archaeological sites are common to find here. The Dieng area covers a cultural and natural environment, with a variety of breathtaking landscapes. Originally formed from a volcanic eruption, the plain expanded into a wide crater in the lake (Sukatno, 2004). When dried up, the lake became a vast plain for settlement and farming.

An attractive mountain destination, Dieng manages to lure more tourists, the numbers of which have increased continuously from 1970 to 1996, the peak year with 132,415 visitors. A deteriorating environment, however, has affected the sustainability of the tourism industry there. Other sites of natural beauty such as the lake, crater, forest and wildlife are affected by the declining quality of the environment. The popularity of Dieng declined until the early decades of the 2000s as the economic crisis hit Indonesia in 1997. The critical quality of the environment has been affected by improper land use which has become one of the main factors for the declining tourist visits. The Dieng Plateau, however, remains an interesting place to visit. The survey revealed that among the visitors to Dieng, 40.91% wanted to relax while enjoying the panorama, 18.19% and 12.12% were interested in visiting the temples and learning the local culture respectively. In addition, other objects are attractive such as the lake, museum, geothermal exploration, flora and fauna diversity and the unique culture including the well-preserved *ruwatan* (ritual for safety). In terms of accommodation, 10.3% visitors preferred homestays, while 3.4% chose to enjoy the rural atmosphere (Raharjana, 2010). The community in Dieng has initiated the objective to conserve nature through tourism services as an alternative to reducing the ecological impact while empowering the community. Nowadays, some residents develop tourist services such as providing rooms for tourists as homestays while working as farmers.

This chapter will describe the social, economic and cultural responses of the Dieng community to visitors. The data presented were obtained from 50 farmer households who own homestays. Simple surveys with in-depth interviews explored the accommodation business in Dieng. Dieng Kulon village was chosen because it is a tourist village where homestays are deemed necessary. Utilising houses for homestays among the potato-growing farmers is worth analysing because they in fact had insufficient knowledge in the homestay business. They, however, observed and interacted with the tourists and finally decided to run homestays.

Literature Review

The development of homestay and Dieng as a rural tourism site is intertwined (Raharjana, 2012). The understanding of tourist activities in the rural areas is quite diverse (Lane, 1994; Puczko and Ratz, 1998; Roberts and Hall, 2001). As Puczko and Ratz illustrated, tourist villages in Europe like Finland began with providing cottages or food services in the suburbs. In the Netherlands, however, rural tourist activities were carried out by camping in the farming areas and doing activities around the farms (Puczko and Puczko, 1998). In Indonesia, the emerging rural tourism (Ahimsa-Putra et al, 2000; Damanik, 2009; Fagance, 1997; Ikaputra, 1985; Nuryanti, 1992; Raharjana, 2005, 2010, 2012) is an attempt to preserve the agrarian assets as tourist attractions. It is argued that tourism and agriculture can be synergised to empower the economy. To this extent, farming activities can be tourist attractions and the tourism sector can promote agriculture to ensure simultaneously a flourishing tourism programme and agricultural development (Pitana and Gaol, 2006).

A number of researchers argue that rural tourism is an integrated system of attractions, accommodation and other supporting facilities in a rural atmosphere. Rural tourism refers to a residential area located in the non-urban countryside, either intentionally or unintentionally, which has been developed into an attractive resort where tourists can stay overnight (Ahimsa-Putra et al, 2000). Ikaputra (1985) has mentioned that rural tourism comprises a settlement with environmental facilities which are compatible with tourist demands to enjoy, or learn about and appreciate. In anthropology (Burns, 1999; Smith, 1989) tourism also involves socio-cultural interaction between the local people and the visitors, done in the context of seeking and providing different experiences in fair economic trade. The interaction affects typically interactive behaviour among the local people and the visitors. To this extent, the community is both the subject and the object of tourism (Damanik, 2009, 2013; Raharjana, 2005; [Dewa Putu, 2013).

Through the development of rural tourism, the local community participates directly in each phase of development. The local community can utilise available assets and resources for economic activities and preserve rural customs, culture and the environment (Permanasari, 2010; Pitana and Darma Putra, 2011). The development of rural tourism is the best example of community-based development with local community empowerment as the main component (Pitana and Darma Putra, 2011). This strategy corresponds to the government-issued four-track strategy of Kementerian Kebudayaan dan Pariwisata (2009), especially in terms of pro-poor, pro-job, pro-growth and pro-environment and through the tourist village this programme is expected to materialise.

On the other hand, the perception of tourism activities is inseparable from the effort to cope with differences (Simatupang, 1999). With their uniqueness such as the natural environment, breathtaking scenery and landscapes, diverse plants, distinctive people and their life pattern, rural areas become an alternative for the experience of the 'Other' (Smith and Eadington. 1992; Lane, 1994). With the shift in the tourist market, tourists demand 'new' experiences (Wanda, et al, 2009) in all aspects, within different physical, social and cultural environments.

In the context of the development of rural tourism accommodation, homestays flourish. Homestays are developed utilising one bedroom in a house for the tourists to stay. Unlike the other types of accommodation, the tourists stay with the house owner (Lynch et al, 2009). Not only do they interact with each other but they also share the local cultural experience (Amirruding, 2009; Hermantoro, 2013). In this, the tourists not only stay with the family but also learn the local culture, language and life style. Deep and intensive social interaction between the tourists and the owner makes the homestay different from other accommodation (Lynch, 2009).

Wall and Long (1996) noted that among 100 accommodation units in their case material from south-central Bali, 14 were homestays. Most (71%) homestays belonged to Balinese (71%) and the rest (29%) belonged to other Indonesians. They have been in operation for seven years with 9 rooms on average. Each homestay employed 5 staff, most of them were unskilled. 70% of them were 21 to 30 years old, 91% were Balinese and were paid Rupiah (Rp) 49.000, on average (1995). The occupancy rate was below 40% and most of the guests (81%) went on tours. Those who stayed in homestays comprised 21% domestic tourists, 33% Australians and New Zealanders, 33% Europeans, 5% Japanese and 8% from other countries. The room rate ranged from Rp. 5,000 to Rp. 20,000 per night single complete with cold water, and Rp. 10,000 to Rp. 30,000 provided with hot and cold water. Most homestays employed family members and a few neighbours. Some of them were experienced in the tourism industry.

In 2005 some Dieng residents started their dual profession: as farmers and tourism workers. The fast growing tourism in Dieng Plateau has generated a range of responses (Ahimsa-Putra, 2011). Dieng residents respond to tourism development and activities in three ways: first, the economic responses, second, social responses and third, cultural responses. As 'economic beings' humans are absolutely free to choose the available alternatives, free to decide. Humans are embedded within a mind frame of making choices or decisions. To this extent, humans are assumed to have an awareness and understanding of the conditions affecting their choice (Ahimsa-Putra, 2003:15). Therefore, the responses of Dieng residents, utilising their house as a homestay, is perceived as the product of rational decision-making in this newly emerging behaviour in response to the growing opportunities of tourism (Ahimsa-Putra, 2011). In addition to the economic responses, homestays generate social responses to the new activities in the form of new social institutions, improved social relations and more networking with outside parties. Homestays not only improve the social relations among the local people but also nurture new values as a result of the encounters between tourists and local people. The cultural responses are characterised in terms of the increasing understanding and the creation of new rules established by the homestay business. In conclusion, the tourist activities in Dieng have generated three different responses for in-depth analysis in the next section.

Results of the Field Study

Development of Homestay Business in Dieng Plateau

'Success will soon have followers'

The above expression implies that when a business is successful it will be imitated by other people. The expression vividly describes what happens in the homestay business in Dieng. Nowadays, homestays provide additional livelihoods for the local residents. Crop failure in potato farming has made the homestay business the growing economic alternative for families. The increasing numbers of unaccommodated tourists initiated the establishment of homestays in Dieng. Forced by foggy weather and unsafe roads, the visitors decided to stay on rather than return home. Unluckily, during the high season, Gunung Mas Hotel, the only available hotel, was unable to accommodate all the guests. Therefore, some families came up with the idea to utilise their house as a homestay.

> Mrs. X and her husband, who are staff in the Tourism Agency, have been running a homestay for quite a long time. Their homestay, as a pioneer along with the legal permit, provides 5 rooms; each is 3x3 metres in size, completed with a garage for 3 cars and several motorcycles. Mrs. X lives with her second child, the first goes to a boarding school. Almost similar with other homestays, her family occupies the back part of her house. This suggests that the rooms for homestay are prioritised over the ones used by the owners. They realize that they still rely on the homestay business despite the husband's fixed monthly income and potato farm (field notes, 2010, emphasis by the author)

The local tourism agency convinces the local residents that they will obtain substantial income from the tourism industry in addition to the agricultural sector. At present, the local residents are eager to carry out economic enterprises supporting tourist activities. From initially 10 homestays the number has surged to approximately 50 homestays. Given that the homestay owners are relatives, they will refer the guests without accommodation to other homestays. In addition, most families in Dieng occupy a big house despite having a small family. It suggests that owning a large-sized house indicates the level of a family's economic well-being.

In general, the homestays in Dieng are adequate and meet the standard seven for foreign tourists. Most homestays have built bathrooms with a water heater, and a sprung bed is available in the bedroom. A fireplace is always available in all homestays. Bedrooms are comfortable with pillows, bolsters, bed cover, and a thick blanket for warmth. In the bedroom, carpet, lighting, and ventilation are available. A TV or DVD is also available in some homestays. Depending on the owners, the facilities are different in different homestays. Generally, the bathroom is proper for use with a shower, seat closet, and hot and cold water. On average, 3 to 4 bathrooms are available for 4 to 5 bedrooms.

Profiles of Homestays and the Owners

50 respondents demonstrate the demographic diversity in terms of age, gender, education and main occupation (seeTable1).

Table. 1. Respondents' Age, Gender, Education and Occupation

Age	%
< 25 years	7.7
26-39 Years	82.1
> 40 years	10.2
Gender	
Male	25.6
Female	74.4
Education	
Elementary School	17.9
Junior High School	30.8
Senior/Vocational High School	58.3
Occupation	
Farmer	38.5
Housewife	35.9
Private	25.6

Source: primary data, analysed in 2010

In terms of age, most homestay owners are women. They also manage the household, aged between 26-39 years and have completed senior high school. Most homestay owners are farmers, housewives and some are entrepreneurs.

Homestays in Dieng were initiated in 2000 along with the rising tourist activities and the activities undertaken by the Dieng Pandawa Tourism Conscious Group with the steady growth over time as Table 2 reveals. The Table shows an increasing number of rented rooms. This consideration is inseparable from the 'economic rationality' in the owner's mind that 'guests are kings'; therefore, they gear up to open rooms for homestays, with varied room rates depending on the facilities. The room rates range from Rp125,000 to Rp150,000. As a model of community-based tourist enterprises, homestays are an important strategy to minimise unemployment while providing additional income for families. The employees are the family members or relatives who serve the guests. As a small business, homestays commonly hire no specific employees.

Table 2. Profile of Homestay Business

Initiating the business in ....(year)	%
< 2000	20.5
2001-2006	51.3
> 2007	28.2
Number of Rented Rooms	
< 2	28.2
3	33.3
>4	38.5
Room Rate	
< 100.000,-	5.1
125.000-150.000,-	84.6
>150.000,-	10.3
Employees	
0 (Not hiring any employees)	43.6
2	41.0
3	15.4

Source: primary data, analysed in 2010

Table 3 presents the facilities available outside the homestays. The facilities support the services to the guests, for instance, the yard to accommodate a large number of guests, the parking lot for the guests' cars, a terrace for the guests to relax on, and the fence for ensuring security.

Table 3. Available Facilities outside the Homestay

Type of Facilities	%
Yard	87.2
Garden	41.0
Parking Lot	79.5
Terrace	97.4
Dry-up Clothe Place	97.4
Waste Dump	97.4
Fence	59.0

Source : primary data, analysed in 201

Table 4. Available Facilities inside the Homestay

Type of Facilities	%
Guest Room	92.3
Living Room	89.7
Dining Room	94.9
Working Room	25.6
Kitchen	94.9
Washing Room	94.9

Source : primary data, analysed in 2010

In addition to facilities outside the homestay, facilities inside the homestay are crucial which include the living room, family room, dining room and kitchen. Almost all homestays in Dieng provide the facilities listed in Table 4.

Table 5 shows two types of beds prepared. Inside the bedroom, there are tables and chairs, windows or ventilation, lamps, clothes hangers, mirrors, a towel drying shelf and cupboard. In certain bedrooms, bathroom and television are available. Comprehensive and high quality facilities in the bedroom ensure that the room rate can be increased to provide a higher income.

Table 5. Available Facilities in the Bedroom of the Homestay

Available Facilities in the Bedroom	%
Bed	
- Single	76.9
- Double	23.1
Tables and Chairs	41.0
Television	23.1
Windows	92.3
Air Ventilation	94.9
Bathroom	43.6
Clothes Hanger	87.2
Towel Dry-up Rack	87.2
Clothes Hanger	94.9
Cupboard	76.9
Mirror	87.2

Source : Primary Data, analysed in 2010

Tourism in Dieng and Community Responses

Tourist activities inevitably trigger new responses in the community. Tourism encourages social and cultural changes in addition to changes in the physical environment which will affect the economic aspect significantly. From initially their status as potato farmers, the local residents nowadays are involved in the tourism industry. The following discussion describes the community responses associated with the developing tourism industry in Dieng.

Economic Responses: Homestay, Newly earned income for Dieng Community

The enhanced response refers primarily to the economic responses the local residents engage in. Tourism has encouraged the local people in Dieng to utilise their house in a different, more productive way, learning from their neighbours' success. The homestay business is closely related to potato farming in the local families. Almost all families have potato farms to cultivate. Because of its seasonality at certain times of the year, the income from potato farming is far below that derived from the homestay business. At present, growing potatoes has become a secondary livelihood for most families. The homestay owners compensate the lower income from their farming activities because they are able to meet the family needs from the homestay business. Here is an example of one household's experience.

> The homestay gives a promising income. During Lebaran 2009, we earned 10million rupiahs just within 1 week. In the school holidays in June 2010, we earned 7 million rupiahs in 15 days. On average, we got more or less 400,000 rupiahs a day; much higher than what we obtained from the potato farming. Normally, we spent the homestay profits to complete the facilities like extra blankets, water heater, and room heater. We obtained our profit after the gross revenue was deducted for family needs, operational costs, and school tuition expenses (field notes, 2010).

In Dieng, the farmer families do not separate out the income from the homestay and that of potato farming. The husband gives the income from potato cultivation to his wife, and the wife reports the homestay income to her husband. This shared income management synergises cooperation between husband and wife in which during the potato harvest and low homestay season, the wife helps her husband in the farm. Likewise, the husband is involved in serving the guests during high homestay season. When having guests in the homestay, the housewife is even busier. Before daybreak, she cooks the breakfast. If the guests demand lunch and dinner, she will be busy preparing the meals. Some homestay owners explained that all this economic activity was done in the interests of family welfare. They realized that they cannot only rely on either the potato farming or the homestay business. Every family is obsessed in getting sufficient income to send their children out of the village for a better education. Sending children for schooling outside Dieng requires a lot of money in that they also need fees for a boarding house or dormitory to stay in.

Social Responses

Tourism activities in a community will certainly generate both social changes and environmental impacts. The following are the kinds of social responses:

Establishing an institution for homestay management

As social beings, a business within the community should be supported by a management structure. The growing number of homestays and the associated activities are under the management of the Dieng Pandawa Tourism Conscious Group (Kelompok Sadar Wisata Dieng Pandawa). The organisation is aimed at maintaining a partnership among homestay owners, collecting relevant business data on a continuous basis, and conducting regular meetings to discuss the problems and development of the homestay business. The homestay owners collectively prepare shared rules and agreements to ensure consistency and regularity in the running of homestay businesses. Setting standards for guest service, cleanliness of bedrooms and bathrooms, and imposing agreed room rates are among the issues which are discussed and decided upon.

Enhancing relations with the guests

'Customers are king' is the slogan of which the homestay owners are fully aware. They know that their guests should be provided with the best services, with which they are expected to come back. The relationship between the guests and the homestay owners as hosts is initially economically motivated in relation to the income that the owners expect to gain. Therefore, the homestay owners gear up to improve the homestay conditions and service. They will be geared up to meet the guests' demands for well-prepared rooms and homestay facilities. In general, the efforts are closely linked to internalising the spirit of *sapta pesona* (seven enchantments [elements or principles to ensure the safety, comfort and satisfaction of tourists]) in tourism especially for the homestay owners. To this extent, all homestays have complied with this spirit. Nearly all rooms offered are well-prepared, clean and secure. The guests should not worry about their luggage while going on tours. In addition, the homestay owners' hospitality has generally impressed the guests enabling a level of sustained contact despite their return home. Apparently, with the best service, the guest-host relations are not merely economic, but also social. This suggests that in addition to the economic objectives are social motives for building social relations to support sustainable guest-host communication.

Expanding social networking with outside parties

Involvement in the tourism industry means a new sphere for the farmers in Dieng. They are no longer only familiar with soil, fertilizers and agricultural middlemen. Through this new economic activity, they have broken the long-existing socio-cultural barriers. Tourism opens wider insights and encourages the Dieng villagers to learn about other people. When engaged in the homestay business, they learn about the guests' interests, backgrounds and personalities. Besides, they also develop social networking with schools, travel agencies, event organisers, production houses and others. Dealing with outsiders has provided a new set of social activities for Dieng residents. Interacting with travel agencies, becoming acquainted with the production houses, building their village along with the university through the Community Field Service (KKN) programme, interacting with the government and other parties are made possible for Dieng residents.

Developing homestay programmes for tourists

Staying overnight in homestays in Dieng is unique for the guests. They are free to become involved in the residents' daily activities. The guests can gather in the kitchen (*pawon*). For Dieng residents, *pawon* which is actually a kitchen is more frequently used for receiving the guests. In the *pawon*, an *anglo* (traditional fireplace) is always available. These facilities have made the homestay experience in Dieng unique. The guests can also become involved in the residents' daily activities such as farming or harvesting potatoes, processing *carica* fruit into typical Dieng syrup, making crafts to take home or touring the village.

Cultural Responses

Accepted 'Tourist Culture' among the community

Tourism is believed to be the agent of change. The influx of tourists in a community for tourist activities stimulates a change in the mindset, system of ideas, values and emerging 'new' interactions, and encourages the local people to behave and act upon the tourist environment accordingly. Tourism has forced the residents to get to know and to develop a "tourist culture'. Inevitably, they have to learn to be a good host, provide the best services and other facilities to the tourists in their homestay for their comfort and to encourage them to return to their homestay. The local residents learn to recognise and understand the 'tourist culture' directly through their contact with the guests and the guidance and direction by the related agencies and universities/colleges or NGOs conducting field services in Dieng. Through tourist activities especially running homestays, the residents are encouraged and encourage themselves to internalise the guest-service spirit.

Preparing new rules for the prospective guests of homestay

The homestay business requires 'new' rules and orders. The rules are collectively agreed by the homestay owners. In this lies the strategic role of the homestay management institution. Requiring the guests to carry their marriage certificate is one unique example of the agreed rule. If they fail to show the certificate, the guests are advised to rent separate rooms. Or the host will politely refuse the guests' demand for staying in the same room.

The rule is strictly imposed to avoid the perception that staying in the homestay in Dieng is 'free', which means that the guests can do whatever they wish after paying. This rule is well monitored and enforced as the homestay owners believe that the income from the business should remain blessed and not violate their religious values.

Conclusion

The running of homestays is the result of the decisions and actions of the Dieng farmers as a rational economic response. The decision has been carefully calculated for its possible positive outcomes. Frequent tourist visits to Dieng have encouraged the local villagers to take the decision to run their own business. Overall this condition is supported by community-based tourism development in Dieng, through rural tourism that encourages full community participation and empowerment. As part of the business unit potential in rural tourism, homestays are beneficial in supporting the long-established activity of potato cultivation by the Dieng farmers. The economic response to secure income to compensate for the lower level of remuneration from potation cultivation dominates the running of homestay businesses among the farmers.

The rapid growth of homestay business generates social and cultural responses, which give specific contributions to local tourism management. The social responses are apparent with the established homestay management institution, the development of new relations and interactions with the tourists, expanded social networking with outside parties and the capability to prepare a viable and successful homestay programme. Meanwhile, the cultural responses can be observed in relation to a more open mindset among the Dieng residents. The open attitude is positive and active but it operates along with the imposition of rules for the homestay guests to ensure that an appropriate moral and ethical environment flourishes in line with the local culture.

Acknowledgements

On the completion of the field study and chapter, I would like to thank the Graduate School of UGM (University of Gadjah Mada), Graduate School of Tourism studies of UGM, Puspar (Center for Tourism Studies) UGM Yogyakarta, Pandawa Tourism Conscious Group of Dieng (Kelompok Sadar Wisata, Dieng Pandawa) Banjarnegara, all homestay owners and farmers in Dieng Kulon, Banjarnegara, Central Java.

References

Abu, A. (2009). ‘Strategies for the successful marketing of homestay programme: some useful lessons’, *International Seminar on Community based Tourism: Learning From the homestay Programme in Malaysia, Towards Developing a sustainable Community Based Tourism: Issues, Impacts & Opportunities.* 4-16 August 2009, Hotel UiTM, Shah Alam Selangor Malaysia.

Ahimsa-Putra, Heddy Shri, Arie Sujito and Wiwied Trisnadi (2000) ‘Pengembangan Model Pariwisata Pedesaan sebagai Alternatif Pembangunan Berkelanjutan’, *Laporan Hibah Penelitian Bersaing*, Lembaga Penelitian UGM Yogyakarta.

Ahimsa-Putra, H. (2003) Prologue: Dari Ekonomi Moral, Rasional ke Politik Usaha’. In H.S. Ahimsa-Putra (ed.), *Ekonomi Moral, Rasional dan Politik dalam Industri Kecil di Jawa*, Yogyakarta: Kepel Press.

—. (2011) ‘Pariwisata di Desa dan Respon Ekonominya: Kasus dusun Brayut di Sleman Yogyakarta’, *Patra Widya*, 12, No. 4, Balai Pelestarian Sejarah dan Nilai Tradisional Yogyakarta.

Burns, M. P. (1999) *An Introduction to Tourism and Anthropology*, London: Routledge.

Damanik, J. (2009) ‘Isu-Isu Krusial Dalam Pengelolaan Desa Wisata Dewasa Ini’, *Jurnal Kepariwisataan Indonesia,* 5 : 127-137.

—. (2013) *Pariwisata Indonesia: Antara Peluang dan Tantangan*,Yogyakarta: Pustaka Pelajar.

Fagence, M. (1997) ‘Ancangan Perencanaan Pariwisata Desa dan Pariwisata Perdesaan: Upaya Mewujudkan Potensi Desa dan Daerah Perdesaan’. In Myra Gunawan (ed.), *Perencanaan Pariwisata Berkelanjutan,* Bandung, pp. 90-100.

Hermantoro, H. (2013) ‘Program Pengembangan Homestay’, *Tentang Kepariwisataan:kumpulan tulisanku seputar ke pariwisataan nasional*, Depok: Aditri, pp.59-64.

Ikaputra(1985) *Desa Wisata Kasongan*, Tugas Akhir Jurusan Arsitektur, Fakultas Teknik, Universitas Gadjah Mada Yogyakarta, unpublished.

Lane, B. (1994) 'What is Rural Tourism, *Journal of Sustainable Tourism*, 2:7-21.

Lynch, P. A, A. J. McIntosh and H. Tucker (2009) *Commercial Homes in Tourism: an International Perspective*, New York: Routledge.

Nuryanti, W. (1992) 'Pariwisata dalam Masyarakat Tradisional', makalah dalam *Program Pelatihan Perencanaan dan Pengembangan Pariwisata*, Jakarta, unpublished.

Permanasari, I. (2010) 'Pengentasan Kemiskinan Melalui Pemberdayaan Masyarakat di Desa Wisata', *Jurnal Kepariwisataan Indonesia,* 5: 55-69.

Pitana, IG, and Haris Lumban Gaol (2006) 'Pengembangan Sinergi antara Sektor Pertanian dengan Pariwisat', *Jurnal Kepariwisataan Indonesia*, Vol.1 No.3 September. Jakarta: Pusat Penelitian dan Pengembangan Kepariwisataan Depbudpar.

Pitana, I Gde and I Nyoman Darma Putra (2011) *Pemberdayaan dan Hiperdemokrasi dalam Pembangunan Pariwisata*, Denpasar: Pustaka Larasan.

Puczko, L. and T. Ratz (1998) 'Rural Tourism and Sustainable Development', paper presented in *Rural Tourism Management: Sustainable Options,* International Conference, Auchinamire, Scotland.

Putu, Dewa Oka Prasiasa (2013) *Destinasi Pariwisata Berbasis Masyarakat*, Jakarta: Penerbit Salemba Humanika.

Raharjana, D. (2005) *Pengembangan Desa Wisata Berbasis Budaya: Kajian Etnoekologi Masyarakat Dusun Ketingan, Tirtoadi, Mlati Sleman DIY*, Sekolah Pascasarjana UGM :Yogyakarta, Environmental Science thesis.

—. (2010) Partisipasi Masyarakat dalam Perencanaan Pengelolaan Pariwisata, Final Report, Hibah Penelitian Dosen Sekolah Pasca Sarjana UGM : Yogyakarta.

—. (2012) 'Membangun Pariwisata Bersama Rakyat: Kajian Partisipasi Lokal dalam Membangun Desa Wisata di Dieng Plateau', *Kawistara* Vol. 2, No. 3 Desember, Yogyakarta: Sekolah Pascasarjana UGM.

Roberts, L. and Hall, D. (2001) *Rural Tourism and Recreation: Principles to Practise*, CABI Publishing : www.cabi.org.

Simatupang, L. L. (1999) 'Pariwisata dan Pengembangan Desa, *Pendampingan Masyarakat Seni dan Budaya,* Jakarta, unpublished workshop module.

Smith, V.L. (ed.) (1989) *Hosts and Guests: the Anthropology of Tourism*, Philadelphia: University of Pennsylvania Press, second revised edition.

Smith, V.L., and W.R. Eadington (1992) *Tourism Alternatives: Potentials and Problems in the Development of Tourism*, Philadelphia: University of Pennsylvania Press.

Sonjaya, J. A. (2005) *Pengelolaan Warisan Budaya di Dataran Tinggi Dieng*, Program Pascasarjana, Fakultas Ilmu Budaya UGM: unpublished thesis.

Sukatno, O. (2004) *Dieng Poros Dunia: Menguak Jejak Peta Surga yang Hilang*, Yogyakarta: IRCiSoD.

Thohir, M. (2007) *Memahami Kebudayaan : Teori, Metodologi, dan Aplikasi*, Semarang: Fasindo Press

Wall, G. and Long,V. (1996) 'Balinese Homestays: an Indigenous Response to Tourism Opportunities'. In R. Butler and T. Hinch (eds), *Tourism and Indigenous Peoples*, International Thomson Business Press: British, pp. 27-48.

Wanda, G.E., H. Mair and D.G. Reid (2009) *Rural Tourism Development: Localism and Cultural Change*, Clevedon: Channel View Publications.

THE POTENTIAL FOR MANAGEMENT IN COMMUNITY-BASED ECOTOURISM OF LILED COMMUNITY, SURATHANI PROVINCE, THAILAND

RUNGRAWEE JITPAKDEE

Background of the Study

According to a World Tourism Organisation (WTO) forecast, by 2020, 20% of tourists around the world (an estimated 1.6 billion) would be nature tourists (WTO, 2002). Thus, ecotourism offers tremendous opportunities, particularly for local communities, by earning income from catering services and offering local products to tourists (Hiwasaki, 2006). Although ecotourism has been promoted in the local community as a 'win-win' solution for developing countries, its assessment shows it is much more complicated (Honey, 2008). Having learned from such experiences, since 2001, the Tourism Authority of Thailand (TAT) and associated agencies have begun to pay attention to the promotion of community ecotourism that can contribute to meet both the needs of sustainable ecotourism and also promote local development (TAT, 2001). The Thai Government is promoting ecotourism in areas with a rich natural diversity which has not so far been affected by mass tourism. There were more than 600 tourist destinations that included natural and cultural resources suitable for promotion as ecotourism in their areas identified by the Government (Chettamart, 2003; Sriphnomya, 2006). One of the communities in Thailand that has tried to institute a management plan and develop a community-based ecotourism destination in their own area is Liled, located in the Phunphin District of Surathani Province (Figure 1). When a community is well-known for community-based ecotourism, there are many agencies and government institutions interested in providing support and promotion without studying the potential of the local community for ecotourism management (McKenzie, 2003; Okpoko, 2006; Peterson, 2010).

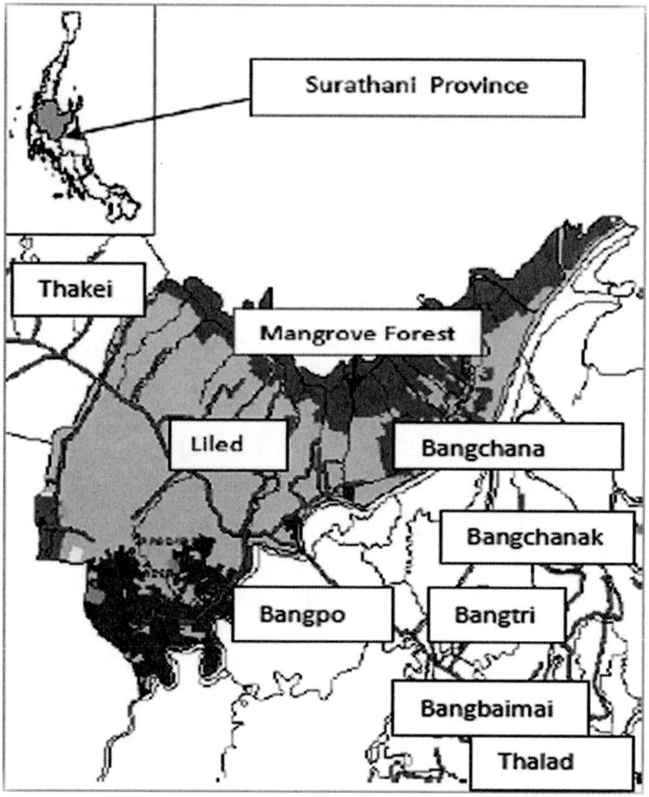

Figure 1: Map of Liled Community

On investigation, the Liled community has not had a comprehensive ecotourism management plan. Therefore, a viable plan needs to be developed by the participating people, raised by the community themselves. This study, itself, was a cohesive cooperation between the researcher and the local community. Finally, the fruitfulness of this study is the recommendations resulting in ecotourism development in the local community. It will be widely useful for everyone interested in ecotourism development, such as local communities, every level of government, NGOs and private sector agencies. They can bring the lessons learnt from the study to manage, improve and maintain ecotourism projects in local areas. For the local community, the local people can lift their awareness and improve the appropriate management of ecotourism.

Objectives of Study

The main objective of this research is aimed at assisting in the development of a management plan for ecotourism in the Liled community that would inherently benefit the entire community and all stakeholders. The study also concentrates on the levels and potentials of ecotourism management and participation by the community.

Research Methods

Quantitative research methods were used for the primary data collection. Questionnaires were distributed to eight villages and 195 samples from those communities were collected by using the simple random sampling method of Krejcie and Morgan (1970); the level of accuracy in the sample size methodology is 95%, with a rate of discrepancy estimated at 0.05 or 5%. Local community respondents provided the information for a self-assessment in community-based tourism management and participation. A sub-sample was then determined for each village taking into account the respective village population (total number of households). A systematic random sampling was employed to select the households for the questionnaire survey. In this regard, a list of households in each selected village was obtained from the Community Development Officer. Households from each village were numbered 1….n. Then, each sixth household was selected from the list for the interview. The researcher was assisted by two local well-educated women who could clearly explain the intents of the questions and provide necessary clarification when administering the questionnaires. In addition, accidental sampling was used to collect tourist data; 130 tourists visiting the community responded with questionnaires on tourist satisfaction and needs.

Qualitative data were also collected by using in-depth interviews of key informants. The key informants consisted of the village committee officials, the head of the Liled Ecotourism Club, chairpersons of the local fishery club, women's groups and local government officials from the Tourism Authority of Thailand office in Surathani Province. The informants had provided qualitative information on the local institutional arrangements established for the promotion of ecotourism. At the end of the study, a local community public hearing and participatory approach together with the researcher were used to develop a tourism development plan.

Results of Study

The findings of this study have shown that the Liled community had a high level of potential attention for development; however, the practical management was no more than fair. According to the tourists' opinions of both Thais and foreigners, the Liled community managed well in ecotourism activities with regard to serving tourists, but the provision of souvenirs was only moderate. Ecotourism facilities, such as transportation networks within the community, parking lots and toilets in the Liled community, needed to be developed.

The study of the people's participation in the Liled community showed that, overall, the level of participation by the Liled community was rated as good. There was participation and cooperation by the community in the process of two-way communication. The first round was 'Top Down', by obtaining a broad policy statement from the central government. Later, the village headman brought ideas for discussion with the local people. The second round was 'Bottom Up', by gathering the opinions and needs from the grassroots level. At the national level, the policies under the 10th National Development Plan (2007–2011), emphasise the important role of the local communities in running the tourism business, especially community-based ecotourism activities. Moreover, the ecotourism strategies encouraged the local tourism industry to establish clubs, organisations or cooperatives to work together towards the direction of conservation and development, and to strengthen the bargaining power of such organisations so that the local entrepreneurs could compete in the market. Such national policies have also been 'mainstreamed' in the ecotourism development plan of the Liled Community.

The Liled communities and institutions have therefore participated in the decision-making process in the promotion of ecotourism, in addition to learning and carrying out activities by setting up various organisations and expanding their networks, both within and outside their communities. They worked together to propose an action plan, in particular, the *Three-year Local Development Plan*. Their plan needed to reflect the nation's strategic plan for economic and social developments. The management plan laid down the regulations and rules for managing the influx of guests while maintaining coastal resources and benefiting the community. The distinctive participation of the Liled community consisted of working as community groups. The Liled community mostly participated as the group involved in trade and conservation. They persuaded the local fishermen's group to preserve the mangrove forests, for example. They set up an ecotourism club within the community, such as homestay programmes with local families. These involved organising labour within the local communities. Communities would be split up into groups with various duties, such as management, liaison, transportation, accommodation reservation and the provision of local tour guides. The club had succeeded in organising their ecotourism activities, most of which are designed in various forms and types, with the main objective of boosting the uniqueness of the locality and conserving the local resources and cultures. The main activities that the club has promoted include mangrove conservation, marine and fish conservation, commercial fishing protection and ecotourism tours over more than 7,000 *rais* (around 2800 acres) of the mangrove forest area. However, the ecotourism participatory process with regard to decision-making and implementation was achieved by only those people who were members of the ecotourism club. The significance of instituting a management plan for ecotourism should be clear to all. Aside from the potential economic benefits, there are the benefits of raising community awareness of the importance of conservation and the potential benefit of allowing fishing communities to conserve coastal resources for future generations and yet still benefit financially.

The result of the local community participation analysis — based on the questionnaire survey using the Weighted Average Index (WAI) (Khumsri et al, 2009) for the weight rank of the participation level — however, revealed that local people's participation in meetings organised for action planning or decision-making in ecotourism development was not so strong (as indicated in Table 1, with a Weighted Average Index [WAI] of 0.55). More than 50% of respondents said that they did not attend any meetings or expressed their opinions, because the decisions made were not usually based on their opinions (Table 1). Therefore, their participation in expressing views and providing suggestions about what to do regarding certain issues was very weak. This reflects the fact that the overwhelming majority of the people tacitly accepted the decisions made by the formal and informal community leaders. Likewise, their participation in training programmes organised for their capacity development was also very weak. The main reason why most members of the local community had less opportunity to attend any training was that the communication system between the training programme organisers and the community always broke down. Some of the community people expressed the view that when local governments or other government agencies held the training sessions, those who could attend were mostly members of the local groups or cousins of the heads of villages. Ordinary people in the community rarely accessed a training session. Moreover, less participation by community members because there was no time to attend meetings owing to the need to earn money was the common answer of the local people here. Moreover, the lack of knowledge leading to the loss of confidence in the decision-making in any involvement process was the root of the participation problem.

Supporting the data from the household survey, 48% of the respondents who had graduated from primary school also still had 4.5% uneducated numbers in the household. This could imply that some of the difficulties of the development community were the result of a lack of education which is important for helping people to develop and learn something new. However, their participation in terms of the voluntary contribution of labour in times of need was relatively strong, as was reflected in the WAI value of 0.70 (Table 1). Regarding their willingness to take part in future ecotourism promotion programmes, nearly 60% of the respondents mentioned that this would depend on the potential benefits that they would gain from their participation. Thus, they indicated that they would actively participate only if the proposed ecotourism programmes and projects could help in improving their economic status.

Table 1: Intensity of Community Participation in Ecotourism Activities

(Multiple responses)

Activities	**f**	**%**	**WAI Value**	**Assessment**
Joined the meetings	80	45	0.55	Occasionally
Expressed opinions on certain issues that needed their consensus	85	48	0.38	Rarely
Attended training programmes	37	21	0.40	Rarely
Joined as volunteer for works initiated by the community	148	83	0.70	Occasionally

Source: Field Survey, 2011

To provide a better understanding of the local participation process as mentioned in the above section, the selected factors that could lead to the success or failure of ecotourism development were considered and the association of the factors with the intensity of each participation process was explored. The predicted independent variables of the respondents included age, gender, number of years in school, original residence, year of residence in the community, ecotourism employment, members in each household, annual income of the household, size of ecotourism labour force in households, and degree of benefits from ecotourism employment. As indicated in the results of the study, the interrelationship between the two variables in terms of the strength of the relationship and the direction between such interrelated variables could be observed. The key factors associated with the intensity of people's participation in ecotourism activities are illustrated in Table 2.

Table 2: Factors Associated with the Intensity of Community Participation in Ecotourism Activities

Factors	Correlation Coefficient			
	Joined meetings	Expressed opinions	Attended training	Joined as volunteer
Age	0.151*	0.040	0.071	0.030
Degree of benefits from ecotourism employment	0.031	0.111	0.142	0.173*
Original residence	0.010	0.011	0.016	0.229**
Size of labour force engaged in ecotourism	0.072	0.032	0.159*	0.178*
Female	0.130	0.050	0.170*	0.026
Male	0.120	0.030	0.130	0.046

** Correlation is significant at 0.01 confidence level (2-tailed)
* Correlation is significant at 0.05 confidence level (2-tailed)

The results of this study showed that local people's participation in ecotourism activities organised for action planning or decision-making in the Liled community was at a low level. The factors that significantly affected the peoples' participation in ecotourism activities included, (i) age, which was significantly associated with joining the meetings, (ii) degree of benefits from ecotourism employment, which was significantly associated with the people's participation in volunteer work on ecotourism activities (at $p<0.05$), (iii) original residence had a significant association with attending the meetings (at $p<0.01$) and, (iv) the size of the ecotourism labour force in households, which was significantly associated with the attendance at training sessions and joining the voluntary work of the local community (at $p<0.05$). Likewise, the gender of the respondents had a significant relationship with the attendance at training sessions (at $p<0.05$), as shown in Table 2.

As shown in the above findings, five factors had been associated with the level of the people's participation in ecotourism activities. The relationship of these factors with the intensity of people's participation is explained below.

Older respondents attended meetings relatively more frequently. As can be noted in many meetings of the community, more people of 50 years old and above were attending meetings compared with the younger ones, because the older people had more free time than the younger ones at a working age.

The degree of benefits that can be obtained from ecotourism employment had a relationship with joining in voluntary work in community activities. Thus, if higher benefits could be gained from ecotourism employment, the participation as volunteers in ecotourism activities could be more frequent.

Original residents meant that their parents were born in the Liled community and were still living in the community. The result showed that original residence is one of the factors that had the strongest relationship with participation in voluntary work. Therefore, if the respondents were the original people in the community, they tended to join more frequently in voluntary work there.

The size of the ecotourism labour force was associated with the people's participation process, especially in attending training sessions and joining voluntary work. This implies that when a greater number of the household members are engaged in ecotourism employment, they had more frequency in attending the training programmes.

Gender was a factor that was associated with participation in the training programmes. Gender was used as a dummy variable with male assigned the value 0 and female the value 1. The result showed that female respondents participated in training programmes more than the male respondents. As a result, the female respondents participated in significantly more training sessions on ecotourism promotion. As noted, there were more women attending the many training programmes conducted in the community, because there were many organised women's groups in the community established for the purpose of developing their livelihoods and thus, were actively joining any training programmes provided.

The above analysis also revealed the rather weak participation of people in the area of decision-making (Table 2). To understand the underlying reason for this variation the respondents were asked why decision-making and action taking in the community could not be achieved in spite of the people's participation in the process. As found in this study, the problems and obstacles identified that had affected the people's participation in ecotourism activities included a lack of information about ecotourism relayed to the local people, the lack of knowledge and understanding about ecotourism, and the lack of effective leaders within the community.

As mentioned in the section on community leadership, most of the community leaders still lacked knowledge and techniques to properly manage the facilities. Thus, they could not empower local communities to participate, to link economic benefits to conservation, and to allow the local community to participate at all stages in the project cycle. Very few community leaders who volunteered in the ecotourism activities had the potential to convey a clear understanding of ecotourism development to other community people and could not work towards a sensible compromise. Moreover, the lack of proper cooperation between the local people and the official governments and the conflict of interests, in particular, corruption in the government system, were the main complex factors that affected the participation of the local people in community activities. The local communities expressed the concern that the government officers in both regional and local governments did not provide the local people with sufficient opportunities to participate significantly in ecotourism (Table 3). This explains why 50% of the respondents evaluated as weak the participation in ecotourism activities of the local people in terms of decision-making and taking action (Table 3).

Finally, the local community public hearing and participation workshop was held in the Liled community. The local community and the researcher collaborated to set out the procedure and the responsible authority in each function for developing the Liled community-based ecotourism plan as in Figure 2.

Table 3: Obstacles in Community Participation in Ecotourism Activities

	(Multiple responses)	
Reasons	**f**	**%**
Ignored by the government	58	65.17
Lack of effective leaders	37	41.57
Lack of knowledge and low education	32	35.96

Source: Field Survey, 2010

The first step in ecotourism management planning was setting meetings and a blueprint of the ecotourism management plan for the community by the community themselves. According to the participatory action of the local people, they used the results from the researcher to brainstorm the processes and issues needing to be developed, such as public relations for ecotourism in their community, accommodation management in both homestays and resorts, raising the awareness both of the local people and visitors, setting a code of conduct for ecotourism management in the area, finding funding and the need for human resources development in ecotourism, and finalising the *Ecotourism Management Plan for the Community*. Significantly, every process requires all stakeholders to take responsibility; in particular, the local community has an important role in achieving involvement in every function and every step. Consequently, the *Ecotourism Management Plan of the Local Community by the Local Community* will be practical.

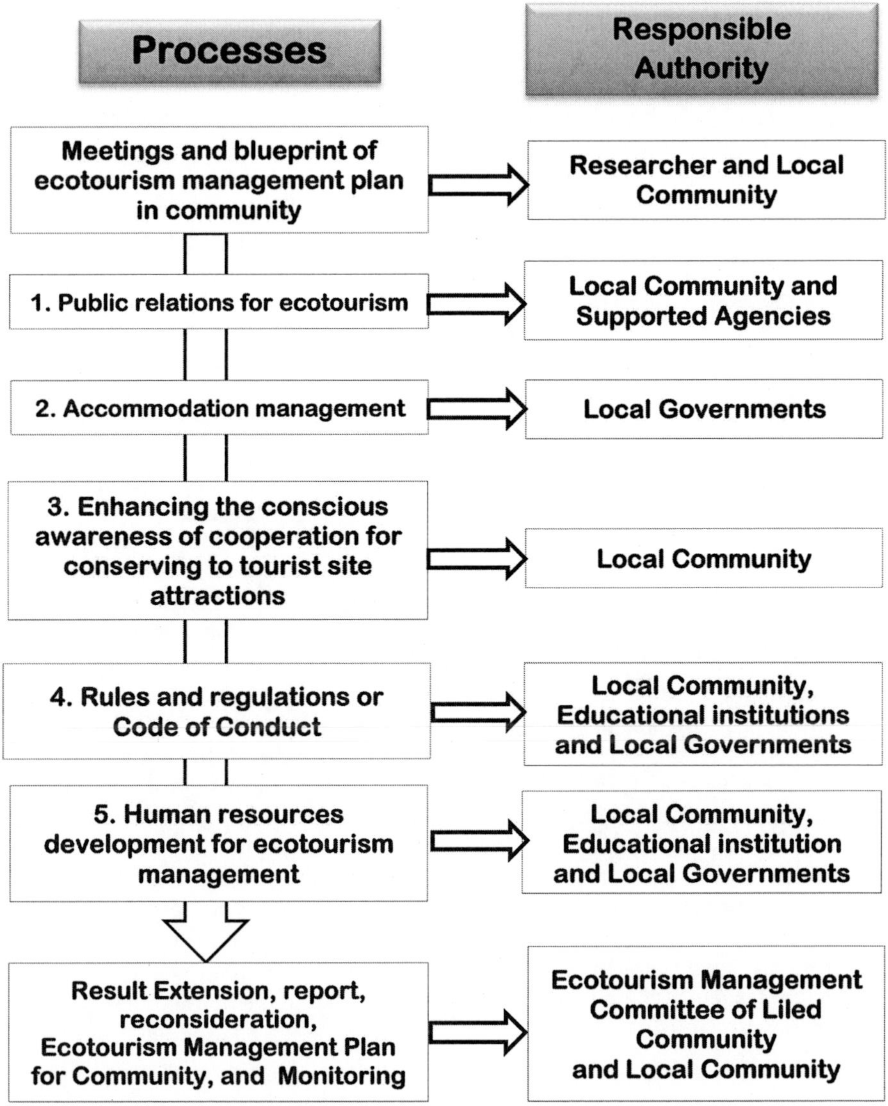

Figure 2: Processes and Responsible Authority of Ecotourism Management Planning of Liled Community

Discussion

As the results of this study have shown, the major factors that could increase the quality and local involvement of ecotourism management in Liled were the high potential in the ecotourism touring programme and service, whereas the tourists responded that the quality and uniqueness of the souvenirs available was not sufficiently adequate. The issues of ecotourism management improvement were the facilities and physiology of tourism destinations, such as a transportation service in the community, parking lots, and toilets in public and tourist areas. This result of the study was similar to the study of ecotourism management potential in the Yaplek community, Samutsakorn Province, Thailand (Thaikamon, 2009). Thaikamon proposed that even though the responsibility of the local people in ecotourism management was very high, the basic infrastructure, such as waste management, and the quality of the trail and tourist information centre were insufficient to present a convincing case for the continuing support of existing ecotourism activities in the areas.

In addition, the result of community participation in Liled was distinctive in the ecotourism projects establishment. Local people gathered in various groups to support ecotourism activities, such as the mangrove forests protection group, ecotourism conservation club, and homestay group. The community seemed to recognise the value of the projects and seemed willing to participate at all levels. This recipe for success is consistent with the research of Eiamsetthi (2005), who suggests that local participation and the division of responsibilities and labour in the hands of the local stakeholders are essential for manning these types of ecotourism programmes. His research also demonstrates that community tourism can be used as a tool to strengthen relationships between members of communities because of the shared and co-dependent nature of the programmes themselves. These tended to get everyone in a community working together for the same goal. In the best cases, community tourism projects, such as the one being attempted in Liled, create unity among the locals.

Recommendations

As indicated in the findings of the study, the extent of community participation in ecotourism activities in the Liled community was rather weak, because of the several obstacles expressed by the local people and these needed to be urgently resolved for the ecotourism development of the Liled community. In this regard, government authorities, in particular the local government, should effectively disseminate information on meetings, training programmes and the benefits to be provided by any ecotourism activities, so the villagers would actively participate in ecotourism activities. It is important to enhance the understanding of the local people of the purpose and importance of conducting ecotourism training activities and, in particular, of the benefits that they would gain from attending and participating in such activities. This should be announced well ahead and prior to the conduct of such activities as meetings, training sessions and conservation efforts. In the process of getting the participants' opinions and decisions for ecotourism development, the authorities should reduce local peoples' feelings of powerlessness in expressing opinions on certain issues that need their consensus. The means of improvement is creating an atmosphere of motivation for their active participation and providing an avenue that would make the community members more comfortable with being involved in the deliberations.

In addition, the results of this study were, for the most part, encouraging for the potential of the Liled community instituting and developing their own community-based ecotourism project with confidence. There should be reinforcement in achieving high levels of cooperation and participation by all stakeholders. One of the most important and equally most promising suggested developments was the establishment of a committee to help oversee the community ecotourism projects in the area. This type of committee should be focused on helping all stakeholders achieve success from community ecotourism and all participants should have the opportunity of being heard. This will empower the local actors to monitor developments themselves without having to rely on outside help from government agencies or outsourcing tasks to companies that have less of a stake in the overall well-being of the community. Importantly, however, communities should be supported with funding from the public sector, thus enabling them to achieve ecotourism goals with less hardship and partake in such projects with more confidence and less worry or financial burdens. The Government must be committed to helping these types of projects to develop and it should be serious about supporting the local stakeholders. It is recommended that stakeholders examine this case study to enable them to better decide in which direction to steer projects and to better identify where best to allocate funding and other resources. The main focus may be most beneficial to all contributors if the focus is on constant and sustainable improvements.

References

Chettamart, S. (2003) 'Ecotourism Resources and Management in Thailand', a paper presented at *the Malaysia-Thailand Technology and Business Partnership Dialogue*, 27–28 July 2003, Langkawi, Malaysia.

Eiamsetthi, P. (2005) *The Pattern of People Participation in Tourism Destination: Case Study of the Suan Hin Pa Ngam Community, Lei Province*, Lei Rajabhat University: unpublished Master's thesis.

Hiwasaki, L. (2006) *Community-based Tourism: a Pathway to Sustainability for Japan's Protected Areas Natural Sciences Sector*, Paris: United Nations Educational, Scientific and Cultural Organization (UNESCO).

Honey, M. (2008) *Ecotourism and Sustainable Development: who owns paradise?* Washington DC: Island Press, second edition.

Khumsri, M., K. Ruddle and G.P. Shivakoti (2009) 'Rights and Conflicts in the Management of Fisheries in the Lower Songkhram River Basin, Northeast Thailand', *Environmental Management*, 43: 557–570.

Krejcie, R.V. and D.W. Morgan (1970) 'Determining Sample Sizes for Research Activities', *Educational and Psychological Measurement*, 30: 607–610.

McKenzie, E. (2003) 'Common-interest Housing in the Communities of Tomorrow', *Housing Policy Debate*, 14: 203–215.

Okpoko, P. U. (2006) *Issues in Tourism Planning and Development*, Nsukka: Afro-Orbis Publishing Co, Ltd.

Petersen, L. A. (2010) *An Examination of Integrated Rural Development in the Goris Region of Armenia*, a dissertation in cooperation with Utah State University, submitted to the Royal Agricultural College.

Sriphnomya, E. (2006) *Ecotourism Policy in Thailand*, Bangkok: Tourism Authority of Thailand.

Thaikamon, A. (2009) *The Potential of Local Community in Ecotourism Management: Case Study of Bang Ya Plek Community, Samuprakarn Province*, Kasetsart University: unpublished Master's thesis.

Tourism Authority of Thailand (TAT) (2001) *The Thailand Ecotourism Information Center,* retrieved from http://conservation.forest.ku.ac.th/ecotourdb/english/About_us/About_us.htm TAT, page consulted 20/06/2011.

World Tourism Organisation (WTO) (2002) *Asia-Pacific Ministerial Conference on Sustainable Development of Ecotourism*, Male, Maldives, 11–13 February 2002, final report.

COMMERCIALISATION AND SANITATION: CRITICAL ISSUES IN ALLOWING LOCALS TO INHABIT THE CORE ZONE OF A NATIONAL PARK: A CASE STUDY OF PHONG NHA-KE BANG NATIONAL PARK IN VIETNAM

TUAN PHONG LY

Introduction

When a rural area in a developing country is designated as a national park (NP) or listed as a World Heritage Site (WHS), tourism becomes the primary driving force of economic growth in the area. However, the government is usually not able to relocate all local communities in the area because of limited budget and resources. Tourists visiting NPs or WHSs expect a special or unique experience that is better than anything they have ever experienced before (Shackley, 2003). An increasing number of tourists prefer to experience authentic local cultures and lifestyles, thus suggesting that allowing locals to stay in the core zones of parks may become a trend in tourism development in developing countries.

Although advantageous for the improvement of rural livelihoods, tourism development also raises a number of complicated issues when locals are allowed to stay in the core zone of a NP. This study is primarily interested in two such issues, namely, the commercialisation of local culture and sanitation problems that have adverse effects on the environment. The researcher acknowledges that other significant problems (such as infrastructure construction, illegal hunting and logging, and increasing number of visitors) are also arising in park management. However, this study focuses on the locals living in the core zone and their management thereof. The human factor is important not only in terms of the commitment to the nomination and management of a WHS, but also in terms of the contribution to the intangible values of a park (Millar, 2012). Murphy (1985) has argued that 'communities are the destination of most travellers. It is in communities that tourism happens; it is an important component of the tourism product and the industry uses the community as a resource, sells it as a product, and in the process affects the lives of everyone' (ibid:165).

The first impressions of tourists in a park are provided by the locals. However, if the locals become too commercialised and become merely concerned with conducting business with tourists, then Vietnam risks losing its local culture, and consequently, tourism development is affected (Nguyen, Dang, Nguyen, Nguyen, and Phan, 2006). Nonetheless, local communities inhabiting the core zone of an NP or a WHS are essential to the preservation of the park environment. Therefore, the major stakeholders of this study are the local communities inhabiting the core zone of the park and the local government that manages such communities.

Phong Nha-Ke Bang (PNKB) NP in Vietnam was selected for the case study because of its typical provincial management model and unique WHS status. This study aims to examine the extent to which tourism affects the lives of locals after PNKB was designated as a NP and then listed as a WHS, and to determine methods of addressing sanitation problems associated with allowing locals to inhabit the core zone of the park. This study also discusses whether the National Park Management Board (NPMB) has managed the two aforementioned issues sufficiently.

Literature Review

Tourism Development and Commercialisation in Developing Countries

Tourism is the largest and fastest growing industry in the world. The Tourism 2020 Vision of the United Nations World Tourism Organization (UNWTO) forecasts that international arrivals are expected to reach almost 1.6 billion by 2020. The growth rate in the Southeast Asian region from 1995 to 2020 is forecast to reach more than 6.3% per year, which is higher compared with the world average of 4.1%. The regional arrivals figure is projected to reach 136 million per annum by 2020 (UNWTO, 2013a). Local governments in developing countries often consider tourism as a primary mechanism for improving the local economy and the living standards of its inhabitants (Tang and Jang, 2009). The top short-term goals of these governments are increasing the earnings of and creating jobs for the rapidly growing working-age population. Governments of developing countries are forced to support the current tourism development despite its incompatibility with long-term sustainable development (Tosun, 2001).

A large number of developing countries, such as Mexico, India, Turkey, and Vietnam, have a strong central government with practical administrative support for local governments; this type of management is called top-down management policy (Campbell, 1999; Tosun, 2000). Tourism in developing countries is argued to be set up from agreements between investors and the local government. The local community neither participates nor is it consulted in the development of tourism sites (Linton, 1987), and a huge communication gap exists between communities and decision-makers. This lack of communication does not only widen the knowledge gap between local communities and the government, but also promotes the isolation of local communities from tourism development (Tosun, 2000). The participation of locals in the tourism business results in the commercialisation of a park (Greenwood, 1989). Lack of sufficient education and communication with the government tempts isolated local communities to generate financial benefits from tourism development, thus ultimately resulting in commercialisation (Bao and Su, 2004; Li, Wu, and Tang, 2006).

Sanitation Issues in the Core Zone

People are generally not allowed to inhabit the core zones of NPs in order to minimise air, water, and land pollution. Such a precaution also reduces the amount of waste generated by tourists and locals (Denman, 2003). Locals inhabiting the core zone undoubtedly increase the appeal of tourism development and promote full-scale protection of local culture. However, tourism development and residents living in the core zone are factors that threaten the protection of biodiversity in the park. For PNKB NP, Ly (2007) reported that local communities pose two main sanitation issues. The first issue is waste management. Locals are used to throwing garbage along the riverside, thus causing downstream contamination and harm to river organisms. The second issue is severe water pollution in the park. The habits of locals of washing their laundry along the riverside and using well water do not only cause water pollution but also damage the natural underground river system of this limestone region. More importantly, locals are convinced that no clean water is available for daily use. Local doctors claim that the use of well water is the primary cause of nephrolithiasis (kidney stones) and cancer in the area. However, no research has been conducted on the use of well water.

Sustainable Tourism and Community Participation

The United Nations World Commission on Environment and Development (1987: 42) defines sustainable tourism as 'development that meets the needs of the present without compromising the ability of future generations to meet their own needs'. This objective is also pursued by UNESCO (UNESCO, 2013a). The development of local communities is considered as an alternative form of sustainable tourism. Murphy (1985) stated that community participation is fundamental to the concept of sustainable tourism, and that participant planning is essential for ensuring that the development of destination areas benefits the local community (Simmons, 1994). Community participation should involve local people because they know what is best for their community (Skelcher, 1993). The strong centralised government management in Vietnam has widened the communication gap between local communities and the government. Moreover, community participation requires a considerable amount of time, money, and skills to organise and sustain (Paul, 1987). Murphy (1985) noted that effective tourism management requires daily operational decisions. However, asking locals to participate in these daily assessments may not be possible under top-down management practice in Vietnam. Nevertheless, the opinion of locals should not be ignored (Skelcher, 1993). In the present study, the researcher attempts to find an alternative method for solving the issue of community participation in countries with top-down management such as Vietnam.

A Brief Introduction to PKNB NP

PNKB NP is located in the western part of Quang Binh Province, approximately 500 kilometres south of Hanoi, which is found in the narrowest part of Vietnam between Laos and the Tonkin Gulf. The western boundary of PNKB NP is part of the Laos–Vietnam border, which is only 42 kilometres from the South China Sea. PNKB NP is situated in a 2,000 km^2 limestone zone in the Vietnamese territory and borders another 2,000 km^2 limestone zone called Hin Namno in Laotian territory. PNKB NP is the largest limestone region in Asia and the second largest in the world (Nguyen et al., 2006). The primordial forests on the site are considered as the richest biological system in Vietnam. The entire core zone of PNKB NP was recognised as a World Natural Heritage Site in 2003 under criteria VIII (geological and geomorphological), thus becoming the fifth WHS in Vietnam (Nguyen et al., 2006; UNESCO, 2013b).

The core zones are divided into three functional areas: (1) Strictly Protected Area (64,894 hectares), (2) Ecological Restoration Area (17,449 ha), and (3) Administrative and Service Area (3,411 ha). Moreover, the Provincial People's Committee (PPC) of Quang Binh approved the extension of PNKB NP area by issuing Decision No. 1678/QD-UBND on 14 July 2008 (PPC of Quang Binh Province, 2010). However, the extension area is not included in the WHS map because the NPMB has not provided any periodic report to the World Heritage Convention since the nomination of PNKB NP in 2003 (PPC of Quang Binh Province, 2010). Table 1 provides a summary of the relevant jurisdictional zoning of the park region, which consists of the core zone (in the WHS) and the buffer zone. The buffer zone has a total area of 217,908.44 ha and includes 13 communes with a population of more than 64,000. The majority of locals are Kinh people, with two ethnic minority groups, namely, Bru Van Kieu (including Van Kieu, Khua, Macoong, and Tri) and Chut (including Sach, May, Ruc, A Rem, and Ma Lieng) (PPC of Quang Binh Province, 2010). The present study focuses mainly on tourism activities in the core zone because this area is the official NP and WHS.

Table 1. Summary of the Jurisdictional Zoning of PNKB NP Region

Land Area of PNKB NP Region		
PNKB NP core zone (ha)		Buffer zone (ha)
Strictly protected area (included in WHS)	64,894	
Ecological restoration area (included in WHS)	17,449	
Administrative and service area (included in WHS)	3,411	

Extension area (PPC of Quang Binh Province, 2008)	31,070	
Special use forest area	8,364.5	
Land without forest area	173.6	
Others	367.5	
TOTAL	125,729.6	217,908.44
Total land area of the PNKB NP region	343,638.04 ha	

Source: adapted from *Sustainable Tourism Development Plan 2010 to 2020: Phong Nha- Ke Bang National Park Region* (People's Committee of Quang Binh Province, 2010: 11).

Major Organisations in Tourism Management

PNKB NP belongs to the provincially managed NP typology. The PPC of Quang Binh Province holds the highest level of authority, and is thus, responsible for managing and monitoring activities in PNKB NP. The NPMB, which is under the authority of the PPC of Quang Binh Province, is directly responsible for the daily operations and management of the park. The NPMB is headed by one director and two vice directors, and is organised into three units [NP Forest and Protection Unit, Scientific Research and Rescue Centre, and Phong Nha Tourism Center (PNTC)] and two functional divisions (Planning and Finance Division and Administration and Organization Division). The PNTC is the most relevant unit because it participates in state-owned tourism activities under the supervision of the NPMB (PPC of Quang Binh Province, 2010).

Since the announcement of the Special-Use Forest Policy in 2006, NPs in Vietnam have witnessed a change through the new management model. Designated as the 'forest owner', the NPMB has the right to manage tourism activities within a park under three different models: state-managed, private-managed, and joint-venture models (Ministry of Agriculture and Rural Development, 2007). In 2010, the PPC of Quang Binh Province allowed the Truong Thinh Group to invest in and operate tourism activities in Paradise Cave by entering into a 50-year forest-renting contract with the group, thus confirming the coexisting management model in PNKB NP. One recreational site in the park can be managed and operated by a state-managed unit, whereas other sites in the same park can be managed by private companies or by a joint venture between the NPMB and for-profit companies.

Methodology

Setting

The researcher focused on locals who live and work in the core zone of the park. Table 2 summarises the major tourism sites in the park. Phong Nha Township is the only area within the core zone that is inhabited by locals. Therefore, this township is considered as a major area for data collection. Moreover, a number of locals working at refreshment stores in Phong Nha-Tien Son Cave and Paradise Cave were included in this study.

Table 2. PNKB NP Tourism Sites and Local Community Distribution

Site Name	Location	Management Unit	Distribution of Locals	Site Description
Phong Nha-Tien Son Cave	Administrative and service area, core zone	PNTC	Yes, with several refreshment stores operated by locals	The first and the signature site of the park, with Phong Nha Water Cave and Tien Son Dry Cave; opened in 1995
Phong Nha Township	Administrative and service area, core zone	PNTC	Yes, the main place of local residents; close to the tourist port station of Phong Nha-Tien Son Cave	The main hub for tourism activities in the park, with aggregated tourism facilities and services (such as guest houses, restaurants, and entertainment facilities)

Nuoc Mooc Spring Eco Trail	Administrative and service area, core zone	PNTC	No	Opened in 2008 as a forest walking trail in the park, with various recreational activities (such as picnic, stream swimming)
Eight Heroic Volunteers Cave	Ecological restoration area, core zone	PNTC	No	Opened in 2008 as an important spiritual and historical site in the province
Paradise Cave	Ecological restoration area, core zone	Truong Thinh Group	Yes, with a few refreshment stores operated by locals	Opened in 2010 as the only privately managed site in the park, with a stunning dry cave system

Data Collection Methods

The primary source of data was semi-structured interviews (Noaks and Wincup, 2004) with relevant locals and managers of tourism sites. The stakeholders in this study comprise three major groups. Group 1 consists of tourism-related locals who work in restaurants, hotels, refreshment stores, or employed as staff in tourism sites within the park. Group 2 consists of non-tourism-related locals. These locals live in the core zone but are not directly involved in the tourism business. They can provide the researcher with a complete picture of the commercialisation of and the sanitation issues in the area. Group 3 consists of local government representatives who were included in the study to obtain a macro view of the management of the two research issues. The key questions included the following: (a) To what extent is the life of locals commercialised by tourism in PNKB NP? (b) How does life in the local community affect the environment? (c) What is the NPMB doing to preserve the local culture and the environment of the park? (d) Do tourism development and environment preservation policies in the park work adequately? Interviews were audio taped with participant consent. The recordings were simultaneously transcribed and translated verbatim by the researcher from Vietnamese to English and were checked for accuracy by several volunteer researchers. Pseudonyms were used in place of the names of the study participants to protect their identities.

Procedures

The field study was conducted in three phases. Phase one was performed in July 2008, phase two lasted from July 2012 to September 2012, and phase three was carried out from February 2013 to April 2013. Most first-hand data were collected during phase one. Revisit field trips during phases two and three were conducted to update and confirm changes regarding the research issues. This prolonged engagement method was employed to achieve a reliable reflection of the study (Padgett, 1998). Finally, 10 people from Group 1, 8 people from Group 2, and 5 people of Group 3 were interviewed. After these interviews for each group, the researcher no longer obtained new information from the participants regarding the phenomenon under investigation. The theoretical saturation principle was applied, and the researcher decided to discontinue data collection and proceeded to data analysis (Glaser and Strauss, 1967).

Data Analysis

Data analysis began immediately after data collection was initiated and continued throughout the data collection process. Content analysis was the guiding methodological orientation in this study (Yin, 2003a, 2003b). Data were managed and coded using NVivo 10 (QSR International, Melbourne, Australia), a qualitative research data management software package (Bazeley, 2007; QSR International, 2013). The analysis confirmed the emergence of three codes: (1) tourism commercialisation issues, (2) sanitation issues, and (3) local tourism management policies. These codes are related to the original objectives of the research.

Findings and Discussion

Commercialisation Issues of the Local Community

Tourism Service and Commercialisation Measurement

The NPMB allows locals to provide certain tourism services, which are listed in Table 3. Most jobs are directly managed by the local government.

These jobs include those of boatmen, photographers, park staff, and non-tourism-related locals. Such management indicates that the government directly decides how the jobs should be handled and how much income is paid (such as for park staff). Meanwhile, photographers and boatmen are given assignments based on a ranking system (that is, they will be called to work based on their assigned numbers). After finishing their assignment, they need to get in line again and wait for the next call. The NPMB has fixed the price for boating and photo shooting services. Therefore, locals only gain income from the services they provide. Locals claimed no sign of commercialisation during the first phase of data collection. Meanwhile, members of the park staff simply accomplish the assignments given to them by the NPMB. Not much competition exists among them because they have the same salary and workload. The management style of the local government is different from that of private companies.

Table 3. Tourism Services and Commercialisation Measurement

Group	Job title	Degree of management by the government	Commercial-isation degree	Description
1	Boatmen	Directly managed, working at Phong Nha-Tien Son Cave	None	Local fishermen, approximately 700 individuals
1	Photographers	Directly managed, working at Phong Nha-Tien Son Cave and Paradise Cave	None to Emerging	Local people, approximately 400 individuals
1	Refreshment sellers	Partly managed, working at Phong Nha-Tien Son Cave and Paradise Cave	Emerging	Local people, approximately 100 individuals

1	Catering services	Partly managed, working at Phong Nha Township	Emerging	Local people, approximately 200 individuals
1	Accommodation services	Partly managed, working at Phong Nha Township	Emerging	Local people, approximately 200 individuals
1	Paradise Cave staff	Partly managed, working at Paradise Cave	Emerging	Local people, approximately 120 individuals
2	Non-tourism-related locals	Directly managed	None	Local people
3	Park staff	Directly managed	None to Emerging	Local people, approximately 200 individuals

Certain signs of commercialisation are observed among tourism services partly managed by the government (including refreshment sellers, catering services, and accommodation services). These services are partly managed by the government; thus, locals who want to offer such services have to bid for a service unit. Locals who win the bidding will then become the owners of refreshment stores, restaurants, or guest houses. The local government simply checks the sanitation standard of these service units. These units have to pay taxes, but are operated independently. Several interviewees claimed that these services are currently commercialised because the owners can set prices on their own. Such practice is a sign of a market-oriented economy.

Impact of a Private-managed Model on Commercialisation Issues

In 2010, the PNTC, influenced by the Truong Thinh Group, changed its management model. Competition resulted in several positive effects. Tourists visiting the park have more choices and receive better services.

Consequently, the number of tourists visiting the park had increased since 2010. To compete in the tourism market, service awareness of the park staff was enhanced, and consequently, the income of the staff was increased. Locals had more working opportunities in the new model than in the old one. Poaching and logging activities decreased to a certain extent. Environmental preservation was also promoted. As strong competition between state-managed and private-managed models was established, interviewees witnessed the emergence of commercialisation among locals with tourism development.

Local Community Attitudes toward Tourism Development

The opinions and attitudes of locals toward tourism development are important because they affect the reaction of locals toward tourists (Murphy, 1985). Most interviewees stated that they feel positive toward tourism development in the park. The interviewees claimed that because of tourism development, the local community has more jobs and living standards have improved. When asked about cultural fusion resulting from tourism development, locals pointed out that their culture remains intact and that they do not feel that it is out-of-date. Locals do not want to imitate the manners and behaviours of tourists for no reason at all. The preservation of their culture is of paramount importance for most locals. Nevertheless, locals are willing to learn useful things such as managing hygienic restaurants and environment-friendly hotels. A few locals considered the negative effects resulting from tourism development (such as environmental damage). However, as mentioned earlier, most locals have positive attitudes toward tourism development. For them, tourism development corresponds to promoting Vietnamese culture, developing the local economy, and facilitating self-improvement.

Local Government Attitudes toward Tourism Development

Vietnam has a strong central government. Therefore, the attitude of the government toward tourism development determines the effects of the tourism industry in the park. In park tourism development, the balance between tourism infrastructure construction and local heritage site protection is difficult to maintain. A number of locals claimed that the NPMB made two wrong decisions in developing tourism infrastructures. First, the Youth Volunteer Monument for the Vietnam–American War in 1975 was relocated to another bank of the Son River to build a tourist car park for the PNTC. This action did not only fail to protect local heritage but also demonstrated negligence. Second, the Xuan Son Ferry was not included in the tourism development plan. This historical ferry, which was used in the Vietnam–American War from 1965 to 1975, is located 50 metres west of the tourism boat station. An interviewee reported that the Xuan Son Ferry is currently being used as a garbage dump.

The exclusion of a historical heritage site in the tourism development of an NP will cause future generations to lose a sense of protection toward local culture. More importantly, this neglectful attitude of the local government also sends a wrong message, that is, financial benefit is the most important aspect of tourism development and the park can disregard or even remove heritage sites to give way to the construction of better tourism facilities for higher revenues.

Sanitation Issues of the Local Community

Litter Disposal

A garbage collection company called Trang An Company, collects garbage daily for locals living in Phong Nha Town. This company was established in 2004 and only served Phong Nha area. The other parts of the park are not included in the service area; thus, all villages in the park (except for Phong Nha Town) still have no garbage disposal service. Interviewees reported that people living in other villages, particularly in slum areas, throw garbage in their backyards. This garbage is collected or burned once a year. Meanwhile, a number of locals who live by the river throw garbage directly into the river.

Garbage from the tourism sites managed by the PNTC or the Truong Thinh Group is collected by another company once a month. Both units have established an environment team (composed of park staff or site staff to collect garbage within the tourism sites). The garbage-collecting company only comes once a month; thus, the NPMB has built a temporary garbage storage pool near the upper stream of the Son River. The Truong Thinh Group also has a temporary garbage storage pool located within the site of Paradise Cave. Locals claimed that the garbage in these storage pools is not treated. Therefore, the garbage storage pools are among the main causes of river contamination during flooding events.

Daily Water Use Issue

Before Phong Nha Village became a WHS, locals traditionally used the Son River for their daily water use (such as cooking, bathing, and washing clothes). A local stated that residents on both sides of the river followed rules in using river water. Locals collected clean water for cooking in the morning. After morning, locals used the river water for bathing and farming. Washing clothes was done at sunset. After the area became a WHS in 2003, more tourists arrived, and locals continuously decreased their use of river water. The toilets for the tourists located near the PNTC have no filters; thus, human waste directly flows into the river. Moreover, a number of locals and tourists throw garbage into the river. The majority of locals prevent their family members from using river water.

The local community gradually switched to using well water instead of river water. However, the use of well water is not favourable to the health of locals and the development of the natural environment. First, well water contains nonstandard amounts of iron and calcium (Nguyen et al., 2006), which are harmful when consumed on a daily basis. Moreover, local doctors argue that the use of well water or river water may be the primary cause of nephrolithiasis (kidneys stones) and cancer among residents in the area. Second, the underground water in this karst region is responsible for shaping the underground cave system of the park. The use of well water directly affects the formation of the natural underground karst system.

The local government recognises the significant risk of allowing locals to use well water. Thus, the local government had planned to build a clean water supply system. The local government lacked sufficient capital and expertise; hence, it asked private companies to bid on the project. A Vietnamese company won the bidding and started the clean water supply project in 2005. The project was scheduled to be completed in three years. However, the project was abandoned in 2007 because of poor infrastructure conditions. The project budget was underestimated, and the clean water fee was too expensive for the average income of locals. To date, no other company has agreed to continue the abandoned project. Lack of capital and expertise is one of the greatest barriers faced by the local government in dealing with environmental protection issues.

Communication between the Local Government and the Local Community

Faced with several significant issues on commercialisation and park sanitation, a number of locals have their own ideas and suggestions but do not have the means to speak out. Locals complained that the local government simply does as it pleases without consulting them. No discussion or communication occurred between these two stakeholders. Community participation has limitations, such as being time-consuming and requiring money and skills to organise. Moreover, locals may lack qualified and professional ideas. However, these people know what is best for their community. Locals claimed that they are not interested in non-participation or pseudo-participation in the local tourism development plan; rather, they require 'real' conversation. As stated by one interviewee: 'We are waiting for some people to come and ask us about the environmental issues, but nobody does'. Thus, communication between the local government and the local community must be established immediately under a top-down management model.

Conclusions

The jobs available for the local community in the park have two types: (1) those directly managed by the local government, such as park staff, boatmen, and photographers; and (2) those partly managed by the local government, such as refreshment sellers, guest house staff, and restaurant workers. The analysis showed that to date, no sign of commercialisation was observed among people directly managed by the local government. However, partly managed tourism services are starting to exhibit signs of commercialisation. When a private company started operating a tourism site, the park witnessed the emergence of commercialisation among local groups with tourism development.

For the issue on sanitation, the local government had implemented a number of strategies for dealing with garbage disposal and daily water use. However, the results of such measures were not as expected and were rather counter-effective. The lack of capital and expertise is among the hardest barriers faced by the local government in dealing with environmental protection issues. Moreover, the lack of an official environmental protection policy is another barrier in tourism development. In conclusion, tourism development and environmental protection policies in PNKB NP do not work adequately and require further improvement.

This research compared the relationship between the local government and the local communities in the park to a reason–result relationship. The lack of communication between these two stakeholders is a major factor that results in the current tourism management issues in the park. However, total community participation, such as those exhibited in several Western countries, is considered illogical and unrealistic in countries with strong central governments such as Vietnam. For countries that do not practice co-management (that is, the lack of participation of locals in tourism management) and that simply operate under a top-down management model, the local government should establish better communication with local communities. The researcher intends to undertake further research on countries that practice top-down management but not co-management. Finally, the co-existing management model for tourism development in Vietnamese national parks should be studied. The extensive exploration of this model can facilitate clear understanding and proper implementation.

The main limitation of the present research design is the application of a single case study strategy. This research focused on an NP managed by a provincial government as a case study. Apart from other NPs managed by provincial governments, eight NPs managed by the central government are also found in Vietnam. Therefore, future research may consider multiple case studies that include NPs under both types of management to investigate the NP system in Vietnam comprehensively. Moreover, only a limited number of locals were interviewed in this study because of time and budget constraints. Further research involving larger samples should be conducted over a longer period to obtain more accurate data.

References

Bao, J. G., and Su, X. B. (2004) 历史城镇的旅游商业化研究 [Studies on Tourism Commercialisation in Historic Towns]. *ACTA Geographica Sinica*, 59: 427–436.

Bazeley, P. (2007) *Qualitative Data Analysis with NVivo*, London: Sage.

Campbell, L. M. (1999) 'Ecotourism in Rural Developing Communities', *Annals of Tourism Research*, 26:534–553. doi:10.1016/S0160-7383(99)00005-5

Denman, R. (2003) *Ecotourism Challenges within a Sustainable Development Agenda*, Power Point presented at the The Tourism Company, Monash University, UK, from https://www.zotero.org/groups/cagrariasdrural/items/itemKey/FU3BMDVV

Glaser, B. G., and A.L. Strauss (1967) *The Discovery of Grounded Theory: Strategies for Qualitative Research*, New York: Aldine de Gruyter.

Greenwood, D. J. (1989) 'Culture by the Pound: an Anthropological Perspective on Tourism as Cultural Commoditization'. In V. L. Smith (ed.), *Hosts and Guests: the Anthropology of Tourism*, Philadelphia: University of Pennsylvania Press, pp. 171-185.

Li, Q., Wu, X. G., and Tang, S. (2006) 古镇旅游开发及其商业化现象初探 [Preliminary Study on Tourism Development and Commercialisation in Ancient Towns]. *Tourism Tribune*, 21: 52–57.

Linton, N. (1987) 'Trends in Tourism and Development : "Third World" Perspective, *Tourism Management*, 8: 96–97. doi:10.1016/0261-5177(87)90008-2

Ly, T. P. (2007). *越南世界遗产项目—风芽格邦国家公园洞穴旅游开发研究* [Vietnam's World Heritage Site: Phong Nha- Ke Bang National Park Cave Tourism Utilisation Research] (Unpublished Bachelor's thesis), Jinan University, Guangzhou.

Millar, S. (2012) 'Stakeholders and Community Participation'. In A. Leask and A. Fyall (eds), *Managing World Heritage Sites*, Oxford: Taylor & Francis, pp. 37-54.

Ministry of Agriculture and Rural Development. (2007) *Quyết định số 104/2007/QĐ-BNN về ban hành quy chế quản lý các hoạt động du lịch sinh thái tại các vườn quốc gia, khu bảo tồn thiên nhiên* [Regulations No. 104/2007/QĐ-BNN on management of ecotourism activities in natonal parks and nature reserves], MARD, the Government of Vietnam, retrieved from
http://www.moitruongdulich.vn/index.php?itemid=1508

Murphy, P. E. (1985) *Tourism: A Community Approach*, New York: Methuen.

Nguyen, Q. M., Dang, V. B., Nguyen, H., Nguyen, D. K., and Phan, D. N. (2006) *Vườn Quốc Gia Phong Nha- Kẻ Bàng [Phong Nha- Ke Bang National Park]*, Ho Chi Minh: Youth Publisher.

Noaks, L. and E. Wincup (2004) *Criminological Research: Understanding Qualitative Methods*, London: Sage.

Padgett, D. (1998). *Qualitative Methods in Social Work Research: Challenges and Rewards*, Thousand Oaks, CA: Sage.

Paul, S. (1987) *Community Participation in Development Projects: The World Bank Experience* (World Bank Discussion Papers 6). Washington, DC: World Bank, retrieved from
http://onlinelibrary.wiley.com/doi/10.1002/pad.4230090420/abstract

Provincial People's Committee of Quang Binh Province (2010) *Sustainable Tourism Development Plan 2010 to 2020: Phong Nha- Ke Bang National Park Region*, Tourism Resource Consultant, GIZ.

QSR International (2013) *NVivo 10 Research Software for Analysis and Insight*, retrieved July 31, 2013, from http://www.qsrinternational.com/products_nvivo.aspx

Shackley, M. L. (2003) *Visitor Management: Case Studies from World Heritage Sites*, Oxford: Butterworth Heinemann.

Simmons, D. G. (1994) 'Community Participation in Tourism Planning', *Tourism Management*, 15: 98–108. doi:10.1016/0261-5177(94)90003-5

Skelcher, C. (1993) 'Involvement and Empowerment in Local Public Services', *Public Money and Management*, 13: 13–20. doi:10.1080/09540969309387770

Tang, C.-H. (Hugo), and Jang, S. (Shawn) (2009) 'The Tourism–Economy Causality in the United States: A Sub-industry Level Examination', *Tourism Management*, 30, 553–558. doi:10.1016/j.tourman.2008.09.009

Tosun, C. (2000) 'Limits to Community Participation in the Tourism Development Process in Developing Countries', *Tourism Management*, 21: 613–633. doi:10.1016/S0261-5177(00)00009-1

—. (2001) 'Challenges of sustainable tourism development in the developing world: The case of Turkey', *Tourism Management*, 22(3), 289–303. doi:10.1016/S0261-5177(00)00060-1

UNESCO (2013a) *UNESCO World Heritage Centre - World Heritage*. Retrieved, from http://whc.unesco.org/en/about/, page consulted 17/08/2013

—. (2013b) *Phong Nha-Ke Bang National Park - UNESCO World Heritage Centre*. Retrieved from http://whc.unesco.org/en/list/951, page consulted 16/07/2013

United Nations World Commission on Environment and Development (1987) *Our Common Future*, Oxford: Oxford University Press, retrieved from http://ukcatalogue.oup.com/product/9780192820808.do#.UePExm0yjDo, page consulted 16/08/2013

United Nations World Tourism Organization (UNWTO) (2013a) *Annual Report, 2012*, Madrid: WTO.

—. (2013b) *Tourism 2020 Vision*, retrieved from http://www.unwto.org/facts/menu.html, page consulted 16/08/2013

Yin, R. K. (2003a) *Applications of Case Study Research,* Thousand Oaks, CA: Sage, second edition.

—. (2003b) *Case Study Research: Design and Methods,* Thousand Oaks, CA: Sage, second edition.

MEANINGS, PURPOSES, AND ACTIVITIES OF SUBURBAN FAMILY TOURISM IN YOGYAKARTA, INDONESIA

JANIANTON DAMANIK

Introduction

Tourist activities are increasingly popular in the life of the Indonesian people. The number of people travelling on tour continues to increase, especially in the last five years. In 2008, in four provinces namely North Sumatra, East Java, West Java, Central Java, 56 to 85 percent of the population travelled out of town (BPS, 2008; Kementerian Pariwisata dan Ekonomi Kreatif, 2013). The travelling habit is very distinctively spotted in various tourist areas during the holiday seasons or weekends. Several mass media reported that a massive number of visitors flocked to the main tourist areas in Jakarta some time ago (Anonymous, 2012a). The similar condition also occurred in the other major cities in Java (Anonymous, 2012b).

The causes of the increased trips are commonly associated with social change. In the context of the Indonesian society, the rapid social changes, among others, are marked by families having fewer children (Van Klaveren, et al., 2010), the declining role of the extended family (LaFave and Thomas, 2012), increased household income, the increasing proportion of women who get involved in the job market, along with high demands to achieve professional employment (Niehof, 1998). Rapid urbanisation at approximately 3.1 to 3.6 percent per year (Firman, 2012), has resulted in a highly dense urban population which has resulted in limited space for relaxation. Rigid and timely work patterns (school, office work, etc.) also demand that the family use their remaining free time efficiently. In short, people are currently enjoying the 'demographic and economic bonuses' which spur the desire to move outside the house for tourist activities.

Most studies on family tourism in Indonesia are relatively superficial. Two important issues are overlooked during the analysis. The first is the logical explanation behind the increased number of people travelling on tour. Does the habit of travelling mean something else beyond just enjoying 'demographic and economic bonuses?' Secondly, tourist activities are so far narrowly perceived as comprising individual movements. This perception ignores the social motives and patterns of collective trips in family travel (Ditjen Pemasaran Budpar, 2008). The family as the analytical unit is essential for understanding motives, meanings and behaviour in tourism and in the context of rapid social change.

The allegedly significant changes in attitude and behaviour towards tourism also occur among the residents of Yogyakarta. In the province, the movement of the population, in terms of out-of-town trips is nationally very high (Directorate General of Marketing for Culture and Tourism, 2008). The status of Yogyakarta as the premier education city receiving students from many other parts of the country can be one of the factors generating the high intensity of travel and tourism. This status is allegedly hidden by the image of the province of Yogyakarta (*Daerah Istimewa Yogyakarta*, DIY) as the national tourist destination.

This chapter aims to further explore the involvement of families in tourist activities in relation to their interpretation of these activities. In particular, two issues become the focus of analysis: first, what does a collective tour mean for families; and second, how does this meaning materialise in the different choices of tourist activities? The critical discussion on this issue will help clarify the concept of 'family tourism' from the tourists' perspective and can help formulate policies in support of Indonesian family welfare.

Tourism and the Family

In this chapter, two main concepts are used interchangeably. The first is the concept of tourism, which is 'a journey for business, pleasure, or education often involving a series of stops and ending at the starting point' (http://www.merriam-webster.com). This concept describes precisely the nature of tourist activities with regard to recreation and pleasure. Tourism is seen as a condition that enables people to evaluate the purpose of their lives (Sutherland, 1957). Some sociologists perceive tourism as a representation of the present activities of individuals alienated from the community environment who seek an authentic experience elsewhere or who wish to keep engaged with past civilisations (MacCannell, cited by Cohen, 2008). Tourism is also associated with escapism from a uniform pattern of life triggered by the constraining forces of the industrial system (Krippendorf, 1984; Hennig, 1999). Economists frequently associate tourism with the availability of leisure time and money; therefore, tourism activities are considered as especially valued commodities or consumer goods (Jaeckel and Wollscheid, 2007). People 'sell' their time by working to earn money and then spend this 'work-time' in the pursuit of 'leisure-time'.

In industrial society, free time is the worker's right allocated to families, friends and neighbours 'to do what they want' (Hunnicutt, 2008). When they work routinely for income, they consciously alienate themselves from the neighbourhood. The isolated time is compensated for by spending time together outside work to experience and engage with their original environment. Thus, leisure time and tourism connect and boost integration and intimacy (Agate, et al, 2009), making it difficult to separate these from everyday life. This view is summed up in Kelly's statement as follows:

> Leisure is human activity that encompasses freedom and constraint, autonomy and multilayered influences, personal identities and social roles, creation and adaptation, self-definition and situational limits, states of mind and physical action (1978).

Tourism activities are indeed a rational choice. Prior to travelling, people consider some appropriate criteria, primarily related to factors with satisfaction scores (Mill and Morrison, 1985). Therefore, a lot of factors affect or determine the decision to travel on tour. Despite the significant role of the economy, and social and psychological factors (ibid), the decision to travel depends on how people perceive it. If people perceive tourism as reinforcing integration (Hazel, 2005) and embodying particular social and personal meaning (Kelly, 1978), they will likely travel on tour with activities positively linked with the above meaning.

Tourism is also associated with the work context in terms of meaning. Tourism is the product of changes in what work means to individuals (Sutherland, 1957; Enzensberger, 1996), and the belief that work should produce pleasure. Work should therefore be interrelated with tourism to enable and construct a balanced life. That is why tourism is inseparable from everyday life even serving as the right identity and lifestyle (Roberts,

2006). It means that work and tourism both become elements in the construction of identities.

The second is the concept of family, which is the smallest unit in society and is socio-culturally created through a legitimate marriage between husband and wife who live together with their children (Hull, 2003). In Indonesia, the family refers to the extended family with a very strong role in the quality of collective life (LaFave and Thomas, 2012), despite the trends towards the nuclear family in the major urban areas (Hull, 2003). Families often serve as a laboratory of social change that indicates shifts in their function and their role in society (Herbert, 1988). The family members contribute, in reinforcing identities, to the economic security of the family in providing financial support. In general, a family associates the actions taken by its members as representing the family as a whole. The family is also authorised to take decisions over any individual decisions taken by its individual members despite recognising the importance of individual rights and autonomy. This understanding implies that seeking happiness and the solution of problems faced by the family members are the basis on which the family is founded, and not on individual interests. Thus, studying individual behaviour should be undertaken in the context of the study of the family (Aslan, 2009).

In terms of tourism the family members view leisure time as functional (Trost, 2008); it enhances emotional ties among the family members and helps solve some of the problems generated by everyday life (Agate, et al, 2009). Tourism also contributes in promoting recreational activities for children to acquire the knowledge, attitudes, values, skills and motivation surrounding leisure time (Iso-Ahola, 1982). Prior to dealing with the new environment (Aslan, 2009), the family commonly applies certain norms i.e. the family head is more authorised in determining the kind of tourism the family pursues. In a developing society, however, harmony and interdependence among the parties involved in determining the tourist activities are preferred (Walker, et al, 2005). Tourism is thus placed in a position similar to other social rites in the spectrum of family activities.

The other studies focus on the motives and effects of family tourism. As mentioned, there are six motives for families to travel on tour (Hazel, 2005). The first and primary motive is associated with physical recovery and rejuvenation (McIntosh, et al, 1995; Venkatesh 2006). Routine work is very prone to stress; therefore, tourism serves as the stress release. Second, tourism is able to reduce the mental and physical burden generated by a stressful environment. Third, tourism reinforces disrupted social relations due to limited space and time among the family members. Fourth, tourism is related to developing people in new activities, such as hobbies and materialising their interests and wishes. Fifth, tourism also nurtures independence in learning to enhance personal responsibility to the new and healthier environment. Sixth, tourism enhances family ties (Hazel, 2005).

Methods of the Study

Two settlements on the outskirts of Yogyakarta, Indonesia were chosen as the location of the study. These are rapidly growing areas, with residents from diverse economic, social and cultural backgrounds; this is an ideal context for examining variations in family tourism experiences.

Mixed-methods were used combining qualitative and quantitative approaches in collecting and analysing the results of the study (Clark and Creswell, 2011; Johnson and Onwuegbuzie, 2004). The data were collected with semi-structured questionnaires previously tested to ensure the validity and reliability of the data. In addition, in-depth interviews were also conducted to explore the understanding and interpretation of tourism. In total, the interviews ranged from 2.5 to 3.5 hours per informant and were conducted repeatedly over a period of approximately one month.

A total of 87 samples were selected purposively for the specific research objective i.e. describing the meaning of tourism. The respondents comprise one of the family members: children aged 15 years and older, father and mother. Four enumerators used semi-structured questionnaires to collect data on family social, economic, and demographic characteristics, travel patterns and perspectives about tourism. During the process, frequent re-scheduling of the meetings with the respondents resulted in longer periods of interview.

The Respondents' Profiles

Tourism activities are strongly associated with the demographic structure of the family. This study recorded it through the gender distribution of the respondents. More than two-thirds of the respondents were male (Table 1). Approximately 93 per cent of male respondents are household heads, compared to 21 per cent with the same status among the female respondents. The figure illustrates that the position of the husbands or men as the household heads remains strong in the society.

Most respondents belong to the productive age group; they have fairly considerable access to various types of jobs. Therefore, the opportunities to gain more income remain huge. Their productive age also indicates that the respondents have better physical abilities for travelling on tour.

Table 1. The Socio-demographic Profiles of Respondents (N=87)

Profiles	**Descriptions**	**N**	**%**
Sex	Male	59	67.8
	Female	28	32.2
Age (years)	20-29	4	4.6
	30-39	22	25.3
	40-49	26	29.9
	50-59	21	24.1
	>59	14	16.1
Education	High School	18	20.6
	Diploma	16	18.4
	Undergraduate	41	47.1
	Graduate	12	18.3
Source: Field Survey, 2012			

The respondents' education level is relatively high. The data are indeed not surprising due to the advanced formal education in Sleman Regency. The number of highly educated people is larger than those in other regencies in DIY as related to the numbers in employment in colleges or universities.

The jobs in the tertiary sector dominate the livelihood of the respondents (Table 2). This has allegedly been associated with the semi-urban geographical location. The jobs in the private sector are quite dominant and in harmony with rapid tourism development and educational services in this area. To illustrate, the trading, hotel, and restaurant sectors contributed 22.8 per cent in 2010 to the Sleman GDP and was the main source of the region's economy (Sleman Regency Administration, 2006). The proportion of livelihoods which are concentrated in the service sector indicates that the society is developing into the phase of capitalism. In terms of the job types, however, approximately 62 per cent of the respondents remain as subordinate workers, in for example the lower levels of business and the bureaucracy. Thus, such tourists are primarily of lower-middle economic class status. Interestingly, the type of jobs still gives significant disposable income for travelling on tour. It simply means that the current occupational condition in Sleman implicitly gives a significant contribution to the people's tourist activities. Table 2 indicates that most (40 percent) respondents received income ranging from 2-3 million rupiahs, followed by the income group of 1-2 million rupiahs (28 per cent). In Yogyakarta Province, the rate of income indicates lower-middle class positions. To compare, the average income per capita of the population in Yogyakarta in 2010 was Rp 249,629 per month or about 3 million rupiahs per year (BPS DIY Province, 2010). If applied to the respondents, every family (assuming that each family comprises five members including the family head), will result in 1.25 million rupiahs per month or 15 million rupiahs per year as the family income. The primary data reveal that the median respondents' income is between 2.0 to 3.5 million rupiahs per month. Thus, the average income of respondents' family members is far above the average income per capita of the DIY population.

Table 2. The Economic Profiles of Respondents (N = 87)

Economic Profiles	Descriptions	N	%
Employment Status	Traders	13	14.9
	Civil Servants/Soldiers	14	16.2
	Employees	41	47.2
	Retired	9	10.3
	Housewives	5	5.7
	Others	5	5.7

Types of Employment	Owners/managers	17	19.5
	Heads/Supervisors	5	5.7
	Staff/tenure employees	54	62.2
	Freelancers/ independent workers	8	9.2
	Others	3	3.4
Income Category per month (Rp.000)	< 1.000	2	2.3
	1.000 – 2.000	24	27.6
	2.005 – 3.500	35	40.2
	3.505 – 5.000	9	10.3
	5.005 – 7.000	6	6.9
	7.005 – 9.000	2	2.3
	9.005 – 11.000	2	2.3
	> Rp 11.500	3	3.4
	n.a**	4	4.5

*Note: ** not stated. Source: Field Survey, 2012*

Table 3. The Meaning of Tourism for Families

Meaning of Tourism	**N**	**%**
Enhancing family/relatives ties	32	36.8
Pleasure and Entertainment	28	32.2
Gratitude to God	24	27.6
Empathy and sympathy	2	2.3
Proving self-existence	1	1.1
Total	87	100

Source: Field Survey 2012

The Meaning of Tourism

The informants' understanding of tourism is fairly good and specific. Almost similar to the experts' opinion (Peterson, 1981), the informants also perceived the concept of recreation as a part of tourist activities arising from the desire to spend leisure time. They distinguished recreation from tourism in that 'recreation is varied in its form' and 'can be done at any time'. Unlike recreation, tourism should be well planned as 'related to effectively and efficiently allotted time, energy and money'. Thus, tourism is commonly subject to extended planning to consider the allocation of the available resources in every family.

For families, tourism comprises three dimensions, i.e. enhancing family links and ties with relatives, pleasure and entertainment, and gratitude to God. The first considers tourist activities and recreation important in providing social and psychological benefits for family members. Over one-third of the respondents interpret tourism as enhancing ties among family and relatives (Table 3). The data can be more specifically explained. In general, the respondents considered the family as the primary focus in everyday life and for seeking happiness. Therefore, each rational action taken always refers to family togetherness and harmony and enhancing social relations with relatives. Apparently, respondents consider that society is facing vulnerable social communality especially due to the stressful working environment (comparing Orthner, 1975; Baker and Palmer, 2006). The respondents viewed tourism as a means of reinforcing the emotional ties within the nuclear and extended family. This phenomenon was also found by other researchers (Shaw and Dawson, 2001). This communal activity becomes the positive medium for maintaining social relations which are undermined in urban society.

Similarly, the choice for tourist activities as a means for enhancing communality is based on a strong logical foundation. Tourist activities free people from routine arrangements such as working, studying, eating, playing and many more, to then engage in loose, flexible and spontaneous arrangements. These activities generate pleasure and pride for the family when they are visiting different places. The common pleasure the families enjoy is much more valued in combination with psychological satisfaction or 'dreamed happiness' which can express stronger togetherness. With tourism, the families feel stronger emotional ties among their members. The children enjoy excitement and a different homely atmosphere.

> It's fun indeed. We played freely there. Mom and Dad just let us play as we wished. Sometimes we were so exhausted playing. No matter anyway, as long as it was not dangerous. Fun…, that's what we wanted...that was so fun ….. (Informant B)

The second dimension of tourism refers to pleasure, an element which was referred to by almost one-third of the respondents (Table 4). Tourism becomes a tool for parents to give pleasure to the children and themselves. The ability of parents to provide fun activities for children with is described as 'a real pleasure'. When travelling on tour, the parents see and feel how the children enjoy their excitement. For children, playing cheerfully at the beach, walking leisurely through shady woods, staring at the breathtaking landscape in the hills, and enjoying breakfast at the hotel serve as landmark events for them to express happiness. For parents, it means enjoyment to see the children's excitement outside the home. Such a condition is apparently hard to create within daily life. Despite the fact that home is the primary place for family gatherings, special events generating common happiness are mostly done outside the home.

> Well, we were so happy. We and the kids looked forward to it. The vacation….costly, isn't it? The time is indeed precious. It isn't easy, you know, to gather with the kids and relatives. There.., the kids played freely as they wished…. That's great to see them laughing happily. (Informant C)

The meaning of this pleasure can be further explored. Pleasure refers to a psychologically relieving condition when someone gets free from routines and obtains positive things. This positive value drives someone to act. Therefore, the informants argued that tourism activities are a means for self-release from routine activities. 'Freeing self from rigid and boring routines' or 'Getting rid of the monotonous activities' are phrases often coined to describe the actions which provide interludes away from the daily errands and where one can find or create a new or different atmosphere. The above points were commonly called 'escapism' in the tourism literature (Burkart and Medlik, 1974), which referred to an effort to reduce the accumulated burden of work. Escaping for a while from one's workload becomes the essence of tourism especially when it is done along with other family members. This medium for escape is used by those with a strict time use and work rhythm particularly among professional-level workers such as supervisors, department heads and business owners.

Interesting to note that tourism also constitutes a spiritual meaning, as an expression of gratitude to God. Around 28 per cent of respondents referred to this aspect of tourism. Despite the fact that spiritual meaning is very subjective, an implicit message is conveyed; tourism leads to a deeper understanding of the divine generosity to human beings. Such a feeling is obtained when 'we enjoy the natural beauty of His creation' in each destination.

Tourist Activities

The respondents chose tourist activities by considering the variety of attractions, interests and buying power. Importantly, they tended to favour natural tourist activities (Table 4). This choice is allegedly related to their residential environment. The dense residential area has induced a cramped feeling and one which deprives people of their original nature. Therefore, nature-based activities such as tracking 'makes us aware of the so good and healthy nature ', and the convenience it provides, 'a gift for the people [who are] surrounded by the walls of houses, factories and dust pollution during the rest of life'. Similar opinions were repeated during the interviews with other informants. The natural attractiveness when on tour was explicitly stated, that 'this sort of natural atmosphere is the one we are looking for'; '[we were] unsatisfied before enjoying the natural scenery' and so on. In conclusion, they can be classified as 'eco-tourists'.

Table 4. The Primary Tourist Activities

Primary Activities	N	%
Cultural tourism (museum, cultural sites, etc.)	8	9.2
Enjoying culinary service	12	13.8
Shopping	2	2.3
Visiting relatives/friends	15	17.2
Natural tourism	30	34.5
Artificial tourism	12	13.8

Natural and artificial tourism	4	4.6
Cultural, natural and artificial tourism	1	1.1
All mentioned	3	3.4
Total	87	100

Source: field survey, 2012

The activity aimed at enhancing social integration like visiting friends and relatives (VFR) is also popular. The activity is the most-chosen one for approximately 17 per cent of the respondents. Compared to the national figure of 45 per cent (Ditjen Pemasaran Budpar, 2008), this number is indeed much smaller. Visiting relatives when on tour is common, for its important social value i.e. enhancing the relationship and closeness while reducing 'feelings of guilt and fear of [being] mistakenly called arrogant and ignorant'. In this context, 'the enhanced friendship ties representing [the] socio-cultural function of tourism' (Kelly, 1978) are affirmed. Nonetheless, the small number of VFR indicates that recreational activities have begun to dominate primary family tourist destinations.

The above interpretation is reinforced by the data about various tourist activities referred to by the respondents in addition to VFR. Enjoying culinary services and artificial tourist activities (water-based activities, game centres, etc.) have become the respondents' preferences. These findings confirm that the growing culinary services today represent the emerging new lifestyle in a developing society (Ansori, 2009). The results of this study also suggest that the culinary services and recreational activities are the respondents' favourite choice. Culinary tourism gives fun and a special experience because the respondents 'have once enjoyed genuine and unique local food'.

Conclusion

Families increasingly feel the monotony of life due to the routine and regularity of work; hence, they need a stress relief channel. This phenomenon is normal in countries which have experienced rapid industrial development with strict occupational distribution (Krippendorf, 1984); this has triggered a high demand for relaxation. To this extent, tourism plays a pivotal role. It occupies a strategic position in family social rituals as the effective medium for physical and psychological rejuvenation. Indeed, tourism becomes a new commodity favoured by family members for generating common pleasure and enhancing social interaction in the nuclear and extended families.

Therefore, it is understandable that the family keeps to the conventional meaning of tourism i.e. relaxation generated by a rigid and stifling domicile due to the constraining work routines. Relaxation is a routine function: the more often families become 'trapped' by their routines, the greater the need for tourism. The primary meaning remains focused on recreational activities which generate pleasure for the families. The meaning determines which types of tourist activities and destinations to choose. The activities are best able to build a different atmosphere, provide physical and psychological rejuvenation, and give pleasure and excitement; sites and activities which fulfill these objectives will inevitably be the favourite choice in tourist destinations. It comes as no surprise that recreational activities directly related to or which are experienced in ‘the wild’ are the ones most families much prefer.

Three policies should be pursued. First, the relaxation function in tourist activities should be facilitated with improved tourism services based on more family than individual needs. Second, increased support is required for tourism programmes in the form of collective holiday incentives to widen the opportunities to enhance family togetherness and social closeness. Third, the extension and diversification of nature-based tourist attractions as the main attraction should be promoted. Therefore, policies on tourism development which are pro-Indonesian families, not pro-international tourists are badly needed.

References

Agate, J. R, R.B. Zabriskie, S.T. Agate and R. Poff (2009) ‘Family Leisure Satisfaction and Satisfaction with Family Life’, *Journal of Leisure Research,* 41: 205-223.

Anonymous (2012a) (http://www.wartakotalive.com/detil/berita/106019/Jumlah-Pengunjung-Monas-Naik-10-Persen) retrieved from http://paa2010.princeton.edu/papers/101335, page consulted 11/11/2012.

Anonymous (2012b) ‘Pengunjung Padati Kebun Binatang Ragunan’, retrieved from http://news.detik.com/read/2012/08/20/155021/1995348/10/60000-pengunjung-padati-kebun-binatang-ragunan, page consulted 03.10.2012.

Ansori, M H. (2009) 'Consumerism and the Emergence of a New Middle Class in Globalizing Indonesia', *Explorations: a Graduate Student Journal of Southeast Asian Studies*, 9: 91-92.

Aslan, N. (2009) 'An Examination of Family Leisure and Family Satisfaction among Traditional Turkish Families', *Journal of Leisure Research,* 41: 157-176.

Baker, D A and R.J. Palmer (2006) 'Examining the Effects of Perceptions of Community and Recreation Participation on Quality of Life', *Social Indicators Research*, 75: 395-418.

BPS Propinsi DIY (2010) *Indikator Ekonomi Provinsi DIY 2010,* Yogyakarta: BPS.

BPS (2008) *Survai Penduduk yang Melakukan Perjalanan, 2007-2008*, Jakarta: BPS.

Burkart, A. J. and S. Medlik. (1974) *Tourism: Past, Present, and Future*, London: Heinemann.

Clark V. L. P. and J.W. Creswell (2011) *Designing and Conducting Mixed Methods Research,* Los Angeles: Sage Publication.

Cohen, E. (2008) 'Tourism'. In W. A. Darity Jr. (ed.), *International Encyclopedia of Social Sciences*, New York: Course Technology, The Gale Group, 8: 398-400.

Ditjen Pemasaran, Departemen Kebudayaan dan Pariwisata (2008) *Survai Pasar Wisatawan Nusantara 2007*, Jakarta: Ditjen Pemasaran Budpar.

Enzensberger, H.M. (1996) 'A Theory of Tourism', *New German Critique*, 68: 117-135.

Firman, T. (2012) 'Urbanization and Urban Development Patterns', *The Jakarta Post* (daily newspaper, May 12).

Hazel, N. (2005) 'Holidays for Children and Families in Need: An Exploration of the Research and Policy Context for Social Tourism in the UK', *Children and Society*, 19: 225-236.

Hennig, C. (1999) *Reiselust: Touristen, Tourismus und Urlaubskultur*, Frankfurt: Suhrkamp.

Herbert, D T. (1988) 'Work and Leisure: Exploring a Relationship', *Area*, 20: 241-252.

Hull, T H. (2003) 'Demographic Perspectives on the Future of the Indonesian Family', *Journal of Population Research*, 20: 51-65.

Hunnicutt, B. (2008) 'Leisure'. In W. A. Darity Jr., (ed.), *International Encyclopedia of Social Sciences*, New York: Course Technology, The Gale Group, 4: 408-409.

Iso-Ahola, S. E. (1982) 'Toward a social psychological theory of tourism motivation: A rejoinder'. *Annals of Tourism Research,* 9(2): 256-262.

Jaeckel, M. and S. Wollscheid (2007) 'Time is Money and Money Needs Time? A Secondary Analysis of Time-Budget Data in Germany', *Journal of Leisure Research*, 39: 86-108.

Johnson R. B. and A.J. Onwuegbuzie (2004) 'Mixed Methods Research: A Research Paradigm Whose Time Has Come', *Educational Researcher*, 33: 14-26.

Kelly, J. R. (1978) 'Situational and Social Factors in Leisure Decisions', *The Pacific Sociological Review*, 21: 313-330.

Kementerian Pariwisata dan Ekonomi Kreatif (2013) *Statistik Wisatawan Nusantara, 2007-2012*, retrieved from http://www.budpar.go.id/asp/detil/asp?c=111&id=1191, page consulted 05.01. 2013.

Krippendorf, J. (1984) *Die Ferienmenschen: Für ein neues Verständnis von Freizeit und Reisen*, Zürich: Orell Füssi Verlag.

LaFave, D. and D.Thomas (2012) 'Extended Families and Child Development: Evidence from Indonesia', retrieved from http://paa2010.princeton.edu/papers/101335, page consulted 11/02/2012.

McIntosh, R. W., C.R. Goeldner and J.R.B. Ritchie (1995) *Tourism: Principles, Practices, Philosophies*, New York: John Wiley and Sons.

Mill, R. C. and A.M. Morrison (1985) *The Tourism System: an Introductory Text*, Englewood Cliffs: Prentice Hall.

Niehof, A. (1998) 'The Changing Lives of Indonesian Women: Contained Emancipation under Pressure', *Bijdragen tot de Taal-, Land- en Volkenkunde*, 154: 236-258.

Orthner, D. K. (1975) 'Familia Ludens: Reinforcing the Leisure Component in Family Life', *The Family Coordinator*, 24: 175-183.

Pemerintah Kabupaten Sleman (2006) *Kabupaten Sleman Dalam Angka* (Sleman District in Figures 2, Sleman: BPS.

Peterson, R. A. (1981) 'Measuring Culture, Leisure, and Time Use', *Annals of the American Academy of Political and Social Science*, 453: 169-179.

Roberts, K. (2006) *Leisure in Contemporary Society*, Oxfordshire: CABI Publications.

Shaw, S. M. and D. Dawson (2001) 'Purposive Leisure: Examining Parental Discourses on Family Activities', *Journal of Leisure Research*, 33: 217-231.

Sutherland, W. C. (1957) 'A Philosophy of Leisure', *Annals of the American Academy of Political and Social Science*, 313: 1-3.

Trost, J. (2008) 'Family'. In W. A. Darity Jr., (ed.), *International Encyclopedia of Social Sciences*. New York: Course Technology, The Gale Group: 3: 83-86.

Van Klaveren, M. et al., (2010) *An Overview of Women's Work and Employment in Indonesia*, Amsterdam: University of Amsterdam.

Venkatesh, U. (2006) 'Leisure – Meaning and Impact on Leisure Travel Behavior', *Journal of Service Research*, 6: 87-108.

Walker, G. J., J. Deng, and R.B.Dieser (2005) 'Culture, Self-Construal, and Leisure Theory and Practice', *Journal of Leisure Research*, 37: 77-99.

http://www.merriam-webster.com.

EMERGING TOURISMS AND CONTEMPORARY ISSUES

CULTURE, TOURISM, AND SOCIAL DYNAMICS: THE CASE OF KOREAN POPULAR CULTURE

EOIN JOSEPH TROLAN

> The booming South Korean presence on television and in the movies has led Asians to buy up South Korean goods and to travel to South Korea, traditionally not a popular tourist destination (Onishi, 2005)

Introduction

Whether it has been Psy and his 'Gangnam Style' in America, Super Junior in France, or the plethora of South Korean dramas on television in the Middle East or South Asia, Korean popular culture has made enormous inroads in promoting Korea and the Korean media industry overseas. In recent years, there has been a major export of Korean popular culture throughout Asia and in certain parts of the Western world. This influx has seen Korean culture in areas of the world which decades ago had very little knowledge of it or Korea as a country. This newfound knowledge or promotion has led to an increase in tourism and the Korean government's involvement in 'brand Korea'. This chapter examines the beginnings and growth of the so-called 'Korean Wave' and how the government is now using this phenomenon to attempt to increase tourism within Korea and to increase the status of Korea.

Korean movies, drama, and music are enjoyed throughout the world and in many respects are re-created by the Hollywood movie and music industries. Only 30 years ago, the Korean movie industry was on its deathbed and yet today Hollywood is making 'Americanised' Korean movies. In Europe, thousands upon thousands of teenage boys and girls are buying CDs and tickets for Korean musicians to witness spectacular shows, upbeat music and to sing along with Korean lyrics. While America and Europe may be the final hurdle or destination for success, Asia has been at the beginning of the Korean Wave and where most of its cultural success has been achieved. The Korean Wave has over the past decade been heavily involved in the export of Korean culture *and* the influx of

Asian tourists to visit movie and music sites within Korea (Jang and Paik, 2012).

From its early beginnings to the present day the Korean Wave has seen an increase of interest in Korea and its popular culture (music, television, movies, food and sports stars). These popular cultural products are now exported to not only Asian countries but countries in the Middle East, Europe and the Americas. The term 'Korean Wave' was originally coined by the Chinese press in the 1990s and has become synonymous with Korean culture and its increased popularity and cultural impact (Tuk, 2012). From this period onwards, South Korea has been at the centre of popular culture in Asia. Though not fully embraced at the beginning, today the Korean Wave has become an integral aspect of Korea's global image and marketability. The demand for Korean dramas and musicians has become so popular that fans have been demanding Korean products at an ever-increasing rate. Korean actors, actresses, and musicians are now breaking into American markets and winning awards at international festivals.

The demand for Korean popular culture has in turn generated several byproducts such as the popularity and demand for Korean language, the demand for car and electronic products, and to 'look' like Korean men and women. The interest in understanding Korea and travelling there as well as the demand for its products and the desire to look like its people have taken the government by some surprise. Thus, with Korea now starting to be viewed as a cultural powerhouse similar to Japan and the USA in Asia and beyond thanks to the Korean Wave, the government of Korea has attempted to take advantage of this through policies to improve its image and attract tourists. The government promotes 'Hallyu' as a form of nation branding whereby Korean music, drama, food, and more recently sport have become incorporated into a form of cultural diplomacy. How much of an impact the government has gained is still in question but with the recent promotion of Psy as a cultural ambassador, it is clear that the government will continue to utilise the Korean Wave as a cultural and diplomatic policy tool. Therefore, this chapter examines the Korean Wave and its impact on the image of Korea and how the Korean government has utilised it to formulate policies to encourage tourism and to improve the image of the country on the international stage.

What is the Korean Wave (Hallyu)?

The Korean Wave is generally understood as comprising Korean cultural products such as television, movies, music, food, and sport (Tuk, 2012). One of the main components of the initial wave was television drama. The first instance of the Korean Wave was in China through television dramas and then in Japan through music. The Korean drama *What is Love* was first shown on Chinese State television in 1997 and the Chinese became infatuated with the storylines and the lifestyles (Korean Culture and Information Services [KCIS], 2013). Additionally, the Chinese could relate to these localised dramas more so than western or American dramas and thus future Korean dramas became highly successful. Historically popular in China, these dramas are now increasingly popular throughout the world for many different reasons according to Jang and Paik (2012). Some of these reasons relate to the themes of drama as relaxing and cheerful, emotional and romantic, and traditional. In the early 2000s Japan began to import Korean dramas and these led to an extraordinary and unparalleled interest in Korean culture and its icons (KCIS, 2013). In part the success of these dramas in Asia was, according to Shim (2006), the fact that they were cheaper to import and the music was much better organised and as such steadily gained airtime in Asian countries such as Singapore, Hong Kong, and Japan. Korean dramas consistently played to new emotions for the Japanese people and had a profound effect on their perception of Koreans.

The Korean Wave grew from Korean dramas to include music or K-pop. This new Korean Wave exploded in Asia and especially Japan thanks to the many girl and boy bands such as BoA, the Wonder Girls, Kara, Girls Generation, Super Junior, and Big Bang. According to the Korean Culture and Information Service, the 1990s saw a huge increase in the success of Korean artists in Japan, China, and Taiwan. During this period, many Korean artists took their concerts outside of Korea and with the increased exposure and management coordination they became blockbusters. This was particularly true in Japan, where Korean artists continually played to sold-out concerts. The female artist BoA was the first foreign success story in the Japanese music scene. Her albums reached number one in the music charts and she is still highly regarded and respected in Japan. One of the main reasons why she became so successful was her marketing strategy. K-pop artists according to Shim (2006) were particularly smart about their marketability because they would release songs in the local language as an attempt to break into the market before releasing their full albums. K-pop has become a mainstay in Asian countries and has begun to make an entrance into the western music markets. Many Korean artists such as Psy, Rain, Super Junior are working with western musicians as a way to promote K-pop and to increase its marketability in those areas.

As such these artists have become cultural icons and have become major factors in the consumption of Korean cultural products and Korean image. A general perusal of newspapers and magazines throughout Asia highlights the growing significance and influence of Korea and its individuals on the fashion trends within the region. The early 2000s saw 'Hallyu' go global with dramas being broadcast in the Middle East, Australia and the American continent. As mentioned earlier, many of these dramas were successful because they played to the emotions of these regions through family values, respect and honour of the family. This increased the perception of a strong wealthy middle class in Korea. Additionally, with the growth of K-pop, many overseas saw Korea through the image of beautiful boys and girls and wanted to act and dress like their idols. The impact of these artists has been increased due, in recent years, to social media, but historically due to the global music and film market. The Internet has played a huge role in the continued growth of 'Hallyu'. Korean dramas and music are some of the most highly watched and followed programmes in social media. Distance is no longer a barrier for 'Hallyu' as citizens of any country can now log on to websites and view their favourite movies or musicians. From what started out as a television drama in China in the early 1990s, 'Hallyu' has been transformed into a global phenomenon within two decades.

Popularity and globalisation

The early 1990s saw the explosion of the Korean Wave and this popularity was due to several reasons. One of the main reasons was the increase of airtime initially for television dramas and then K-pop. In relation to K-drama, one of the main reasons for its popularity was down to the beauty of the individuals in the television dramas and music. In Korean television programmes and in K-pop the majority, if not all are attractive people. From an examination of television programmes it is immediately obvious that the female characters are all very attractive and seductive (either as strong and independent or passive and infantile), while, the male characters are sensitive, emotional, and sexy. These characteristics attract people who strive for both external and internal fulfillment.

K-pop became the spearhead for the next level of the Korean Wave. Shim (2006) has stated that prior to the 1990s most music was dominated by American popular music. The Korean music industry then created a hybrid genre where they would utilise Korean and American music styles and dance. The Korean Wave was a hybrid culture according to Kim and Ryoo (2007) where there is a promotion of Asia and modernity without potential stereotyping within the Hollywood or Western entertainment industry. Whether it was television or movies or music, the Korean Wave infused Asian modernity, Western traits, and Eastern traits and created a trans-hybrid cultural product. Howard (2002) stated '…more and more musicians appropriated foreign music styles'. This appropriation gave a change in style to the younger Korean generation and opened the market to regional exportation. Kim and Ryoo (2007) have discussed how K-pop stars were breaking into the Asian region and the American market. Artists such as Rain, Girls Generation, and Wonder Girls were on regularly in Asia and had begun to break into the American market. Indeed, Rain had been one of the most successful Asian music artists playing to sold out crowds and being named as one of *Time Magazine*'s 100 top influential stars in 2011.

The initial popularisation of Korean popular culture was aimed at Japan, China, and South Asia and was considered an emphatic success. The next step was to go global. Globalisation was initially created through traditional media but it was the new media that really globalised the Korean Wave. The exposure from social media made the popularity and globalisation of the Korean Wave easily accessible for those outside of Asia. Social media such as Facebook to Twitter, and YouTube means that K-Drama or K-pop is now at the fingertips of the world's youth. The internet has turned what was once a regional cultural force into a global opportunity for Korea to export Korean cultural products. Specifically, Korean artists are and have utilised the internet to showcase their talents at relatively little cost compared to traditional methods. The most recent example of this phenomenon was Psy and his song 'Gangnam Style'. This video first went viral on social media before most traditional media sources were aware of it. Once the video on YouTube had become such an extraordinary success and the most watched video ever on YouTube, the traditional media finally took notice. Once traditional media, both in Korea and outside, noticed the rising popularity they 'jumped on the bandwagon', and Psy became one of the most popular entertainment figures of 2012. Eventually, Psy and his song became so popular that he performed the song for presidents and at mega sporting events watched by billions.

There are now a large number of websites dedicated to K-drama and K-pop. K-Drama websites allow foreign residents to watch these dramas with subtitles effectively nullifying the language barrier and potentially encouraging people to learn Korean. K-pop has the largest number of websites and highlights the concept of the 'new Korean Wave' with music at the forefront. Many of these websites delve into a mixture of culture and music and again expose foreign residents to Korean culture through music. Social media has led to major impacts for the Korean entertainment industry and tourism, and in turn, an opportunity for governmental branding of 'Korea'.

Korean Wave impact

The globalisation of the Korean Wave has led to impressive impacts on the entertainment industry, the tourism industry, and Korea's image. The entertainment industry has seen increased profits for its management and increased exposure for its musicians and actors. These individuals are role models and icons for the younger generation in Asia and in many other parts of the world. Their popularity has led to increased sponsorship and marketability for them. Additionally, Kim and Ryoo (2007) have drawn attention to the fact that the Korean entertainment industry now exports more films and television programmes than in previous decades and its actors and directors are becoming more famous every year. K-pop stars are on advertising billboards in Southeast Asia; K-pop is extremely visible throughout everyday life. Tuk (2012) stated that since the Korean Wave there has been an increase of television drama exports from 6 million in 1993 to more than 180 million in 2010. Such high profile exports have led to an increased interest in Korea itself as well as its industries. Additionally, according to an article in the *New York Times*, early 'Hallyu' success helped to promote Korean industries and cultural exports which have increased from barely anything to over $600 million (Onishi, 2005). More recently, in 2011, the Ministry of Culture, Sports, and Tourism (MCST) announced that exports of both cultural and other materials have increased steadily towards the multibillion dollar level in countries in the Middle East, Central and South America and Central Asia, all significantly, areas that have imported 'Hallyu'. The rate of exports has also risen in such countries as Vietnam and Thailand. Specially, concerning Vietnam, the exports have risen by over 100%, which given the history between Korea and Vietnam, demonstrates the impact of 'Hallyu'.

The Korean tourism industry has seen a huge influx since the beginning of the Korean Wave. From as early as 2002 after the World Cup, Korea noticed an increase in positive imagery thanks to a well-organised and successful tournament. Therefore, the government wanted to continue to encourage the perception of Korea as a political, economic, and social powerhouse in Asia and increased its use of 'Hallyu' as a promotional tool (Kim, 2010). Lee (2003) highlighted that thanks to the success of 'Hallyu', there has been an increase of tourists from Asia, and Park (2004) specifically stated that there was a 50% increase of Taiwanese tourists in 2004 when compared to 2003. Kim and Ryoo (2007) reiterated the steady climb in tourist numbers thanks in part to 'Hallyu' and this increase has led to the increased purchase of Korean cultural goods.

Shim (2011) has highlighted that many tourists visited the locations where the dramas were filmed. The number according to Shim was well over 130,000 and they came mainly from China and Southeast Asia. Many of these tourists see 'Hallyu' as a blend of Western and Asian cultures and easier to adopt than Western culture only, according to Choi (2001). This adoption of a blended culture or hybridisation has led to an increased popularity of not just Korea but for the 'Hallyu' participants. According to Nakagawa a large number of fan clubs has emerged around the world at the heart of the increase in tourism (2010). Indeed, it is not rare to see Korean fashion on the streets of Southeast Asia, China, and Japan. So popular are many of the singers and actors that 'Hallyu' fans have reverted to visiting Korea to get plastic surgery to look like their idols (Shim, 2011; Anonymous, 2002a, 2002b). In total, over 11 million people visited Korea, many from the China/North Asia region (ibid).

The image of Korea has changed drastically thanks to the Korean Wave. Korea has seen tremendous growth since its birth as an independent nation-state after the Korean War yet many people throughout the world had no idea of what Korea was as a nation, culture and society. With the Korean Wave, there has been increased interest in Korea, increased interest and understanding of Korean culture, increased study of the language, increased consumption of Korean goods and the formation and solidification of a positive image of Korea (Shim, 2011). A perfect example of this was the K-pop recent concert in Paris where tickets sold out within 15 minutes. Organisers stated that there would only be one show but such was the demand for another show and the fact that French K-pop fans protested, the organisers relented and held another show. This show sold out in 10 minutes (Anjaiah, 2011). Additionally, this positive image has been transferred to the Korean electronic industry. The use of

Korean actors or musicians as spokespeople for the company product has seen demand for those products increase and according to Shim (2006) Koreans have now realised the importance of culture in the promotion of everyday products. As recent as 2010, the government has stated that they plan to utilise the Korean Wave to promote tourism linked commercials overseas and thus promote Korea as a national brand (Yang, 2010).

Government policy and use

Historically the government has been involved with the media and entertainment industry as a form of domestic propaganda rather than economic or international promotion. From the late 1990s according to Shim (2006), the Korean government created a plan to enhance the standing of the Korean entertainment industry. Universities were tasked with producing the next generation of directors, producers, and actors. Film studios were actively promoted by the government and money was spent on creating agencies that primarily focused on promoting tourism based on Korean culture (and K-Drama locations). Today while the government owns many of the media outlets, there are numerous private organisations and the philosophy is no longer domestically orientated but rather internationally focused and promoted. The overall success of Korean industry in global markets has given the Korean government confidence to promote its culture as the next marketable product. Thus, the success of the recent Korean Wave underlined to the Korean government the potential growth and marketability through cultural promotion. Han and Lee (2008) and Ravina (2009) stated that the Korean government viewed the Korean wave not just as a cultural export but also as a marketing and business phenomenon. With the help of new technology and social media, Korean culture as a commodity is now available in the far distant corners of the world and has attracted foreign media to Korea. Thus, the government has promoted Korea as the 'Hollywood of the East' (KCIS, 2013) and has taken a major role in the promotion and penetration of cultural products in the overseas market through the Ministry of Culture, Sports, and Tourism (MCST). Additionally, the Korean government has increased the budget and increased their overseas foothold through specialists who promote 'Hallyu' and the interest in Korean culture (Cho, 2012).

The Korean government has taken several steps to continue the influence of the Korean Wave. A major step was the creation of 'Hallyu' agencies under the umbrella of the MCST. These departments focused on promoting ‘Hallyu’ through different avenues such as food events, sports events, or celebrity events, but especially through music concerts (Staines, 2012). Staines also described how the MCST are reportedly spending over 13 billion on musical festivals in the coming few years. The government has levied these organisations to travel to other countries such as India, Thailand, Indonesia, America, Brazil and parts of the Middle East to promote the Korean Wave. Governmental agencies such as the Korean Tourism Board and the Korean Culture and Content Agency utilise ‘Hallyu’ as a consumer cultural product and are a mainstay for tourism in many of their media outlets, especially on-line media. One of the major steps was to open Korean cultural centres in many foreign countries; according to Coll (2011) the government opened centres in Australia, Spain, and the Philippines. These cultural centres also are used to promote the Korean Language and according to Chung (2013) the popularity of ‘Hallyu’ has led to an increase in interest in the Korean language. In fact, the number of language centres overseas has now increased and the numbers have risen dramatically from 80,000 to 160,000 in the space of a few years. The government has taken a keen interest in this area and is helping fund these language centres overseas.

The government has also supported the Korean Broadcasting Commission (KBC) to promote films and television overseas and to visit international film festivals. This according to Tuk (2012) has resulted in Korean dramas being played in South America, Central Asia, and Africa. One example of using the Korean Wave as a tourist attraction was the use of movie sets and television sets as tourist destinations (ibid). Kim (2011) also stated that the KBC went to several Southeast Asian countries and these trips had a positive effect on exports and tourism. The MCST and the Korean National Tourism Organisation (KNTO) regularly publish news articles about ‘Hallyu’ through their digital media sites and produce in-depth reports on the popularity of K-drama and K-pop. These reports and the articles are positively promoting the brand Korea and promote visiting Korea through Korean Wave tourism. The KNTO has also developed travel programmes and travel tours to help encourage more tourists to visit Korea and visit the places of the modern ‘Hallyu’ idols.

The Korean Wave serves as revenue and a branding tool for the Korean government and agencies. The Korean government while not actively taking all the credit for the Korean Wave is now heavily involved in maintaining the status quo and continuing the growth of the Korean Wave. Prominent actors and actresses are used by governmental agencies to promote Korea as a tourist destination and this use of Korean actors and musicians has allowed Korean businesses to break into regional markets. Korean businesses are now using the Korean Wave as an avenue to promote their profits. According to the Korea Creative Culture Agency (2006) the Korean wave or 'Hallyu' has improved Korean business access and profits both regionally and internationally. Samsung, LG, and KIA/Hyundai have all used K-pop idols as figureheads in their product promotions. Indeed, the government has viewed the Korean Wave as a stepping-stone for increasing the popularity of K-drama and K-pop to the purchase of cultural products, purchase of other products, and eventually, a positive impression of Korea. The overall benefit to the continued promotion and growth of the Korean Wave or 'Hallyu' is not just about cultural promotion but also about the economic promotion of Korea. Kim (2011) highlighted four stages of the Korean Wave as 1) popularise Korean culture; 2) increase the purchases of Korean cultural products; 3) then increase the purchase of other Korean products; 4) promote a positive impression of Korea. From these stages, one can clearly discern the function of the government in the Korean Wave: start with cultural promotion and end with economic promotion.

Conclusion

The expansion of 'Hallyu' has taken place at a very fast rate. You can now see and hear Korean drama or music in nearly every continent in the world. The initial phenomenon garnered the interest of the Korean government and they have played a role in the continued expansion and growth of 'Hallyu'. The government's role in creating agencies and offices in different countries in an attempt to promote Korean culture has added to the success of Korean drama and music and has changed the philosophy of 'Hallyu'. The first initial steps of the Korean Wave were to promote Korea and its culture – the end steps are increased international economic growth for Korean industries and the positive image of Korea. The success of the Korean wave is based on several factors but the prime reason is that dramas and music seen worldwide are adaptable to different viewer perceptions. From the conservative family views that attract many western viewers to the non-sexual love stories that attract the Middle East, and the wealthy lifestyles that attract viewers from South Asia. Korean dramas have something for everyone and according to many researchers are successful because they are apolitical and are adaptable to the needs, interests and preoccupations of the majority of cultures around the world.

The involvement of the government is not to change the content of the Korean Wave but to enhance its visibility, thus, they bring out news reports, positive stories about Koreans overseas and their success. This means that many of the general population believe that Korea is well known throughout the world and the nation has a positive national brand. The recent success of Psy and his single 'Gangnam Style' and his new role as a governmental spokesman for Korea has highlighted that 'Hallyu' is not slowing down and the government are at the heart of its growth. The Korean Wave has led to an increase in tourists visiting Korea for shopping and pleasure. Tours from China, Thailand, Vietnam, and Japan regularly come to Korea to visit K-Drama television and movie sites and to view at first-hand Korean culture. 'Hallyu' has been a resounding success and has done more to promote Korea than any political or diplomatic policies. If you ask most people today who is South Korea's most famous son or daughter – the majority would mention a K-pop artist or K-Drama actor rather than Ban Ki Moon the Secretary-General of the United Nations. This demonstrates unequivocally the power of the Korean Wave whether you agree with it or not!

References

Anjaiah, V. (2011) 'Korean Culture Spreads across the Globe', *The Jakarta Post,* retrieved from http://www.thejakartapost.com/news/2011/07/18/korean-culture-spreads-across-globe.html, page consulted 18/07/2013

Anonymous (2002a) 'Taiwan Women Hanker after Korean Looks', *Straits Times*, March 12th.

Anonymous (2002b) 'China Girls Seek Surgery to Look Like Korean Stars', *Straits Times*, August 5th.

Cho, Hae Jong (2012) 'Reading the "Korean Wave" as a Sign of Global Shift', *The Korea Journal,* Winter 2006.

Choi, Y. (2001) 'Asia Dreaming of Korea's Pop Singers and Actors', retrieved from http://www.pomnada.com/dpsa.html, page consulted 11/07/2013

Chung, A.Y. (2013) 'Hallyu Boosts Boom in Hangeul, Korean Studies', *The Korea Times*, retrieved from http://www.koreatimes.co.kr/www/news/culture/2013/07/135_135063.html, page consulted 19/07/2013

Coll, M. (2011) '*Korea is Killing its Own Wave*, retrieved from http://www.cnngo.com/seoul/visit/maxwell-coll-korea-killing-its-own-wave-564122

Han, H.J. and J.S. Lee (2008) 'A Study on the KBS TV Drama "Winter Sonata" and its Impact on Korea's Hallyu Tourism Development', *Journal of Travel and Tourism Marketing,* 24: 115-126.

Howard, K. (2002) 'Exploding Ballads: The Transformation of Korean Pop Music'. In T.J. Craig and R. King (eds), *Global Goes Local: Popular Culture in Asia,* Vancouver: University of British Colombia Press, pp. 80-95.

Jang, G.J., and W.K. Paik (2012) 'Korean Wave as a Tool for Korea's New Cultural Diplomacy', *Advances in Applied Sociology,* 2: 196-202.

Kim, M. (2011) 'The Role of the Government in Cultural Industry: Some Observations from Korea's Experience', *Keio Communication Review*, 33: 163-182.

Kim, E.M. and J.W. Ryoo (2007) South Korean Culture Goes Global: K-Pop and the Korean Wave, *Korean Social Science Journal,* 34: 117-152.

Kim, H. (2010) 'Korean Culture Key to Promoting Positive National Image', *The Korean Herald,* retrieved from http://www.koreaherald.com/view.php?ud=20051123 000044, page consulted 07/07/2013

Korean Culture and Information Service (KCIS) (2013) 'The Korean Wave. A New Pop Culture Phenomenon', retrieved from http://www.korea.net/Resources/Publications/About-Korea/view?articleId=2215#, page consulted 12/06/2013

Korea Creative Content Agency USA (2006) 'The Korean Wave. Entertaining More than Half the World', retrieved from http://www.kccla.org/english_/5download_.asp?cPage=3, page consulted 19/06/2013

Lee, S. (2003) 'Seoul Survivor', *Straits Times*, April 8.

Nakagawa, U. (2010) 'Korea's Hallyu Boom', *The Diplomat*, retrieved from http://thediplomat.com/new-emissary/2010/10/27/koreas-hallyu-boo/, page consulted 18/06/2013

Onishi, N. (2005) South Korea Adds Culture to its Export Power, *The New York Times,* retrieved from http://www.nytimes.com/2005/06/28/world/asia/28iht-korea.html, page consulted 27/07/2013

Ravina. M. (2009) 'Introduction: Conceptualizing the Korean Wave', *Southeast Review of Asian Studies,* 31: 3-9.

Park, Y. (2004) 'Korean Wave Fever Calls Tourists from Taiwan', *Munwha Ilbo'* retrieved from http://munwha.com/culture/200401/09/2004010901013026106005 .html, page consulted 23/07/2013

Shim, D.B. (2006) 'Hybridity and the Rise of Korean Popular Culture in Asia', *Media, Culture, and Society,* 28: 25-44.

—. (2011) *Waxing the Korean Wave*, Asian Research Institute, Working Paper Series No. 158.

Staines, J. (2012) 'Government to Expand Korean Wave and Overseas Cultural Exchanges, retrieved August 15 from http://culture360.org/news/korea-government-to-expand-korean-wave-and-overseas-cultural-exchanges/attachment/koreanwave/

Tuk, W. (2012) *The Korean Wave: Who are Behind the Success of Korean Popular Culture*, Leiden University: unpublished Master's Thesis.

Yang, S. (2010) 'Korea Aims for Tourism Powerhouse in Asia by 2020', *The Korean Herald,* retrieved from http://www.koreaherald.com/view.php?ud=20091126000051, page consulted 09/07/2013

EXPERIENCE A CHANGE IN LIFE: LONG-STAY TOURISM FOR JAPANESE RETIREES IN CHIANG MAI, THAILAND

MIWA SHIBUYA

Introduction

This chapter examines one configuration of Japanese migratory flow, namely long-stay tourism or *Rongustei* as acknowledged by the Japanese, with a focus on Chiang Mai, Thailand as a case study. Long-stay tourism consists mostly of outbound seniors who aim to stay for a long duration, enjoy a well-to-do and relaxed lifestyle whilst engaging a new environment and culture, and then eventually return to Japan. This genre of tourism entails both features of migration and conventional overseas tourism. In turn, long-stay tourism blurs the demarcation between tourism/tourists and migration/migrants (Toyota et al., 2006; Ono, 2008). Today, the concept of long-stay tourism prevalently permeates ideas of retirement for Japanese grey citizens. According to the Long Stay Foundation which is a government-authorised public interest corporation, by its definition, in 2011 about 1.4 million Japanese people were estimated to experience long-stay tourism[1].

On the global spectrum, long-stay tourism falls into the same category as International Retirement Migration which has been popular in the European Union since the 1960s (Williams et al., 2010). Compared to the intra-EU mobility of senior citizens, Japanese retirement migration is relatively a new advent. The earliest history of long-stay tourism in Japan can be traced back to 1986. In that year, the 'Silver Columbia Plan' was

[1] The definition of long-stay tourism by the Long Stay Foundation is 'Staying for a relatively long period (more than two weeks) in one place abroad not only enjoying leisure life but also promoting international goodwill through learning its culture and contributing to its society while maintaining a livelihood resource in Japan' http://www.longstay.or.jp/ (page consulted, 08/12/2013).

launched by the Ministry of International Trade and Industry (presently, the Ministry of Economy, Trade and Industry). This was, in short, a scheme to construct retirement homes for Japanese 'elderlies' in several countries. However, the programme was abandoned soon after much criticism, both domestic and international, particularly from other countries who regarded this plan as an attempt by Japan to dump its elderly population on foreign nations. Domestically, many Japanese 'elderlies' were not willing to resettle in a foreign country as a permanent resident (Miyazaki, 2008). Long-stay tourism emerged as a mitigating alternative to the unpopular radical plan. Consequently, the government indirectly supported the concept of tourism which had been geared up by an ageing population in Japan. Today, people aged over 65 years old and above comprise 25% of all Japanese nationals in 2013 (*The Asahi Shimbun*, September 16, 2013).

On the side of the receiving region, Southeast Asia, in response to a growing population of greying citizens in developed countries including Japan, the establishment of 'retirement visas' took place. Compared to Western destinations, the sales point of long-stay tourism in the region is, first and foremost, the lower cost of living. The contrast in living costs, attracted many Japanese seniors who were able to afford a 'hedonistic consumption' lifestyle in the region within a limited budget (Shirai, 2012). The Tourism Authority of Thailand (TAT) regards foreign senior travellers as a strategic growth segment to increase foreign revenues (Aswin, 2008). In turn, the Thai government began to offer people aged 50 years and older the 'retirement visa' in 1998. For Japanese nationals, there are two kinds of retirement visas to stay for a long period in Thailand; Non-Immigrant Visa 'O' (Visa O) and Non-Immigrant Visa 'O-A' (Visa O-A). Visa O-A is issued in Japan while Visa O in Thailand. There are several different conditions between Visa O and Visa O-A. Regarding monetary conditions, applicants need to prove a bank statement of the latest month in Thailand indicating a deposit of the amount equal to or no less than 800,000 baht (about US $25,000) or an income certificate with a monthly pension of no less than 65,000 baht, or a certificate showing a deposit account in a bank in Thailand plus a pension income which is no less than 800,000 baht a year (C.L.L Club, 2012a). Compared to Visa O-A, fewer documents are required to acquire a Visa O and procedures are easier at a lower cost. Also, many seniors mentioned that screening was far more lenient, therefore Japanese retirees tended to prefer Visa O to O-A.

Thanks to a variety of desirable conditions, according to a survey by the Long Stay Foundation in 2011, Thailand was chosen the second most desirable country for Japanese long-stay tourism following Malaysia. As Japanese pensioners became entrenched in one of the most favorable inbound markets in Thailand (see, Prathurng, 2006), Chiang Mai became a particularly desirable receiving city. Though it is very difficult to know the official number of Japanese long-stayers in the city, one expat club, the Japanese Association in Chiang Mai estimates about 2,000 Japanese long-stayers reside there. During winter time in Japan from November to March, adding seasonal stayers to sedentary ones, the number of Japanese stayers rises to 4 to 5,000 people (personal interview January, 2013). Two areas are business developed spaces, no further than a 20-minute drive and most of the Japanese seniors tend to aggregate there. As Chiang Mai is home to a growing number of Japanese sojourners and expatriates, Japanese cultural spheres such as eateries, karaoke clubs, apartments, and golf clubs catering to Japanese seniors, are more and more conspicuous in the city.

A limited number of scholars approach the Japanese retirement migratory phenomenon from the perspective of the migrant actor. Most of them focus on major push and pull factors in creating the outbound movement of the Japanese elderly and their migration life in Asia (Kubo and Ishikawa, 2004; Ono, 2008; 2010; 2012b; Kuramata, 2003; Thang, Sone and Toyota, 2012) or in Western destinations (Ishikawa, 2004; Shinozaki, 2007; Thang and Sone, 2011; Thang, Sone and Toyota, 2012).

These previous studies brought to light detailed reasons for Japanese elderly people leaving their country mainly as follows; economic reasons, mild climate and geographical proximity, seeking care givers, establishment of visa, and also pursuit of *ikigai*[2] activities and difficulties in living in Japanese society in the context of social norms. Most of the studies restrict findings to the actors' intended purpose to migrate, but further investigation has not been done on how their motives were embodied or reformed after migration. Kuramata's survey (2003) indicates that about a half of the Japanese residents in Chiang Mai had been interested in living in a different culture before they decided to move. Even so, once Japanese seniors resided in Chiang Mai, they appeared to linger within the Japanese ethnic constituency. It is necessary to understand how their initial motives and their migration experiences are (dis)connected.

---

[2] Gordon Mathews translated the term *ikigai* as 'that which most makes one's life seem worth living' (1996 vii).

Moreover, some research has focused on retirees' adaptation to Thai society and relationships with the locals. Most of the studies reveal that both Japanese (Kuramata, 2003; Kawahara, 2010; Thang, Sone and Toyota, 2012) and Western seniors (Howard, 2008; 2009) have few interactions with Thai citizens and less adaptation to Thai society. Language and cultural barriers hamper them from making themselves comfortable in their retirement life. Koch-Schulte's work (2008) showed that a growing number of Western retirees brought about socio-cultural and economic changes on the community level in Udon Thani since the Westerners created an ethnic demarcation from Thais. While these studies portray the alienation of foreign seniors in Thai society, none of the studies attend to the interaction among resettled seniors in the ethnic community which they inhabit.

Therefore, this chapter will throw some light on the relationships and interactions between Japanese seniors who tend to be aggregated and how they live within the ethnically ascribed boundaries in Thailand. Since a large scale exodus of Japanese retirees has continued for over a decade, it is necessary to understand what kinds of interactions can be observed and what dynamism is now being produced among the retirees in a peculiar setting of 'being away from home'. In addition, the chapter will consider what kinds of experiences the Japanese elderly gain and in what ways their life has changed through living overseas. This will help us comprehend how the experiences can be integrated into their motives for living overseas.

All findings were based on in-depth interviews with 32 Japanese retirees (20 males and 12 females) aged from 58 to 77 years old in Chiang Mai. All of the informants resided in Thailand for no less than six months a year. I also interviewed other business operators and representatives of Japanese expat associations. Data collection was collated in about three months between 2012 and 2013. In-depth interviews were usually carried out on a face-to-face basis and multiple interviews were conducted with about a half of the informants. They were approached through two ways: snowball samplings and visiting particular sites where Japanese were likely to assemble such as malls, and Japanese condominiums and apartments. In addition, I stayed in one Japanese popular condominium for a month between March and April, 2013, so I could obtain adequate information that I could not have acquired in an interview methodology.

Interactions among Japanese retirees in Chiang Mai

Cohabitation of the rich and the poor Japanese in Chiang Mai

The gap between the poor and the rich amongst the elderly is wider than any other age groups in Japan (Tachibanaki, 2011). On the one hand, the average savings of the elderly household[3] is 140% higher than that of all other types of household (Korei Shakai Hakusho, 2012). On the other hand, in July 2013, the highest proportion of households on social welfare was the elderly households. Putting it simply, the social recipients are not capable of making a living, thus depend fully on the government for financial support (*The Asahi Shimbun,* October 3, 2013). For these less affluent seniors, Southeast Asia has become a lifeline to stretch their pensions (see Ono, 2008, 2010).

Chiang Mai epitomises the status quo of the elderly in Japanese society. On the one hand, Japanese senior citizens who wish to have a long-stay in Thailand but are concerned about budget tend to settle down in Chiang Mai (Kawahara, 2010; Kuramata, 2003). On the other hand, the city also accommodates a wealthy Japanese group which is willing to have a luxurious lifestyle without economic incentive. Therefore, significant differences in economic strata with a different primary motivation appear amongst Japanese retirees in this city (Toyota, 2006).

Although the Thai government accepts only people ‘having-money’ with the retirement visa conditions, Chiang Mai appears to be inundated with more and more ‘not-having’ Japanese who are not able to meet visa requirements today. These economically less fortunate people depend on the visa agency to solve the issue. Seventy year-old Mr. Harada told me he came to Thailand four years ago to save his pension to build a house in Japan in the future. Yet, one year after migration, he married a Thai woman and they bought a home for themselves and his two-year stepson. Because of this big expenditure, he ran out of cash to deposit into a Thai bank necessary to apply for his retirement visa. Mr. Harada found a Japanese visa agency on the Internet in which the sales point was no need of money to acquire a long-stay visa. After he paid a charge, in that year he received an ‘official’ Visa O in Bangkok.

---

[3] The definition of an elderly household is one consisting of individuals aged 65 years or over, with or without unmarried dependents under 18 years old, representing 20.5 % of the entire households in 2011 (The Statistics Handbook of Japan, 2012).

How is such a thing possible? My findings were that visa corruption took place in collaboration between Japanese visa agencies and Thai officials. Japanese clients who were not entitled to hold a visa officially requested the visa acquirement from the visa agency. The agency called upon an affiliated Thai agency to undertake the rest of the processes. The Thai middleman and the Japanese retiree went together to a certain bank in Bangkok. Then, the Thai person deposited 800,000 baht into the bank and made the bank statement under the client's name for the visa documents in advance. Upon the acquisition of the retirement visa for the clients, the Thai agency pulled the 800,000 baht out of the bank. When the application screening for Visa O was done, the Thai agency paid a commission to the police with which the agency had a connection so the police turned a blind eye. As a precondition, the Japanese visa agency required non-criminal records and that the Japanese clients should be over 50 years old. All the processes cost 49,000 baht the first time. After the second time, it would charge 47,000 baht every year (personal interview, March, 2013).

Other visa agencies implicitly noted that officers in the immigration bureau were involved in this corruption too. On visa advertisements, the sort of phrase, 'you can get a visa without money', could be easily found on bulletin boards, non-subscription papers in Chiang Mai or on the Internet. Several visa agencies, including the one above, told me that it was not just a few Japanese who had attained the retirement visa in this way. There is no way to investigate the number of the needy who acquired a visa in a questionable manner. Today, economically deficient Japanese seniors cohabit with the affluent Japanese as 'authorised aliens' in Thailand.

Ruptures based on economic capital

In this context, hierarchical ruptures based on economic capital emerged among Japanese seniors. This was an ironic outcome when many Japanese expected no such distinction. The majority of my respondents tended to conceptualise the retirement life overseas as something to reset their past; who they had been and what they had done in Japan. Most of my respondents were no longer concerned about their social status and previous occupation once they reached retirement age. Japanese seniors perceived the retirement life in Chiang Mai as an erasure of the social background associated with Japan, thus equalising the level of status of retirees. For instance, 69-year-old Mr. Tsukada was engaged in the Self-Defense Forces for decades until retirement age and then worked as a care worker to make a living in Japan. Once he was fired, he came to Thailand for financial security. He told me about relationships with other Japanese seniors in Chiang Mai as follows:

> I don't know how many great things one has achieved in Japan, but everybody is the same now, self-defense forces, the policeman or the president. It may have been a president at a place at that time. But when the presidential term finished, it does not matter. Just a person, we are the same ordinary people (November, 2012).

Like Mr. Tsukada, many of my respondents shared the idea of dismissing social background and admitted that all the long-stayers in Chiang Mai were 'just retirees'.

In addition to an indifference to social position in Japan, their increased economic power also appeared to play a role in making the collective of Japanese retirees equal. Suffice to say that almost all of the Japanese have more purchasing power to access a consumption-centred lifestyle in Thailand than in Japan. Thus, in Thailand people seem to have more opportunities to intersect with different economic classes by attending luxurious activities that were only a privilege to the wealthy in Japan. In this respect, social and economic positions in Thailand are no longer as influential as they were in Japan. Migration appears as an opportunity for Japanese seniors to build new relationships without status distinctions in the Japanese community in Chiang Mai.

In reality, hierarchies based on different lifestyles ruptured the perceived social coherence of the Japanese retiree community in Chiang Mai. Although Japanese seniors gained more chances to meet a variety of Japanese people since they came to Chiang Mai, the amount of economic capital determined what level of lifestyle individuals could have and they gradually scrutinised those who they could share the same life patterns with through friend-based interactions. For instance, 61-year-old Mrs. Kojima was a self-employed showcase-decorator in Japan. She came to Thailand because her financial situation in Japan became a struggle after retirement. Thus, she tries to be frugal with her money with a budget under 10,000 baht a month in Chiang Mai. Mrs. Kojima said that her selection of Japanese friendships was influenced by material differentiation.

> The hard thing is that sometimes when I go out to eat with other people, even if it is not their intention to show off their wealth, it is just natural for them to comment about it. But after eating, let's say it cost 200 baht. For me, if I spend 200 baht, I think, 'Oh, I have spent as much as 200 baht!'

> while another person comments 'today I just spent 200 baht only'. It hits me hard. I feel I am not able to hang out with these people (February 2013).

The group of respondents on a tight budget excused themselves from hooking up with the more affluent whereas the wealthier ones also refrained from accompanying the more frugal group due to different leisure pursuits. Economic differences are a decisive element for Japanese retirees as to whom they connect with in a relocated settlement.

In *Economy and Society* (1978), Max Weber proposed that the concept of 'status' and 'status group' developed in modern society. According to Weber, economic classes and status groups overlap with each other but are not exactly identical. He categorised 'class' into three modes, namely, property class, commercial class and social class and all are significantly determined by the market. In contrast, according to Weber, status emerges outside of the market arena. There is a specific pattern of lifestyle, behaviour and consumption called 'tastes' and a distinctive pattern espoused by each group of people. He called the social congruency based on cultural practices 'status'. Further, these cultural practices confer, in Weber's term 'honour' which is either positively or negatively ascribed to individuals of a particular status level through society's evaluation. This brings about status stratifications embraced by members in a society. The same status group creates a boundary, restriction and repulsion with other groups according to the status order.

In the case of Japanese retirees in Chiang Mai, broadly speaking, at least three different groups arose based on their principal motives; 'leisure-pursuit group', 'seasonal migrant group' and 'economic migrant group'. I define the 'leisure-pursuit group' as the type propelled to migrate to Thailand by the pursuit of a different life from that in Japan. The 'seasonal migrant group' is the type which seeks a mild climate as well as a healthy life. The 'economic migrant group' is the type driven to live in Thailand mainly to secure a retirement life with a limited financial resource. Compared to the economic migrant group, the other two groups tend to be more mobile and can afford to engage in more consumption-oriented activities. Japanese retirees in the economic migrant group often seem to spend their life frugally or refrain from having an exorbitant luxurious lifestyle. In turn, a superior honour is given to leisure-pursuit and seasonal migrant groups wherein inferior status is conferred on the economic refugee group. In short, broadly two hierarchical status groups arise in Chiang Mai; 'economic refugee status' and 'non-economic refugee status' based on their monetary sources. Subsequently, a feeling of antipathy began to emerge between the two statuses.

Ruptures based on Taste, Behaviour and Dress

Max Weber (1978; 306) argues that status expresses itself in four forms: 'connubium', 'commensality', 'monopolistic appropriation of privileged modes of acquisition or the abhorrence of certain kinds of acquisition', and 'status conventions (traditions) of other kinds'. The third mode of acquisition or in other words, the element of possessing certain items, ensures one's membership of a particular status group.

As consumption practices become a primary pillar of retirement life in Thailand for the Japanese, their expression of material wealth comes into play in distinguishing between them and other Japanese of a different status. For instance, 63-year-old Mr. Taki was a food-related company owner and began coming to Thailand more than a decade ago to seek cheap amenities for a short duration. He frequently went to play golf in a luxurious brand automobile. Every time he went out, he dressed up. Mr. Taki explained that he had many Thai friends with high official status and Japanese friends who worked here for a Japanese company. It was necessary to wear certain formal clothes and drive a certain brand of vehicle for him to mingle with these high status people. He demonstrated his association with a higher class and standards attributed to worth or status by wearing elegant attire and riding in a high-class vehicle,

By the same token, exhibiting a luxurious lifestyle created fissures among the Japanese. For instance, 58-year-old Mr. Yamada, who was a self-employed photographer in Japan and migrated to Chiang Mai because of economic difficulties, told me that Japanese retirees playing golf were the type in Chiang Mai whom he did not want to associate with. Here was his narrative:

> I don't want to hang out with people playing such a thing (golf) because they boast about themselves. There are many (Japanese) people who dare to put on golf wear to walk in the street....I think guys playing golf are sort of snobbish. I did not play golf in Japan, neither…[do].. I feel more reluctant to approach men playing golf than men in dirty clothes. 〔Golfers are〕 people like those who wear leather shoes with a formal suit (February, 2013).

According to him, the retired golfers had a bourgeois mentality, in his terms, 'they boast about themselves'. This was a nuisance for Mr. Yamada since he perceived golf wear as a sign that symbolised their superior position in a relocated site. In contrast, he felt in more proximity with other Japanese retirees with an unkempt appearance who seemed to have more in common with him. Consumption practices produced some distance and antipathy in displaying statuses.

Not only visible symbols but also less palpable marks or behaviour are signs creating cleavages. Weber asserts that status is typically founded on three components; lifestyle, formal education, and occupational prestige. He claims education corresponds to forms of behaviour. That is, distinctive behaviour such as ways of speech is significantly attained in the process of education. To a lesser degree, superiority and inferiority were observed among the Japanese retirees via behaviour. For instance, 64-year-old Mr. Yazawa's narrative shows that social and economic backgrounds in Japan are not completely erased but still involved in creating a coming together of similar people in a new setting. He was educated up to middle school. Until he retired, he worked as a clerk at a telecommunication company. Mr. Yazawa insisted that it was no longer valid to consider an educational degree as higher social status as in the past once Japanese seniors in Chiang Mai were detached from a working position. Nevertheless, he found it awkward to speak with other Japanese seniors who used to belong to a high social position. He thought his position was not equal to theirs even after migration.

> Mr. Yazawa: When I talk with people who had a high status, they speak to me at a working level. Sometimes, it is fine but I think 'hey, you are already retired from work'. I cannot keep up with them because I am dumb. But I cannot say I am dumb. I want them to talk from the level of one of the same Japanese as I am.
>
> Author: Why do you feel that they talk to you at working level and you feel yourself lower than them?
>
> Mr. Yazawa: Maybe the way they speak.....I feel they speak to me from the higher position….They do not belong to the same level as mine (April, 2013).

Mr. Yazawa sensed a demarcation between social classes which were supposed to have diminished but remained salient in forms of speech. The speech of high positioned retirees was also a signal to the uneducated Mr. Yazawa that made him feel inferior about his educational background.

This attitude towards others' behaviour constrained him from overcoming the differences in educational and social backgrounds with other Japanese retirees.

Behaviour, preferences, consumption and lifestyle, all these become symbols illuminating retirees as to which collective group they belong. Ironically, many informants considered retirement life in Chiang Mai as their new life under an equal status with others, but they tended to associate with people having the similar level of monetary consumption and behaviour. In the end, fissures emerged to create a hierarchy of two orders.

Importantly Weber argued that economic unities interrelate with status, but are not exactly the same. Like Weber's argument, concerning Japanese seniors in Chiang Mai, though economic resources were linked to the two statuses, economic conditions did not lead my respondents to stay in a fixed collective group. My respondents in both statuses were not segregated clearly but actually came into contact with each other in a transnational space. In other words, there was no discerning criterion of demarcation in lifestyle between the two. But my respondents positioned themselves and others by being sensitised to individuals' subtle 'codes' such as which area their residences were located in, how many times they played golf, what food they often ate, what kind of clothes they wore, and which association they belonged to.

Further marginality for poor retirees

Status distinctions amid Japanese retirees become more complicated in the transnational setting. The wealthier residents displayed discriminatory views towards economically less-fortunate retirees in Chiang Mai. Two reasons were pointed out as to why the Japanese rich desire to remove these 'pension refugees' from the Japanese retiree community. Firstly, the wealthier Japanese were concerned when poor Japanese expatriates become representatives of the whole senior Japanese enclave and have the effect of causing all Japanese retirees to be classified as vulgar or coarse. 63-year-old Mrs. Ohe articulated her apprehension about the growing population of poor Japanese retirees in Chiang Mai as follows:

> At first, when I began to come here, I thought that even if people do not have money like the poor who need to rely on social security in Japan, here they can live. So, I thought this sort of person should come to live here. But now I mind their coming because these people look dirty in what they

> wear. They put on tired-looking clothes. I think people wear neater clothes in Japan. Old [Japanese] men in Chiang Mai are in rags....I don't want poor [Japanese] people to come really. I feel ashamed. Feeling ashamed means, as the same Japanese, I want to be thought that Japanese know good manners by Thais....I don't care if *Farang* (Westerners) are dirty or Koreans are dirty. It is not my business, but I don't want dirty Japanese to come (February 2013).

Firstly, Mrs. Ohe considered that Chiang Mai could become home to the Japanese who were not able to make a living in Japan. In the beginning, she was more sympathetic towards other Japanese consigned to a poor retirement life as one of the same nationals. However, later on, the reflection that the Japanese retirees have on the Thai viewpoint entered into considerations about those who are appropriate stayers overseas and who do not shame other Japanese. Since Mrs. Ohe regarded herself as staying in Chiang Mai from an objective perspective, as a member of the Japanese enclave evaluated by Thais, she became more exclusionary with regard to less-wealthy people. From her premise, her view on poor Japanese was the same as the view of the locals towards Japanese retirees. She ascribed a negative evaluation to Japanese people in unclean dress and denied being associated with this same category. In this sense, class dimensions are a cause of conflict among Japanese expatriates. The lower status group is labelled as a shameful representation of Japan.

The second reason has to do with mutual misunderstanding or incomprehension as the bottom line in the relationships among Japanese retirees, particularly a dubious perception of the poor Japanese. All too often, poor Japanese are viewed as potential 'troublemakers' by other Japanese. In order to understand fully why well-to-do seniors are warned against interacting with poorer Japanese, firstly I shall explain some characteristics of the Japanese community and the relationship between Japanese retirees.

Though many Japanese tend to connect up with other Japanese mainly because of a deficient proficiency in other languages, they are actually wary of each other like 65-year-old Mr. Ohta. He intermingled only with Japanese in Chiang Mai since he could not converse with other nationals; however, he was quite skeptical of other Japanese retirees as he had heard many rumours about Japanese swindlers. He compared the seniors in Chiang Mai to Thai women whom he had actually been warned of before coming to Chiang Mai. He said, '*After I came here, I realised that I need to be careful of Japanese more [than Thai women]. I have not been cheated but many stories come into my ears*'.

The existence of 'bad Japanese' who try to cheat others for money was frequently shared in the Japanese enclave. Distrust was considered as a proper demeanour amongst the Japanese. Their warning against other Japanese is also enhanced by a publication. One of the Japanese expatriate associations in Chiang Mai, C. L. L. Club published a guidebook for Japanese long-stayers in the city. In the book, a column written by an anonymous long-stayer advises visitors to distrust the kindness of both the locals and the Japanese regarding business deals.

> There are many cases in which the Japanese cheat other Japanese. So please be very careful. It is normal that money, let's say, even hundreds of baht called kickback is involved even though it is a deal between your close friend and you when a local intervenes.... Do not believe in people familiar with the place and approach you saying, 'I can find you' a house or a car, nevertheless, with no credentials. If the person is Japanese, you are more prone to trust, therefore, it is more dangerous (C.L.L. Club, 2012b: 24, author's translation).

In this context, financially marginalised Japanese retirees are viewed as suspicious characters in the community. I often heard suspect comments from the affluent amenities-seekers like 67-year-old Mr. Sato. He had once advised a manager of his apartment not to rent a room to poor looking Japanese. He said the following:

> Harmful people are males who cannot make a living on a pension and are married to a Thai. You should be careful of Japanese men who marry Thai women. To cheat, Thai women are necessary (October, 2012).

In his mind, poorer Japanese people are more likely to cheat other Japanese because it is a necessity for them to survive in Chiang Mai. Also, he pointed to Thailand's regulations and restrictions imposed on foreign nationals in some circumstances when conducting businesses such as non-entitlement to buy land. Therefore, he noted Thai women's complicity in fraud. This sort of discourse circulated in the Japanese community as well. The warnings embodied an exclusive attack on pension refugees and created a fissure in the relationship between the affluent and the needy.

As the poor Japanese are suspected as potential swindlers, material differences play a decisive part for the well-to-do Japanese in deducing who is good/bad, reliable/unreliable, safe/dangerous and harmless/harmful. As a consequence of these divergent pluralities, status rupture ended up consolidating the asymmetry between the dominant and the dominating in Chiang Mai.

Escaping from Japan is an ideal retirement life?

Self-emancipation in Chiang Mai

I shall now shift my attention to seniors' subjective experiences in investigating the changes in their lives through migration. Many interviewees described the life in Chiang Mai as 'carefree', 'less stressful' and 'less tiring'. These respondents who preferred a retirement life in Thailand over one in Japan attributed the reason to Japanese social norms and obligations. The pursuit of their ideal lifestyle in their late life-stage was derived from distancing themselves from the rules observed in Japanese society and this allowed the retirees to seek a desirable way to live and develop self-actualisation. By self-actualisation I mean when Japanese seniors become able to express themselves in ways that are considered unacceptable in the Japanese society due to its restrictive normative standards.

From this perspective, female respondents prominently claimed their appearances and demeanour changed in relation to age between the two countries. They tended to state that in Japan, for a proper mature lady, there were social rules about what to wear and how to behave. In other words, their 'what I want to be like' had been suppressed due to normative mores in their home country. For instance, 61-year-old Mrs. Ohe resided in Thailand and Japan off and on every year. While she said she liked both lifestyles in Japan and Thailand, she also noted that what she benefitted most from by living in Thailand was her choice of apparel. When I interviewed her, she was in a frilly short skirt that she bought in Japan, but only as 'special clothes' to put on in Thailand. She explained the reason;

> Mrs. Ohe: I was thinking that I wanted to wear the skirt [in Japan]. When I come here, I can wear with no hesitation.
>
> Author: Oh, you look good. Please wear it in Japan, too.
>
> Mrs. Ohe: (Smile) Thank you. But I can't do it. I would be left out [of other female circles in Japan]. And I don't want to be left out because I want to stay mingling. I don't desire to wear this outfit as much as I mind being left out. (November, 2012)

Mrs. Ohe feared the reaction of her friends in Japan if she had worn her favourite outfits. She speculated that her neighbours would have laughed at her behind her back as it seemed to them that she was trying to look overly young against the conventional model of an 'ideal' female in her

60s. In fact, I thought she was in her late 40s or so in these clothes. A different selection of clothes to wear was a visible embodiment of conflict between whom she wanted to be and who other Japanese expected her to be in Japan.

A conservative Japanese society restricted the desire of 'what I want to do' for individuals; however, once in Thailand, this all changed. For instance, 71-year-old Mrs. Imai came to Chiang Mai four years ago as her husband was bored with country life in Saitama and longed for a more exciting retirement life overseas. Since migration, like her husband, she has engaged in several language and hobby classes. One of them was ballet lessons that she could not have tried in Japan. For her, learning ballet was a form of self-emancipation. Here was the dialogue between Mrs. Imai and her younger sister who had just come to Chiang Mai from Japan.

> Mrs. Imai: Well, I can be into any hobbies without hesitation in Thailand even if I would be too embarrassed to go for some of them in Japan. For example, I had learned ballet before and I was asked by my friend, so I began it again [in Thailand].
>
> Sister: Yeah, you cannot dance ballet in Japan because of your age.
>
> Mrs. Imai: I know. I am wearing leotards (laugh)! It is very good to be able to live in a way to stay true to my heart (August, 2013).

In Japan, Mrs. Imai and her sister supposed people would have thought negatively of her performing ballet in leotards because it is an inappropriate hobby and attire for someone at the age of 71. On the other hand, she validated her desire and could commit herself to ballet in Thailand. Like Mrs. Imai, many Japanese seniors became more active in the resettled domain. The first reason is that they can make use of cheap amenities. In addition, some Japanese seniors were able to try what they wanted to do once free from Japanese societal norms as to what individuals should do according to their social attributes.

The shackles of ingrained ideologies and prescriptive norms were saliently pointed out by my female informants. To a lesser degree, male informants also felt subjected to this pressure in Japan. Here was a comment about Japanese culture by 63-year-old Mr. Sakamoto who has lived in the USA for over a decade.

> There is something like this [in Japan]; because people do this, you have to do it too, Girls around 20 years old have to be in certain outfits. People

> over 60 years old should wear certain clothes and behave in certain patterns and talk about certain topics. There is no such rule [in Chiang Mai]. Yes, it is comfortable (October, 2012).

Individuals are inevitably categorised into a certain role in society whether they like it or not based on their attributes. The word らしさ（*Rashisa*）in Japanese language describes the concept and pattern of behaviour prescribed for citizens as a social role norm. For instance, regarding male societal roles, 男らしさ（*Otoko-Rashisa*）*Otoko* means 'man' in Japanese and *Otoko-Rashisa* shows the concepts and patterns to make a man man-like. In the same way, 老人らしさ（*Rojin-Rashisa*）*Rojin* means 'the elderly' and *Rojin-Rashisa* shows the concepts and patterns to make the elderly elderly-like. Everyone is entangled with this *Rashisa* which guides individuals to behave in a certain way and play a certain role. If one deviates from *Rashisa* which is assigned to individuals, it is considered inappropriate or unpleasant behaviour.

Because of the anxiety about what others think, therefore, many informants put much energy into monitoring their own conduct such as going out appropriately dressed, observing rules as a member of their community, or interacting with their neighbours regularly, so as not to offend others in Japan. In this way, the informants were performing their own-*Rashisa* in public in accordance with their age. In the meantime, in Thailand, because of the absence of public scrutiny the informants no longer needed to consider their assigned character. They could experiment with 'deviant' activities. In short, many informants had played dual characters in the two countries, which I shall explain next.

Radical Change of Character and Identity

Living in Thailand was interlaced with the conception of an 'outlaw terrain' in which people need not conform to the customary practices of Japan. Most of the informants found individualistic life more comfortable in Thailand when not following approved and established roles. Thus, a new silent maxim was produced. The alteration of a given role in Japan should not be questioned in the Japanese community in Thailand. Many Japanese female respondents felt that no other Japanese retirees would speak ill of their 'improper' clothes behind their back. As a consequence, some seniors were radically switching their character of who they are between Japan and Thailand. Here was a comment by 62-year-old Mrs.

Nakase about one senior female who had one identity in Japan and another in Thailand.

> Recently, a woman in her 70s was wearing a ribbon (showing a gesture of big ribbon like the one of Minnie Mouse) on the top of her head and it was oddly cute. It could be said to be cute. It is impossible to happen in Japan, isn't it (smile)?……We were talking about the old lady with the ribbon; 'it is cute'. When the lady was gone, the Japanese person next to me who was her neighbour in Japan said to us that she is a normal old lady in Japan (December, 2012).

Retreating from social structure not only influences a change in visible identity but also the psychological viewpoint of the actor too. Mrs. Ohe found a shift in the way she perceived herself from the perspective of age. By wearing young-generation clothes and socialising with liberal Japanese retirees she said, '*I became rejuvenated here. My feelings became rejuvenated more than in Japan*'. In Japan, she was put into the group of 'women in their 60s' and performed the role, consequently feeling more aged.

The American anthropologist Ruth Benedict (1946/1967) investigated the patterns of Japanese cultural behaviour and their underlying values. She initiated the concept of 'shame culture' to explain behaviour in Japanese society. The 'shame culture' is when an individual's moral and ethical conduct are based on external standards, thus, inhibiting people from carrying out immoral conduct since they are concerned about public reaction. Japanese society maintains its morals by individuals putting a check on others' conduct. Because 'shame' is a pillar of policy of behaviour in Japan, on a daily basis, Japanese nationals pay careful attention to public evaluation about their own conduct in every sphere. The speculation of what others think is a fundamental indicator when deciding how to behave properly in Japanese society.

As a substitute for the concept of a 'shame culture', many idiomatic phrases emphasise the importance of abiding by the majority opinions, culture, and customs in Japan such as 和を以て貴しと為す（*Wa o Motte Totoshi to Nasu*） [important to harmonise with others] or 郷に入っては郷に従え（*Go ni Ittewa Go ni Shitagae*） [practice the manners and customs of the living place]. Sympathisers in harmony with the majority are considered virtuous in Japanese society. External pressure plays a role in reconciling each group or collectivity of Japanese based on their attributes in the way they are supposed to live in congruency with others. As a consequence, individual discretion is diminished.

According to Benedict (ibid.), performing assigned roles and obligations of what other people expect of you are particularly important but troublesome to practice, especially in the case of family relationships. Therefore, for the Japanese elderly, migration is sometimes utilised as a way to escape from the bothersome roles and fragmented commitments to family as well as community neighbours in Japan. For instance, Mrs. Nakase was prudent about deviating from the proper female model in her 60s, for her relative was a person of high status in Japan. But in Chiang Mai she could do whatever she wanted without worrying about damaging the family name of her relative by being an eccentric aunt. Similarly, some informants strategically made use of the geographical distance between Japan and Thailand in order to be disembedded from their local context in Japan. For instance, 72-year-old Mrs. Nakano was tired of living close to her family members and acquaintances in Japan because she needed to pay heed to her own behaviour in front of these people on a daily basis. One of her obligations she found bothersome was at her age, she was continuously compelled to participate in funerals and other festivities to pray for the dead in Japan. Living in Thailand was a good excuse for skipping these occasions without much criticism from family members.

In Thailand, Japanese seniors were able to be anonymous and unbound. Being physically released from their local context through migration erased the standards that restricted certain behaviour and positions in the community. This gave them more discretion to do whatever they wanted and be whoever they wanted to be. They were free to express and explore the 'otherness' they had heard and fantasised about.

Having said that some respondents were exempted from their obligations in Chiang Mai, notions of Japanese family roles and social norms were still entangled in their life abroad. For instance, 70-year-old Mr. Nakamura felt guilty for his decision to prioritise his desire for the quest overseas over his family role as a widowed husband in Japan. His wife's family expected him to pray for her regularly in Japan. In the interview, Mr. Nakamura excused himself by saying, 'If I listen to my brothers and families of my wife, I can do nothing'.

Since developing a sense of individualisation and diversified values regarding their life in retirement, Japanese retirees were able to choose how to live a life based on their own will. This new conceptualisation of how to live one's own life also brought about conflict, dilemma and guilt, particularly, after previously delegating every choice in life to determined cultural prerogatives whether it was compatible with one's will or not. In the age of global modernity, the choices for Japanese grey citizens expanded their options and opportunities beyond the territory of one specific nation or era.

Concluding Remarks

This chapter has added to the literature on Japanese seniors' migration experiences from previous work in terms of relationships with other Japanese in a particular destination. The research showed that although retirees expected no hierarchical structure in the relocated domicile, they were split into dichotomous levels according to economic statuses, lifestyles, tastes and behaviour. Due to this diversification, my informants faced personal ruptures and repulsion based on arising and existing statuses.

A similar cleavage was also observed in Oliver's and O'Reilly's work (2010) on British retirees in Spain. British retirees assumed relocation would erase social classes which they once belonged to in England. However, the hierarchies were retained through, in Bourdieu's term (1984), cultural capital and *habitus*. Yet, in the case of my informants, cultural practices and economic classes were far less relevant than the British case since as other scholars have already pointed out, unlike Europe, social classes do not necessarily determine or influence cultural activities in Japanese society (see Uchida, 2008).

Also, the unfolding drama played out in the long-stay destination of Chiang Mai produced a specific dynamism in retirees' communication. This research showed the widespread discourse of 'cheating Japanese' in the Japanese community which made my informants more cautious about other Japanese. Furthermore, the informants of superior status tended to consider the values of less affluent Japanese as vulgar and a shameful representation of the nation. In addition, the chapter has demonstrated the exclusive phenomenon in which wealthier Japanese retirees desired to rid the Japanese community of other lower status Japanese in Chiang Mai. In the end, the economically less-fortunate Japanese seniors may find themselves more marginalised.

Further, the chapter has demonstrated what kind of migration life my informants experienced and how the experiences made differences in their lives. According to Giddens (1991), today people in developed countries dwell in *high modernity* in which individuals are disembedded from the particularities of locality, with time and space separated. The consequences of high modernity have given rise to the dismantling of the strong traditional forms of classifications, identifications and obligations. Therefore, people living in high modernity gain expanded discretion. In other words, people are forced to make decisions about every choice in life in accordance with one's own standards rather than the specific meta-narrative role shared by members of a community in a previous epoch. Accordingly, Giddens claims, a lifestyle consists of a continuity of plural choices and what to choose is interwoven with self-identity. He referred to this whole phenomenon as 'life politics'.

The chapter has illustrated that Japanese long-stay tourism is one form of 'life politics'. Japanese seniors adopted an anonymous persona by disembedding themselves from local Japanese contexts and constructed their new identity in the relocated terrain. They formed a new kind of relationship with other expatriates and community mores which do not force individuals to be subject to Japanese social norms. Sometimes the change was fraught with complications, but overall many respondents were satisfied with self-actualisation and a newly gained identity. Japanese retirees' motives for long-stay became more multifaceted as they became engulfed in the wave of migratory experiences. The multiplicity of unexpressed desires and available choices in lifestyle are important factors for the Japanese seniors to continue to stay in Thailand today.

Lastly, and worthy of note, the desire of self-emancipation and rearrangement of their character and lifestyle was much stronger among my female respondents than my male ones. In this regard further investigation on Japanese long-stay tourism and the needs, desires and experiences from a gender perspective is necessary.

References

Aswin, S. (2008) 'Travel Motivations of Japanese Senior Travelers to Thailand', *International Journal of Tourism Research,* 10: 81-94.

Benedict, R. (1946) *The Chrysanthemum and the Sword; Patterns of Japanese Culture,* Harcourt: Houghton Mifflin (1967) 菊と刀 (Matsuji Hasegawa, translator) Tokyo: Shakai Shiso Sha.

Bourdieu, P. (1984) *Distinction. A Social Critique of the Judgment of Taste,* London: Routledge and Kegan Paul.

C.L.L. Club (2012a) *Biza no Syutoku to Tetsuduki [How to Obtain Visa and Procedures],* first edition. Chiang Mai: C.L.L. Club.

—. (2012b) *Chen Mai Seikatsu Gaido [Chiang Mai Life Guide]*, 9th edition. Chiang Mai: C.L.L Club.

Giddens, A. (1991) *Modernity and Self-Identity. Self and Society in the Late Modern Age,* Cambridge: Polity.

Howard, R. W. (2008) 'Western Retirees in Thailand: Motives, Experiences, Wellbeing, Assimilation and Future Needs', *Ageing and Society*, 28: 145-163.

—. (2009) 'The Migration of Westerners to Thailand: an Unusual Flow from Developed to Developing World', *International Migration*, 47: 193-225.

Kawahara, M. (2010) 'Tai Chenmainiokeru Nihon Jin Rongusuteiya no Tekio Senryaku to Genchi Shakai no Taio [Adaptive Strategy of Japanese Senior Long-Term Stayers and Local Community Responses in Chiangmai]', *Nenpou Tai Kenkyu,* 10: 35-55.

Korei Shakai Hakusho (2012) 'Chapter1: Koreika no Jyokyo [Situation of Ageing]' from http://www8.cao.go.jp/kourei/whitepaper/w-2012/zen bun/pdf/1s2s_2_5.pdfpage consulted05/10/2013

Koch-Schulte, J. (2008) *Planning for International Retirement Migration and Expats: a Case Study of Udon Thani, Thailand*, University of Manitoba: unpublished Master's thesis.

Kubo, T. and Y. Ishikawa, Y. (2004) '"Rakuen" oMotomete－Nihon Jin no Kokusai Intaildo [Searching for "Paradise": Japanese International Retirement Migration]', *Jinbun Chiri,* 56: 74-87.

Kuramata, T. (2003) Chenmainiokeru Nihon Jin Rongusutei Sha no Jittai Chousa [The Survey on Reality of Japanese Long-Stayers in Chiang Mai]', *Chenmai Ken Doboku*, Toshikeikaku Jimusho.

Mathews, G. (1996) *What Makes Life Worth Living? How Japanese and Americans Make Sense of Their Worlds*, Berkeley and Los Angeles: University of California Press.

Miyazaki, K. (2008) 'An Aging Society and Migration to Asia and Oceania', *Senri Ethnological Reports,* 77: 139-149.

Oliver, C. and K. O'Reilly (2010) 'A Bourdieusian Analysis of Class and Migration: Habitus and the Individualising Process', *Sociology,* 44: 49-66.

Ono, M. (2008) 'Long-Stay Tourism and International Retirement Migration: Japanese Retirees in Malaysia', *Senri Ethnological Reports,* 77: 151-162.

—. (2010) 'Long-stay Tourism: Elderly Japanese Tourists in the Cameron Highlands, Malaysia', *Senri Ethnological Studies,* 76:95-110.

Prathurng H. (2006) 'Japanese Senior Tourists: an Untapped Potential in Thailand's Tourism Industry', *The Journal of Behavioral Science*, (1):55-61.

Shinozaki, M. (2007) 'Nihon Jin no Kokusai IntaiIdou: Nyuii Rando no Jirei [Japanese International Retirement Migration: A Case Study of Japanese Retired Couples in New Zealand]', *Nihon Nyujirandogakushishi* 4:75-81.

Shirai, Y. (2012) 'Choki Taizaigata RyokoniokeruYuin no Kosatsu: Kairaku Shohi no Shiten Kara [The Motives for Extended Stay Tourism: From a Hedonistic Consumption Point of View]', *Chiiki Seisaku Kenkyu*, 15: 65-79.

Tachibanaki, T. (2011) *Muen Shakai no Shotai; Ketsuen・Chien・Shaen ha Ikani Hokai Shitaka [The Reality of Non-connection Society; How Were Blood Bond, Habitat Bond and Occupational Bond Demolished].* Tokyo: PHP.

Thang, L.L. and S. Sone (2011) '(Re)Engagement for a New Life: Mature Japanese Women Living in Western Australia', *Nihon Go・Nihon Gaku Kenkyu,* 1: 45-66.

Thang, L.L., and M. Toyota (2012). 'Freedom Found? The Later-life Transnational Migration of Japanese Women to Western Australia and Thailand', *Asian and Pacific Migration Journal*, 21: 239-262.

The Asahi Shimbun (2012) 'Nihonjin Jyosei no Jyumyo, Sekaiichikara Tenraku Daishinsaiga Eikyo [The Life Expectancy of Japanese Females Fell from the World Top Catastrophic Earthquake Affected]', 27 July.

—. (2013) '65 Saijyo, Sojinko no 25%, 80 Saiijyo ha 930 Mannin [People Aged 65 years Old and Above, 25% of the Whole Population, People Aged 80 years Old and Above is 9.3 million]', 16 September

—. (2013) 'Seikatuhogo no Jyukyusha 7Gatsu Hutatabi Zouka Setaisu ha Saita Kousin [Increasing Recipients of Social Welfare, July, Again Break Records of Number of Households]', 3 October.

The Statistical Handbook of Japan (2012) From http://www.stat.go.jp/english/data/handbook/index.htmpage consulted 06/18/2013

Toyota, M. (2006) 'Ageing and Transnational Householding: Japanese Retirees in Southeast Asia', *International Development Planning Review*, 28: 515-53.

Toyota, M., A. Bocker and E. Guild (2006) 'Pensioners on the Move: Social Security and Trans-border Retirement Migration in Asia and Europe', *IIAS Newsletter 40* based on the papers presented at the ASEF-Alliance Workshop 5-7 January 2006, Singapore: 30.

Uchida, T. (2008) *Chini Hatarakeba Kadoga Tatsu,* Tokyo: Bungei Shunjyu.

Weber, M. (1978) 'Political Communities', in *Economy and Society: An Outline of Interpretive Sociology*, California: University of California Press, pp. 901-938.

Williams, A.M., R. King, A. Warnes and G. Patterson (2010) 'Tourism and International Retirement Migration: New Forms of an Old Relationship in Southern Europe', *Tourism Geographies: an International Journal of Tourism Space, Place and Environment,* 2: 28-49.

EVALUATING LINKAGE BETWEEN LOCAL BRAND PRODUCTS AND TOURISM: EVIDENCE FROM RURAL JAPAN

YASUO OHE

Introduction

Branding of farm products generates benefits to the local community by increases in the income of producers through the price premium paid for brand products, as these products are differentiated from those of other producing areas. In addition to the direct economic effects of branding, when tourism development in the producing areas is achieved and is well coordinated with brand farm products, the economic benefits will be more widely spread not only to producers but also to the local community, thus providing indirect economic effects. For this reason, quite a few producing areas have been making efforts to brand their own products and encourage tourism development. Other effects on the local community that we can assume are non-economic social effects. In particular, it is often pointed out that tourism activity enables local residents to assess their own community and come to embrace community pride and self-confidence. These non-economic effects are supposed to nurture crucial conditions through the enhancement of motivations among stakeholders concerned with the sustainable development of tourism in rural areas facing tight resource constraints in terms of manpower and capital.

Thus, based on a literature review and data collected by a questionnaire survey to all of the agricultural cooperatives in Japan this chapter examines statistically the relationships among the direct and indirect economic effects and non-economic social effects and explores what profiles of producing areas work on these effects. In conclusion, it is proposed that there are policy implications in relation to this research which requires a strengthening of the connection between local brand farm products and tourism strategies.

Literature Review

Local food production has attracted growing attention in recent years in that it has a high potential to leverage the sustainability of rural development (Vaz et al., 2009). In addition, local food is often discussed in connection with tourism in rural areas where resources for tourism are relatively limited (Renko et al., 2010; Sims, 2009, 2010). In this context, local food can play an important role in sustainable diversification of farm and rural economies. Policymakers also aim at reinforcement of this complementary relationship between local food and tourism (for instance, for the European policy context, see Sims, 2010). Such a complementary relationship is expected to generate a wide range of effects on the local community (ibid); these include economic effects and social effects such as identity issues (Everett and Aitchison, 2008; Brandth and Haugen, 2011). Of these effects, this chapter focuses on the economic effects that accrue to the local community and classifies these as direct and indirect economic effects. The direct economic effects are sales and employment accrued from local food due to the development of production, processing and distribution systems. The indirect economic effects are generated as a result of diversification of the rural economy through taking advantage of brand names of local food. Indirect economic effects are the sales and employment generated from visitor spending on accommodation and dining in local rural tourism facilities and restaurants. If the indirect effects increase, then sales of local products will also increase because visitors will buy local food on site or through the Internet. Thus, if these two effects are simultaneously generated, a large economic benefit will be generated for the local economy.

In this respect, the complementary relationship between local food and the tourism-related sector must work well. Rural cultural heritage has been recognised as being closely connected with this complementarity (Szlanyinka, 2009; Ohe and Ciani, 2011). Types of tourism that are named after a crop, beverage or food-related activity are examples of complementarity between food and tourism; examples are food tourism (Hall et al., 2003), wine tourism (Hall et al., 2000; Kim, Yuan, Goh and Antun, 2009), culinary tourism (Montanari and Staniscia, 2009; Horng and Tsai, 2010) and organic agriculture and agri-ecotourism (Kuo et al., 2006). Authenticity is a crucial issue in both local food production and food-related tourism activity (Sims, 2009).

Previous studies of the economic effects on local food and tourism are differentiation of tourism destinations (Haven-Tang and Jones, 2005), effects of food consumption by tourists (Skuras et al., 2006; Kim, Eves and Scarles, 2009), backward economic linkage (Telfer and Wall, 2000) and hedonic pricing evaluation (Ohe and Ciani, 2011).

The relationship between local foods and tourism, however, is not always guaranteed from the beginning but must be established through much effort (Telfer and Wall, 1996), However, it cannot be denied that such a relationship is worth exploring to evaluate the potential for development of tourism in rural areas either in developed or developing countries (Bélisle, 1983). In particular, we need to clarify under what conditions this connection works most effectively, which would allow suggestions to be made to rural communities on developing tourism by taking advantage of local food and heritage.

Turning to tourism in rural areas, a programme for rural tourism, which is called 'green tourism' in Japan, was inaugurated in 1994. The number of farmers who provide rural tourism activities has grown gradually, but many issues remain problematic such as lack of management skills and ageing of the rural population (Ohe, 2008). These obstacles involve issues that are commonly observed not only in rural Japan, but also in rural communities in other parts of the world.

Thus, this chapter focuses on the current supply-side situation of local brand farm products and sheds light on the direct and indirect economic effects of food-related tourism and how these two effects are connected. Here this is termed a complementarity hypothesis, and data from a questionnaire survey are examined. Until the present report, this complementary relationship has not yet been fully tested statistically although descriptive case studies have been conducted. The reason for focusing on local brand farm products rather than local food in general is to control for issues of authenticity of local products. The term local food is too ambiguous for investigation. Finally, I present policy recommendations toward strengthening the complementary relationship between local brand products and tourism development.

Data

The research team has defined local brand farm products from a wide perspective, in that they are considered as locally connected farm products, which includes those having regional collective trademarks designated by the national government not according to the individual producer but according to the producing area, a trademark and/or designation at the prefectural level, and a reputation as a local product despite no official designation. The questionnaire survey of all agricultural cooperatives in Japan was conducted from January to February in 2009. The survey was conducted jointly by the Organisation for Urban-Rural Interchange Revitalisation and the research team in consultation with the Ministry of Agriculture, Forestry and Fisheries (MAFF), which was the funding body for this survey project. Survey sheets were distributed to each agricultural cooperative and returned by surface mail; 225 out of 757 cooperatives responded (29.7%). That response rate is about normal for this kind of survey. The questions asked concerned various aspects of local brand products and the cooperatives such as what they produce, size of production, history of production and branding, positioning of the local brand, and quality standards, among other issues. Information was also elicited on the effects of local brand products, such as direct and indirect economic effects and non-economic social effects, and issues including tourism development as well as necessary support measures for the future. This survey was the first comprehensive one in terms of local brand farm products in this country as far as is known.

Profiles of surveyed agricultural cooperatives that produce local brand farm products

First, we examined profiles of local brand farm products and producing areas from the survey results. The average number of producers in each cooperative was 406. The average sales per cooperative were 1165 million yen (8.32 million euros when 1 euro=140 yen), with the average sales per producer being 2.9 million yen (about 21 thousand euros). The composition of local brand farm products is shown in Figure 1-1. Vegetables and other field products are dominant (45.8%) followed by fruit (19.1%) and rice (15.6%). This disparity is because the variety of vegetables is far greater than the variety of other crops. Beef, which includes ‘Matsuzaka beef’, a world-renowned quality beef, and ‘Wagyu’ Japanese endogenous beef, was not a major local brand product in terms of share, i.e. less than 10% among total local brand farm products. This relative scarcity supports the evidence of how precious is Wagyu beef.

As to the positioning of local brand farm products, about 40% of the respondents positioned their goods as extra high-end and high-end and about one-fourth indicated that their goods were slightly high-end (Figure 1-2). Thus, it is safe to say that local brand farm products are positioned as high-end goods.

Figure 2-1 shows the history of production of brand farm products. It tends to vary from one producing area to another, although nearly 30% of cooperatives, respectively, had either a more than 50-year production history or a production history of more than 10 years but less than 30 years.

Regarding the history of brand formation (Figure 2-2), those cooperatives with a history of brand formation of greater than 5 years but less than 15 years accounted for nearly 40% of the cooperatives, which was the highest percentage among the durations of brand formation examined, and was followed by those with a history of brand formation greater than 15 years but less than 30 years, which accounted for nearly 30%. Only 14.7% of cooperatives had a history of brand formation of less than 5 years. Among products, the brand formation period for rice was shorter than for other products with statistical significance (5%); the portion of those areas producing rice with less than a 15-year history of brand formation was 20.6% while 8.5% had a history of 15 years or more; this is because of the more recent emergence of better tasting varieties of rice that resulted from competition in breeding among major rice-producing prefectures. Thus, there is role sharing between the cooperatives and prefectures, with the prefectures responsible for development of the new varieties and cooperatives responding by production and marketing. This point demonstrates the difference between the definition of a local brand farm product in Japan and the geographical indications by the European Union in that the European Union especially respects traditional production methods and local heritage while its Japanese counterpart permits producing areas to explore brand formation with new products.

With respect to name recognition of local brand farm products, only 2.2% of the respondents answered that they recognised local brand products from abroad, indicating that cooperatives were oriented toward the domestic market (Figure 3-1). Of the cooperatives, 35.6% indicated that their local brand farm products were recognised nationwide while more than 50% indicated that their products were recognised within neighbouring prefectures or only in the area of production. These facts are in sharp contrast with the European geographical indications that are eagerly oriented toward international recognition and marketing abroad.

It is essential for producing areas to have unified criteria for quality control to secure authenticity in local brand farm products. Of the responding cooperatives, 62.2% had unified criteria and 20.9% had a rough standardisation for quality but no explicit criteria (Figure 3-2).

In short, vegetables and other field products were the most common local brand products and areas producing these had a long history of production and branding while there was a shorter history for rice production and branding due to the emergence of newly-bred varieties due to intensified competition among producing areas.

Effects of local brand products

Now let us take a look at the effects of local brand products. First, as to direct economic effects, about half of the respondents expressed satisfaction in that the effects were greater (10.7%), or almost the same as expected (40.4%). The remaining respondents felt that the effects were less than expected (21.3%) or that they could not judge the effects yet (21.8%; Figure 4).

In relation to the indirect economic effects, i.e. mainly the tourism aspects, less satisfaction was expressed than for the direct effects. Specifically, only about one fourth of respondents stated that the effects were greater than expected or almost the same as expected. In contrast, effects were reported as less than expected by 32.4% of the respondents, and 35.6% indicated that they did not know yet whether the effects were favourable or unfavourable (Figure 4). The most probable reasons for this low level of satisfaction as to indirect economic effects are the difficulty in attaining indirect effects and also difficulty in measuring these effects.

The non-economic effects on local communities, which can be generalised as social effects, are shown in Figure 5. First, one of the expected social effects of local brand products is increased name recognition of the local community. This indicates an effect on society outside of the local community. Over half indicated that this effect was greater or almost the same as expected. Other social effects were related to the impact on the community by local brand farm products. Second, as to revitalisation of the local community, expressions were divided almost equally between indications of meeting expectations and not meeting expectations. Third, a similar pattern was revealed regarding increasing local residents' interest in their community. Fourth, the effect on the understating of local food and culinary heritage inside and outside of the local community was evaluated a little more favourably than the other two effects. In short, about half of the respondents were satisfied with the social effects on the local community.

Fifth, well-coordinated cooperation with local governments provides significant leverage for the development of local brand farm products. Figure 6 shows that respondents were divided between satisfaction and dissatisfaction with the current state of cooperation with local governments; 43.1% of respondents were satisfied, 31.1% were neither satisfied nor dissatisfied while 20.5% were dissatisfied.

To summarise, half of the respondents gave a positive evaluation on the direct economic effects while only the one fourth expressed positive feelings on the indirect economic effects. Respondents tended to acknowledge the existence of social effects that exerted benefits not only in the local community but also beyond the community.

Statistical tests on direct and indirect economic effects of local brand farm products in connection with various factors

Here, we conduct statistical tests to examine the complementary relationship between direct and indirect economic effects and social effects of local brand farm products, and profiles of the producing areas. To avoid the complexity of statistical tests on the direct and indirect effects, we classified the answers into two categories, that is, whether they were positive or negative. Responses as 'greater than expected' or 'almost the same as expected' were classified as 'Yes,' while responses of 'less than expected' or 'do not know yet' were classified as 'No'. Authors used this classification for the direct effects and indirect effects, respectively.

From the results of the statistical test shown in Table 1, nearly 90% of those who acknowledged satisfaction with the direct economic effects also acknowledged the presence of indirect economic effects while only about 40% of those who did not acknowledge direct economic effects acknowledged the indirect effects. From these results, we confirmed the complementarity hypothesis between the direct and indirect economic effects with statistically high significance (1%). Since indirect economic effects represent effects on the local tourism business as mentioned, it is safe to say that there is a positive relationship between local brand products and tourism. The above results indicate that the direct economic effects come first and are followed by indirect economic effects, which is consistent with what we noted by simple observation and suggests endogeneity between the two economic effects. Furthermore, we can also observe the complementary relationship between the two economic effects and social effects on the local community such as improvement in name recognition of the local community, increasing interest in the residents' own community and an understanding of the local food heritage, and then eventually a revitalisation of the local community. These social effects enhance self-confidence and local pride of those in the local community and can become a further driving force for tourism development.

Product-wise, we also statistically confirmed complementarities between the two economic effects and also between the two economic effects and social effects such as for rice, vegetables and upland farm products, fruits and beef (Tables 2 and 3). Interestingly, the percentage of those who acknowledged indirect economic effects was relatively higher in fruit- and beef-producing areas than in rice- and vegetable-producing areas. This is because paddy and vegetable fields are the most common agrarian landscape, and it is often difficult to differentiate one's own local community from that of rivals. Put differently, it is safe to say that beef- and fruit-producing areas are more adaptable to tourism.

To summarise, we can say that local brand products widely exerted not only economic effects but also exerted effects on local residents in terms of increasing interest in their local community, which leads to enhancing confidence among local residents in the long term. We should be reminded, however, that not all local brand-producing areas enjoyed all of these effects, as expected.

Table 4 shows results of a statistical examination of how the profiles of local brand products and producing areas are connected with the two economic effects. Profiles that had a connection with direct and indirect economic effects with statistical significance were those that had high-end products, a history of over 15 years of brand formation and had their own quality standards. Other profiles such as the size of the area of the brand product, number of producers and history of production had no connection with the two economic effects. These facts indicate that it takes time to form a brand that exerts complementary direct and indirect economic effects and that quality management is crucial. Also shown was that a good partnership with local government is an important factor in nurturing branding of farm products.

Table 5 statistically compares what sort of intellectual property rights work on the generation of economic effects. Among various intellectual property rights, the results of statistical tests revealed that only specific intellectual property rights actually work. Interestingly, in the case of local brand farm products the regional collective trademark worked effectively on the indirect economic effect, with 5% significance, while it had no significant effect on the direct economic effect. This means that the regional collective trademark is effective for tourism development.

Table 6 shows the results of statistical tests on the connection between the expected two economic effects and the actual evaluated effects. Acknowledgement of direct economic effects was significantly associated with expectations of raising the recognition of local community and pride (5% significance). On the other hand, acknowledgement of the achievement of indirect economic effects was significantly associated with the expectation of wider effects on the local community than was the acknowledgement of direct economic effects. Such specific effects were succession of local cultural heritage and creation of new business (1% significance) and protection of brand and rediscovery of local resources (10% significance). The results indicate that the indirect economic effects have a closer connection with non-economic social effects in terms of heritage succession while enhancement of community pride is closer to the direct economic effects. In this respect, we can say that among non-economic social effects the enhancement of community pride comes earlier and then is followed by rising interest in the succession of the local heritage.

There are many issues to be overcome in the development of local brand farm products (Table 7). Specifically, advertising and promotion activity was a common issue among those who acknowledged direct and indirect economic effects. In contrast, quality management and securing human resources capable of marketing were stated as issues for indirect economic effects.

Finally, Tables 8 and 9 show various actions actually undertaken for the development and maintenance of local brand products. There were common efforts made by those producing areas that had acknowledged both direct and indirect economic effects. These actions included making a plan for branding local products, establishing a system for branding such products, defining a linkage between the locality and the product, and developing new products. Other actions were management of quality and quantity of goods, advertising, and forming partnerships with local tourism and restaurant sectors. Thus, it is safe to say that these are the necessary common conditions to generate direct and indirect economic effects of local brand products. Developing human resources to implement brand management was a common issue in acknowledgment of both direct and indirect economic efforts, although the significance level was only 10%.

Now let us examine actions undertaken that are specifically connected with each economic effect. With regard to direct economic effects, a higher percentage of those who acknowledged direct economic effects took actions in defining the value of the local products, naming the products and creating a logo and securing funds for activity than those who did not (1% significance; Tables 8 and 9).

With respect to an indirect effect, per contra, higher percentages responded that they established a system to prevent illegal use of production technology or seed varieties and took action for succession of the local heritage than those who did not acknowledge an indirect effect (5% and 1% significance, respectively; Table 9).

To summarise, the results of this study indicated that considerable efforts were made by utilising common managerial resources with a long-term perspective for generation of direct and indirect economic effects in the producing areas. In this context, it is safe to say that there is much room left for these areas to tighten the relationship between local brand products and tourism-related business. At the same time, the results also showed that there are differences in terms of necessary conditions between the direct and indirect effects. The indirect economic effects require local producers to look more carefully at issues of cultural heritage and the local community, which suggests the importance of a wider perspective including non-economic social effects.

Conclusion

This chapter empirically investigated the relationship between local brand farm products and tourism activity from the results of a questionnaire survey on the effects and issues related to local brand farm products that was targeted at agricultural cooperatives in Japan. The main points revealed from the investigation are as follows.

The results of statistical tests on the relationship between the direct economic effects from the local brand farm products and the indirect economic effects, mainly tourism, and non-economic social effects empirically clarified that there was a complementary relationship between the two economic effects. There were common factors that were effective in relation to the two economic effects and specific factors in relation to each of the economic effects. Common factors for the direct and indirect effects were establishment of a plan and system for action for branding, a clear definition of products based on the locality, quality and quantity management of brand products, and advertising. The specific factors for indirect effects have closer connection with a wider perspective such as local cultural heritage and partnership with tourism and culinary sectors.

There was also a complementary relationship between the two economic effects and non-economic social effects. These non-economic social effects that raise community pride and interest in the residents' own local heritage in the community will become factors for promoting further tourism development in the area.

At the same time, those producing areas that acknowledged the two economic effects have a relatively long history of branding formation of products. Consequently, in order to strengthen the complementary relationship, concerned people in the producing areas need to have wider and longer perspectives in local resource management than that of solely promoting local brand products. Put differently, this complementary relationship between local brand farm products and tourism enables producers and residents in the local community an important opportunity to realise and nurture community pride and confidence. Thus, these points should be considered when support measures are designed for diversification of farm and rural economies.

Acknowledgements

This study was funded by the Grants-in-Aid for Scientific Research, No. 24658191, Japan Society for the Promotion of Science (JSPS).

References

Baumol, W.J., J.C. Panzar and R.D. Willig (1988) *Contestable Markets and the Theory of Industry Structure,* New York: Harcourt Brace Jovanovich, revised edition.

Bélisle, F. J. (1983) 'Tourism and Food Production in the Caribbean', *Annals of Tourism Research*, 10: 497-513.

Besanko, D., D. Dranove and M. Shanley (2000) *Economics of Strategy,* New York: John Wiley and Sons, second edition.

Brandth, B. and M. S. Haugen (2011) 'Farm Diversification into Tourism - Implications for Social Identity?' *Journal of Rural Studies*, 27: 35-44.

Everett, S. and C. Aitchison (2008) 'The Role of Food Tourism in Sustaining Regional Identity: a Case Study of Cornwall, South West England', *Journal of Sustainable Tourism*, 16: 150-167.

Hall, C.M., L. Sharples, B. Cambourne and N. Macionis, N. (2000) *Wine Tourism around the World: Development, Management and Markets*, Oxford: Butterworth- Heinemann.

Hall, C.M., L. Sharples, R. Mitchell, N. Macionis and B. Cambourne (2003) *Food Tourism around The World: Development, Management and Markets*, Oxford: Butterworth- Heinemann.

Haven-Tang, C. and E. Jones (2005) 'Using Local Food and Drink to Differentiate Tourism Destinations through a Sense of Place: a Story from Wales-dining at Monmouthshire's Great Table', *Journal of Culinary Science and Technology*, 4: 69-86.

Horng, J-S. and C-T. S. Tsai (2010) 'Government Websites for Promoting East Asian Culinary Tourism: a Cross-national Analysis', *Tourism Management*, 31: 74-85.

Japan Patent Office (2008) '*Designated Regional Collective Trademark* (in Japanese)', issued in August 2008, Tokyo: Japan Patent Office, pp 1-20.

Kim, Y. G., A. Eves and C. Scarles (2009) 'Building a Model of Local Food Consumption on Trips and Holidays: a Grounded Theory Approach', *International Journal of Hospitality Management*, 28: 423-431.

Kim, Y. H., J.J. Yuan, B.K. Goh and J.M. Antun (2009) 'Web Marketing in Food Tourism: a Content Analysis of Web Sites in West Texas', *Journal of Culinary Science & Technology*, 7: 52-64.

Kuo, N-W., Y-J. Chen and C-L. Huang (2006) 'Linkages between Organic Agriculture and Agro-ecotourism', *Renewable Agriculture and Food Systems*, 21: 238-244.

Montanari, A. and B. Staniscia (2009) 'Culinary Tourism as a Tool for Regional Re-equilibrium', *European Planning Studies*, 17: 1463-1483.

Ohe, Y. (2007) 'Multifunctionality and Rural Tourism: a Perspective on Farm Diversification', *Journal of International Farm Management*, 4: 1-23.

—. (2008) 'Characteristics and Issues of Rural Tourism in Japan'. In C. A. Brebbia, and F. D. Pineda (eds), *Sustainable Tourism III,* Ashurst: WIT Press, pp. 305-316.

Ohe, Y., and Ciani, A. (2011) 'Evaluation of Agritourism Activity in Italy: Facility-based or Local Culture-based?' *Tourism Economics*, 17: 581-601.

Panzar, J.C. and R.D. Willig (1981) 'Economies of Scope', *The American Economic Review*, 71: 268-272.

Renko, S., N. Renko and T. Polonijo (2010) 'Understanding the Role of Food in Rural Tourism Development in a Recovering Economy', *Journal of Food Products Marketing*, 16: 309-324.

Saloner, G., A. Shepard and J. Podolny (2001) *Strategic Management*, New York: John Wiley and Sons.

Sims, R. (2009) 'Food, Place and Authenticity: Local Food and the Sustainable Tourism Experience', *Journal of Sustainable Tourism*, 17: 321-336.

—. (2010) 'Putting Place on the Menu: the Negotiation of Locality in UK Food Tourism, from Production to Consumption', *Journal of Rural Studies*, 26: 105-115.

Skuras, D., E. Dimara and A. Petrou (2006) 'Rural Tourism and Visitors' Expenditures for Local Food Products', *Regional Studies*, 40: 769-779.

Szlanyinka, E. (2009) 'Role of Cultural Values in Rural Development'. In T. d N. Vaz, P. Nijkamp and J.L. Rastoin (eds), *Traditional Food Production and Rural Sustainable Development: a European Challenge*, Surrey: Ashgate , pp 101-118.

Telfer, D. J. and G. Wall (1996) 'Linkages between Tourism and Food Production', *Annals of Tourism Research*, 23: 635-653.

—. (2000) 'Strengthening Backward Economic Linkages: Local Food Purchasing by Three Indonesian Hotels', *Tourism Geographies*, 2: 421-447.

Vaz, T. d. N., P. Nijkamp and J.L. Rastoin (eds.) (2009) *Traditional Food Production and Rural Sustainable Development: A European Challenge*, Surrey: Ashgate.

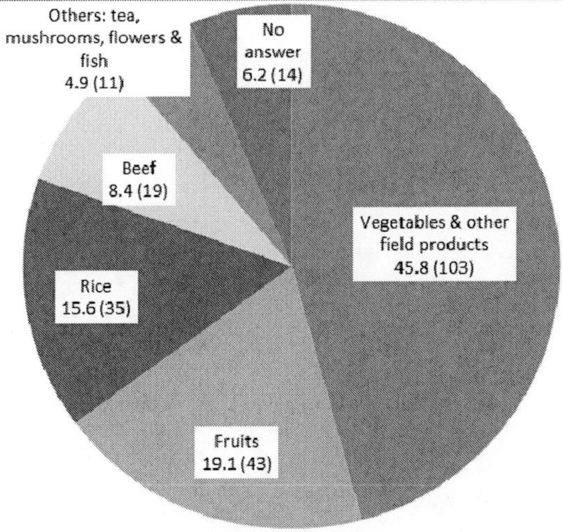

Source: Questionnaire survey to all agricultural cooperatives in Japan conducted jointly by the Organization for Urban-Rural Interchange Revitalization and the authors in 2009. The response rate was 225 out of 757 cooperatives (29.7%).
Note: Numbers are percentage and sample size.

Figure 1-1. Composition of local brand products

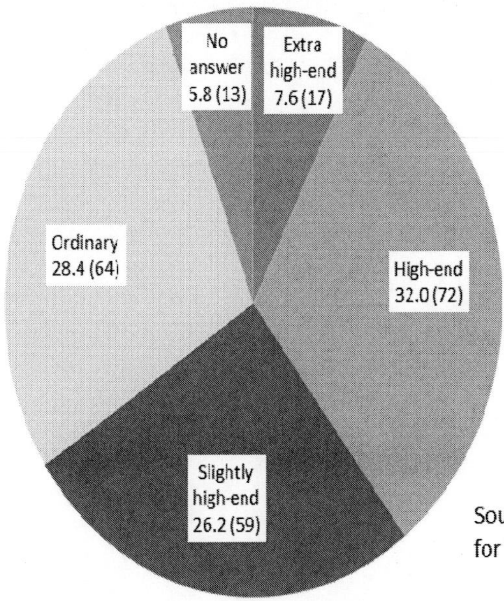

Source: Same as for Figure 1-1.

Figure 1-2. Position of local brand products

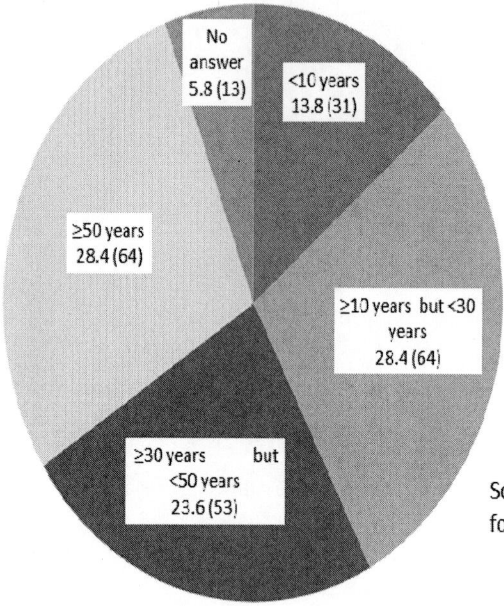

Source: Same as for Figure 1-1.

Figure 2-1. History of production

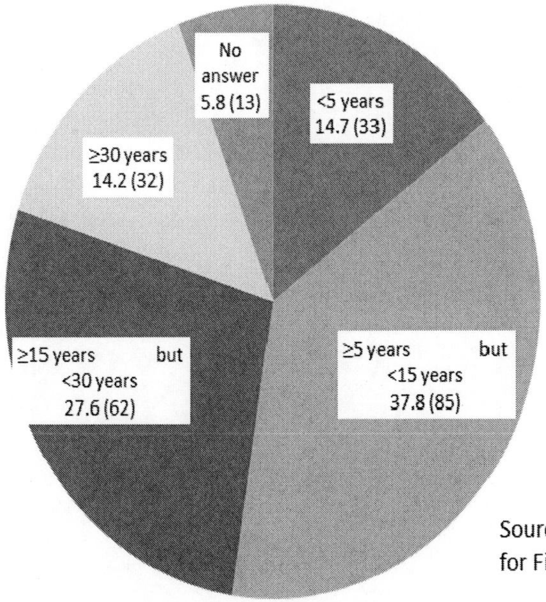

Source: Same as for Figure 1-1.

Figure 2-2. History of local brand formation

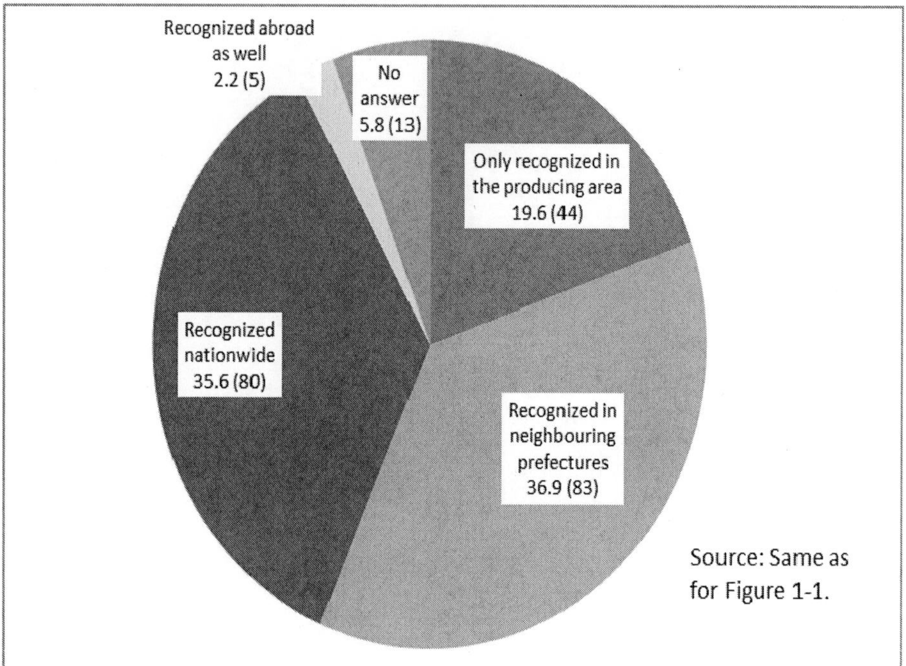

Figure 3-1. Degree of name recognition

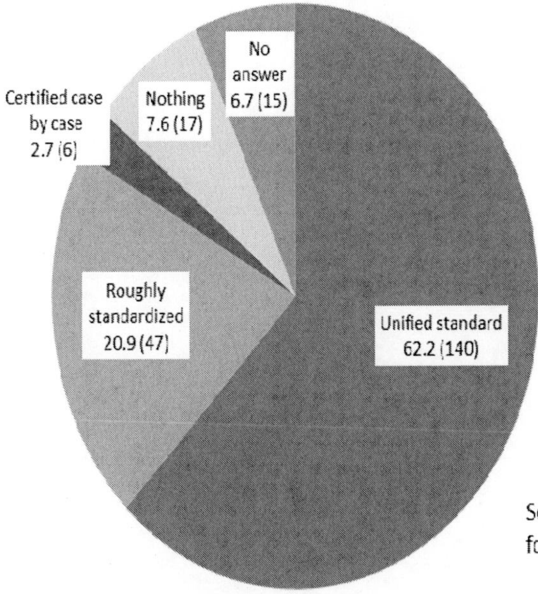

Source: Same as for Figure 1-1.

Figure 3-2. Existence of quality/certification standard

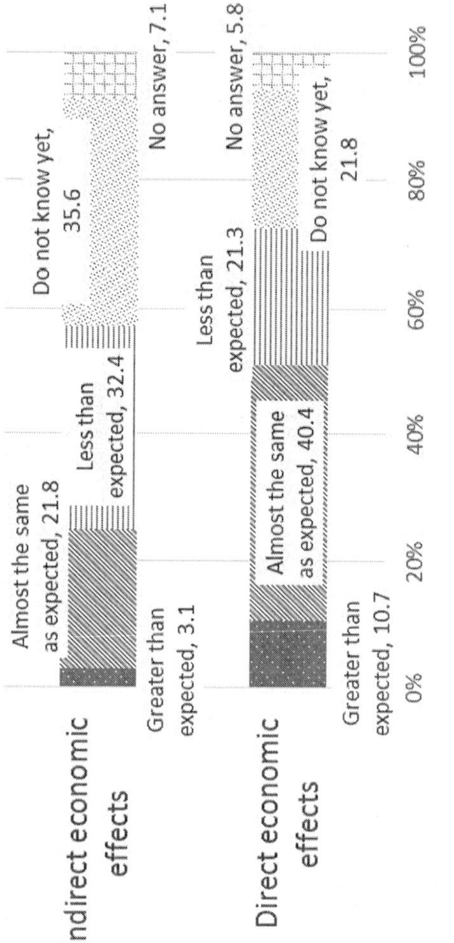

Source: Same as for Figure 1-1.

Figure 4. Evaluation of direct and indirect economic effects

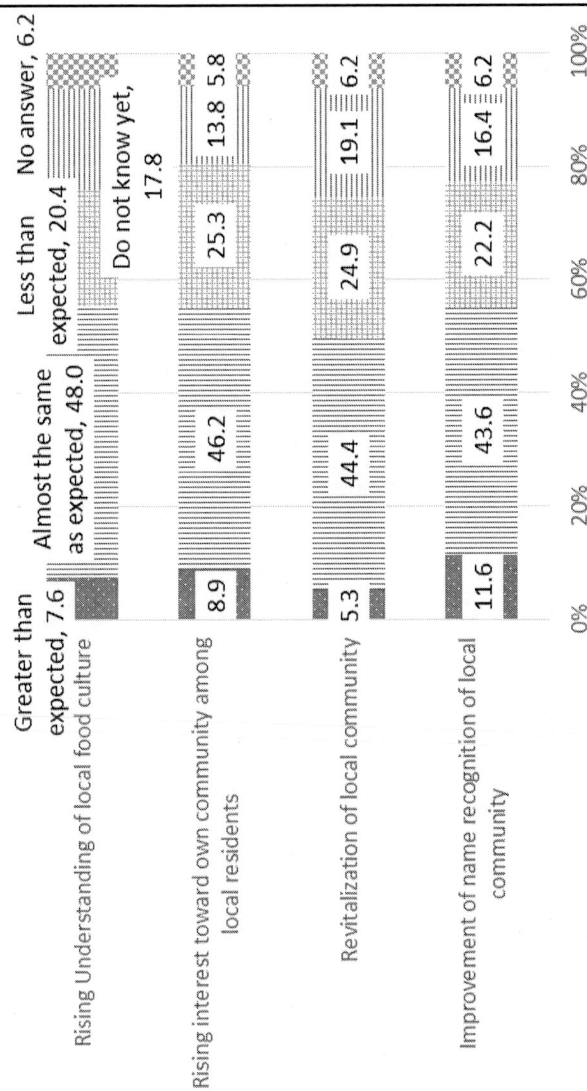

Source: Same as for Figure 1-1.

Figure 5. Non-economic effects on local community

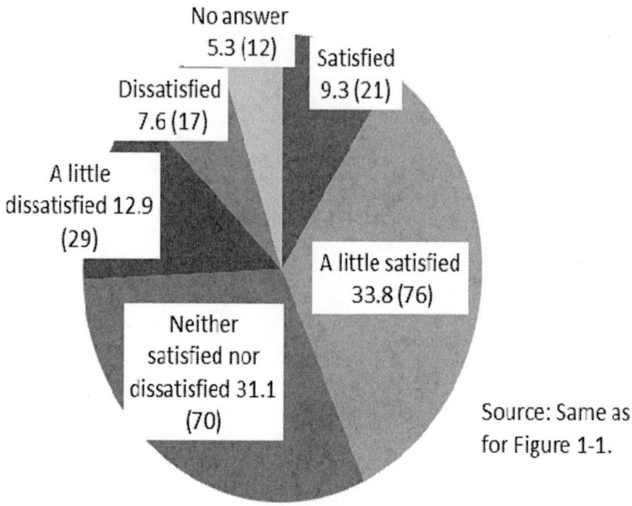

Figure 6. Partnership with municipality

Table 1. Connection of direct and indirect economic effects of local brand farm products with non-economic social effects (%)

Effects (greater than expected or as expected=1, others=0)	Direct economic effects			Indirect economic effects		
	Yes	Test Result	No	Yes	Test Result	No
Direct economic effects	-	-	-	87.5	>>>	39.1
Indirect economic effects	42.6	>>>	6.4	-	-	-
Improvement in name recognition of local community	72.2	>>>	37.3	94.6	>>>	42.0
Revitalization of local community	72.2	>>>	26.4	87.5	>>>	37.3
Increasing interest in own community among local residents	77.4	>>>	31.8	89.3	>>>	43.8
Increasing understanding of local food culture	74.8	>>>	35.5	85.7	>>>	45.6

Source: Same as for Figure 1-1.

Notes: Statistical method was Chi-square test and >>>, >>,>, =>, = are 1%, 5%, 10% and 20% (reference) significance level and not significant, respectively. Sample size was 225.

Table 2. Product-wise connection among effects (%): direct economic effects

Effects (greater than expected or as expected=1, others=0)	Direct economic effects (Yes)			
Local brand farm products	Rice	Vegetables	Fruit	Beef
Indirect economic effects	87.5**	88.0***	86.7**	100.0**
Improvement in name recognition of local community	66.7**	71.2***	66.7^{ns}	61.5^{+}
Revitalization of local community	66.7*	75.9***	77.3**	81.8***
Increasing interest in own community among local residents	73.7***	73.3***	74.1**	63.4^{+}
Increasing understanding of local food culture	66.7**	71.7***	76.0**	61.5^{+}

Source: Same as for Figure 1-1.

Notes: Statistical method and sample size are the same as in Table 1. Sample sizes for each product are 35 (rice), 103 (vegetables), 43 (fruits) and beef (19). ***, **, *, +, ns are 1%, 5%, 10%, 20% (reference) and not significant, respectively.

Table 3. Product-wise connection among effects (%): indirect economic effects

Effects (greater than expected or as expected=1, others=0)	Indirect economic effects (Yes)			
Local brand farm products	Rice	Vegetables	Fruit	Beef
Direct economic effects	41.2**	39.3***	50.0**	55.6**
Improvement in name recognition of local community	44.4***	44.2***	46.7**	38.5^{+}
Revitalization of local community	53.3***	38.9***	59.1***	45.5**
Increasing interest in own community among local residents	36.8**	36.7***	51.9***	45.5**
Increasing understanding of local food culture	44.4***	33.3**	52.0***	38.5^{+}

Source: Same as for Figure 1-1.

Notes: Statistical method and signs of statistical significance and sample size are the same as in Table 2.

Table 4. Connection between economic effects and profiles of local brand products and producting areas (%)

Profiles	Direct economic effects			Indirect economic effects		
	Yes	Test Result	No	Yes	Test Result	No
Position of local brand (extra high-end or high-end product=1, others=0)	46.1	>>	32.7	53.6	>>	34.9
History of local brand formation (15 years or more=1, others=0)	49.6	>>	33.6	58.9	>>>	36.1
Degree of brand name recognition (nationwide or abroad=1, others=0)	48.7	>>>	26.4	42.9	=	36.1
Existence of quality/certification standard (yes=1, others=0)	76.5	>>>	47.3	83.9	>>>	55.0
Partnership with municipality (a little satisfied or satisfied=1, others=0)	49.6	>>	36.4	53.6	>	39.6

Source: Same as for Figure 1-1.

Notes: Statistical method and signs of statistical significance and sample size are the same as in Table 1.

Table 5. Connection between economic effects and employed intellectual property rights (%)

Employed intellectual property rights (yes=1, no=0)	Direct economic effects			Indirect economic effects		
	Yes	Test Result	No	Yes	Test Result	No
Regional collective trademark	27.0	=	23.6	37.5	>>	21.3
Trademark in general	38.3	=	31.8	35.7	=	34.9
Patent	2.6	=	1.8	5.4	>=	1.2
Design right	2.6	=	0.9	1.8	=	1.8
Breeder's right	0.9	=	0.9	0.0	=	1.2
Local certification framework	24.4	>	15.5	28.6	>	17.2
Nothing	16.5	=	22.7	10.7	<	22.5

Source: Same as for Figure 1-1.
Notes: Statistical method and signs of statistical significance and sample size are the same as in Table 1.

Table 6. Connection between expected economic effects and actual evaluation (%)

Expected effects (expected or a little expected=1, others=0)	Direct economic effects			Indirect economic effects		
	Yes	Test Result	No	Yes	Test Result	No
Increase in producer income & employment	90.4	>	81.8	94.6	>>	83.4
Revitalization of related industry	67.0	>	55.5	73.2	>>	57.4
Increase in exports	28.7	=	24.6	32.1	=	24.9
Increase in no. of tourists	46.1	>>	30.9	66.1	>>>	29.6
Protection of brand (prevention of plagiarism)	56.5	=	52.7	64.3	>	51.5
Increase in recognition of brand among consumers	81.7	>>	69.1	83.9	>	72.8
Increase in recognition of local community & pride	93.0	>>	84.6	94.6	=	87.0
Revitalization of local community	79.1	>>	63.6	92.9	>>>	64.5
Succession of local cultural heritage including culinary aspects	75.7	=	68.2	87.5	>>>	66.9
Rediscovery of local resources	63.5	=	55.5	69.6	>	56.2
Creation of new business	53.9	>=	43.6	64.3	>>>	43.8

Source: Same as for Figure 1-1.

Notes: Statistical method and signs of statistical significance and sample size are the same as in Table 1.

Table 7. Connection between economic effects and various issues (%)

Issues (yes=1, no=0)	Direct economic effects			Indirect economic effects		
	Yes	Test Result	No	Yes	Test Result	No
Maintenance & improvement of quality	50.4	=	48.2	62.5	>>	45.0
Advertisement & promotion activity	38.3	<<<	52.7	28.6	<<<	50.9
Development of human resources capable of brand management and marketing	47.0	=	39.1	57.1	>>>	38.5

Source: Same as for Figure 1-1.
Notes: Statistical method and signs of statistical significance and sample size are the same as in Table 1.

Table 8. Connection between economic effects and actions actually taken (%) I

Actions (intensively taken or taken =1, others=0)	Direct economic effects			Indirect economic effects		
	Yes	Test Result	No	Yes	Test Result	No
Making plan of action for branding of local product	55.7	>>>	28.2	58.9	>>>	36.7
Forming system for branding local product	53.0	>>>	24.6	60.7	>>>	32.0
Defining linkage between locality and product	38.3	>>>	22.7	46.4	>>>	25.4
Defining product value such as taste, nutrition etc.	48.7	>>>	28.2	48.2	>	35.5
Marketing/needs survey	33.9	=	26.4	39.3	>	27.2
New product development including processing	31.3	>>>	15.5	41.1	>>>	17.8
Maintenance & improvement of quality	75.7	>>>	47.3	76.8	>>>	56.8
System of securing production amount	67.8	>>>	45.5	75.0	>>>	50.9

Source: Same as for Figure 1-1.

Notes: Statistical method and signs of statistical significance and sample size are the same as in Table 1.

Table 9. Connection between economic effects and actions actually taken (%) II

Actions (intensively taken or taken =1, others=0)	Direct economic effects			Indirect economic effects		
	Yes	Test Result	No	Yes	Test Result	No
System to prevent illegal use of production technology and seed varieties	32.2	=	24.6	41.1	>>	24.3
Naming, creation of logo or package design	62.6	>>>	36.4	60.7	>	46.2
Advertisement & promotion activity	73.0	>>>	44.6	76.8	>>>	53.3
Developing human resources capable of brand management and marketing	23.5	>	13.6	26.8	>	16.0
Securing funds for activity	37.4	>>>	16.4	30.4	=	26.0
Promotion of exports	9.6	=	5.5	8.9	=	7.1
Succession of local heritage including culinary aspects	27.0	>	16.4	39.3	>>>	16.0
Partnership with tourism and restaurant sectors	31.3	>>	18.2	48.2	>>>	17.2

Source: Same as for Figure 1-1.

Notes: Statistical method and signs of statistical significance and sample size are the same as in Table 1.

GASTRONOMY AS A CREATIVE CITY STRATEGY: A SITUATION ANALYSIS OF GEORGE TOWN, PENANG

SUET LENG KHOO
AND NURWATI BADARULZAMAN

Introduction

In recent years gastronomy has assumed a pivotal role and its contribution towards developing and regenerating urban spaces and places is gaining prominence. In recognition of this, the UNESCO Creative Cities Network Flagship has served to draw attention to the importance of cities as catalysts in local economic growth and development. This Flagship advocates that cities should be branded accordingly, based on their niche economic activities and attractions which best showcases their city in today's highly competitive and globalised world. To this end, creative and innovative place-branding labels have since emerged such as 'City of Fashion', 'City of Literature', 'City of Design', and even recognition is bestowed upon the gastronomic prowess of a city, thus, 'City of Gastronomy'.

This chapter explores the viability of branding and strategising George Town, Penang as a 'City of Gastronomy', given the city's myriad of unique traditional and ethnic-based cuisines that are also acknowledged as part-and-parcel of George Town's invaluable intangible cultural heritage (State Government of Penang [SGP], 2011). Given the limitations of time and manpower, this study only endeavoured to examine one traditional cuisine, namely, *nasi kandar* to understand the extent to which the novelties of this dish could be used as a strategy to contribute towards strengthening the local economy, enhancing tourism sustainability as well as preserving the authenticity of George Town's urban place and space.

George Town's gastronomic treasures are well-known worldwide and recent food accolades include being ranked in CNN Go's Asia's 10 Greatest Street Food Cities in 2012 and 12th placing in The New York Times Frugal and Food Category (Penang State Tourism Development, nd). Given these international acknowledgements, however, the strength of gastronomy in George Town has yet to assume the same status and importance as that in Popayan and Chengdu (Sichuan Province) whereby these cities have successfully promoted and advocated their status as centres of gastronomy. Thus, this study is timely to further explore how gastronomy can be a creative city strategy to promote and showcase in the international arena George Town's gastronomic strength.

This chapter is organised into five sections comprising an introduction, a review of the relevant literature, an outline of the methodology, the key findings based on a survey of 412 respondents in George Town's World Heritage Site, and finally, the provision of some pragmatic suggestions with regard to urban planning and cultural development policies.

Literature Review

A review of the relevant literature has pointed to an obvious fact that in the study of gastronomy, the concept cannot be detached and is in fact related to areas such as heritage and cultural tourism, hospitality (Boyne, Hall and Williams, 2003; Scarpato, 2002) and gastronomy's origins and ties to the heritage of a particular location and destination (Hwang, van Westering and Chen, 2004). Studies in Hong Kong have also shown that the rise of gastronomy is inextricably linked to a destination and the destination's image (Kivela and Crotts, 2006: 51). In their study, Kivela and Crotts have argued that the unique gastronomy native to a particular location is a 'reasonably valid construct' for destination branding and marketing purposes which in turn spurs repeat visits to a destination.

More specifically in management and branding literature, researchers have introduced labels such as 'destination branding, place branding, destination image' (Mak, 2011), 'destination brand, location brand' (Kerr, 2006) and 'place marketing, place branding' (Gertner, 2011). From a tourism perspective, studies have examined the 'identity of a place' (McCabe and Stokoe, 2004) and explored the 'destination image' to boost tourism (Chen and Tsai, 2007). In articulating the importance of place and space, a range of research has since emerged, particularly in urban development with the notion that cities, instead of nations, are competing amongst themselves. With regard to cities novel phrases like 'place branding' (van Gelder, 2008a, 2008b), 'city branding' (Crombie, 2011; van Gelder and Roberts, 2007), 'place marketing' and 'place branding' (Metaxas, 2010; Zenker and Martin, 2011) have emerged in scholarly discourses recently.

In this study, specific reference is made to UNESCO's Creative Cities Network Flagship which hinges on the notion that culture can play a prominent role and function in urban regeneration and the need for policy-makers to consider the role of creativity in development planning. The Creative Cities Network aspires to the development of the 'Creative Industry' and 'Creative Economy' concepts which, according to the United Kingdom's Government Department for Culture, Media and Sport (DCMS), is defined as: 'those industries which have their origin in individual creativity, skill and talent and which have a potential for wealth and job creation through the generation and exploitation of intellectual property'.

More pertinently, UNESCO's Creative Cities Network has acknowledged the role of cities in leveraging creativity for growth and socio-economic development with reference to three key drivers. First, cities possess the whole spectrum of cultural actors encompassing the creative industry chain, from the creative act to production, consumption and distribution. Second, as ideal incubating locations for creative talent to cluster, cities are endowed with great promise to promote creativity. In turn, cities within the network can capitalise on these potentials for global and local impact. Third, cities are unique entities; they are able to influence local cultural industries and simultaneously they are large enough to function as 'gateways' to international markets.[1] A survey of related creative cities websites further accentuates the need to position culture and community in the centre of urban innovation. In this connection it has been argued that 'Culture is the Oxygen of Cities'.[2] Similarly, this notion was also echoed by another initiative in the UK called the 'Creativity and Culture in your

[1] 'Why cities?: UNESCO Culture Sector', http://portal.unesco.org/culture/en/ev.php-URL_ID=26390&URL_DO=DO_TOPIC&URL_SECTION=201.html), retrieved on 6 August 2013.

[2] About Creative Cities International, http://creativecities.org/about-2/, retrieved on 8 August 13.

Community' website. Simply put, this website aims to inspire and provoke us to re-imagine our city and our place within it.[3]

In the context of this study, we look specifically at re-positioning gastronomy activities in a society and community with reference to *nasi kandar* in George Town. With George Town's rich and diverse cultural heritage, gastronomy is certainly an intangible heritage and cultural asset. Gastronomy scholars have recognised its 'cultural value' (Miller, 1978 cited in Scarpato, 2002: 10) and further acknowledged gastronomy as a 'cultural artefact' (Barthes, 1979 cited in Scarpato, 2002: 10). Asian scholars have also proposed that street food is a 'must have' in any popular city (Goh, 2012). In George Town, the endless array of gastronomic treasures has popularised and bestowed upon George Town the title of the 'world capital of street food'. [4] Undoubtedly, George Town's traditional gastronomic culture is a crucial urban asset that has contributed towards the city's inscription as a UNESCO World Heritage Site on July 7, 2008.

In this study, we examine the way *nasi kandar*, which is a home-grown George Town gastronomic treasure and cultural signature has contributed towards (or against) the city's route to becoming a gastronomic city. *Nasi kandar* represents and is characteristic of George Town's vibrant Indian Muslim community with a spread of traditional restaurants such as Line Clear Nasi Kandar, Dawood, Cravan, Nasi Kandar Beratur, and Ramzan which has created an indelible presence in George Town's space and place. Literally, *nasi kandar* which means 'yoked rice' (eaten with different types of curries) was traditionally carried on shoulder yokes by itinerant Indian Muslim hawkers. [5] *Nasi kandar* was first introduced to Penang in the 1990s when the Indians first set foot there. At that time, they were working around the port and using whatever local ingredients they could obtain to concoct various kinds of curries (*The Star*, 26 September 2009). The next section will briefly discuss the methodology for this study.

---

[3] Creativity and Culture in your Community, http://creativecities.org.uk/ retrieved on 8 August 13.

[4] Khoo Salma Nasution, 'Cultural Heartland, Food Paradise', http://www.tourismpenang.net.my/heritage_article_01.html, retrieved on 21 December 2011.

[5] Ibid.

Methodology

A survey was undertaken in George Town's World Heritage Site (WHS) from March to May 2012. The WHS consists of the Core and Buffer Zones. Referring to a list from Penang's Licencing Department, there are presently 15 *nasi kandar* establishments found within the WHS. Due to constraints of time and manpower, this study only selected five out of these 15 establishments to execute the survey. These five *nasi kandar* establishments are amongst the most popular in George Town where both local and foreign tourists like to patronise and have their meals (see Table 1.0 for the numbers of respondents surveyed in the five establishments). A standard questionnaire was used to elicit information from both local and foreign tourists. Ten enumerators were administered to survey the tourists using the questionnaire. Two enumerators were stationed at each *nasi kandar* establishment during this period until completion. This study managed to survey 412 local and foreign tourists (Pictures 1a – 1d feature Kassim Mustafa Nasi Kandar situated along Chulia Street).

In brief, the questionnaire was divided into four main sections. The questions in the questionnaire were formulated and adapted following a review of related literature on city branding (Kivela and Crotts, 2006; Du Rand, Heath and Alberts, 2003; Boyne, Hall and Williams, 2003; Ab. Karim and Chua, nd). In the first section, demographic information on the tourists surveyed (i.e. gender, age, country of residence, purpose of visit, length of stay) was collected. Section two was on the measurement of 'perceived image of *nasi kandar* in George Town', captured in a 31-item, 5-point Likert type scale. In section three, the 'level of satisfaction with *nasi kandar* in George Town' was measured using a 17-item, 5-point Likert scale on dimensions related to dining atmosphere, convenience, core value/quality and gastronomic icon. The agreement level for each item on the 5-point Likert scale ranged from 'Strongly Agree (= 1)' to 'Strongly Disagree (= 5).' Lastly, section four was designed to gather information regarding the 'respondents' experiences of *nasi kandar* in George Town' based on emotional attributes that duly represent their experiences as used before in Shenoy's research (2005).

Table 1.0: Number of respondents surveyed in the five *nasi kandar* establishments

Street	Name of Shop	Tot al	%	%
Jalan Masjid Kapitan Keling	Nasi Kandar Beratur	81	19.7%	
	total	***81***		***19.7%***
Lebuh Chulia	Kapitan's Nasi Kandar	111	26.9%	
	Kassim Mustafa Nasi Kandar	11	2.7%	
	Restoran Ros Mutiara	164	39.8%	
	total	***286***		***69.4%***
Penang Street	Line Clear Nasi Kandar	44	10.7%	
	total	***44***		***10.7%***
No info/ no answer	No info/ no answer	1	0.2%	
	total	***1***		***0.2%***
	Grand Total	***412***	***100.0 %***	***100.0 %***

(Source: fieldwork survey, March – May 2012)

Pictures 1a, 1b, 1c & 1d: Nasi Kandar Kassim Mustafa Situated Along Chulia Street, Penang

(Source: fieldwork survey, August 2013)

Findings and Discussion

From the survey, we can claim that *nasi kandar* is being viewed positively by local and foreign tourists alike when 93% (n = 384) said that they will recommend this spicy dish to their friends and relatives (see Figure 1.0).

In Figure 2.0, it is also pleasing and promising to note that tourists have high levels of satisfaction with the *nasi kandar* that they have savoured in George Town. The percentage that concurred with this statement and highlighted *nasi kandar* as ‘good’ was quite consistent between local tourists (64.2%, 147 respondents) and foreign tourists (62.8%, 115 respondents). This showed that both categories of tourists were satisfied with *nasi kandar* being George Town’s gastronomic icon or tourism product to promote the city’s food culture.

Figure 1.0: Decision to Recommend *Nasi Kandar* to Friends and Relatives

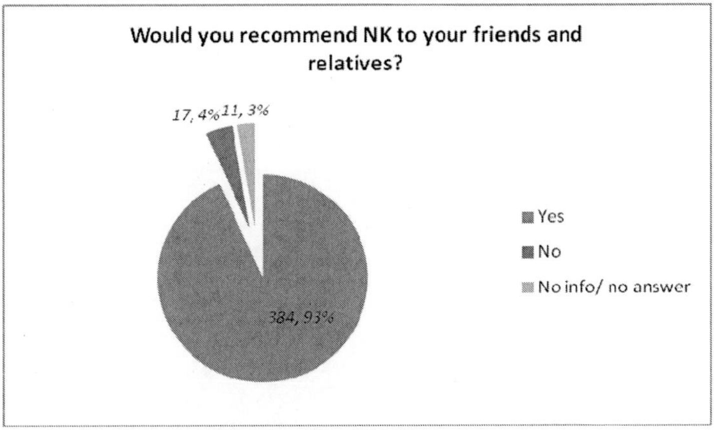

(Source: fieldwork survey, March – May 2012)

Figure 2.0: *Nasi Kandar* as a Gastronomic Icon of George Town's Food Culture

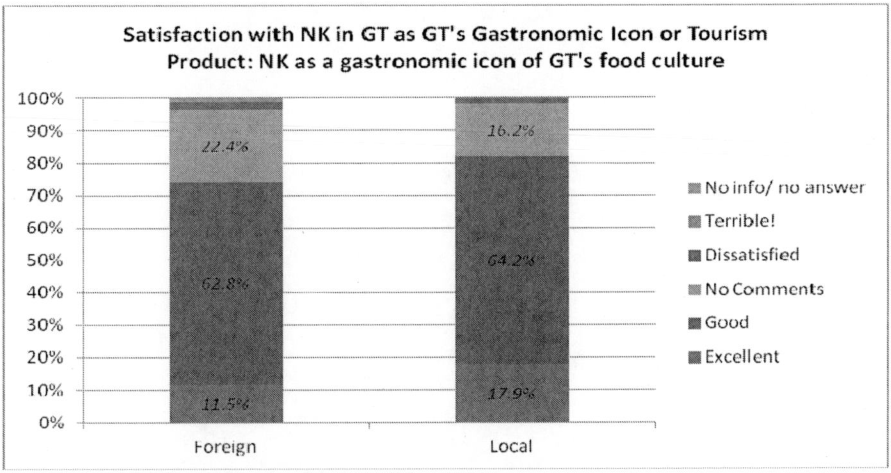

(Source: fieldwork survey, March – May 2012)

In terms of availaibility of information on the legacy, food history and cooking methods of *nasi kandar* in George Town, though more than half of both types of tourists commented positively, however, about one third (33.9%, 62 respondents) of foreign tourists and 27% (62 respondents) of local tourists chose not to comment (as illustrated in Figure 3.0 they were not (even) certain on the availability of information on the legacy, food history and methods of cooking of *nasi kandar* in George Town (in Pictures 2 and 3, we can see that Nasi Kandar Ros Mutiara and Ramzan Nasi Kandar are located in the heart of George Town).

Picture 2: Nasi Kandar Ros Mutiara, Chulia St

Picture 3: Ramzan Nasi Kandar

(Source: fieldwork survey, August 2013)

Figure 3.0: Availability of Information on the Legacy/Food History/Cooking Methods of *Nasi Kandar* in George Town

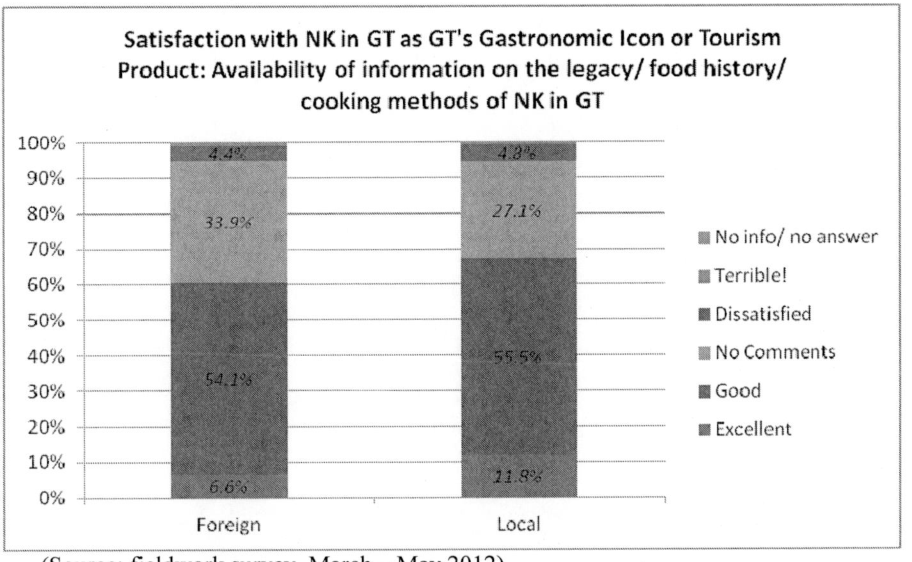

(Source: fieldwork survey, March – May 2012)

Overall, both categories of tourists were satisfied with the availability of *nasi kandar* food menus in English where foreign tourists scored higher (71.6%, 131 respondents) than local tourists (65.5%, 150 respondents) (see Figure 4.0).

Figure 4.0: Availability of Food Menus in English

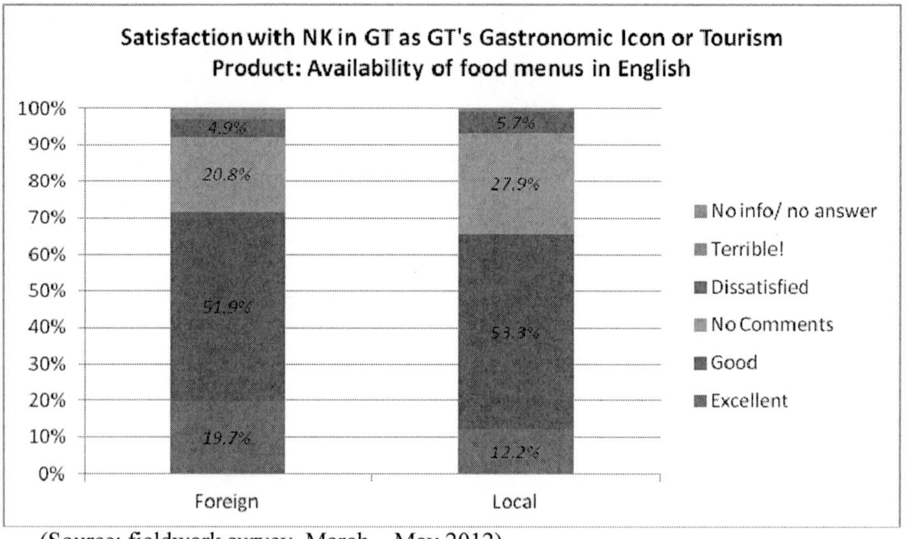

(Source: fieldwork survey, March – May 2012)

Similarly, the tourists interviewed were rather satisfied with the ability of *nasi kandar* food providers' to converse in English (as illustrated in Figure 5.0 more foreign tourists [69.4%, 127 respondents] commented positively compared to local tourists [63.3%, 145 respondents]).

Figure 5.0: Ability of *Nasi Kandar* Food Providers to Converse in English

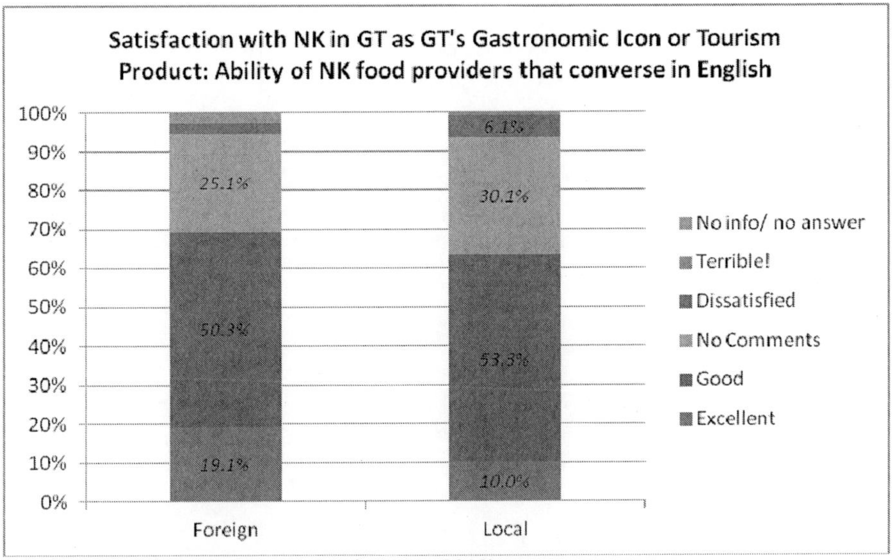

(Source: fieldwork survey, March – May 2012)

From Figures 6.0 and 7.0 respectively, overall, the tourists were very satisfied with the accessibility and variety of *nasi kandar* outlets in George Town. For instance, 23% (93 respondents) opined that there was 'excellent' accessibility whilst more than half (57%, 236 respondents) regarded the accessibility of *nasi kandar* outlets in George Town to be 'good'. Tourists were also extremely satisfied with the variety of *nasi kandar* outlets in George Town with a quarter (25%, 105 respondents) saying 'excellent' and 57% (234 respondents) highlighting that the variety was 'good'.

Figure 6.0: Accessibility of *Nasi Kandar* Outlets in George Town

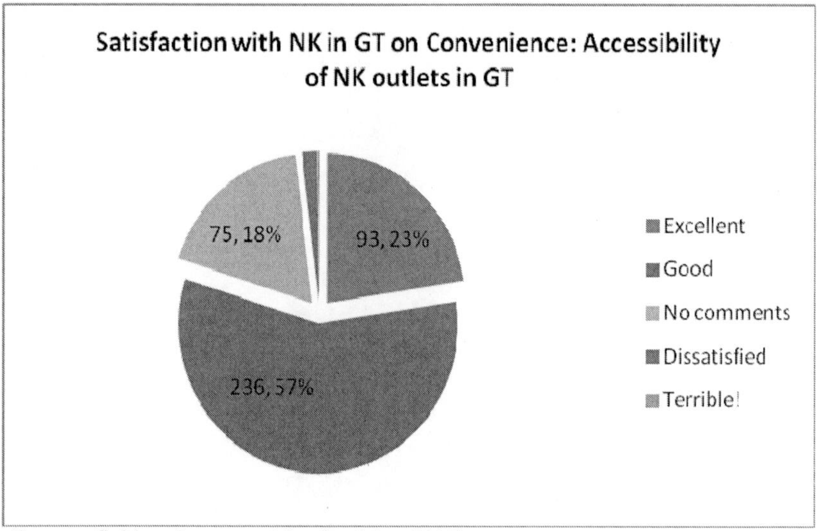

(Source: fieldwork survey, March – May 2012)

Figure 7.0: Variety of *Nasi Kandar* Outlets in George Town

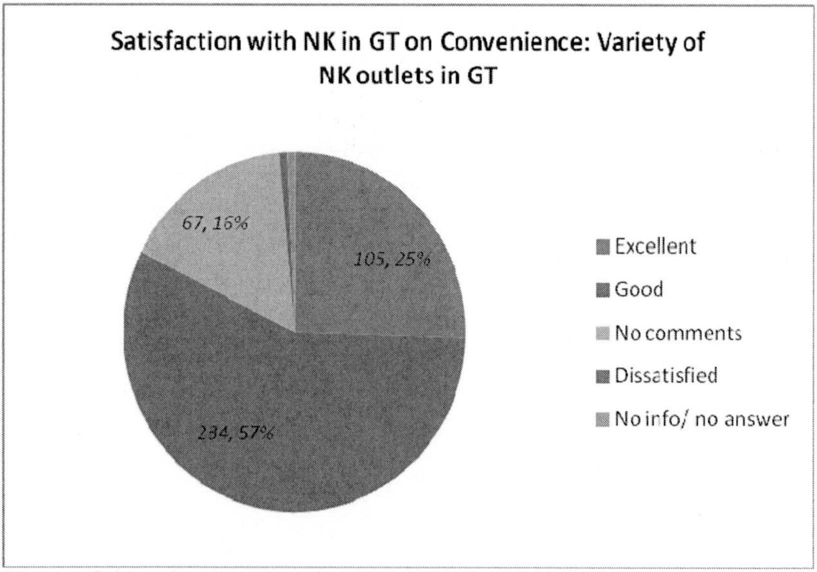

(Source: fieldwork survey, March – May 2012)

From this study, we also managed to reveal the perceptions of tourists in terms of the relationship between *nasi kandar* and branding George Town as a 'City of Gastronomy.' Figure 8.0 shows that more than half (62%, 256 respondents) of the respondents agreed that the mention of 'urban gastronomy' in George Town made them think of *nasi kandar.* Only a small percentage of 12% (51 respondents) disagreed with this statement and 25% (102 respondents) were unsure and did not provide any comments.

Figure 8.0: Urban Gastronomy in George Town and *Nasi Kandar*

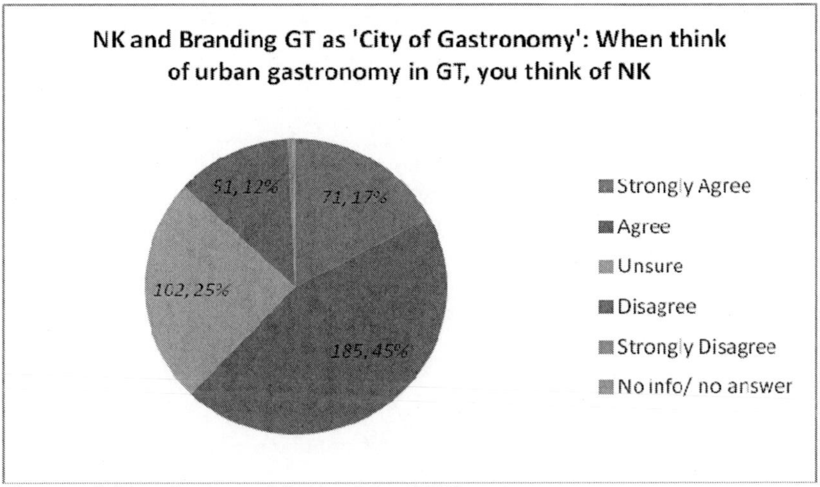

(Source: fieldwork survey, March – May 2012)

As shown in Pictures 4a and 4b, *nasi kandar* outlets are ubiquitous and easily available and accessible in George Town. Thus, the ubiquity, availability and easy accessibility of *nasi kandar* qualify this dish to be considered as the most important element in the urban gastronomy of George Town and one which should be promoted.

Pictures 4a and 4b: Easy availability and accessibility of *Nasi Kandar* as urban gastronomy in George Town

(Source: fieldwork survey, August 2013)

Subsequently, the next four dimensions are related to *nasi kandar* and George Town's branding rights as a City of Gastronomy (see Figures 9.0 to 12.0). Overall, tourists are agreeable that George Town has a vibrant *nasi kandar* community that serves the local populace and tourists. 15% (60 respondents) strongly agreed whilst more than half (57%, 234 respondents) agreed.

Figure 9.0: George Town's vibrant *Nasi Kandar* community that services the local populace and tourists

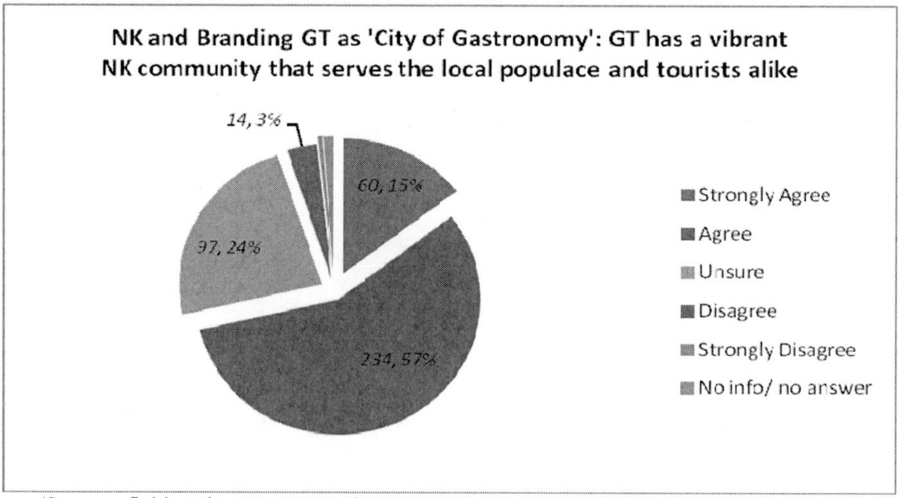

(Source: fieldwork survey, March – May 2012)

An equally high percentage (69%, 286 respondents) of tourists concur that *nasi kandar* is distinctively unique to George Town (see Figure 10.0).

Figure 10.0: *Nasi Kandar* is distinctively unique to George Town

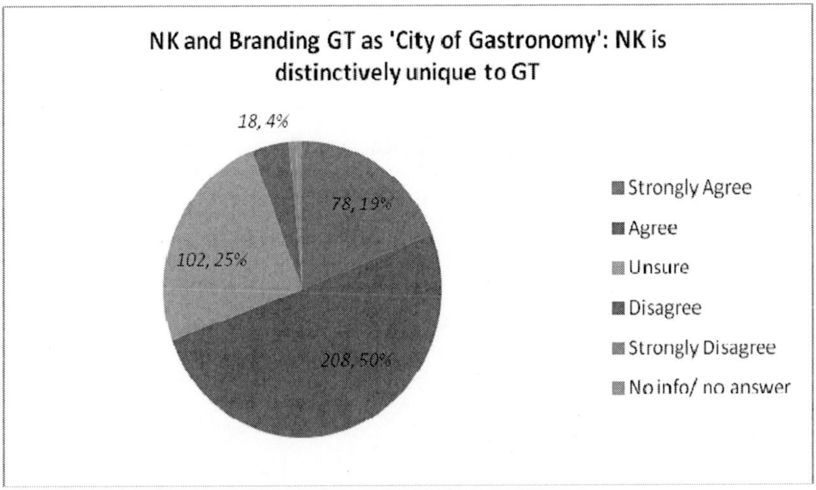

(Source: fieldwork survey, March – May 2012)

Likewise as illustrated in Figure 11.0, a high percentage of 70% (287 respondents) of tourists opined that George Town is the ultimate space and place for *nasi kandar*.

Figure 11.0: George Town is the ultimate space and place for *Nasi Kandar*

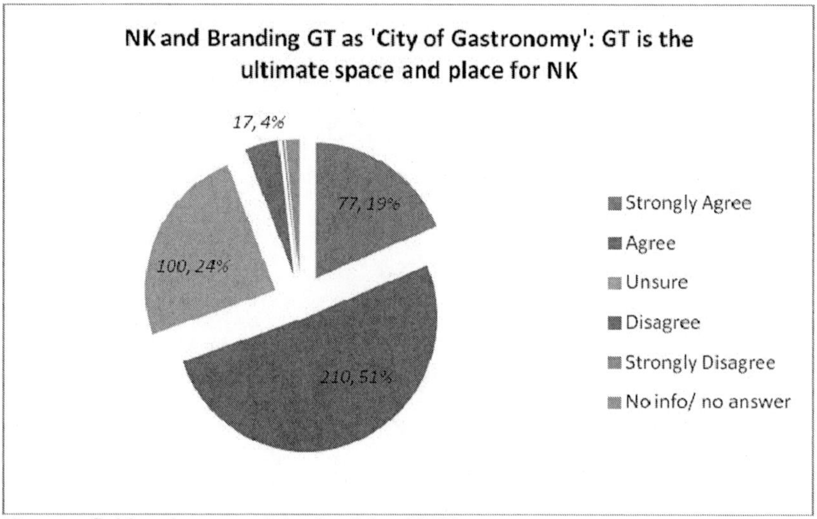

(Source: fieldwork survey, March – May 2012)

Consistently, another indicator revealed that 70% (288 respondents) of the tourists surveyed agree that George Town distinctively carries the image, identity and branding for *nasi kandar.* This revelation certainly augurs well for the city en route to being recognised and branded for its gastronomic prowess (see Figure 12.0).

Figure 12.0: George Town distinctively carries the image, identity and branding for *Nasi Kandar*

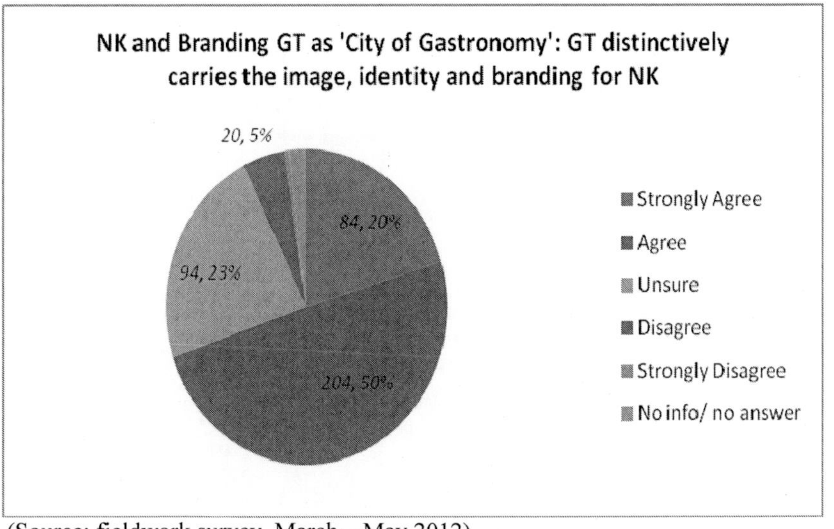

(Source: fieldwork survey, March – May 2012)

Nasi kandar as George Town's key attraction is further demonstrated when 61% (253 respondents) of the tourists claimed that *nasi kandar* in George Town is worth travelling the world to gorge on (see Figure 13.0). This suggests that George Town as a destination can utilise *nasi kandar* as a branding tool for culinary/heritage tourism.

Figure 13.0: *Nasi Kandar* in George Town is worth travelling the world to gorge on!

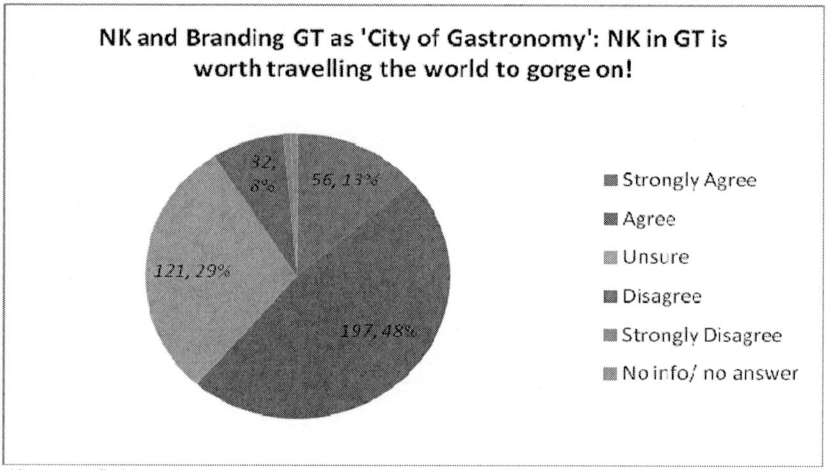

(Source: fieldwork survey, March – May 2012)

To further affirm the ability of *nasi kandar* as George Town's branding tool towards becoming a City of Gastronomy, this study found that the majority of the respondents (77%, 274 respondents) agree that *nasi kandar* qualifies George Town to be branded as a 'City of Gastronomy' (see Figure 14.0 and Pic tures 5a and 5b).

Figure 14.0: *Nasi Kandar* qualifies George Town to be branded as a 'City of Gastronomy'

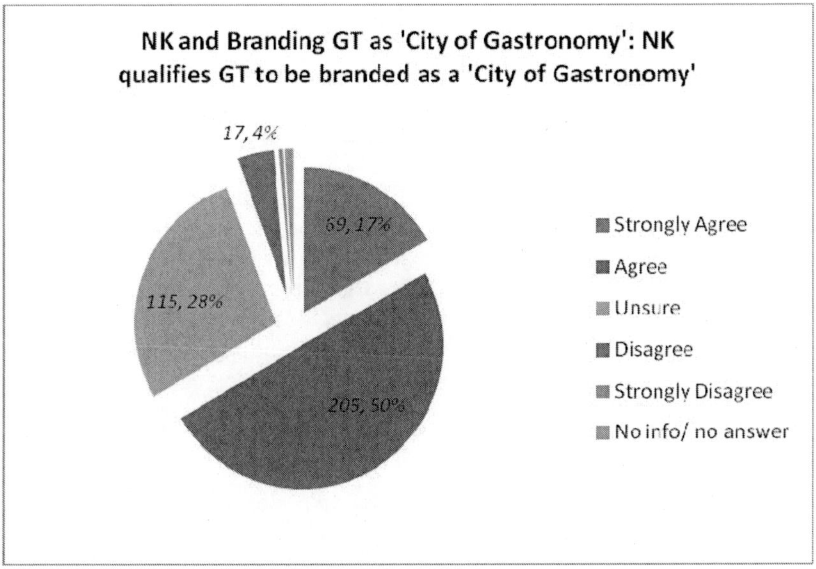

(Source: Fieldwork survey, March – May 2012)

Pictures 5a & 5b: *Nasi Kandar* as urban gastronomy qualifies George Town as a City of Gastronomy

(Source: fieldwork survey, August 2013)

Conclusions and Implications

This chapter presented the emerging trend of culinary and local delicacies being considered as a vital component of tourism attractions in many cities worldwide. The City of Gastronomy is one of the many designations conferred by the UNESCO Creative City Network in which a city showcases its niche area in cultural and creative activities as an integral part of the city's economic strengths and socio-cultural assets. Culinary tourism, gastronomic tourism or food tourism, these terms are often used interchangeably, refer to the unique and memorable experiences of tasting the food and drink of the country, region or area, and this trend of tourism is now gaining importance in the global tourism experience. Tourists often opt for dining out at their destinations; hence savouring the local food is very important to tourists apart from enjoying the local climate, scenery and lodging or accommodation. Culinary tourism owes its roots to the cuisines of cultural tourism, and it is also linked to agritourism, rural tourism, and urban tourism.

The chapter has examined the gastronomy experiences offered by George Town World Heritage Site in Penang State, Malaysia with special reference to the local delicacy of *nasi kandar*. Empirical evidence from the study revealed that *nasi kandar* has a strong image and identity amongst both Malaysian and foreign tourists, and it is agreed more generally that *nasi kandar* is a very unique dish that may qualify George Town to be a City of Gastronomy. However, more coordinated effort is necessary by all stakeholders to realise this important mission. Nonetheless, the study has shown that a city's gastronomic appeals are a very important factor that contributes to the tourists' quality of experiences while travelling abroad. The city's unique gastronomy may also persuade the tourists to return to the destination time and again to resample its distinctive cuisine. Hence, it is imperative that all policies, strategies and campaigns for destination marketing emphasise aspects of food in order to entice more tourists to experience the culinary delights of the city of George Town, namely the delicious *nasi kandar*.

Acknowledgement

This study was funded by Universiti Sains Malaysia's Short-Term Research Grant (304/PSOSIAL/6311122).

References

Ab. Karim, M. S. and B-L. Chua (nd) 'Malaysia as a Culinary Tourism Destination: International Tourists' Perspective', *Journal of Tourism, Hospitality & Culinary Arts,* pp.63-78, retrieved from http://www.jthca.org/Download/pdf/V1%20IS3/chap%204.pdf, page consulted 26/08/2013.

Boyne, S., D. Hall, and F. Williams (2003) 'Policy, Support and Promotion for Food-Related Tourism Initiatives', *Journal of Travel and Tourism Marketing,* 14: 131-154.

Chen, C-F. and D. Tsai (2007) 'How Destination Image and Evaluative Factors Affect Behavioural Intentions?' *Tourism Management,* 28: 1115-1122.

Crombie, B. (2011) 'Branding Cities and Clusters for Economic Development', *The ISM Journal of International Business,* ISSN 2150-1076, 1 (3, December, 2011).

Du Rand, G.E., E. Heath and N. Alberts (2003) 'The Role of Local and Regional Food in Destination Marketing', *Journal of Travel and Tourism Marketing,* 14: 97-112.

Gertner, D. (2011) 'Unfolding and Configuring Two Decades of Research and Publications on Place Marketing and Place Branding', *Place Branding and Diplomacy,* 7: 91-106.

Goh, B.L. (2012) 'Cities and Culture', *The Sun Newspapers,* 28 August 2012.

Hwang, L-J. J., J. van Westering and H-H. Chen (2004) 'Exploration of the Linkages Between the Gastronomy and Heritage of Tainan City, Taiwan', *Advances in Hospitality and Leisure*, 1: 223-235.

Kerr, G. (2006) 'From Destination Brand to Location Brand', *Journal of Brand Management*, 13: 276-283.

Kivela, J., and J.C. Crotts (2006) 'Gastronomy Tourism: a Meaningful Travel Market Segment', *Journal of Culinary Science and Technology,* 4: 39-55.

Mak, A.K.Y. (2011) 'An Identity-centred approach to Place Branding: the Case of Industry Partners' Evaluation of Iowa's Destination Image', *Journal of Brand Management,* 18: 438-450.

McCabe, S. and E.H. Stokoe (2004) 'Place and Identity in Tourists' Accounts', *Annals of Tourism Research,* 31: 601-622.

Metaxas, T. (2010) 'Place Marketing, Place Branding and Foreign Direct Investments: Defining their Relationship in the Frame of Local Economic Development Process', *Place Branding and Public Diplomacy,* 6: 228-243.

Penang State Tourism Development (nd). Brochure entitled 'Penang Street Food. "Food Paradise of Asia"', Penang: Penang State Tourism Development, retrieved from http://www.visitpenang.gov.my/portal3/where-to-eat.html, page consulted 10/11/2013.

Scarpato, R. (2002) 'Gastronomy Studies in Search of Hospitality', *Journal of Hospitality and Tourism Management,* 9: 1-12.

Shenoy, S.S. (2005) *Food Tourism and the Culinary Tourist*, Clemson University: unpublished PhD thesis.

State Government of Penang (SGP) (2011) *Draft Special Area Plan. George Town Historic Cities of the Straits of Malacca,* Penang: SGP.

Van Gelder, S. and H. Roberts (2007) 'Branding Brings a Place to Life', *Branding,* Issue 63, October-December 2007, retrieved from www.placebrands.net, page consulted 23/09/2012.

Van Gelder, S. (2008a) *How to Improve the Chances of Successfully Developing and Implementing a Place Brand Strategy*, Amsterdam: Placebrands Ltd., retrieved from www.placebrands.net, page consulted 23/09/2012.

—. (2008b) *Place 2.0,* Amsterdam: Placebrands Limited.

Zenker, S. and N. Martin (2011) 'Measuring Success in Place Marketing and Branding', *Place Branding and Public Diplomacy,* 7: 32-41.

PROMOTING TAI FOOD FOR HEALTH TOURISM IN MAE HONG SORN PROVINCE, THAILAND

NARONG SIKHIRAM
AND SONGSUDA POOSAWANG

Introduction

Geographical and Historical Context

Mae Hong Sorn is located in the northern part of Thailand and surrounded by mountains. Ban Pha Bong is home to diverse ethnic groups, such as Tai Yai or Tai and Karen. Therefore, it boasts its unique lifestyle and culture and is an interesting learning centre for outsiders. Furthermore, there are also abundant natural resources for tourism such as hot springs, hill tribe villages and viewpoints to take in the dramatic upland landscapes.

Ban Pha Bong is a relatively small village dating back more than 150 years and linked more closely to Burmese rather than to Thai or Lanna culture. During the late nineteenth century the community leader was Ku Ei Tang, who was elected to that position. Villagers built the temple Jong Pha Bong north of the village in 1875, and the abbot at that time was Pra U Wa So who was also teacher of the Tai language for the community when there was still no formal education. In 1875 Ku Ei Tang and the local residents built a large Buddha image. In 1889, Jong Noi Num and his family built another small Buddha image. Then much later in 1981, Pa Ka Mon and Kam Poo Hoi Lek had faith in the Buddha and built another two images. These four Buddha images were named in the Tai language.

Local Food and Health

Healthy food is any kind of food considered to be beneficial to health beyond normal dietary requirements. Food provides energy and the essential nutrients needed. The four important elements to achieve a healthy food intake are nutrient adequacy, variety, moderation and balance. Food adequacy involves having six main nutrients: carbohydrate, protein, fat, vitamins, minerals and water. The nutrient requirement depends on age, gender, weight and height, health conditions and physiological need. Variety means combination of all five categories (group 1: starch, starch products and starchy roots; group 2: meat, meat products and soybean; group 3: vegetables; group 4: fruits; and group 5: fat and oil). It is vital that human bodies receive all essential nutrients for daily needs. Moderation in food consumption is the skill that needs to be learned, such as keeping the portion sizes reasonable when eating every meal and learning to eat slowly because eating slowly gives enough time for the nervous system to send the right signals of satiety at the right time to the brain to prevent over-eating. Moderation means restriction of food and nutrient intake in order to prevent harmful effects on health. A balanced diet, from a nutritional perspective, should be attained between food intake and physical activity. When equality is met between food intake and physical exercise, body weight is maintained. The balanced diet should provide energy from the right proportion of carbohydrate, protein and fat in the ratio of 50-55: 10-15: 25-30, respectively.

Unhealthy diets and physical inactivity are major risk factors of chronic diseases. Reports of international and national experts and reviews of the current scientific evidence recommend goals for nutrient intake in order to prevent chronic diseases. For appropriate dietary requirements, the World Health Organisation (WHO) (http://www.who.int/dietphysicalactivity/diet/en/print.html) recommends that individuals should 1) achieve energy balance and a healthy weight; 2) limit energy intake from total fats and shift fat consumption from saturated to unsaturated fats and towards the elimination of trans-fatty acids; 3) increase consumption of fruits and vegetables, and legumes, whole grains and nuts; 4) limit the intake of free sugars; and 5) limit salt (sodium) consumption from all sources and ensure that salt is iodised.

Other recommendations include omitting consumption of sufficient calories to avoid malnutrition, but eating adequate food for optimal health and disease prevention (AlKerwiA'a, 2013). This transition has impacted the significance of the 'diet quality' concept. Beyond the provision of meeting basic nutritional needs, adequate nutrition is required for normal physical growth, mental performance, and to maintain better health (ibid). The concept of healthy food is multidimensional. It not only refers to the concepts mentioned above, but also nutrient density, generally defined as a ratio of nutrient content to the total energy content.

This participatory study involved collaboration among community homestay members, community leaders, government health officers and direct participation of researchers in the object of study (Marshall and Rossman, 1999; Robson, 2002). Marshall and Rossman state that 'Participant observation is to some degree an essential element of all qualitative studies' (ibid: 106). The data were collected by interviews, discussion groups, in-depth discussions, observations, and brainstorming with the following activities: academic researchers created a forum held with villagers and local leaders to explain the purpose of the research and project activities; a focus group was held among researchers to analyse the problems and difficulties, limitations and potential of members who were involved in Tai food preparation for tourists; ingredients were measured in Tai dishes and local cooking practices were observed; and the nutritive values of Tai food using INMUCAL Nutrition Software were calculated.

The study was conducted between March - December 2012 at Moo 1, Ban Pha Bong, Muang District, Mae Hong Sorn. The research aimed to develop healthy traditional Tai food to promote Health Tourism. Another aim of the study was to establish a training centre and a learning resource for other homestay groups, students, and members of the general public. The study was carried out as a participatory study which included seminars and workshops on hygienic conditions for Tai food management for the participants. The training also covered other food production related topics; including, introduction to food and nutrition, basic knowledge in food and health, food safety and sanitary management, the 'healthy food' concept, food display, food preparation, preservation and practice.

Participants joined a focus group in which they collaborated in healthy food preparation and management. They also took part in the SWOT analysis. Participants also collaborated in designing a Khan-Tok set (Khan-Tok is traditional Lanna food served on a low round table). In addition, they have learned from the workshops to improve the quality of healthy food; including, setting criteria for raw materials, and using appropriate utensils in the production process. The participatory study method has various advantages, the 'immersion offers the researcher the opportunity to learn directly from his own experience of the setting' (Marshall and Rossman, 1999: 106).

Methodology

Procedure for collecting data

Primary data were collected through interviews, discussion groups, in-depth discussion, observations and brainstorming. Data include transcripts of audio-taped meetings of community homestay members, community leaders, and local government public health officers. Field data collection also included direct participation of researchers in every part of the community tourism participation activity. Secondary data were reviewed from books and research on Lanna indigenous foods, northern Thai food style, the traditional food service called Khan-Tok, the nutritional value of local plant food resources, and other literature related to the production of healthy Tai food.

Analysing data on community food management for developing healthy Tai Khan-Tok food

Interview sheets were distributed to collect data on: personal information, cooking experience, the 'healthy food' concept and their knowledge in healthy Khan-Tok food. Other sources of data came from focus groups and the evaluation of cooking skills and food display by participation techniques, measurement of ingredients used for Tai recipes and calculated nutritional value. In addition, SWOT analysis was conducted regarding their local identity, physical strength, knowledge and Tai food culture. Personal data such as cooking skills and knowledge in healthy food and a healthy Khan-Tok concept were also examined. Ingredients of Tai dishes cooked by female residents were weighed for calculating nutritional value by INMUCAL Nutrition Software. Group discussions and focus groups on nutritive values of the Tai dishes were held. Basic and applied knowledge in incorporating indigenous ingredients was provided to female residents of Ban Pha Bong. The women's group cooked and set healthy Tai food for tourists and the nutritive values were evaluated and calculated using INMUCAL Nutrition Software. Finally, data were analysed by comparing various ways of food management to create the healthy Tai food model. Workshops and training were held for community members who were involved in food preparation for tourists. The evaluation process was conducted by tourists who were journalists, government officers, and others.

Research findings

Ban Pha Bong is an agricultural community. Local residents live on the cultivation of organic vegetables, organic rice and other products from organic farming. This community is surrounded by mountains and rivers. It is an ideal place for travel and leisure, for example, a bike trip that explores community lifestyles. In addition, community members still maintain their cultural traditions as expressed through their dress, language, food, and cultural performances. Visitors can enjoy learning about Tai culture.

Food in Ba Pha Bong, Mae Hong Sorn was influenced by Burmese traditions, and prepared with such local raw materials as organic rice and chicken from their farms, and fish from rivers. This area is a production site for soy bean, used for the production of fermented soybean called Tua Noa (similar to Nutto in Japan or Tempeh in Indonesia). Moreover communities also grow sesame for sesame oil and souvenir production.

Ban Pha Bong's potential and opportunity to become a health tourism destination

As Ban Pha Bong still maintains its traditional characteristics, such as being a farming community with a distinctive Tai culture, it has a high potential to become a tourist destination. An evaluation of the village's potential can be summarised as follows: *potential of the group of women and its managemen*t: female residents of Ban Pha Bong have clear division of duties in the food preparation process; *potential of good quality food resources*: the community grows organic vegetables, and it grows a sufficient amount of crops to accommodate tourists; these can also be developed into healthy snacks or souvenirs for tourists; *potential of the cooking member*s: the members of the community involved in cooking can provide Tai food with an unique taste. Moreover, Tai food is classified according to eating styles, and there were also Tai performances during the Khan-Tok dinner, with *Pi Paat* musician groups and dances by young people; *opportunity to promote Tai food for health tourism:* Tai food is distinctive and cooked from raw materials available locally. It was found that the local community was eager to learn about healthy food by encouraging Tai women who were involved in food preparation for tourists to learn how to cook healthy food and to develop a dining, hospitality and service model.

SWOT analysis regarding Ban Pha Bong's Identity, strength, knowledge and Tai food culture

The results of the SWOT analysis indicate that women's groups had strengths and opportunities that might support the development of healthy Tai menus for tourists. With regard to weaknesses, it was found that they had limited knowledge of healthy eating and had no standardised recipes. As a consequence, the research team set up the training programme to increase their knowledge in healthy cooking, food handling and food management.

Strengths	**Weakness**
- Cooking expertise - Healthy habit concerns. - Open-minded and ready to change. - Maintain Tai traditional culture. - Local organic vegetables used.	- Limited knowledge of healthy eating. - No standard recipes. - Preferences for salty taste.
Opportunity	**Threat**
- Increase in the number of tourists. - Healthy tourism model. - Supported by the government.	-Their workload in family care and farming.

Cooking experience, healthy food concepts, and healthy Khan-Tok food

Tai women have been cooking Tai food since they were teenagers and they learn how to cook from their senior female family members. Mostly they cooked Tai food for their family and some of them cooked Tai food for tourists in guest houses and homestays. With regard to the perception of healthy food or healthy eating habits, we established a focus group and used open-ended questionnaires related to diet and health; what they could or could not eat and the reasons for this; how were their cooking skills; and issues surrounding their eating habits and personal hygiene. We focused on the perception of appropriate eating portions (see Table 1).

Table 1. The level of knowledge in healthy eating perceptions of female residents.

Healthy Eating Perceptions	Level
Eating habits and health	Good
Eat much and problems with health	Good
Sugar and body wt. and diabetic	Good/fair
Low fat and blood lipid and body wt.	Good
Sodium and blood pressure	Good/fair
Enrichment nutrient diet	Fair
Good practice in cooking, eating and hygiene	Fair
Eating portions	Bad

From Table 1, we can establish that the local women, primarily responsible for cooking and delivering cooked food, have a good level of understanding of eating and health, but they still lack understanding in the appropriate levels of sugar and salt consumption. Their choices of food did not provide good sources of nutrients. They had a fair level of knowledge of cooking practices, eating habits and personal hygiene. They ate a lot of saturated fatty acid from pork, the Gaeng Hang Lay Moo dish, and they have no knowledge of eating portions.

Nutritive value of Tai food

At this stage, the study was conducted by letting the women's groups cook their own recipes and we then collected the data by weighing the ingredients. Then the research team calculated ingredients menu by menu. Other methods included focus groups and evaluation of cooking skills and food display by participation techniques. The measurement of Tai food ingredients and the calculation of Tai food nutritional values were analysed by INMUCAL Nutrition Software.

It was found that some of their original menus contained high saturated fats, cholesterol and sodium content (more than 2500 mg per serving). Some of their menus had low sugar content, high fibre from vegetables, and high beta carotene from dark green vegetables. The set menu also contained a large amount of carbohydrate from sticky rice.

Figure 1 Focus group discussed their strengths and weaknesses.

Figure 2 Measuring Tai food ingredients.

Table 2: Nutritional value of Tai food before improving healthy diet.

Menu	Energy (Kcal)	CHO* (g)	Protein (g)	Fat (g)	Vit A (RE)	Ca (mg)	P (mg)	Fe (mg)	Na (mg)
 Kang Fug Tong	267	7	43	8	137	196	4.79	4.77	1572
 Kang Pak Keaw	151	15	3	15	521	383	206	7.26	1243
	124	6	4	16	21	124	262	3.33	1105

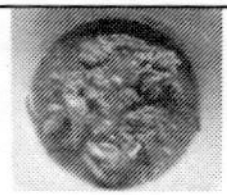	Nam Prik Nok									
		297	33	13	12	26	293	142	581	205
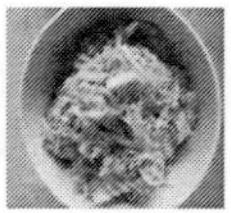 Ma Muang Sa Nab										
	Lab Tai	336	17	16 (Chol** = 130 mg)	31	2054	185	325	8.81	1042

* CHO = Carbohydrate ** Cholesterol

Kang Fug Tong (pumpkin curry with chicken) is a good source of sugar, fibre, fat, protein and beta carotene. However, this dish contains a high level of sodium (Na) from seasoning and curry paste.

Kang Pak Keaw (green vegetable curry with dried fish) is an indigenous Tai dish. The important step of cooking was how to choose types of vegetable that are rich in flavours. Kang Pak Keaw contains Tua Noa as seasoning. This dish is low in calories, a good source of beta carotene, however, it also contains a too high level of sodium content from shrimp paste, salt, and Tua Noa.

Nam Prik Nog (chilli dip) is normally served with fresh and steamed vegetables. Nog in the Tai language means grinding ingredients, such as grilled chilly, garlic and steamed fish with mortar. This dish could preserve nutrient loss from cooking, because it is served with vegetables that contain high fibre, a good source of protein. Fat content in this dish is obtained from fish. However, it is necessary to decrease the amount of sodium.

Ma Muang Sa Nab (mango and herb salad with ground dried fish) is tasty and a good source of calcium. It may be served with fresh vegetables to increase fibre consumption.

Laab Tai (minced pork seasoned with a variety of herbs and spices) is served with fresh vegetables. It is tasty, but contains high saturated fat and cholesterol from pork and it is visceral, with high sodium content from seasoning. On the other hand, it was a good source of protein, iron and retinol.

Developing healthy Tai food recipes

The groups of women cooked their own Tai food dishes. We measured and weighed ingredients. We calculated the nutritional value of Tai food by INMUCAL Nutrition Software and recommended healthy Tai food recipes by decreasing sodium, fat and cholesterol, reducing/replacing some ingredients, adding good sources of fibre, preparing appropriate serving size portions and setting a Tai menu based on nutritional value and writing standard recipes (standard household measuring), for example, replacing saturated fat and cholesterol with soy protein, fish or organic chicken.

Figure 3 The standard recipe handbook.

Tai food set menu for tourists

After they had standardised recipes, the research team let them follow standardised recipes and set up Tai food set menus for three meals: breakfast, lunch and dinner. The Tai food sets were as follows:

Figure 4: Khan-Tok breakfast for four people

Table 3: Nutritional value of Tai breakfast

Menus	serving	Energy (Kcal)	CHO* (g)	Protein (g)	Fat (g)	Vit A (RE**)	Ca (mg)	P (mg)	Fe (mg)	Na (mg)
Khao Tom Kruang	4 cup	1432	256	56	20	68	152	600	6	3132
Yam Tua Pae Lor	1 cup	357	46	17	12	39	73	302	8.2	551
Tua Pu Ueun	1 cup	143	15	6	7	0.4	33	97	1.2	8
Boiled egg	4 eggs	344	4	28	24	818	84	511	6.9	396
	Total	2276	321	107	63	925	342	1510	22.3	4087
	Per 1 Person	569	80	27	16	231	86	378	5.6	1022

* CHO = Carbohydrate ** Retinal Equivalent

Table 4: Nutritional value of Tai lunch set.

Menus	serving	Energy (Kcal)	CHO* (g)	Protein (g)	Fat (g)	Vit A (RE**)	Ca (mg)	P (mg)	Fe (mg)	Na (mg)
Cooked Rice	4 dish	904	208	16	2	0	40	128	2	232
Ma Muangsa Nap	1 dish	297	33	12	13	26	293	142	5.8	205
Kang Pakkeaw	1 dish	155	15	16	3	3	383	206	7.3	1243
Lab Tai	1 dish	431	10	41	25	22	61	462	4.8	610
Nam Prik Oop	1 dish	361	58	19	6	0	56	173	1.7	930
	Total	2148	324	104	49	51.03	833	1111	21.6	3220
	Per 1 Person	537	81	26	12	13	208	278	5.4	805

* CHO = Carbohydrate ** Retinal Equivalent

Table 5: Nutritional value of Tai dinner set.

Menus	serving	Energy (Kcal)	CHO* (g)	Protein (g)	Fat (g)	Vit A (RE**)	Ca (mg)	P (mg)	Fe (mg)	Na (mg)
Kaw Souy	4 dish	904	208	16	2	0	40	128	2	232
Kang Fug Tong	2 dish	616	87	36	13	352	112	478	6.2	878
Mu Oop	1 dish	391	26	39	14	72	112	478	6	878
Pak Koodsa nab	1 dish	721	30	24	56	941	140	460	14	565
Nam Priknok	1 dish	198	18	19	5	122	75	230	3.7	84
Total		2830	369	134	90	1487	479	1774	31.9	2637
Per 1 Person		708	92	34	23	372	120	444	8.0	659

* CHO = Carbohydrate ** Retinal Equivale

Table 6: Nutritional value of Tai dinner set.

Menus	serving	Energy (Kcal)	CHO* (g)	Protein (g)	Fat (g)	Vit A (RE**)	Ca (mg)	P (mg)	Fe (mg)	Na (mg)
Kaw Souy	4 dish	904	208	16	2	0	40	128	2	232
Pla Nam Pai Ong	1 dish	360	25	30	15	21	191	188	8.2	926
Lab Tai	1 dish	431	10	41	25	22	61	462	4.8	610
Mak Lang Hung	2 dish	638	28	43	39	31	124	469	10.0	1017
Yam Tua Poo	1 dish	306	17	15	20	34	119	202	3.8	97
Total		2639	288	145	101	108	535	1449	28.8	2882
Per 1 Person		660	72	36	25	27	134	362	7.2	721

* CHO = Carbohydrate ** Retinal Equivalent

Figure 5: Tai lunch set for four people

Figure 6: Tai set dinner for four people

Fig.7: Tai dinner for four people.

Conclusion

The Ban Pha Bong women's group was able to offer a range of healthy Tai food set menus for tourists in three meals, breakfast, lunch and dinner. This engaged research project suggests that a programme of healthy food provision can enhance the prospects for developing tourism, and particularly homestay tourism, in these upland areas of northern Thailand. What this project illustrates is that there are now elements of tourism, which include food and health, which can contribute to the development of specialist or niche kinds of tourism in rather more remote places.

Acknowledgment

The authors would like to thank the Upper Northern Provincial Charter I for funding support, all villagers and the leader in Ban Pha Bong, Mae Hong Sorn province., and all the staff involved in the project *The Developing of Healthy Tourism Community Model in 4 Provinces Upper North of Thailand*.

References

AlKerwiAla'a (2013) *Diet Quality Concept: A Review*, *Nutrition,* doi: 10.1016/j.nut.2013.10.001.

Auksorntub, T. (2006) *Nutritive Values and Fiber of Lanna Food,* Unpublished Master of Science (Nutrition Education), Chiang Mai University, Chiang Mai, Thailand *(in Thai).*

Boonmakard, P. (2001) *The Study of Traditional Yong Foods*, Unpublished Master of Science (Nutrition Education), Chiang Mai University, Chiang Mai, Thailand *(in Thai).*

Kantaruksa, P. (2004) *Comparison of Nutritive Values between Chemical Analysis and Calculation From Thai Food Composition Table*, Unpublished Master of Science (Nutrition Education), Chiang Mai University, Chiang Mai, Thailand *(in Thai).*

Karnjana Kaewtep and Kanoksak (1987) *Self-reliance: the potential in the development of rural areas,* Bangkok: Catholic Council of Thailand for Development *(in Thai).*

Legkerm, C. (2009) *Nutritional Value and Harvesting Inbox of Some Locally Grown Vegetables in Chiang Mai*, Unpublished Master of Science (Teaching Biology), Chiang Mai University, Chiang Mai, Thailand *(in Thai).*

Marshall, C., and G.B. Rossman (1999) *Designing Qualitative Research,* California: Sage Publications, third edition.

Mile, M. B., and A. M. Huberman (1994) *Qualitative data analysis: An expanded edition,* Thousand Oaks, CA: Sage.

Mills, G. E. (2007) *Action research: A guide for the teacher researcher*, Upper Saddle River, NJ: Pearson.

Nimsakul, S. et al. (2003) *Lanna food and wisdom in health care,* Chiang Mai, Thailand (*in Thai*).

Robson, C. (2002) *Real World Research: a Resource for Social Scientists and Practitioner-researchers,* Oxford: Blackwell Publications.

Suton, N. (2002) *Study of Zinc and Copper Content in Local Native Vegetables Chiang Mai Province,* Unpublished Master of Science (Nutrition Education), Chiang Mai University, Chiang Mai, Thailand *(in Thai).*

Valaisatein, P., S. Ob-oon and C. Hasannaree (2003) *Process and Techniques for Community Developer*, Bangkok: The Thailand Research Fund *(in Thai).*

Wongkamolshun, R. (2010) *Num-prik-ta-dang a native food for health from Thai herbs of shallot, garlic and chilli with fibrinolytic promotion*, Associated Med. Chiang Mai University, Thailand *(in Thai).*

CONTRIBUTORS

Nurwati Badarulzaman has been a Lecturer at the School of Housing, Building and Planning, Universiti Sains Malaysia since 1994. She holds a Bachelor of Urban Studies and Environmental Planning from the University of Wisconsin, Green Bay, USA, a Master's degree in Urban and Regional Planning from Virginia Tech, USA and a PhD in Employment Planning from Sheffield University, UK.

Catherine Cheung is an Associate Professor and Associate Dean in the School of Hotel and Tourism Management (SHTM) of the Hong Kong Polytechnic University. She is an active researcher and writes regular reviews for several hospitality and tourism journals. She has been involved in more than 15 research grant projects for both internal and external grants. She has received two awards from SHTM on Research Excellence and Service Excellence.

Janianton Damanik holds a PhD from Universität Bielefeld, Germany. He is Professor of Community Empowerment in the Department of Social Development and Welfare, and Director of the Center for Tourism Studies at Gadjah Mada University, Indonesia. His teaching and research interests include community welfare, poverty alleviation, community tourism, tourism planning, destination management, and tourist mobility. He is co-editor of *Poverty Alleviation through Tourism (bi-lingual)* (2005), with H. A. Kusworo and D. T. Raharjana.

Peter Hervik is an anthropologist and Professor in Migration Studies at the Department of Culture and Global Studies, Aalborg University, Denmark. He has conducted research among the Yucatec Maya of Mexico and on the news coverage of religious and ethnic minorities in Denmark. His books include *Mayan Lives Within and Beyond Boundaries. Social Categories and Lived Identity in Yucatan* (1999, 2001), and *The Annoying Difference. The Emergence of Danish Neonationalism, Neoracism, and Populism in the Post-1989 World* (2011).

Michael J. Hitchcock is Professor of Tourism Management and Dean of the Faculty of Hospitality and Tourism Management at the Macau University of Science and Technology. He was formerly Dean of IMI Switzerland, Luzern. He is currently conducting research on the Macau World Heritage Site and the Chinese female tourist gaze.

Mae Claire G. Jabines is an Assistant Professor in Social Science at the University of the Philippines, Cebu. She has a Master's degree in Political Science. She teaches history, political science and geography. Her research focuses on local history, political science and tourism. She is an advocate of promoting local history and tourism.

Rungrawee Jitpakdee is a Lecturer in the Tourism Programme and a Deputy Dean of Walailak Management School, Walailak University, Thailand. She is an expert on community-based ecotourism management and has undertaken research for several local communities particularly in the South of Thailand. She graduated with two Master's degrees in Business Administration (International Tourism and Hospitality Management) at Griffith University, Australia and Public Administration at Prince of Songkhla University, Thailand. She holds a doctoral degree in Rural and Regional Planning and Development at the Asian Institute of Technology, Thailand.

Amnaj Khaokhrueamuang is a PhD candidate in the Department of Tourism Science at Tokyo Metropolitan University (TMU). His main research focus is the sustainability of rural tourism development in Thailand, supported by the Asian Human Resources Fund of the Tokyo Metropolitan Government. He has a Master's degree in Ecotourism from Srinakharinwirot University (SWU). He maintains a specific interest in Japanese long-stay tourism in Thailand.

Sasiwimon Khongmueang served for four years as a Lecturer at Chiang Mai University affiliated with the Department of Modern Management and Information Technology and Hospitality Center, College of Arts, Media and Technology. Currently she is a PhD Fellow at the Department of Culture and Global Studies, Aalborg University, Denmark. Her research interests focus on community-based tourism management and development, tourist behaviours, the anthropology of tourism, cross-cultural studies, immigration and transnational marriage.

Suet Leng Khoo is a Senior Lecturer at the School of Social Sciences, Universiti Sains Malaysia. She holds a Bachelor of Arts (Geography) and Master of Science (Urban and Regional Planning) from Universiti Sains Malaysia and a PhD (Development Studies) from the University of Melbourne, Australia. She has undertaken research on human capital development, urban development and heritage conservation. Her latest research interests are related to planning cities of the 21st century to become Creative Cities.

Victor T. King is Emeritus Professor of Southeast Asian Studies, University of Leeds and Professorial Research Associate, School of Oriental and African Studies, University of London. He was recently Eminent Visiting Professor at Universiti Brunei Darussalam and currently Visiting Professor at Chiang Mai University. His research interests focus on the sociology and anthropology of Southeast Asia. His publications include *The Peoples of Borneo* (1993), *Anthropology and Development in South-East Asia* (1999), *The Modern Anthropology of South-East Asia* (with William Wilder) (2003/2006), *The Sociology of Southeast Asia* (2008/2011), *Tourism in Southeast Asia: Challenges and New Directions* (2009) and *Heritage Tourism in Southeast Asia* (2010) (with Michael Hitchcock and Michael Parnwell), and *The Historical Construction of Southeast Asian Studies: Korea and Beyond* (with Park Seung Woo) (2013).

Tuan Phong Ly is an Assistant Professor of the Faculty of Hotel and Tourism Management, Macau University of Science and Technology. He is an expert on national park management and ecotourism in Vietnam and other Southeast Asian countries. He holds a Master's degree in Arts and Heritage Management at the University of Sheffield, UK and a PhD degree in Tourism Management at The Hong Kong Polytechnic University.

Thi Hong Hai Nguyen is a PhD candidate at the School of Hotel and Tourism Management of the Hong Kong Polytechnic University. Her current study focuses on tourist perceptions of authenticity. Her research interests focus on heritage tourism, consumer behaviour and tourism experiences.

Shu Nimonjiya is a PhD candidate in social anthropology at Tokyo Metropolitan University. His research focuses on nomadic people, especially their mode of thought. He has carried out fieldwork among the Mlabri in Thailand and among homeless people in Japan on which he has published several papers.

Yasuo Ohe is Professor of Rural Economics at the Department of Food and Resource Economics and Vice-Dean of the Faculty of Horticulture, Chiba University, Japan. His main research interests are in the economic analyses of rural tourism and farm diversification. He is an editorial board member of *Tourism Economics*. He serves as Chair of the Appraisal Committee of the Rural Tourism Programme in the Japanese Ministry of Agriculture, Forestry and Fisheries.

Songsuda Poosawang is a Lecturer in the Home and Community Division, Department of Human Relations, Faculty of Humanities, Chiang Mai University, Thailand. She is an expert in nutrition, diet therapy, community nutrition assessment and Thai traditional (indigenous) culinary art. She has undertaken research on Thai recipe development, health tourism and rural tourism development in northern Thailand. She holds a Master's degree in Nutrition from Mahidol University.

Ploysri Porananond is Associate Professor of Tourism Studies, Chiang Mai University, Thailand and is currently Head of the Centre for Tourism Studies and Academic Services. She was awarded her PhD from Leeds Metropolitan University. Her research interests focus on festival tourism, cultural tourism and the cultural industry, as well as tourism and the transformation of local traditions. Her previous research has focused on tourism and development in ASEAN countries and her publications include *Modernity and evolution of a festive tourism tradition: the Songkran Festival in Chiang Mai, Thailand (2008), Tourism and the Transformation of Ritual Practice with Sand Pagoda in Chiang Mai, Thailand (2014-forthcoming).*

Destha Titi Raharjana is a researcher at the Centre for Tourism Studies, Universitas Gadjah Mada, Yogyakarta. He is interested in tourism research, particularly in the field of community development, rural tourism, ecotourism and tourism impacts. He is also a Lecturer at the Department of Tourism in the School of Vocational Studies, UGM Yogyakarta and STP AMPTA, Yogyakarta.

Miwa Shibuya has undertaken research on globalisation and immigration and changes triggered by these phenomena in a welfare system within the nation state. She graduated with an MA from Chiang Mai University in 2014. Currently she works in India.

Narong Sikhiram is a Lecturer in the Home and Community Division, Department of Human Relations, Faculty of Humanities, Chiang Mai University, Thailand. He is an expert in food conservation and preservation, food product development, food safety, food security and Thai traditional (indigenous) culinary art. He has undertaken research for Thai restaurants in the USA and Australia, and in health tourism and rural tourism development in northern Thailand. He holds a Master's degree in Food Science and Technology from Chiang Mai University.

Eoin Joseph Trolan is Lecturer in the Department of International Sport and Leisure at Hankuk University of Foreign Studies, Korea. His research interests are in sports diplomacy, branding, and tourism. Originally from Northern Ireland, he has spent the last 21 years living and researching sport overseas. Active in sport he regularly travels throughout Asia, promoting and playing the traditional Irish sports of Gaelic football and hurling.